Jewish Studies as Counterlife

Jewish Studies as Counterlife

A REPORT TO THE ACADEMY

ADAM ZACHARY NEWTON

FORDHAM UNIVERSITY PRESS

New York 2019

Copyright © 2019 Fordham University Press

All rights reserved. No part of this publication may be reproduced, stored in a retrieval system, or transmitted in any form or by any means—electronic, mechanical, photocopy, recording, or any other—except for brief quotations in printed reviews, without the prior permission of the publisher.

Fordham University Press has no responsibility for the persistence or accuracy of URLs for external or third-party Internet websites referred to in this publication and does not guarantee that any content on such websites is, or will remain, accurate or appropriate.

Fordham University Press also publishes its books in a variety of electronic formats. Some content that appears in print may not be available in electronic books.

Visit us online at www.fordhampress.com.

Library of Congress Cataloging-in-Publication Data available online at https://catalog.loc.gov.

Printed in the United States of America

21 20 19   5 4 3 2 1

First edition

for my beloved son

CONTENTS

	Preface and Acknowledgments	ix
	Introduction	1
	Interchapter I: JS *Davka*	30
1.	Jewish Studies as Lever	35
	Interchapter II: The Dialectics of Ownership	55
2.	Jewish Studies and the Pitchfork	60
	Interchapter III: "Past its own aim, out to another side"	83
3.	*Mochlos* or *Makhlokes*: JS and the Humanities	87
	Interchapter IV: Speaking of JS; and Its Vicissitudes	123
4.	*Bildungsheld* or *Pícaro*, Canon and List: A Heterotopology for JS	127
	Interchapter V: *Bildung* and Built-ins	161
5.	Ventilating the Tradition: Rashbam and the Coen Brothers	165
	Epilogue: Knotted thread, middle game: an *envoi*	191
	Notes	201
	Works Cited	239
	Index	273

PREFACE AND ACKNOWLEDGMENTS

This book tells the story of a Jewish Studies that hasn't fully happened—or at least, not yet. In its myriad twists and turns, it is a story slanted frankly against the grain, as befits a project that interrogates boundary and frame: Jewish Studies if not as counter-fact, then as *counterlife*. A charitable colleague once called the book's aim "messianic"; certainly, it aspires beyond the given—toward what novelist Robert Musil liked to call "the utopia of essayism."[1] As I finish this book in the spring of 2019, I intend such messianism to sound, or even stand, against the troubled state of our polity, marked as it is by the return of "the same hatred of the other human, the same antisemitism" (Levinas) to the mainstream of American life.

Since I explain the book's title and subtitle in greater depth in the introduction, at this juncture I will merely underscore the figural expressivity they both possess for having been drawn from works of literary fiction, for a new *rhetoric* for JS (as the academic practice of Jewish Studies will be abbreviated in this book)[2] represents one of its primary aims.

Although my account speaks often and at length to other knowledge practices, it cannot but be informed by my own disciplinary training in literary studies and philosophy. It is infused and energized by the interplay between classical exegetes, Talmudic passages, Jewish intellectual history, modern literary sources, and post-traditional thinkers of a theoretical cast.

How redoubtably Judaic sources like the Rashbam, Shlomo Ibn Gabirol, Leopold Zunz, and Gershom Scholem convincingly share discursive space with Bill Readings, Seamus Heaney, Giorgio Agamben, and Jean-Luc Nancy will be one of the (bilingual) lessons the book is designed to model, as an exercise in theorizing Jewish Studies around the problematics of profession, practice, and institution.

"Such-and-such *Studies*": Many cross-disciplinary programs on the landscape of the humanities, social sciences, and natural studies now anchor themselves in, and through, that remarkably protean formulation. *Jewish* Studies, one might argue, remains exceptional for reasons internal to its history within the university that only incidentally coincide with certain modes or expression of Jewish exceptionalism. Even its name incorporates a margin of variability.

While usually denominated "Jewish Studies," sometimes the semantically nonidentical adjective "Judaic" doubles for "Jewish," seeming to express an exclusive concern with the religion of *Judaism* (whether the case or not). Sometimes the modifier coordinates with a secondary term, such as "and Holocaust," or "and Near Eastern," or "and Israel." Less commonly, the whole phraseology is refashioned—for example, "Program in Jewish Culture and Society" or "Institute for the Study of Modern Jewish Life."

The story of Jewish Studies, or the story told *by* Jewish Studies, is a complicated one—not as long (long-standing) as some, but not as short (recently begun) as others. While this book's mainspring does not qualify as historicist—indeed, the historicism that continues to dominate so much of the scholarship undertaken under the aegis of JS exposes the field to liabilities even as it confers benefits—I do devote substantial space to Jewish Studies as narratable *histoire* and *récit*.

For many practitioners of Jewish Studies, in tandem with the many lay audiences in synagogues or community centers that they often find themselves addressing as scholastic experts on "the Jews," Jewish History and the History of Judaism *just are* Jewish Studies.[3] What looks therefore like the field's rationale—at its best a grand act of reclamation[4]—could be said to derive from both the intellectual hegemony of nineteenth-century *Wissenschaft des Judentums* and a religio-cultural predilection for narrated or juridical fact, empirical documentation, and archival traditions.[5] As *project*, however, and more than mere *amalgam*, I conceive of JS otherwise.

Already figured by its title, this book's diagnostic and prognostic energies focus on JS as something other than the status quo. Writing about the crisis-state in which the academic humanities are routinely purported to find themselves, cultural historian Louis Menand writes, "If one part of the university is continually enacting a crisis of institutional legitimation, it is performing a service for the rest of the university. It is pursuing an ongoing inquiry into the limits of inquiry."[6] Although Jewish Studies doesn't typically see itself as having undergone legitimation crises, this book contends that it might be salutary—for the field as well as the university at large—if it did.

As the question of legitimation shadows JS from its very start—identified by Gershom Scholem as its "chthonian aspect" crossed with a restively repressed "demonic" element[7]—so crisis provides one engine for (self-)cri-

Preface and Acknowledgments xi

tique. At any rate, if Menand valorizes the humanities, for all their vicissitudes and occasional controversy, as a kind of "systems check" on the entire institutional affair, so I wish to make a similar case for Jewish Studies as an admittedly niche kiosk in the contemporary university's marketplace of ideas.

In this book, my intention is to address readers who reside both within and outside the boundaries of Jewish Studies as knowledge practice(s) and credentialed sodality. Where one readership concerns itself primarily with documenting Jewish history and the history of Jews and Judaism (even when such discourse is not explicitly historiographic), the other positions JS relative to its own acts of disciplinary adhesion and the claims of "field."

To some insiders, a meta-project on JS will just seem beside the point—even if *"always historicize"* (the intentionalist rallying call for disciplinary self-interrogation) can, from another vantage, devolve into the iron grip of genealogy and fatality of guild. To some outside, the plastic and multiple significations of "Jewish" might, at the same time, suggest possible overreach—as if, at the level of its boundaries, JS presumed to be everything and everywhere while still managing to contract into yet another of the contemporary university's silos.

It is my possibly quixotic hope that both readerships become so interested in the capacity for leverage this book imagines for JS that they become new and engaged interlocutors for reimagined terms of debate. At bottom, the modest version of a swerve[8] that this book proposes is to ask: What do we mean when we say "Jewish Studies," when we conjoin its component terms, when a field takes up its past and projects its future? Like the other pointed questions populating the chapters to follow, the following observation by the late Bill Readings about the university's circuits of communication is meant to sustain its relevance throughout:

> What a sender says takes its place amid a crowd of idiolects in the listener, and their conversation acquires its sense in a discursive act of which neither is the master. . . . It is to speak in a way that respects what might be called the abyssal space of reading by the other: the fact that we never know to whom our words may speak.[9]

Where *mayn eygene tayere froy*, Miriam, is concerned, I think I have come to know well enough to whom my words have spoken, and may speak, still so firmly anchored as we are in our—now familial—heart of wonder. I am, nevertheless, inexpressibly grateful to her as the unflagging witness (and peerless *darshanit*) for what has felt like a valedictory undertaking. Whatever "moving of th' earth" may bring, "inter-assured of the mind" are we, says Donne confidently, as he promises his wife not breach but expansion. Many of this book's sentences owe enduring gratitude for her unerring eye and ear, including those myriad hundreds left on the cutting room floor. Rarely has "acumen" deserved both pronunciations. *Mir farmakhn di oygn / Un vern tsuzamengetsoygen / Durkh loshn-drot-papir / Ikh tsu dir du tsu mir.*

In an essay discussed later in the book, philosopher Franz Rosenzweig wittily revises Ecclesiastes 12:12 by connecting *Bildung*, the formation of character, with *Büchermachens*, the making of books. While that pairing—for Rosenzweig, exemplarily academic—does not necessarily add up to any Jewish pursuit per se, my own book would be nowhere without it. In two previous books, I quoted Emmanuel Levinas on the vagaries of book-making, which, as discrete moments in an ongoing heteronomous discourse, "are interrupted, and call for other books and in the end are interpreted in a saying distinct from the said."[10] Barring the unforeseen, my part in that economy feels here rather like a closing statement—even if *Bildung* has more in store for me.

Accordingly, I feel especially grateful to the editors of Fordham University Press and to my eloquently responsive referees. With the exception of the fifth chapter, a previous version of which appeared under the title, "A Tale of Two Jewish Studies: From Ron Meshbesher to the Rashbam," in *Studies in American Jewish Literature* 36. 2 (2017), this book was through-composed, one chapter leading directly into the next. Any possible losses thus incurred in more lengthy incubation, it is hoped, have been offset by a general gain in immediacy (my affinity for em-dash/parentheses withal).

Commenting on a comparison between words on the one hand and goads and nails on the other—appearing, as if on cue, in the verse from Ecclesiastes directly preceding "Of making many books there is no end"—Rabbi El'azar ben Azariah further elaborates the analogy in a famous passage from the Babylonian Talmud, or *Bavli*. He compares life-affirming words of Torah to the "goad [that] directs the cow to her furrow to bring forth sustenance for life to the world" (b. Ḥagigah 3b).[11] To give that figural screw my own irreverent turn, I can only trust that those goads exerted on my career over the past decade by institutions, disciplinary cohorts, programs, and individuals that led directly to this project have resulted in words of avowal guiding their charge away from impasse, culvert, or precipice *l'darkhei ḥayim* (toward paths of life) instead.

Preface and Acknowledgments xiii

My simpatico stepsons and agents of grace, Y2K (among other sobriquets), showed admirable patience when reading and word processing stole time away from precious games of baseball in the cul-de-sac or another viewing of *The Treasure of the Sierra Madre, Mon Oncle*, or *Once Upon a Time in China*. I love, prize, and thank them both.

Last, I give boundless thanks to and for my miraculous *yingl*, Emmanuel Ḥasdai (Josiah), who will be three by the time this book appears and to whom it is dedicated. Although he transcends the totality of this parent's accomplishments, its progress was accompanied throughout by his, from blessed zygote to even more adored toddler. From the *Bavli* again: a *baraita* ("outside teaching") from Tractate b. *Kiddushin* 29a inventories a list of paternal responsibilities for sons, which include circumcision, redeeming him if firstborn, transmitting Torah, finding a wife, and teaching a trade—the lion's share of which, א"יה, still lie ahead.

Regarding the *stamma*'s supplementary obligation—"Others say: teaching him how to swim as well"[12]—intrepid little "Manujaya" and I are already on our way to fulfilling its counsel for immersive prowess in the Steinian element: "With the exertions of your hands and feet in the water, make the deep, deep sea keep you up." Bath, pool, stream, or surf, even when an ocean tumbles by: deep down and deep inland there, still bathe you in eternal mildness of joy.

Heard not long ago declaiming, "I am a great idea!"—as verily you are—Manu, Manoushi, Manolito, Munyele, Mannikin, little Papi, Forefinger Sam, Emoji, Bimbelyush, Sticklet, Mr. Go-Again, Admiral Halsey, ShowMeDickens (among an ever-expanding cache of nicknames): May you live a long and accomplished life of deftly maneuvered surfaces and depths, buoyancy and momentum, deep-diving, nimble locomotion, and simple oceanic joy, *niño lindo de Papi y Mami*, my capable boy!

Introduction

> Philologists, when discussing their science, never get down to the root of the subject: they never set forth philology itself as a problem. Bad conscience? Or merely thoughtlessness?
>
> —FRIEDRICH NIETZSCHE, "We Philologists"

Stopping short of Nietzsche's ascriptions, this introductory chapter sets forth Jewish Studies itself as a problem—from its philological and historicist origins in nineteenth-century Germany to its current state in North American colleges and universities. Two animal fictions by Franz Kafka, personalized by two Jewish Americanists in professions of critical faith, jointly set the stage for an exposition of the book's twofold title, followed by a brief history of the field and an initial consideration of its dilemmas in content and form, with reference to several contemporary critics and scholars. Getting down to the root of *this* subject calls for a certain deliberateness beforehand. If periphrastic at first, these preliminaries eschew any intent (as voiced on the facing panel by Nietzsche's younger, Jewish contemporaries, Brod, Weltsch, and Herzl) to "talk about being Jewish forever."[1] With more proportionate ends in sight, this chapter concludes with four overarching questions posed to and for JS, plus an outline for the rest of the book.

Two (Jewish) Professors Ape a Dog

THE MUSIC OF AMERICA

"Ontogeny recapitulates phylogeny," in the memorable formula of biologist-philosopher Ernst Haeckel. Recast it here as *ethnography recapitulates zoology* and we are ready to follow a somewhat winding but accretive and elucidating chain of allusions from professor to canine to simian back to professor, and thence to Jewish Studies.[2] Why begin this way? Because the following examples of mediated connection to the academy—both autobiographical and scholastic—prepare the ground for my main subject: the contingent advent of Jewish Studies on the university landscape and the enigma of its arrival.

When the late Sacvan Bercovitch first listened to "the music of America"—the "redemptive promise of language" he found in its classic literary tradition—what he heard "sounded like ideology," or even worse, Muzak, "a long series of scholarly ventures in culture formation."[3] Taking up the mantle of Emerson's concentrically progressing American Scholar, he interpolates his own series of increasingly particularized "border-crossings" (6), a personal mosaic that picks up where America's, and that of the then-reigning American Studies, leaves off.

To perform this move in an intentionally refractive manner, he turns to a piece of literary fiction—one of Kafka's more elaborate animal stories, "Investigations of a Dog" ("Forschungen eines Hundes")—and demonstrates how "a great parable of interpretation as mystification" can also be "a great parable of the limitations of cultural critique." The Montreal-born son of Yiddish-Socialist parents in frictional relation to all things American, Bercovitch discerns a peculiarly apt analogy with the ways in which both Kafka and his canine first-person unfold their peculiar and double-edged "epiphany of otherness" (3). In so doing, he also provides a prototype for the investigations I propose to undertake here.

Readers familiar with Kafka's text will recall that an accidental encounter in his youth with a group of younger musician-dogs prompts the story's older canine narrator, now absented from "canine community," to initiate an ultimately unfinished inquiry into the species-life of *Hundschaft*. While the dog may imagine that mystery is ultimately mastered through reference to a higher reality, such mastery is actually deferred according to Bercovitch, since "to magnify the categories of our containment is to diminish our capacities for understanding of it" (4). In other words, try-

Introduction 3

ing to comprehend his fellows' self-expression, the dog merely becomes ensnared in his own.

Bercovitch seizes on precisely these self-confessed and otherwise repressed limitations, which he calls the "hermeneutics of transcendence," as the springboard for his own revisionary relationship to the kind of literary criticism that preceded his arrival on the professional scene. His preferred instrument, a "reversal of traditional comparativist methods," showcases the "*enabling* ambiguities of limitation" (5) instead, educating a capacity to be "nourished" by boundaries, underscoring the historical and particular that lie behind what is otherwise made to seem essential and universal.

"It is Kafka's *donné* that we have no choice but to interpret" (3), Bercovitch maintains. "If dreams of transcendence are indices into the traps of culture, then inquiry into the trapping process may provide insight into our own and others' non-transcending condition" (5). It is Bercovitch's *donné*, in turn, to have interposed the figure of Kafka so as to pinpoint the intellectual and discursive gap into which a newly Americanized self can insert his own liberating, self-authorizing critical practice. Far from being oblique, the appeal to literary fiction here is precisely what gives the autobiographical moment its peculiar slant. No less insightful about Kafka's text than the then-current state of American Studies, the refraction stands as its own lesson. Recontextualized now and here, it preinscribes and models my own. As Bercovitch's narrative stands in relation to Kafka's, so this prelude stands in relation to both.

The Music of America, Take 2

"Strangeness," writes cultural historian Josh Kun, "is identity's uncomfortable, but required, double."[4] A decade after Bercovitch, and in validation of his insights for a new generation of American scholars, another self-confessing, music-lured, nonrepresentatively Jewish academician arrives at the same Kafka text about canine misprision. In Kun's reading, from within the context of a nonmetaphorical American music, when our informant dog encounters the world of his fellow canines' sounds and their communal harmonies, he "understands his [own] listening as a way of confronting and living with difference and strangeness" (15).

Innately "suspicious of harmonies," Kun's dog "performs a *critical listening*," disclosing himself as still a listener-at-a-distance, "defined by his difference, whose 'investigations' de-center the chauvinism of the dogs he encounters" (17). The point of recapitulating Bercovitch's intellectual progress for Kun, with a twist, is to introduce to the field of American cultural studies not just the vibrancy but also the peculiar relevance of minority discourse.

Kafka is thus twice enlisted by scholars seeking to justify their place in those higher cultural precincts where both interpretive shrewdness and the negotiation of difference constitute the core pursuits of twenty-first-century humanistic inquiry. For each of them, a generation apart and differentially positioned against the grain of national ideology and cultural heritage, "Kafka's dog offers a way out," in Kun's words (15)—an investigatory and a critical posture.

Likewise, Jewishness itself comes to represent a mode of critical possibility. In a San Francisco Synagogue, "feeling like Kafka's dog" in relation to his own Jewishness, Kun is struck by the Reform prayer book's evocation of the shofar as "a stranger among sounds" (13), which licenses, as Bercovitch would say, its own enabling ambiguities of limitation.[5] That the shofar, Kafka, and Bercovitch would all become associated, for Kun, as parallel instances of a liberating "strangeness" only underscores its dissentient and utopian power for him as critique—as Bercovitch absorbed a similar lesson several decades before, informed in its own way by culturally Jewish habit.

In summary, then: Two academicians in revisionary, self-referential relation to their discipline, linked by the displacing energies of Jewish desire, construct a mimetic chain to explain their own self-understanding as it impinges upon their standing within an academic field, an affiliation ratified for them by Kafka's prior license to illuminate, through productively estranging, the drama of intellectual personhood.

What does all of this have to do with JS? it may be reasonably demurred. Since neither Bercovitch nor Kun typifies "Jewish Studies" in any formal sense—notwithstanding proficiency in Yiddish translation (Bercovitch) and Jewish-American music (Kun)—the answer to that question will require a further move and a second Kafka text whose animal first-person offers a fresh opportunity for borrowed voice.

An Ape Dogs a (Jewish) Professor

Curiously enough, "a way out" is the identical phrase used by Rotpeter (Red Peter), the performing ape in Kafka's "A Report to [for] an Academy" ("Ein Bericht für eine Akademie").[6] Although in this highly specialized subgenre of Jewish professing-by-way-of-Kafka that I have minted here, the canine teachings inculcated into Kun's and Bercovitch's cross-cultural sensibilities may have something just as acute to say about the particular style and pathos of investigation known as *Wissenschaft*: nevertheless, the ape and his report to an audience of academicians will better serve as a springboard for our concerns here.

Trauma looms over his past (his name derives from one of two wounds he sustained during capture), and possibly his present, too.[7] Claimed on the one side by an *äffisches Vorleben* (apish past), a free but nonverbal life in the West African Gold Coast (present-day Ghana), and on the other, by a quasi-human, European here-and-now, Rotpeter reveals himself to be an uncanny Kafkan double: an animal through whom the human is glimpsed and made strange:

> In variety theaters I have often watched, before my turn came on, a couple of acrobats performing on trapezes high in the roof. They swung themselves, they rocked to and fro, they sprang into the air, they floated into each other's arms, one hung by the hair from the teeth of the other. "And that too is human freedom," I thought, "self-controlled movement." What a mockery of holy Mother Nature! Were the apes to see such a spectacle, no theater walls could stand the shock of their laughter.[8]

Freedom from his own *Affentum* eventually presents him with two choices: either being confined to the Zoological Garden, which amounts to no more than "a new barred cage," or performing on the Variety Stage, which assures him (so he says) of a "way out" (*Ausweg*)—"the way out of human beings" (*diesen Menschenausweg*). Concluding a monologue that satisfactorily demonstrates his painstakingly acquired, albeit aped, (*nachäffen*) humanity, he confides,

> On the whole, at any rate, I have achieved what I wished to achieve. You shouldn't say it was not worth the effort. In any case, I don't want any human being's judgment. I only want to expand knowledge. I simply report. Even to you, esteemed gentlemen of the Academy, I have only made a report.

A (Jewish?) Ape Schools the Professoriate

He has already reminded his amply credentialed audience that such report was requested of him by "the Academy" to begin with, tailored specifically to an account of his previous life as an ape. However, he cannot honor this request except "in the narrowest sense," because of the obscuring of his apish consciousness and memory by the sedimented overlay of the human.

Like his counterpart, the *Wissenschaftlich* dog, who has nonetheless come to appreciate freedom in the midst of compromised *Forschungen*, Kafka's ape insists on the limited victory or power of *Bericht*, a word that means not only "report" but also "account," "statement," "chronicle," and "commentary."

He simply (*nur*) reports, he tells us, wishing only "to expand [or in the Muir translation, 'to impart'] knowledge." To the *hohe Herren von der Akademie*, he has *berichte nur* (only reported), the adverbial suggesting that he is delivering merely another kind of variety showpiece. While it may gesture toward his coveted *Ausweg*, his way out, it still falls short of conferring real freedom—a goal or condition overestimated by humans, the ape tells us, and one he demanded neither then nor now.

The assemblage of "esteemed gentlemen" before him would be surprised to discover that, in having initiated the requested performance and its mimetic—apish—trick, they have become reciprocally implicated in its performative trap. For needless to say, *berichten nur* describes what academicians themselves do, too. They, likewise, inhabit a specialized form of theater which routinely obliges them to deliver a very similar kind of display text. In a work that remains canny about any hard-and-fast species difference, Rotpeter cleverly locates such proximity in an initial disclaimer before his story formally commences:

> Speaking frankly, as much as I like choosing metaphors for these things—speaking frankly: your life as apes [*ihr Affentum*], gentlemen, insofar as something of that kind lies behind you, cannot be farther removed from you than mine is from me. But it tickles at the heels of everyone who walks here on earth, the small chimpanzee as well as the great Achilles.

A satire of *Bildung*, of self-formation and cultivation—and thus, in parallel with "Forschungen eines Hundes"—"Ein bericht für eine Akademie" conjures a tale of transformation, its anthropoid narrator subjected to a kind of accelerated evolution by which a new identity enhances his given one. The academy, he seems to conclude, licenses no less, as Bercovitch and Kun have both demonstrated for us through their separate "transferences to America."[9]

On the Margins of the Academy: From Kafka to Roth

One name for such identity-transfer from within the arena of Jewish American/para-academic culture is *counterlife*. I began this prelude by proposing how mediated connection to the academy ushers in my main subject, the enigma of JS's arrival on the university scene. We have now almost arrived, ourselves.

Neither my coinage nor Kafka's, the conceit of "counterlife" belongs to another twentieth-century writer, the late Philip Roth, for whom Jewishness is compounded of angst and comedy, choice and nemesis, analysis terminable and interminable. In its single appearance in the novel of the same name, "counterlife" is narrator Nathan Zuckerman's word for Jewish self-fashioning and, indeed, for any imaginatively contestatory version of the self.

Espoused or embodied on a supranational scale by Zionism, it expresses the desire "to reverse the very form of Jewish existence" associated with precarious insularity and exclusionary otherness always and everywhere. "The construction of a counterlife that is one's own anti-myth was at its very core . . . a species of fabulous utopianism, a manifesto for human transformation as extreme—and, at the outset, as implausible—as any ever conceived. A Jew could be a new person if he wanted to."[10]

Astutely observed by novelist William Gass in an early review of Roth's novel, the construct of "counterlife" licenses its own morphology: counterlife, counterlives, counterliving.[11] Even further, it promises a *mise en abîme*, since the original freestanding "life," to which all the other counterlives—selfhood, national belonging, time's arrow—presumably refer, hasn't ever attained its authoritative, self-identical form. This would be "the problem of priority,"[12] which, as Kafka shows us, possesses certain other interpretive applications: the human prior to the animal, the uncultivated life prior to the institutional.

The Counterlife's narrative design and its characters' individual plots all coalesce around this idea of replication, inversion, and fictionalization, of imagined self-cancellation and beginning again, all grounded in a kind of negative dialectics or supersessionism: anti-myths conjured only in relation to originary and enduring myths. In addition to suggesting the improvised and impersonated as the stuff of selves both individual and collective, the term's valences for Roth include a kind of productive duplicity and poetics of displacement—for example, Bercovitch by way of Kafka, Kun by way of both. Such a program for refashioned identity finds its echo at novel's end in another mini-manifesto for the malleable life:

> The burden isn't either/or, consciously choosing from possibilities equally difficult and regrettable—it's and/and/and/and/and as well. Life *is* and: the accidental and the immutable, the elusive and the graspable, the bizarre and the predictable, the actual and the potential,

all the multiplying realities, entangled, overlapping, colliding, conjoined—plus the multiplying illusions! (306)

As an admitted superfluity of conjunction, such fluid praise of "and" also speaks reflexively to my own concatenation of Bercovitch and Kun, Kafka and Roth, and the foregrounded drama of primary source and scholarly commentary. Indeed, it rather nicely describes the syntactic logic of this book. Furthermore, where one critic construes the figure of "counterlife" as signifying "exactly the rejection of our multiple performances in a move that becomes *counter* or against life,"[13] I prefer to see a balance between it and the related concept of lived parataxis.

In tandem, the two formulas reflect a productive ambiguity that resides at the core of my own topic. Where the infinitely coordinate syntax of "and/and/and/and/and" faithfully reproduces Nathan Zuckerman's aspirations, so "either/or" spells out the more restrictive, even tragic, conditions facing Kafka's simian. In parallel to both cases, however, readers must parse a fable of transposition, narrated as self-revising fiction or species life history, each conducting its own anatomy of counterlife.

Fusing Kafka and Roth in this fashion yields me the title, subtitle, and rhetorical mainspring for this book. In common, their narratives conduct a retrospect of a self enmeshed, inscribed by semi-mystified discursive forces. The idea that *Hundschaft* in the dog-story lends itself to quasi-*Wissenschaft*, or that the ape-story presents as *ein Bericht* under the auspices of *eine Akademie* proves all but irresistible as allegory for the staging of academic practices and personal experience in the chapters to follow.

Because *counterlife* expresses both utopianism and transformative possibility, it licenses a similar redirection of its figural uses. That the inquiry I undertake at the same time traffics so readily in such permutations and the manifold connections to Jewish Studies they presuppose, returns me in kind to the title of Roth's novel and its license for transposition and re-commencement. How, finally, does this prelude speak to the organizing properties and developmental conditions of JS?

Jewish Studies–as–Counterlife

Given a conflicted institutional history and a frictional present, a story as well as plot, *counterlife* feels peculiarly apt for describing the academic pursuit we know as Jewish Studies, which began its life as a kind of *counter* to prevailing institutional norms, and which has also lent itself to the improvisatory, to the appeal of *Ausweg*, in the midst of overdetermined scholasticism. Its intrinsic problem of priority—for it can claim to be as self-fashioning as it is imitative and belated—led none other than counterhistorian Gershom Scholem to lament at mid-twentieth century, "perhaps we do not realize the extent to which we are orphans and alone in our project" (71).

Within the contours of this project, Jewish Studies–as-counterlife signifies a kind of lived institutional poetics. In allegiance with a specifically *linguistic* project that has been dubbed "Philosophical Marranism," this book seeks to nudge Jewish Studies beyond its manifest discursive boundaries, to "marry the speech of strangers and let the Hebrew talk through it"[14]: to *counter* JS—in apparent paradox—with the help of that selfsame Jewish Studies.

As both this book's topic and symbolic field, JS denotes, variously, a data-field; an interdiscipline; a program; a center, or institute; a departmental major or minor; a vocation; and an academic pursuit. It signifies a compound of scholastic enterprise, habitus, and professional guild, vigorously pursued and practiced, and yet in some part still mystified to itself as a university structure. JS is sometimes conjoined to related but also semiautonomous programs like Holocaust Studies and Israel Studies; under the gaze of an extramural public and underwritten by philanthropic sponsorship, JS might also plausibly suggest its own version of "multiplying realities, entangled, overlapping, colliding, conjoined." To what end a transdisciplinary syntax of "and/and/and/and/and" might similarly be put, would be just one query to ponder here.

Originally conceived in a positivist and utopian (if not quite messianic) spirit in twentieth-century Germany and migrating thence to pre-State Palestine, subsequently reimagined as an uneasy version of ethnic, multicultural, and even area studies in the mid- to late-twentieth-century American university, JS straddles a charged line between chauvinist myth and academic anti-myth—hence, one could argue, its own latency of counterlife.

In its own ongoing report to the academy, JS tells a double narrative with one voice, history, consciousness, and setting in unsynchronized relation to a precedent other. In distant echo of Kafka's dog, it compels interpretivity of its own "source material" and through its multiple methodologies and disciplinary configurations. In rough parallel with Rotpeter, it can be said to have had two geneses: a start and a restart.

Consequently, any Deuteronomic retelling of its goals and purposes has its work cut out for itself, as "neo-demonic" as it must be dynamic—in the case of this book's own parataxis, a report, a chronicle, a series of investigations, an extended manifesto with glintings of memoir. Like few other multisided pursuits, and almost uniquely in the academy, "Jewish Studies" stands for a congeries of disciplines, methodologies, and subject areas.

Its objects of inquiry include not only the figures of Kafka and Roth but also more specialized *topoi* like medieval Hebrew poetry, Yiddish modernism, Judezmo in cyberspace, Israeli cinema, Kaifeng Jewry, Anatolian art of Late Antiquity, the Jewish graphic novel, klezmer-salsa, early modern legal codes, the Cuban-Jewish diaspora, Feminist Jewish ethics, contemporary Ḥaredi and ecstatic Judaisms, demography, Mizraḥi literary culture, radical Jewish music, Second Temple archaeology, New Talmud studies, and the boundaries of Jewish languages and literatures. It subsumes the entire diachronic range of Jewish discursive traditions, lived experience, and material culture.

But JS also shares the concerns of other interdisciplines organized around modern markers of particularity (ethnic, racial, cultural, religious, and regional) at a cultural moment when, as Semitic philologist Ernest Renan put it, "nations . . . are [still] something fairly new in history."[15] And yet, the historicity it takes for granted reaches back to premodern notions of peoplehood, all the way to the Bronze Age. It speaks to, and about, itself through multiple disciplinary speech genres, such as philology, *Geschichtsbewußtsein*, philosophical reasoning, theological argument, textual commentary, vernacular culture, ethnomusicology, cinema, Hebrew/Yiddish, non-Jewish languages, and postmodern *Wissenschaft*, i.e. theory.

Unifying such a vast corpus would seem self-evident: After all, does the mechanism not inhere right there in the indexical "Jewish" preceding the nominative "Studies?" And yet, that very identifying term is what one recent critic of the enterprise regards as a "biologistic-identitarian" construct, a consequently "impossible" signifier and empty relay between undertheorized notions of "population" and "culture."[16]

What makes all of Jewish Studies *Jewish*, according to this viewpoint, is highly contestable, bestowing no inarguable sanction for the institutional, indeed canonical, terrain thus named, claimed, and staked out. Haunted by a "spectral Jewish archive" and its predicative displacements, probably no example is more critically edifying than the many JS mission statements that adduce "the Jewish experience," as if it were at all times and everywhere self-evident.

Bericht *as Stagecraft*

Such fictions of invariance return me once more to Kafka's story of interspecies similitude. One of the story's modern critics deems the ape's performance a necessary "failure of identity," since, like his other feats of imitation (drinking, smoking, dressing, and reporting), it is conducted theatrically. To play, quote, recite, and perform oneself is something less than authorizing, coinciding with, or *being* that self.[17]

Kafka's ape subsists, then, in the *gap* between one thing and another, flanked by a repudiated *Affentum* on the one hand, and an approximated *Menschheit* on the other. Retrieving the formulation directly above, we might call Rotpeter not only an impossible subject but also an impossible anthropoid, sharing his metaphysical theater with comparably impossible writers and readers, Jewish academicians and academician Jews, and most of all, Jewishness itself.

As we have seen with our researcher-manqué dog, the temptation to deploy the ape as effigy or persona beckons. Regarding "A Report to an Academy" and similar Kafkan texts, literary critic Dan Miron asks, "What are [they] if not dramatic monologues waiting for performative realization?"[18] If a dog's investigations can shadow forth those elected by two scholars, why not one "report to an academy" staged in echo of another— in conformance with Bercovitch's proviso that while the "symmetries are not precise . . . they point to certain common principles of exegesis" (4)?

Could Rotpeter, then, be a figure for this author's own professional counterlife and its border-crossings, say, from the Gold Coast of professing literature in non-Jewish languages to the Variety Stage of Jewish Studies? Not quite. But I hasten to emphasize how powerfully the scene of instruction on display in Kafka's story resonates as an allegory for the evolution of Jewish Studies itself—from para-institutional "Judaistic science" (*Wissenschaft des Judentums*), to university life and counterlife, to (potential) epiphany of otherness.

All Rotpeter wants, he says, is "a way out," an animating desire common to groupings both filiational and affiliative, part and parcel of species and institutional life alike. To that degree, at least, if Kafka's ape aptly serves the function of mask here, let the prosopopœic speaker behind it stand revealed as Jewish Studies itself.

If the ape knew his St. Augustine, for instance, he might channel that famous admission from the *Confessions* to encapsulate his—and to our ears, Jewish Studies'—dilemmas: "Mihi quastio factum sum, et ipse est languor meus" (I have become a problem to myself, and that is my infirmity.)[19] In specific regard to JS, what might prompt such self-reckoning? The Nietzschean version for philologists is recorded in the epigraph to this introduction. An Augustinian, as well as post-Freudian, answer would be *desiderium*, or desire.

Jewish Studies Structured as a Desire

In the preface to her own excursive report for the academy, literary/cultural studies scholar Marjorie Garber hits upon the phrase "disciplinary libido" to explain the lure of *Ausweg* inside the very professional precincts which she now critically but also affectionately surveys:

> In combining the most "disciplined" and the most "undisciplined" of forces, [my] title *Academic Instincts* is meant to sound like a contradiction in terms. But this is a book about the energies that keep scholarly disciplines from becoming inert and settled. It is about the instincts not of individuals but of fields—what might be called the *disciplinary libido*. In each chapter, I consider the ways in which a field differentiates itself from, but also desires to become, its nearest neighbor, whether at the edges of the academy (the professional wants to be an amateur and vice versa), among the disciplines (each one covets its neighbor's insights), or within the disciplines (each one attempts to create a new language specific to its objects, but longs for a universal language understood by all).[20]

Those three tensions, Garber explains, arise from a constitutive doubleness within academic disciplinary and social, discursive fields. As she expresses it, "The contrasts around which these disputes revolve do not signify real opposites, but rather depend upon one another for their strength and effectiveness" (ix). Not unlike the *apish* and the *human* in Kafka's "Report," competing purchases on knowledge-circulation—scholar versus autodidact, or the discipline of history versus the discipline of literature—are always co-implicating each other. In this case, the fences between neighbors *articulate* the site of troubled connectivity, libido being merely the obverse of *amour propre*—features that are no less common to Jewish Studies than to other academic habitats.

Thus, the question is, will any academicized "report" link audience to lecturer and vice versa? Whatever such speech acts may say contrastively, they also perform a tale *about* that entanglement. When Sir Philip Sidney (Garber's example) juxtaposes poets with astronomers, mathematicians, philosophers, and historians, he is merely drawing attention to the way all scholarly knowledge-practices can be understood as being "structured as a desire" (62), as phantasmal as the individual psychic dramas embodied by and played out among their practitioners, aspects of the university's not-fully metabolized excess.[21]

Even more scandalously, far from being maintained in their integrity, contamination has always been the open secret of formalized academic pursuits, not least when they share so many methodological or topological borders. "'Purity,'" Garber mordantly observes, "is always another name for another impurity" (67). Or as Louis Menand expresses a similar point about the professional anxiety that ensues from ostensible correctives to disciplinary myopia, "Interdisciplinarity is the ratification of the logic of disciplinarity," even—and here, Garber and Menand converge on the same intuition—the "fetishization" of disciplinarity.[22]

So, maybe the true pathos of this conflict of modern faculties is to be found not among neighboring disciplines or even between disciplines and interdisciplines, but rather *at the root of disciplinarity itself*, which, Garber explains, is "constituted by the asymptotic approach" to its own ego-ideal; in short, "disciplines envy themselves" (90). Or as the punchline to the celebrated Jewish joke about competitive masochism among rabbi, cantor, and *shnorrer* renders it, "Look who thinks he's nothing!"

To bring Garber and Menand up to date: A decade or so after the publication of their books, the very politics of disciplinarity for the humanities typically cedes prominence to the far more intractable matter of their economics. As the labor pool in higher education undergoes radical alteration and the tenure system enters its twilight, we have even been challenged to "end the university as we know it."[23] Presuming, however, that a Jewish Studies–to-come will yet figure on the institutional horizon, I seek to highlight here the *desire lines* peculiar to the structures and vested interests of academic Jewish thought.

This is the terrain explored with specific relation to the subdiscipline of Jewish philosophy by both Agata Bielik-Robson and Willi Goetschel.[24] Yet to designate this particular intellectual history as subdisciplinary (or counterpositional) is to miss something distinctive about "Jewish philosophy" in its necessarily unstable relation to the academy and its agency as "critical supplement." Says Goetschel,

> Jewish philosophy represents neither an alternative to philosophy in general nor any kind of counterphilosophy. Rather, we can call Jewish philosophy those moments in the thought of Jewish philosophers where interventions of their thought attend to lacunae that prompt us to rethink the project of philosophy and reimagine it critically (6).

At a certain productive distance from the university, the various instantiations of Jewish philosophy in their family resemblance function in the aggregate as a kind of *differend*. Bielik-Robson thus calls the practice (or vocation) "Jewish clinamen, or the third language of Jewish philosophy" (1). Goetschel prefers the locution of philosophy's *dybbuk*: "the marginalized, muted, and repressed that returns and haunts the claim to universalism that excludes and silences what enriches it" (7).[25] The work of (largely German-)Jewish philosophers, in its historically specific contexts, constitutes a particularized intellectual discourse that remains oblique to the "disciplining" of philosophy, which Kant's post-Enlightenment *Der Streit der Fakultäten* formalized as a thoroughly academic profession.

To that extent, what makes Jewish philosophy do its *dybbuk*-work is not any identifiable Jewishness (as though it were another sort of "Judaistic science"), but rather its capacity for "critical reflection on what it means to do philosophy" (56) in the first place—as both a universalizing intellectual project and a disciplinary construct. It thus offers a countertext to institutionalized reasoning that stops short of historicizing or even critiquing its institutionalization (one of several "blindspots" afflicting academic philosophy as a canonical, professional pursuit). Or, in Bielik-Robson's words, it does "counter-philosophy with the help of philosophy" (4).

After Adorno, Lessing, and Benjamin, Goetschel calls his individual case studies of specific figures like Heine, Spinoza, Mendelssohn, and Rosenzweig "critical models," "rescues," and "redemptive readings." More audaciously, Bielik-Robson calls hers "philosophical Marranos." By aspirational analogy, my own readings of various texts and intellectual figures in this chapter and those that succeed it obey a similar logic.

Like Goetschel's and Bielik-Robson's more local case for Jewish philosophy as a (counter-)disciplinary rethinking of academic philosophy's "task" positioned beyond "identity and exclusion of difference," I want to make a general argument for Jewish Studies in the relational, differential challenge it might pose for the academic humanities. Like Garber, I seek to draw out the intrinsic *vitality* alongside, *even owing to*, the multifariousness of the data-field and, consequently, the "impossible" Jewishness that impinges as now perhaps its defining feature upon contemporary Jewish Studies in the academy.

"Teaching and writing at a college or university," Garber confesses, "is a job for optimists and for idealists, whatever discursive or critical mode we may use" (xii). I might take this apologia for an "intervention and a credo" even one step further. The view of Jewish Studies that I unfold here self-evidently chafes against the status quo, inclining toward the liberating possibilities of what the next chapter calls the *as if*.

If I make bold enough again *not* to wave away the ascription "messianic" adduced in my preface, the JS I envision, in the spirit of Kafka's messiah, may well arrive only when it is no longer needed; but I truly hope not. Like Goetschel, I would like to think my aims here are less reflexively postmodern than dialogical and postcontemporary[26]: sensitive to both Jewish Studies' belatedness as well as the author's own, "from a vantage that comprehends itself as decidedly positional, i.e., relational and differential" (10).

In "A Report to an Academy," Kafka's narrating ape demurs at directly espousing any messianism for his individual prospects. Yet, his conjuring of "a way out," even if it only selects out a receding horizon, offers a preliminary way for me to formulate my hybrid report here, as a meditation on the state of Jewish Studies in the North American academy: where it has been, where it finds itself now, and what an imagined futurity may hold in store. In echo of Jacques Derrida's sanguine salute to the humanities' near horizon, I propose to call it a *Jewish Studies–à-venir* (to come); or, in imitation of another Derridean *jeu d'spirit*: thanks to *"Jewish Studies," what could take place tomorrow.*[27]

Three-and-One-Third Ways of Looking at Jewish Studies

In order to underscore how elusive such a putatively straightforward undertaking that really is, let me enlist some anecdotal pronouncements. The first belongs, conveniently, to Marjorie Garber, who, while exploring the ambivalence around the development of interdisciplinary structures and research areas in the university, observes in passing,

> It is as if new formations, like "science and literature" or "environmental studies" or "medical humanities" or "criminal justice" or "the new Jewish studies," to name just a random few of the "interdisciplines" in which students can now take courses and degrees, put in question the integrity and methods of science, literature, theology, philosophy, medicine, or law. (75)

Garber's footnoted reference to a 1999 article in the *Chronicle of Higher Education* notes the tension for humanities scholars who are seen as either "too Jewish for the humanities" or insufficiently "Jewish" for traditional JS programs, "which have stressed expertise in biblical literature and history" (160).[28] Thus "find[ing] themselves between two worlds," such scholars also find themselves unnervingly proximate to our narrator's dilemma in Kafka's story: that is, never human (academic) enough; or compensatorily, *too* academic.

The second pronouncement rehearses the question of "difference" so central to the field now as one of a set of interdisciplines authorized by the university's political economy and predicated on the minoritized subject, which, however, may or may not recognize "the Jew" as a member in good standing. Such tension underlines the dilemma with which a more recent piece on "the new Jewish Studies" from *Inside Higher Ed* concludes: "'This all begs the question: What kind of difference is Jewishness?'"[29]

At any rate, and as I explain later in this introduction, importing such constructs within the bounds of JS or otherwise "pushing" its boundaries, as undertaken by some of its practitioners, does not necessarily equal a more concerted dialogism with(in) the humanities at large. Cultural Studies (ca. 1990s), in other words, need not be the only academic *lingua franca* in which JS should latterly aspire to acquire proficiency.[30] Surely, the tongues in which JS speaks—aside, of course, from the linguistic hegemons of Hebrew and Yiddish—exceed the binary choice of either a rebranding that would align it with other "studies"-based programs, or the tried and true brand of Jewish Studies exceptionalism as its own claim to singular academic "identity."

Third, at the epicenter of Jewish Studies research, a recent issue of the *AJS Review* features a review by the late scholar Yaakov Elman of fellow Talmudist Daniel Boyarin's 2015 book, *A Traveling Homeland: The Babylonian Talmud as Diaspora*.[31] "By concentrating on Christian theological elements," Elman writes critically of Boyarin, "the Western field of Talmud study misses the huge amount of Hellenism to be found in rabbinic and Zoroastrian texts alike" (170). So far, such concerns remain confined to the subfield of Talmudic Studies within the putatively more comprehensive field of JS.

We observe an intriguing slippage, though, as Elman adduces the historicity of that academic enterprise, the reason for which, he says, "would seem to lie in the sociology of knowledge. The academy is a post-Christian institution, for the most part, but it is post-*Christian*, and Christianity's problems with Pharisees and talmudists is well-documented" (170). Where and in what manner can Talmudists in the modern university, as Elman puts it, "make a place for themselves and their fields of study," given that two-thirds of the Babylonian Talmud is halakhic in bent, concerned with the particularities of Jewish law and ritual?

"Some have done narratology, some have done Jewish-Christian relations (but not Jewish-Zoroastrian ones!), some choose theology, but theology of a Christian cast." If one wishes to concentrate solely on *halakhah*, the two likeliest professional profiles, according to this view, are Qumran studies, where that orientation is encouraged, or law school, which represents "the only other path for the would-be Jewish studies academic."

"It was no accident," Elman concludes, "that academic halakhic studies flourished for a time in Boyarin's alma mater, the Jewish Theological Seminary. That regime, and that regimen, could not continue in the new world of academic Jewish studies" (171). And yet, by this conclusion of the short review, even this purported "new world of academic Jewish studies," that is, cutting-edge Judaics, seems fully consonant with the aims and dictates of nineteenth-century German *Wissenschaft des Judentums*, rooted in classical Jewish sources and the history of Judaism.

Finally, for the one-third, we turn to Boyarin himself. A little more oddly, given this particular scholar's vaunted disciplinary promiscuity, the intriguing title of one of his own review essays discloses an eerily similar proprietary aggrandizement. While "Jewish Studies as Teratology" might seem to predict a meta-reflection on the entire field (even featuring a talking ape or investigative dog), the subtitle after the colon, "The Rabbis as Monsters,"[32] indicates its purview will be far more restrictive.

As a sharp critique of Lawrence A. Hoffmann's *Covenant of Blood: Circumcision and Gender in Rabbinic Judaism*, why Boyarin did not opt for the more accurate title "*Rabbinics* as Teratology" is a fine point that the essay, a local disagreement between scholars of Talmud and liturgy/ritual, never quite addresses. But an interrogation of "Jewish Studies" *tout court*, as its title portends, it most certainly is not.

So we have seen that JS may be enlisted as one telling instance of the tilt toward interdisciplinarity in the contemporary American university; it can also be prominently excluded from such precincts altogether, and it can be reduced to describe only the study of the religious texts of Judaism together with its history. Of course the latter would surprise those practitioners who inhabit "the new world of academic Jewish studies," yet who specialize in Yiddish modernism, Israeli graphic novels, or Jacques Derrida's Jewish-Maghrebi identity. Ironically enough, given that such "new Jewish Studies" (ca. the early 2000s) "is at home with questions about minorities, difference, transnationalism, diasporas, and identities—increasingly hot topics in a globalizing current,"[33] the immediate relevance of such constructs for the premodern historicity adduced in the Elman book review would be undeniable.

Alongside the question of disciplines or practices, might one also be asking about intellectual community in a more affiliative sense? To put that more pointedly, is it likely that the respective readerships for Sergei Dolgopolski's triptych of books that juxtapose the discourses of Talmud and continental philosophy, for Marc Caplan's intertwining of African and Yiddish peripheral modernisms, and for Zachary Braiterman's interface between Buber-Rosenzweig and German expressionism overlap even *within* the bounds of Jewish Studies (except in the book review sections of the professional journals)?[34]

Do these otherwise disconnected subfields—rabbinics, Yiddish modernism, modern Jewish philosophy, each conceiving of a different cognate discourse-partner, that is, postmodern thought, comparative literary studies, the visual arts—resonate with each other on the same frequencies? Would a conversation *among* the faculty and graduate students who populate those same subfields be likely to take place at the relevant professional meetings, except to exchange pleasantries in passing? What might be the gain in an affirmative answer to these questions?

Five "Field Surveys": A précis

Imagine another possibility, then—modern German *Wissenschaft* imbricated with postmodern *Yidish visnshaft*—that compounds itself in robust transdisciplinary dialogue with the post-Christian, post-historical university at the boundaries of humanistic inquiry.[35] A discernible urgency has already made itself felt in the field a decade into the twenty-first century. How else to explain the publication of five meta-reflections on it in as many years, each framing some disciplinary aspect of JS in order to make a larger judgment upon the whole.

If we agree with Andrew Bush's *Jewish Studies: A Theoretical Introduction* that "Jewish studies has reenacted the intellectual history of the Western universities where it has come to find a home,"[36] inserting its Jewish content into the secularized receptacles of disciplines, methods, and practices with their own institutional histories—then the question becomes: Does such reenactment (in all the belatedness that word implies) chiefly determine its present and future shape, and does it aspire to more than tenancy, remapping the same terrain in order "to find a home?"

Of these five accounts—*Educational Theory and Jewish Studies in Conversation* (2013), *The Impossible Jew* (2015), *Jewish Studies: A Theoretical In-*

troduction (2011), *Jewish Studies at the Crossroads of Anthropology and History* (2011), and *The Study of Judaism* (2013)—two of them (Andrew Bush's *Theoretical Introduction* and Harvey Shapiro's *Educational Theory*) imagine the enterprise in terms of what other intellectual practice(s) it resembles, as in the rhetoric of *midrash*, that is, *le-mah ha-davar domeh* (to what may this be compared): a correspondence course, environmental studies, and educational theory. Yet both of these accounts leave the enterprise more or less bounded as currently configured.

The jointly edited *Jewish Studies at the Crossroads* advocates a new direction for JS beyond an already substantial investment in "disciplinary pluralism," in order "to rethink the analytical categories and frameworks with which the field continues to work."[37] While the theoretical gain is substantial, the topography traversed by history and anthropology in co-disciplinary formation likewise treats the encompassing bounds of Jewish Studies as a given instead of in dialogic relation to academic terrain not already marked "Jewish."

The remaining two books mirror each other in their reformulation of the multidisciplinary terrain *pars pro toto*. Aaron W. Hughes's *Study of Judaism* worries that Jewish Studies may be "too Jewish" in the specific context of religious studies, parochial, and parochializing. Yet, to the extent that the book's primary concerns, including those related to JS scholars' own ethno-religious identity and the ideological agendas of private foundations, cluster around the disciplinary work denominated by its title, JS (in the spirit of the late Jacob Neusner) comes to signify effectively *Judaic Studies*.[38]

Benjamin Schreier's *Impossible Jew: Identity and the Reconstruction of Jewish American Literary History* argues for a Jewish Studies beyond ethnicity, beyond Jewish identity as known, given, and invariant, the presumptively shared bond between Jewish books and their Jewish readers. How do we intervene in the reifying of the categorical, essentializing, ethnographically and anthropologically coded study of Jews[39]—for which task the epistemological challenge becomes "now and for the future of Jewish American literary studies . . . to pursue a thorough critique of categorical Jewishness"?[40] As that very statement clarifies, however, "Jewish Studies" decants into Jewish literary study, and even more specifically, modern Jewish American literary history, thus mapping only one particular subdivision of an obviously more encompassing JS real estate.

A "reading of and through Jewish Studies"[41] that seeks to take account of the whole, variegated terrain it now boasts in the academy remains before us to undertake. For example, when Bush complicates a prevailing conflation of such terrain with Ashkenaz, a standard mapping of German-Jewish European hegemony onto the evolution of Jewish Studies, he advocates a more polycentric approach, using Sepharad as one example of a more mixed, hybridic, heterogenous national history. "It is possible," he writes, "to provincialize Ashkenaz by studying its constant interaction with other Jews beyond its border . . . a form of practicing Jewish studies as liberation politics, though the liberation is now from within" (44).

If, at its most tendentious, *Wissenschaft des Judentums* and its historico-philological/theological afterlife in modern Jewish Studies have sought to isolate and archive "the Jewish," the idea here is to track its permeability and to recuperate alterity, the various kinds of otherness residing within the borders of the same, a counterhistory and countermemory, so to speak, to a Eurocentric "science of Judaism." I take that strategic move here as a prompt to be exercised meta-discursively for the field of Jewish Studies—to disembed, provincialize, and otherwise *alter* (maybe even liberate) its own sense of itself.

Bush begins and ends his book by invoking the antecedent tradition of Talmud Torah, of religiously grounded Jewish education. Invoking anthropologist Talal Asad's notion that the "grammar of a concept" can be altered,[42] he invites us to consider the difference between participial *learning Jews* (that is, Jews who learn) in the traditional setting of a yeshiva, and gerundive *studying Jews*, that is, a procedure executed by academics (mostly Jews themselves) in the university, where the Jewish subject gets turned into an object. The distinction is not unique to Bush's book. It can be found, for example, in a professedly question-settling article from 1976, "Where Does Jewish Studies Belong?"[43] It underpins Jacob Neusner's related books about JS and the humanities, which I examine in Chapter 3.

Perhaps most piquantly, the difference is limned by Emmanuel Levinas in his 1953 essay, "Means of Identification," in which he isolates the Western mentality of refusing "to adhere to anything before it performs an act of adhesion," emblematic for him of both assimilationist identity in general and the academy in particular.[44] If adherence signifies a personal choice that can also be later revoked (Levinas speaks of a possible "estrangement"), then adhesion suggests something more communitarian.

An "act of adhesion" means that one now monitors oneself from the outside, by means of *comparison*, from the vantage of shared group identity and elective affinity.[45] "To compare oneself to others involves analyzing and weighing oneself up, reducing the personal identity that one is to a series of signs, attributes, contents, qualities, and values. The institution that embodies such a mentality is called the university" (51). Since any other choice regarding Jewish tradition amounts to an anti-modern act of bad faith, "it is [the Western Jew's] duty to reformulate everything in the language of the university."[46]

As a sober judgment about the academy and its sundry reports, this most certainly qualifies. Positively understood, however, acts of adhesion resemble what Edward Said extolled as affiliative forms of intellectual belonging and community beyond or outside of one's "inherited location," and what Stathis Gourgouris has more recently named "the *poiein* of secular criticism," an interrogative practice over and above a theory, a "process of bringing otherness to bear upon the world, as opposed to receiving otherness as an external property."[47] To perform an act of adhesion in this sense is to choose or practice *critique*, to espouse a discipline (*espousal* being a quite powerful expression of *adhesion*), while interrogating it at the same time.

Here, then, is one challenge posed by and to JS, which is not so much interdisciplinary as interlocative and interdiscursive. Who is the addressee for and within Jewish Studies? Who—or what—will be its institutional Other? Which acts of adhesion, which declarations of belonging that also unhome and desituate, will it perform beyond the well-established confines of Judaistic science?

"The very fact of questioning one's Jewish identity means it is already lost," writes Levinas. "But by the same token, it is precisely through this kind of cross-examination that one still hangs on to it. Between already and still Western Judaism walks a tightrope" (50). That is how "Means of Identification" begins. Where Jewish Studies is concerned, let us imagine the tightrope suspended between adverbs of place and not just of time, not so much the condition of its "belonging" or its "inherited location" but rather its traversal between here and there.

Anthropologist Jonathan Boyarin quotes the formulation approvingly in his postscript to *Thinking in Jewish*, "Yiddish Science and the Postmodern," refashioning Levinas's "between already and still" as "the general problematic of postmodernity: living in history, overcoming history . . . living through just this contradiction" (197). And yet, "To a great extent, one can say that postmodern thought takes shape in the recognition that, actually, this is no contradiction." From the vantage of the postmodern, from within its structure of feeling, "human history . . . is not created once and for all," because "the past is always being created anew according to the needs of the present," hence, the emphasis on an alternate identity formation, programmatically marginal and centrifugal, which Boyarin labels "critical post Judaism."

Schreier approvingly cites Boyarin's analysis in his own book in an analysis of identity that diverges radically from Levinas's. Far from being self-evidently *about* Jews and their history, Schreier wants to reconceptualize JS "as operating precisely as the displacement of the assumption that Jewish studies is the study of the Jews" (1). The move feels analogous to Bercovitch's counterpoint between the traps of culture (or historicism) on one hand, and de-transcendentalizing inquiry into the trapping process on the other.

Whether or not, as Levinas argues, "before one starts comparing himself to anyone else . . . one just is a Jew," the one facing us[48] does not so easily correlate with stable, unifying and unified features that we might normatively assign to a given, scrutable Jewish identity. A real-life Jewish fraud like Binjamin Wilkomirski/Bruno Dössekker or the self-reinvented Lev Nussimbaum/Kurban Said (the very exemplar of Rothian counterlife), drives the point home.[49] *Pace* Levinas, it is now the university—paradoxically enough, as an engine for critique—that supplies both analytics and vocabulary for critiquing any number of presuppositions about identity and about who one "just is."

Whereas Bush endorsed othering an academic discourse from within through recourse to counterhistory and countermemory, thus "provincializing" what purports to the referential norm, I wish to extend Schreier's powerful insight about legibility to a more field-wide, meta-disciplinary intervention. Let this project stand, then, as a *recognition scene* staged for Jewish Studies, by which its own given and legible features of identity, its own "population," so to speak, are placed productively in question. Beyond the laudable aim for a *conversability* of JS outside its borders, reflecting its own "interwoven praxial, discursive texture,"[50] impelling it should be a more energetically politicized self-critique, a placing and displacing of the field itself, a counter-archive to its regulative predicates of identity.[51]

As a flanking maneuver to the five meta-reflections summarized above, I wish to gather together what I have said and unify it under this heading: If JS is to evolve beyond those regulative predicates (as it already has beyond an original positivism), it must undertake its own investigations, its own report to the academy in respect to both its "content" and the otherness it can bring to bear upon an institutional world. One way to begin that process would be to speak differently about it in a genuinely new key: a *concerted* rhetorical dialogism over and above *laissez faire* heterogeneity, multispecialization, and concatenations of expertise.

Thus, the title of a 2009 MLA symposium, "Does the English Department Have a Jewish Problem?"[52] (as valid as it may still be) could just as well be instructively inverted: *Does Jewish Studies Have an "English Department" Problem?* In other words, which are its elective (and resisted) affinities? Does JS function as a genuine crossing point for what Dominick LaCapra, in his critique of Bill Readings, calls "articulatory practices"?[53] Will its own future horizon leave open indeterminate, ostensibly closed, pre-legitimated categories, which nevertheless signify, in Schreier's phrase, a persistent "axis of desire?"

Even if an individual Jewish Studies program boasts illustrious faculty or particular field strengths, even if it innovates according to fresh or previously underutilized thematic foci, and even if it convenes cutting-edge international conferences, it may still have its work cut out for itself in establishing a pivoting point for a Jewish Studies–to-come. Call that work, after Benjamin, *eine schwache messianische Kraft* (a weak messianism) or less grandiosely but still provocatively: Jewish Studies as counterlife.

(The) Four Questions

I have described my purposes here under the heading of "manifesto," although I have committed a rather flagrant violation of the genre's protocol for brevity. Playing off (and within) a more specifically Judaic scaffold—and with similar cheek—we might also avail ourselves of the Hebrew *"haggadah"* to describe a text woven by disparate threads, like that Mishnaic tapestry of narrative, law, ritual, song, praise (and invective) recited at the *Seder* table on the annual Jewish festival of Passover. On the model of its most widely-known section "the four questions," through which the process of *haggadah* (telling) is formally initiated, I submit the following organizing queries.

No. 1: Notwithstanding named chairs or honorifics, can one meaningfully be said to profess Jewish Studies, to be a "professor of Jewish Studies" as opposed to being, say, a Jewish historian, a scholar of Medieval Jewish philosophy, an expert in modern Semitic languages, a specialist in Jewish art, literature, music, folklore, sociology, and the like? Is JS a classically embedded platform of vertically or laterally integrated fields, pedagogies, and areas of research, solidly perched upon its twin nineteenth-century piers of philology and history, the "Jewish" more or less interchangeable with "the Judaic"? Or is it, rather, something more ad hoc, variable, and locally contingent, depending on how a given program has been founded, staffed, and directed? Does it boast a genuinely critical mass, the whole greater than the sum of its parts? Or is it loosely aggregated instead, a platform for enlightened self-interest? What would be the minimum amount of teaching and research coverage to justify the administrative nomenclature of "JS" (some programs numbering as few as four faculty and others as many as thirty)? And finally, in the larger context of the humanities: Does the increasingly common push for early and relentless professionalization in graduate training merely paper over the time-honored habit of professorial self-reproduction, all the more ethically questionable in a contracting academic ecology? All such questions speak to JS as a network anchored in disciplinary structure. The unasked question, however, would take shape as a more-than-merely interdisciplinary inquiry into intellectual community, as what makes the university matter.[54]

No. 2: Which other possibilities open up for the structure and location of Jewish Studies within the bounds of the university beyond strictures of field or discipline? How, in a word, does JS "recommence"—a concept (retrieved in my epilogue) that Sacvan Bercovitch adapts from Emerson, signaling dynamic and recursive change?

No. 3: What does it mean to practice and profess Jewish Studies in the post-historical university, the university without an idea, the dereferentialized university, the university of Excellence? All such characterizations, if not immediately familiar to readers (belonging as they do to a single source-text), shall be explained subsequently.

No. 4: Is there a more efficacious way of asking the field's animating question now other than by way of disciplinary hegemony and specialization—that is, "Where does Jewish Studies belong?"—which inadvertently highlights its belatedness on the academic scene while holding it to an overarching criterion of "fit"? Or will the matter of belonging always stand over the enterprise as not just an administrative question but a quintessentially Jewish one, reproducing, if again only by accident, a familiar conundrum about Jews and the places and groupings to which they either do or don't "belong"?

In Chapter 1, "Jewish Studies as Lever," I elaborate these four heuristics both diagnostically and figurally. In thus reframing some of the field's organizing assumptions, my particular interest here is to "work the frame" itself: to mobilize borders, to set forth inside relative to outside "as a problem," and, in echo of the ever-insistent *answerability* Bakhtin assigns to art, to pursue the latent *interrogativity* of JS.[55]

Appealing thus to thinkers not immediately associated with the customary frontiers of JS at a reflexive level allows me, in Chapter 2, "Jewish Studies and the Pitchfork" (the most syncretic in the book), to amplify and thicken the inquiry by means of a further constellation of figures. As ad-

mittedly unconventional as such thinkers or figures may be vis-à-vis JS—
and a challenge thereby posed for some readers—in an obvious sense I am
importing strangeness as we already saw that move refined by Bercovitch
and Kun. Yet, my intent here, as throughout the subsequent chapters, is to
read Jewish Studies, to stage it in the performative sense, to propose a contraversion of its current mode of self-reflection, and to project an open
future for its reframing possibilities.

Chapter 3 is entitled "*Mochlos* or *Makhlokes*: JS and the Humanities."
"*Makhlokes*" (Ashkenazi pronunciation) connotes "dissensus," "separation,"
"faction," "dispute" (like German "*Streit*" in Kant's *The Conflict of the Faculties*). Its trilateral root חלק (*HLK*) can signify either "to divide" or "to be
smooth or viscous." How, in light of this Mishnaic concept, does JS position itself with respect to academic humanities: as a mode or leverage, or
as a node of energetic conflict and contestation?

A conservative, polemical answer to that question was posed thirty years
ago by the late and prodigious scholar of rabbinic Judaism Jacob Neusner
in several books about the disciplines, research methodologies, and modes
of Jewish Studies in specific relation to the "new Humanities." With a
wealth of reformulation having accrued to the latter term in the last decade or so, Chapter 3 reopens Neusner's presentation of the case vis-à-vis
a contemporaneous deployment of the same phrase by Derrida.

Chapter 4, "*Bildungsheld* or *Pícaro*, Canon and List: A Heterotopology
for JS," foregrounds an extra-disciplinary structure for "Jewish Studies"
outside the bounds of the university proper. British rabbinics professor
Philip Alexander's keen observation about JS feels especially pertinent here:
"Jewish Studies has emerged as an autonomous field that is strictly speaking neither secular nor religious, but academic."[56] I turn, therefore, to the
precedent of Franz Rosenzweig's Freies Jüdisches Lehrhaus Frankfurt,
whose short heyday in the 1920s has bequeathed a model for extra-academic
Jewish education, subsequently refashioned by others.

What would JS look like if it weren't tied to the institutional vicissitudes
of academicized knowledge practices, if the reproduction of the academic
system and social field, the *magister-discipulus* relation, were not its determinative economy? Is, or can, Jewish Studies be a kind of heterotopia
within the university's borders? What would it mean for JS—as Rosenzweig envisioned for his students in Lehrhaus—to bring the outside in? As
counterexample to Neusner's essays in Chapter 3, Rosenzweig's, along with
brief treatments of Heidegger and Foucault, determine the slightly denser
focus in Chapter 4. Implications of the chapter's title, with its tension be-

tween hero and adventurer and closed or open catalog, are taken up in the concluding pages.

Chapter 5, "Ventilating the Tradition: Rashbam and the Coen Brothers," covers a performative and unlikely coupling of rabbinic commentary and postmodern filmmaking that pivots around the vagaries of storytelling. With this chapter, I aim to circulate air not only within the crowded spaces explored in the first four, but also inside the classical textual precincts JS has traditionally made its own.

If this book had been authored by a different category of disciplinarian—historian, social scientist, or theologian—this final chapter would most likely not be juxtaposing a twelfth-century Northern-French Torah commentator and twenty-first-century American filmmakers, or the contrasting narrative strategies in Genesis 24 and *A Serious Man*. But in conducting just that sort of interreading, *Jewish Studies as Counterlife: A Report to the Academy* concludes on the note on which it began, picking up the thread of a Jewish Studies story that hasn't quite materialized or been recounted with a level of invention that matches its own unfolding.

The epilogue, "Knotted thread, middle game: an *envoi*," weaves that conceit into a set of final reflections about Jewish Studies in its counterlived aspect as *un fil renoué*, a motif from Emmanuel Levinas's late philosophy. It also returns to a formulation from one of his earlier essays we have briefly touched upon by reconsidering the question of affiliative belonging. A brief reflection on Bruce Robbins's notions of secular vocation and professional identity segues to a final section, the most conventionally manifesto-like portion of the book. We return full circle to Sacvan Bercovitch, whose Emersonian reflections on the "alternative possibilities" discoverable in chess's middle game, alongside those of Stanley Cavell, offer a final heuristic for JS, concluding the book.

If we were to dust off an old-fashioned model of story-structure, the introduction and the first two chapters sketch the outlines of a *plot*. Chapters 3 and 4, focused on the intellectual figures of Jacob Neusner and Franz Rosenzweig, add the ballast of *character* and *setting*. Chapter 5 and the epilogue, respectively, carry through a performative commitment to *theme* and *point of view*. More intrepidly summarized: An experimenting,[57] *ein bericht*, a post-traditional *haggadah* for a rather different sort of *seder* (Heb. for "order"), *Jewish Studies as Counterlife* narrates and reimagines the fortunes of one distinctive habitat within the modern university's institutional ecology.

While rehearsing some of its past and seeking a window on the present, I do not intend so much to foretell its future as hold open for it a principle

Giorgio Agamben has called *la potenza*, a worldly force that does not expend itself but rather gets sustained in retention.[58] As the allusions to Kafka and Roth should illustrate, along with the other motifs sketched in this introduction, I want not only to theorize or conjure Jewish Studies but to *figure* it: to recast it through a series of elastic, catalytic tropes.

To that extent, my use of the term "allegory" to describe Rotpeter's report or Bercovitch-Kun on "Investigations of a Dog" may actually miss the mark in specific relation to JS; a more precise word is probably needed to get at the fissures each of Kafka's texts exposes. In his essay on hermeneutics, "What Is tradition?," Gerald Bruns contrasts the premodern modes of allegory and satire as different approaches to the past and its otherness. Allegory typically justifies itself as "appropriative discourse with claims to universality," seeking to translate the alien by domesticating it, smoothing over its rough edges. As such, it epitomizes "the mode of interpretation of the institution, whose task is to identify everything in terms of itself, not just (of course) academically, but to lay claim to it, to keep it under control."[59]

By contrast, satire represents the discourse of the Other against the Same: counterallegory—more Kafka and Roth, than, say, Philo as a reader of the Holy Scriptures. (Bruns's own contrast is totalizing Descartes vs. exilic Petrarch.) "From a hermeneutical standpoint," argues Bruns, "the encounter with tradition is more likely to resemble satire than allegory, unmasking of the present rather than a translation of the past" (204). Since it often entails a return of the forgotten or repressed, it lends itself to interventions like Scholem's grand lesson in counterhistory. Such a frictional notion of tradition is satire's gift to the academy—and by extension its analytic utility for Jewish Studies, especially regarding its resistances, its othering of self, the difference(s) of its belonging, and the conflict of interpretations in which it lives.[60]

A gast af a vayl zet a mayl: *The Memoir in the Manifesto*

Interpolated between chapters are five interchapters recounting scenes of quasi-clerical life in JS. As anecdotal vignettes in distant echo of Bercovitch and Kun, they make no pretense of belonging to "the subgenre of contemporary academic memoir [whose instances] anticipate and impact contemporary considerations of humanism and the state of the humanities,"[61] however, they might obliquely filter such considerations.

In the original Greek, an *anekdota* denotes a small unpublished item—in English, a "narrative generally of an amusing and biographical incident."[62] The incidents separately related here are intended to convey the general spirit of a Talmudic concept known as *se'or sheba'isa* (leaven in the dough): in itself an extrinsic element, which, however, assures the benefit of fermentation or procreation (for example, b. *Berakhot* 17a and b. *Yoma* 69b).

A parallel within a more modern Jewish discursive tradition would be the role Primo Levi welcomes for himself as a Jew in his memoir *The Periodic Table*: Necessarily at the margins, in the interstices, both vulnerable and catalytic, pr'ecariously yet galvanically impure, "In order for the wheel to turn, for life to be lived, impurities are needed, and the impurities of impurities in the soil, too, as is known, if it is to be fertile. Dissension, diversity, the grain of salt and mustard are needed. . . . I am the impurity that makes the zinc react, I am the grain of salt or mustard [*sono io il granello di sale e di senape*]."[63]

Notwithstanding Levi's contention ventured elsewhere that he "did not believe that there is much affinity between Kafka and me,"[64] his conceit is positioned here in much the same way as was Kafka's fiction earlier in this introduction: a "thrown voice" for Jewish Studies, and more indirectly, for my own experiences in and with it.

I subscribed there to Bercovitch's proviso about common principles of exegesis that can effectively correlate imprecise symmetries; here we can invoke the phenomenon well known to Levi the chemist, of "chirality": the asymmetric relationship between mirror-image molecules and ions. If one such compound cannot be superimposed upon its seeming "double," then likewise, the interchapters, while coinciding with each other in certain basic respects, narrate discrete experiences. The through line is the "counter" in, of, and athwart JS.

The interchapters make no bid for typicality. Reflecting neither the top echelon nor the outskirts of JS programs at institutions large and small, public and private, they occupy a middle ground. If somewhat like canine investigations or a reacclimated primate's report—each having the force of the singular or supplementary—they still fall within hailing distance of the norm. As I stipulate in one of them, the case for their inclusion is less personal than structural, even diagnostic: as so many x-rays revealing a portion of academia's "body." Like the radiographs exposed to his fellow bus-passengers by a garrulous Israeli in a *New Yorker* essay by David Grossman, the interior thereby becomes a filter for the exterior as a "noisy swarm" outside is made "visible through a single pair of kidneys,"[65] (mirror of the psyche and seat of conscience in *Tanakh*).

Like comparable instances of *travail* (as Derrida names the university's vocation), JS hardly lacks occasions for burlesque. But while their edge is ever so slightly satirical, the interchapters are calibrated as much for self-satire—hence, the cover illustration by Yiddish puppeteer-artist Yosl Cutler[66]—as they are for institutional critique. Together, they comprise a personal record of seasons spent reaping to the edges of a jointly worked field and gathering the gleanings.

INTERCHAPTER I

JS *Davka*

"The Questionnaire," a now staple feature of the biannual AJS *Perspectives* magazine, poses this roving reporter–like question in its Spring 2012 issue: *Why did you go into Jewish Studies?* The responses from a range of scholars in disciplines like history, religious studies, and Hebrew literature narrate accounts of being both placed and displaced (some even linked specifically *to* place, such as Berlin and Jerusalem) as statements about professional identity and disciplinary affiliation. Had I been one of the designated respondents, I might have begun with something like the following: Did I actually do so? Could I even be said to be *in* it now?

It is true that several of my books (including this one) have been marketed under the publishers' category of "Jewish Studies." I serve on the editorial board of more than one journal in the field. Annual dues have guaranteed me membership in the Association for Jewish Studies (AJS) at whose annual conference I have presented periodically. I even logged a stint as the ad interim director for a Jewish Studies program on its way to more stable and well-funded status.

My teaching has included JS courses in a number of subject areas. In print, I have treated the likes of Levinas, Henry Roth, Yeshayahu Leibowitz, Bruno Schulz, rabbinic *darshanim*, Dan Pagis, Rabbi Joseph B. Soloveitchik, the late Aharon Appelfeld, Yiddish American poets, Elias Canetti, Cynthia Ozick, Emmanuel Ringelbum, the Rashbam, Kadya Molodowsky, Walter Benjamin, and Ben Katchor. Yet in all candor, I think whatever answer I might supply to the query above would still be haunted by the question: Have I *davka* ever "gone into" JS?[1]

In my first academic position, I taught English and American literature and theory. Observing a gradual drift in my career trajectory into more areas and matters academically Jewish, a senior colleague expressed some concern about the risk of losing purchase on a "field" by venturing too far outside it—*Ausweg*, so to speak, by mistake. The intent, I took it, was something like re-occidentation: Stay in literary studies or lose your bearings.

In truth, I never forswore my "primary" affiliation, as I rather fondly look back on it now from my unchurched vantage of JS. Nor, typically, was any mechanism of dual or multiple citizenship needed, nor letters of transit that facilitated unmolested passage between departments. I often wonder whether it is simply the contingent choices of the institutions with which one's lot gets thrown.

Perhaps there would be rather different stories to tell with other contingencies in other institutions in force. I discovered that, barring exceptional translocational fortune or talent, one practices one's secular vocation under the aegis of a *particular* school motto, on a *particular* campus, within a formal niche of research, and teaching whatever is its individual concentration or distribution of Jewish valences: interpersonal, intellectual, aspirational, or stubbornly factual.

And yet, whether I was formally affiliated with JS or lurking and working in its penumbra, another text by Kafka, from roughly the same period as the animal fables treated in our introduction, now occurs to me. Composed in 1920, given the title "Gemeinschaft" ("Community") by Max Brod and published in 1936, it supplies perhaps the definitive parable about an *a posteriori* community whose "continual being-together" can never quite escape an all-too-contingent origin-story—the Derridean "event of founding":

> We are five friends, one day we came out of a house one after the other, first one came and placed himself beside the gate, then the second came, or rather he glided through the gate like a little ball of quicksilver, and placed himself near the first one, then came the third, then the fourth, then the fifth. Finally we all stood in a row. People began to notice us, they pointed at us and said: Those five just came out of that house.

Since then we have been living together, it would be a peaceful life if it weren't for a sixth one continually trying to interfere. He doesn't do us any harm, but he annoys us, and that is harm enough; why does he intrude when he is not wanted? We don't know him and don't want him to join us.

There was a time, of course, when the five of us did not know one another, either, and it could be said that we still don't know one another, but what is possible and can be tolerated by the five of us is not possible and cannot be tolerated with this sixth one. In any case, we are five and don't want to be six. And what is the point of this continual being together anyhow? It is also pointless for the five of us, but here we are together and will remain together; a new combination, however, we do not want, just because of our experiences.

But how is one to make all this clear to the sixth one? Long explanations would almost amount to accepting him in our circle, so we prefer not to explain and not to accept him. No matter how he pouts his lips we push him away with our elbows, but however much we push him away, back he comes.[2]

We could style this as an "inside narrative" (as Herman Melville cannily subtitled *Billy Budd* in the margins of its manuscript), which would also thus suit the contours of both "Investigations of a Dog" and "A Report to an Academy." Inside narratives differ from official or historical reports. Unlike the newspaper account of Billy's crime reserved for the penultimate chapter of Melville's novella, they are tainted by the personal. So it is with the inside narrative offered here, a "socio-analysis"[3] told by a sometime-insider who also positions himself both outside and on the slant.

The import of Kafka's social discourse[4] about community in this tale differs dramatically from what we find under the same heading in an essay published just seven years later on the eve of World War I by Martin Buber, inaugurating his monthly magazine *Der Jude* (for the second volume of which, as we have already learned, Kafka published his "Zwei Tiergeshichten."

> In the tempest of events the Jew has the powerful experience of what *Gemeinschaft* means.... The most essential weakness of the Western Jew was not that he was "assimilated" but that he was atomized; that he was without a connection; that his heart no longer beat as one with a living *Gemeinschaft* . . . ; that he was excluded from the life of the people and their holy *Gemeinschaft*. . . . Now, however, in the catastrophic events that he experienced with his neighbors, the Jew

discovered with shock and joy the great life of *Gemeinschaft*. And it captured him.[5]

For Buber (whom Kafka, to his independently minded credit, deemed both "remarkable" and "dreary"),[6] Jewish fellowship, camaraderie, and sodality coalesce when Jewish security itself is imperiled. Rather embarrassingly for him, the First World War did not provide the catalyst for an integrative German-nationalist Jewish peoplehood and the "aesthetic of unity"[7] that he imagined (and subsequently recanted); the benefits of geopolitical chaos that it seemed to herald, for Buber, became particularly lethal to the Jews of Weimar, Germany, and only ensured their doom.

Absent such hazard (or at least, sufficiently distanced from it), and given Buber's own skepticism about the *Wissenschaft* legacy, Kafka's more modest and self-ironizing vision—"It could be said that we still don't know one another"—limns a rather different horizon for the legatees of a Science of Judaism in the academy.

And it is with respect to such cautious *Gemeinschaft*—the guild-mentality of its scholar *clercs*—that we turn to the next chapter, where questions of community and communities of the question take center stage. As both plurals inflect a project as overdetermined by tradition as Jewish Studies, it would be sage to keep in mind Bruns's distinction between allegory and satire, because as much as JS might appeal to the former to construct a desired unity, it is more likely the spirit of the latter, as a determined encounter with otherness, that will benignly superintend a postcontemporary project burdened by the past but still tasked with an open future.

CHAPTER 1

Jewish Studies as Lever

> For although the boundary as such is necessary, yet every single specific boundary can be stepped over, every fixity can be displaced, every enclosure can be burst, and every such act, of course, finds or creates a new boundary. The pair of statements—that the boundary is unconditional in that its existence is constitutive of our given position in the world, but that no boundary is unconditional since every one can in principle be altered, reached over, gotten around—this pair of statements appears as the explication of the inner unity of vital action.
>
> —GEORG SIMMEL, "Life as Transcendence," in *The View of Life: Four Metaphysical Essays with Journal Aphorisms*

After a compressed history of modern JS centering on the figure of Gershom Scholem (no mean metaphorist himself), this first of two linked chapters adds to the initial figuration of Jewish Studies a further constellation of images pertaining to location and movement/force: the boundary, the ruins, the city, and the lever. It would be a lonely field, however, if it were populated only by metaphors, no matter how evocative. Hence this further ensemble of curated voices, whose reverberant, interdiscursive effect offers one paradigm in the context of JS, makes for a more dialogically inflected humanities. Like the deceptively prosaic matter of what constitutes a "Jewish language,"[1] both this and the succeeding chapter endeavor to *think* the project of Jewish Studies adventurously by considering genres over and above disciplines, and by pursuing emergent rather than settled questions.

Partes extra partes

Let us imagine we are coming upon the nomenclature of "Jewish Studies" for the first time. Electronic device at hand, we Google the term to determine identifying criteria and discover, among its first hits, the directories of more than two hundred Jewish Studies programs (including those in Israel, the UK, and Canada) on the Association for Jewish Studies (AJS) website, as well as those listed on the Academic Jewish Studies Internet Directory.[2] Were we statistically inclined, we might then pursue a comprehensive study of all these programs as reflected on their websites, developing metrics that would reveal institutional history, faculty distribution, areas of expertise and nature of appointment, course offerings and programming, joint ventures with other departmental structures, or extramural constituencies.[3]

But even short of such assiduous compilation, we discover that the range in content, design, core, and affiliated faculty for such programs is extremely broad—so broad, in fact, as to make unifying criteria elusive. Differences among such programs are telling, depending on how and when they have been configured, staffed, and funded. Centers, institutes, and programs that couple Jewish Studies and some other entity, say, Israel Studies, make the picture—and the concomitant identity politics—even more complicated and ideologically freighted.

(With apologies to conscientious encyclopedists), Wikipedia proves similarly dissatisfying.[4] Its JS entry, listing thirty-two of the most prominent programs, defines "Jewish (or Judaic) Studies" variously as corresponding to "an academic discipline," demonstrating an "interdisciplinary" character, and constituting "a distinct field" to which are related those other "fields that include Holocaust research and Israel Studies, and in Israel, Jewish Thought." A focus on field and discipline obscures the roles played by department and stakeholder. Because JS is administered so variously and is so inconsistently populated by faculty and students, an invariant template will prove elusive. Certain programs coalesce around a single originating faculty presence and disciplinary tilt; others develop more collaboratively, across research fields; still others develop through the demands of students, local Jewish communities, and/or influential donors.

But would it then be just a matter of reordering its component elements within the flexible contours or Platonic ideal of a JS "data field"?[5] Even within such a field, the multiple components of JS appear less dialogical than aggregated, a mix of loose and fast fish.[6] As I suggest at the end of this chapter, however, that status can also make for productive possibility, a property known to readers of Jean-Luc Nancy as *partes extra partes* or "parts outside of parts," where the *outsideness* of any subjectivity, its exposure to others, matters more than any sovereign interiority.

Still, even if our concerns here involve sovereignty as much as structure, asking the *quid*—What is JS?—from the perspective of the *quo* or even *cui*—Where, within which boundaries, should JS reside, and to whose authority should it answer?—may provide some support, since at the very least it prompts a meta-inquiry into the placing/displacing of Jewish Studies.

What if we were to take an alternate approach, then, by returning to the AJS website to consider the umbrella professional organization itself, which, from the top-down, identifies a learned, credentialed society. Established in 1969, its official name, "The Association for Jewish Studies," encodes more than one semantic possibility. One of these might be JS as a vehicle for *kibbutz*—*communitas*, *Mitsein*, *ensemble*—a colloquium of academic practitioners gathering to speak in print or in person about their respective fields, research areas, pursuits, and vocations. Alternatively, perhaps the studies themselves comprise what aspire to be dialogistically "associated."

At its inception, this "associative" aspect of Jewish Studies took both forms, in fact. Thanks largely to the late Judaics scholar Jacob Neusner, it was expressed as a question about *belonging*, posed as an explicit matter of Jewish membership on the one hand, and Jewish advocacy on the other: (1) Did non-Jewish scholars of Hebrew Bible criticism, for example, at that freighted fault line between two professional organizations—one mostly Christian (the Society for the Study of Biblical Literature), and the other mostly Jewish (the AJS)—belong within the fold of the latter?; and (2) Does the extramural Jewish community—the world of Jewish communal institutions, services, and synagogues—have a stake in the academic enterprise; that is to say, do they belong inside, too?

Quite clearly, in the almost fifty subsequent years, such questions remain open and perhaps permanently so, making JS only an artificially unified and settled affair. And yet, despite some continuingly *arrière-garde* tendencies, exactly such ongoingness might justify the field's self-understanding in the vanguard of "new Humanities," where limits and categories of belonging, of inside and inside, of content and directionality, remain productively in question.

As we saw at the end of the introduction, according to Martin Buber already in 1901, only the smaller component of the JS data-field is embodied by a "science of Judaism," its greater portion belonging to various other disciplines through mechanisms of "tracing and linkage." With a prehistory of specific learning habits and practices exclusive to *yeshivot*, its comparatively late genealogy encompasses several discernible stages or guises, almost all inflected by some version of apologetics: *Wissenschaftlich* (early nineteenth century), Semiticist (late nineteenth century), nationalist (early-twentieth-century Palestine), ethnic-particularist (late-twentieth-century United States), and what we might call, after the ambivalent "post" in "postmodernism," post-traditional, post-Western, post-*Wissenschaft* (early twenty-first century).

Scholem on Wissenchaft: *Content and Aspect*

It took several decades into the twentieth century before the academicized embodiment of Jewish Studies began the transition from seminaries to the university proper.[7] Not insignificantly, "Jewish Studies also emerged as a Western academic discourse in an age of European colonialism and nation building."[8] This point is particularly salient in regard to the establishment of Hebrew University in 1920s pre-state Palestine, while reminding us that Jewish Studies has always been subject to temporal refashionings, such as orientalist, postwar perennialist, 1967- and-after.

With Salo Baron's appointment as the Miller Chair in Jewish history at Columbia University in 1929 and Harry Wolfson's appointment as Littauer Chair in Hebrew literature and philosophy at Harvard in 1925 (both scholars having also taught at Stephen Wise's Jewish Institute of Religion[9]), Jewish Studies as such commences in American universities. Both scholars excluded themselves from participating at the inception of the AJS four decades later, a fact that leads us to note an internal resistance or differentiation in almost ritualized recurrence throughout its history (often reflecting generational schism). This seems to mark Jewish Studies as frictional (and recurrently factional) at its core.[10]

It is worth pondering for a moment whether the nomenclature of "Jewish Studies" is thus properly singular or plural (or more provocatively, *both*). In Israeli universities, JS is known as *mada'ei hayahadut* ("knowledge practices of Judaism") rather than *mad'a hayahadut* ("science of Judaism"). The singular denotes a fiction of unity (to that degree, commensurate with a much older tradition of religious self-understanding encompassing all manner of text and commentary within a single normative hermeneutic). By contrast, the plural almost by definition discloses, even stipulates, fault lines and variegation.

From its origins in critical-historical consciousness and disciplinary exactitude, a heterogeneity of methodologies has by now become perhaps the defining feature of JS, which assumes quite different configurations depending on region, faculty or student demographic, organizing philosophy, and programmatic thrust. Where once philology, Jewish history and philosophy, the Biblical canon and its commentaries, and *yam hatalmud* ("the sea of the Talmud") appeared illimitable and inexhaustible all by themselves (even if room was eventually made for the likes of Kabbalah, Hasidic wonder tales, and modern Hebrew poetry), the field of modern academic Jewish Studies appears now more like a world map of states and nations, with borderlines as far as the eye can see.

Visual and material cultures, various national literatures and languages, cultural anthropology, ethnography, disability and body studies, et alia crowd a field formerly confined to the formerly sovereign triumvirate of Biblical/Post-Biblical Literature, Jewish History, and Jewish Thought. Jewish Studies in 2018 differs as much from Jewish Studies circa 1969 as the latter did from Jewish Studies circa 1929.[11]

Even the superordinate term shifts according to predilection both ideological and disciplinary: *Wissenschaft des Judentums*, Jewish Studies, Judaic Studies, Judaistica, Jewish Civilization, Hebrew Culture Studies, *mada'ei hayahadut*, and so forth. A simple comparison of Hebrew literature scholar Arnold Band's 1967 essay, "Jewish Studies in American Liberal-Arts Colleges and Universities," and the 2008 AJS Membership survey (as well as more recent questionnaires on the state of the field in the association's *Perspectives* magazine) will plainly convey this shift in both the practices and institutionalization of JS over the last fifty years.

At any rate, the structure and location of JS continue to depend on Jewish Studies' twin origin-stories: first, as *Wissenschaft des Judentums* in Europe and Palestine, and next, as one of several identity-based minority programs of study in the American university.[12] These competing cultural and historical origins bequeath to us an institutional hybrid that is discursively unique, spanning a set of foundational texts nearly three millennia old and the most current and immediate expressions of its postmodernity. Subsequent chapters in this book frame the problem as a narrative sequence from the cultural ideals of *Bildung* and *Wissenschaft* to the fissured and fissuring politics of identity within the academy's sociology of knowledge.[13]

This was already Scholem's point of departure back in the 1944 essay "Reflections on Modern Jewish Studies," twenty years after the establishment of the Hebrew University of Jerusalem, when he asked whether this was the heritage and the goal that a previous generation had so intensely awaited:

> Is there something wrong in the house of wisdom and science, so that one ought to think of repairing the house? Is it not stated that during

the birth pangs of Messiah, the hidden things will become revealed—
and also by rights, that the revealed things will become hidden? And
whether this is said in praise or denigration—do not even the revealed
things in the Science of Judaism also contain hidden elements? (52–53)

That intuition, of course, bespeaks Scholem's full scholarly investment in the claims of what his biographer David Biale terms "counterhistory," the great reservoir of Judaism's mystical traditions eschewed by historical criticism only to its detriment.

This would be Scholem's version of the Jewish search for a usable past, the counterhistorical corrective to the *Wissenschaftler*'s historical science, and a clarion call for a more comprehensively contoured Jewish Studies. The intuition lies also at the heart of Scholem's two essays, the prewar critique from which I just quoted, and "The Science of Judaism Then and Now" from 1959, more measured, less demonizing, that views JS through the lens of the State of Israel's establishment and the Shoah, whose twin meaning "must remain of overwhelming significance for the Science of Judaism and cannot be assessed too highly."[14] Scholem invokes the "great catastrophe of the Jewish expulsion from Spain in 1492" as the comparable event in Jewish history that required the passing of at least two generations before "it could render itself accountable and come to grips with what had happened."

In both essays, Scholem laments a tradition of *Wissenschaft*, whose apologetically driven relation to the Jewish past was ambivalent at best. Salvaged as a relic, suited for academic inquiry no less than other bygone religious and cultural traditions, that legacy may seem to have been reclaimed by being founded on a new platform. And yet, under *Wissenschaft*'s aegis, "you see before you giants, who for reasons best known to themselves, have become gravediggers and embalmers" (59). Scholem quotes Moritz Steinschneider's memorable retort to a Zionist student of his who extolled the renaissance of the Jewish people and its hidden values, "Please, sir, we have no other task but to conduct a 'proper funeral' for all that" (60).

In place of this well-intended salvage mission, which—while it may have liberated rabbinic literature from the rabbis also, in archiving, codifying, historicizing, and scientizing—risked merely "embalming" it, Scholem declaims,

> new concepts, new categories, new intuition, new daring are required: a 'critique of the critique,' the dismantling of the dismantling. From now on, the creative destruction of scientific criticism which examines

hearts and innards via the documents of the past will serve a different function: not the washing and embalming of the dead body, but the discovery of its hidden life by removing the masks and curtains that had hidden it, and the misleading inscriptions.

For Scholem, these represent constitutive problems, which require a revisionist approach from what now discloses their "proper place: the renewal of the nation from its tragic and tumultuous history" (67). A transvalued historical consciousness revivifies the scientific method.

That was 1944. Looking back, Scholem is just as keenly critical of his own intellectual moment as motivated by the national homiletics and national rhetoric (his phrases) of Zionism. From a vantage point in the shadow of the Holocaust which has taken the lives of a whole generation of scholars, he wonders aloud whether he and his peers have not been ruthless enough in their "profound surgery which was meant to uproot from our flesh the multi-colored plague that spread therein." "We had hoped," he writes, "for healing and received instead terror" (70).

Fifteen years after the Holocaust, and a decade since Israel's founding, the tone of the 1959 essay is less doleful and more pragmatic, as Scholem surveys an academic landscape for Judaic studies—the more accurate term for what he is analyzing—now shared between "the major centers of activity in Israel and America," where he can point to Saul Lieberman, Harry Wolfson, and Salo Baron, "men who are re-creating a scholarly heritage in our generation" (312–313), as contemporary figures no less distinguished than were historians Zecharias Frankel and Heinrich Graetz in their generation, and the secularizing Simon Dubnow in his.

A mere ten years later (1969), on terrain the eminent American literary critic Alfred Kazin called "native grounds," that landscape shifted in a way Scholem could probably not have predicted. Historian Salo Baron and scholar of Hebrew literature and philosophy Harry Wolfson, the two then most prominent members of the American Academy for Jewish Research (AAJR), pointedly elected *not* to attend the inaugural meeting at Brandeis of the Association of Jewish Studies (an organization compared unfavorably with the American Academy of Religion by Jacob Neusner and held in contempt in subsequent decades).[15] And just as significantly, that colloquium and the professional organizing and development that followed in its wake were the direct consequence of a widely circulated article published three years earlier by Arnold Band—the same year that Jacques Derrida first presented his work, the soon-to-be-famous "Structure, Sign, and Play," at an American conference.

What compels our attention here, and why I also allude to Derrida in passing, is Band's professed specialization. For this was not "literature" in the sense Leopold Zunz understood the term in his 1818 article, "Etwas über die Rabbinische Litteratur," or the way it functions in the name chosen by Christian Hebraists in the same century, "The Society for Biblical Literature." Nor was it what Scholem had in mind almost a century and a half later when he conceded the vast work yet to be done on "the great works of Jewish literature" whose aesthetics "is still totally lacking," as befits a research area within the transhistorical ambit of Judaic studies that has "not yet been scientifically evaluated" (313).

To cite a distinction Scholem deploys in correspondence with Walter Benjamin (1933–1940), "Jewish (and particularly Judaic) contents" are what fundamentally galvanize Scholem as opposed to, say, "Jewish aspects"— Benjamin's term for those elements in his autobiography, *Berliner Kindheit um Neunzehnhundert*, that were neither Zionist nor demonstrably tied to expressions and forms of traditional Jewish content. Scholem and Benjamin triangulated around Kafka, as their correspondence famously illustrates. But their Jewish intellectual horizons diverged sharply. Even if Benjamin uses Kabbalistic tropes in his essays or loosely distinguishes between *aggadah* and *halakhah*, his sensibility is a highly literary and even vernacular one compared to Scholem's rootedness in medieval and early modern source traditions.

For several decades by this point, literary scholars like Ahad Ha'am, Ba'al Makhshoves, Meir Viner, Shmuel Charney (Niger), Shoshke Erlich, Shimon Halkin, Leah Goldberg, Baruch Kurzweil, Yosef Klausner, and Dov Sadan, many of whom were affiliated with Israeli universities, had been contributing to a growing corpus of criticism on Hebrew and Yiddish writers.[16] Yet Scholem, a practicing poet and literarily cultivated, did not have such work in mind as a modern sphere of "Jewish content" in either of his aforementioned essays.[17] A scant ten years after his 1959 essay, however, Jewish Studies in the American university found itself at the point of including within its scholarly precincts not only the secular traditions of modern prose fiction composed in Hebrew and Yiddish, but also novels, essays, and short fiction by Jewish authors in a diaspora of non-Jewish languages.

German, Polish, Russian, French, Spanish, and preeminently American English were now increasingly linked to "Jewish" in academic literary histories by means of that redoubtable punctuation mark, the hyphen, signaling a different set of frontiers for a Jewish Studies previously confined to Jewish languages alone. This marks the same moment when new, not specifically Judaic aspects of Jewish Studies also became visible on American campuses in parallel with the rise of the ethno-racial interdisciplines: African American and Africana, Chicano/Chicana and Latina/Latino, Asian American, and Native American studies.

Reminted JS also coincides with the introduction into literary studies, rhetoric, and philosophy departments of structuralist and post-structuralist thought in their graduate and even undergraduate curricula, soon to produce its own subset of hyphenate Jewish fusions as well as a distinct set of Jewish scholar-critics.[18] It parallels the personal intellectual history Sacvan Bercovitch charts in "The Music of America." In short, while the remapping of the habitat for the humanities in American universities and Jewish Studies' second life both saw a parallel upsurge almost fifty years ago, JS consistently played the laggard.

Allowing for its early origins subordinate to "the hegemony of the Christian West over academic knowledge," Susannah Heschel observes that, "it is no wonder that JS became transformed into a conservative field whose goal was the incorporation of Jewish history into the larger framework of Western civilization."[19] And yet, the fact that at the time of this book's composition, one of its most traditional components—Talmud study—enjoys a resurgence of radical critical approaches underscores its still unfulfilled potential to play more of a vanguard role generally, as boundaries among disciplines (if not the more stubborn fixtures of departments) continue to be redrawn.

Readings, Derrida, Bakhtin: Ruins, "as if," and the Boundary

As this section heading intimates, each word after the colon is associated with a particular thinker who contributed to a theoretical conversation in late-twentieth-century academe. Bakhtin, of course, was known long before that in non-American contexts. He is included here because of his unflagging attention to borderlines within and between utterances, genres, and persons, which I will transpose here to the very question of the university that both Readings and Derrida subject to sharp critique. I begin with Bill Readings, from whose diagnostic portrait of the American academic scene, *The University in Ruins*, the first term is drawn.

While now more than twenty years old, Readings's book continues to hold its own amidst a cottage industry of more recent and, no doubt, more timely interventions for a new century. It has had its critics as well as its admirers.[20] Some of Readings's readers still quibble with the trope of "ruins" itself, which at the time it was published (1996) meant no more or less that the university's intellectual practices could no longer credibly make transcendental claims for themselves or purport to be their own culturally sanctioned reward.[21]

Whether in successive treatments by Kant-Humboldt (Germanic), Newman-Arnold (British), or Hutchins-Adler (American), Readings argued, the traditional understanding of the university has by now outlived itself. "The story of what [Allan] Bloom calls 'the adventure of liberal education' ... no longer has a hero" (7). "The University system does not need such subjects any more [for] the liberal individual is no longer capable of metonymically embodying the institution [as] the centered subject of a narrative of University education" (9), whose double-edged mission is "the production of national subjects under the guise of research into an inculcation of culture" (89).

From within the contours of JS (albeit absent in Readings's book), the trope of ruins resonates quite powerfully. One thinks, for instance of Walter Benjamin, who saw in ruins "allegories of thinking itself." Or Scholem, whose critique of *Wissenschaft des Judentums*, which was concurrent with the very German intellectual history charted by Readings, meant renewing and rescuing Jewish literature, through the particular lens of Kabbalah, from "the ruins of the past."[22] Likewise, historical Jewish contexts both ancient and modern come readily to mind: first-century Temple structures and razed cities in the Levant, decimated populations and cultures in twentieth-century Europe.[23]

Readings's book does not knowingly intend such contexts, alluding instead to a long intellectual history stretching from Greco-Roman through Renaissance and Romantic evocations to Freud. For Readings, the university remains dependent upon the two uses of ruins that characterize modernity: one, nostalgia for a lost or bygone origin, and two, appropriative mastery, the past extolled as guarantor of knowledge in its unimpeded progress, as the University of Chicago's motto proclaims: *Crescat scientia; vita excolatur* (Let knowledge increase; life is being perfected).

To that degree, traditional departments of French or German or English might be seen as corresponding to figurative sites of ruin when they configure their national literatures as dominated by the past and their primary function as custodial and preservationist.[24] We might also think of ruins, in accord with the late Comparative Literature scholar Svetlana Boym, as fundamentally linked with anxieties about human history, about aging, mortality, and legacy, and thus implicitly, with the scholarly-academic-pedagogical project of the humanities. Even if specifically Jewish narratives or structures don't figure into Readings's constellation of references, that may be another reason to read his book now as if, in the shadow of the university as a ruined institution; it had Jewish Studies (for example, Mendelssohn or Heine) and the new humanities consciously in mind.

As if: the conditional locution that animates Jacques Derrida's reflections on the humanities roughly contemporaneous with Readings's book—how they have been constituted thus far and how they might take unconditioned shape in some conditional future. "Does not a certain 'as if' mark, in thousands of ways, the structure and the mode of being of all objects belonging to the academic field called the Humanities, whether they be the Humanities of yesterday or today or tomorrow?"[25]

Within that modern genealogy, a whole philosophy of the "as if," of the *als ob* or the *comme si*, can be traced from Kant to Hans Vaihinger and Wittgenstein to Derrida. But it is Derrida who specifically enlists it for a consideration of the future of the liberal arts in his essay, "L'Université sans condition." To *profess* a discipline means to produce an event, affirmatively and performatively, and one which, Derrida insists, he himself will speak about as if he "were engaging in a profession of faith." To be a "professor" is to acknowledge one's responsibility to and for the future,[26] "to link the 'as if' to the thinking of an event . . . that might eventually find its place" (213). Reciprocally, the work of the new humanities begins with the fundamental task of genealogy, since any institutional community is founded upon a set of conventions, of "as ifs" that authorize its various doings and thinkings.

For Derrida, the academic "as if" takes shape, among other possibilities, as a "politics of the virtual." Virtualization represents for him the most powerful instance of imagining the university otherwise (even beyond the advent of a digital humanities): "It upsets the university's topology, worries everything that organizes the places defining it, namely the territory of its fields and its disciplinary frontiers as well as its places of discussion, its field of battle, its *Kampfplatz*, and the communitary structure of its 'campus'" (210).[27] Moreover, the university's habitat has always been part and parcel of the "as if," just as the work of the humanities from now on, whether pragmatic or utopian-messianic, archivalist or theoretistic, begins with the fundamental task of genealogy.

> The Humanities of tomorrow, in all their departments, will have to study their history, the history of the concepts that, by constructing them, instituted the disciplines and were coextensive with them. There are many signs that this work has already begun, of course.

> Like all acts of institution, those we must analyze will have had a performative force and will have put to work a certain "as if." (230–231)

This critical historicism would most certainly apply to the case of nineteenth-century *Wissenschaft des Judentums*—a self-instituting project that proceeded on the assumption that German universities, which neither employed Jewish professors beyond the rank of unsalaried adjunct (*Privatdozent*) nor included the study of Jewish discursive traditions and Jews in its curriculum, could be persuaded of the non-marginality of these same persons and traditions. Call it the great maskilic, Enlightenment project of the Jews' *as if*—a concrete institutional instance of "the legacy of German Jewry"[28] whose wager on historical progress should be measured against watershed events like the riots against Jews in Germany of 1819, the official rejection in 1848 of Leopold Zunz's request for a new chair in this history of Judaism, Wilhelm Marr's promulgation of *Antisemitismus* in 1881, and the wholesale expulsion of Jewish academics from the German university system in 1933.

In Jonathan Boyarin's view, what *Wissenschaft* connotes is exactly *modernity*; academically speaking, it connotes an operation that aims to consider, define, and control its object. Its stress is on continuity, "rather than, say loss or forgetting," which, Boyarin suggests, coincides with a sensibility more postmodern than modern (192).[29] As for the original *Wissenschaftler*, though—culturally marked, whether garbed in *yekkes* (short jackets) or not—scientizing Judaism was a largely straightforward matter of applying rationalistic German scholarship and historical criticism to Jewish texts.

Scholem spoke more bluntly in terms of "surgery," a recuperative program which, after an interregnum in Semitics departments and brief detours like Franz Rosenzweig's Freies Jüdisches Lehrhaus, held conservative sway for two twentieth-century afterlives of the Science of Judaism: in Israel from the 1920s onward and in American seminaries like the Jewish Theological Seminary (JTS) or specialized institutions like Dropsie College in Philadelphia, antecedent of The University of Pennsylvania's Center for Advanced Judaic Studies.

An allegiance to *Wissenschaft* as a structure of master disciplines and subaltern pursuits haunts the academic project of Jewish Studies to this day. Boyarin notes in another essay, "there has 'historically' been a disciplinary hierarchy in Jewish studies, with the historians standing near the very top, the literary critics expected to stick to literature and not transgress the boundaries of popular culture, and the anthropologists gradually coming in from nowhere at all."[30] Needless to say, perhaps such hierarchization does not bode particularly well for a Kun or even a Bercovitch (who translated Yiddish poet Itsik Manger and Sholem Aleichem when he wasn't writing about the Puritans, Hawthorne, or Melville),[31] let alone the specialist in Israeli dance and Palestinian cinema, or those intrepid enough to chart entirely novel JS terrain in dialogue with institutional peers outside its nominal confines.

Jewish Studies programs so structured obviously leave themselves open to a concerted dialogism from within (the various specializations that populate the JS data-field) and without (other interdisciplines, the humanities at large). If a restrictive set of disciplinary knowledges was once envisioned as Jewish Studies' proper home, it now lies properly positioned across or "transgredient" to them (to use a Bakhtinian term).[32]

In asking the field's questions, *staging* a field comprising multiple disciplinary formations, I am shifting the question of terrain to the question of boundary. As Bakhtin wrote late in his life, "Every cultural act lives essentially on the boundaries: in this is its seriousness and significance; abstracted from boundaries it loses its soil, becomes empty . . . the realm of culture has no internal territory: it is entirely distributed along the boundaries, boundaries pass everywhere, through its every aspect."[33]

From such a perspective, disciplines, departments, and constituencies within the academic social field and their several rhetorics all answer to the translocational force of граница (granitsa) or borderline. (Since "discipline" itself is such a regulative, bounded, and potentially sterile concept, we might well be better off here thinking in terms of Bakhtinian "speech genres" to describe an interlocative situation in which academic pursuits share and cross boundaries, re-accenting each other in the process.)

To make the institutional culture of Jewish Studies dialogical, both in self-relation and extension outward, is to put into action this concept of the mobile, omni-directional frontier. Alongside that admittedly abstract ideal, I want to proceed on the assumption that "Jewish Studies" more accurately names an academic unit rather than a field of study, given the differential configurations it takes across the range of American universities and colleges that include it in their curricula. Boundaries become the means whereby, as Bakhtin says of his own emergent ideas, it is productively more "difficult to separate one open-endedness from another."[34] This is the Janus-faced quality of boundaries, the fact that "the boundary partakes of both its 'this side' and its 'that side'" (3), making of lived experience a "unity of boundary-setting and boundary-transcending" (14).

Of Levers and Jewish Studies: Kant, Derrida, Bahti

To speak of thresholds in this way is also to speak of *leverage*—as in the class-two lever of a door, where the load moves in the same direction as the effort, and which serves as one mechanism for crossing a boundary; or the class-three lever of the human elbow joint which opens or pushes through a door. It's a metaphor one finds, conveniently, in one of the very earliest "policy statements" for Jewish Studies, Leopold Zunz's "On Rabbinical Literature," published in 1818. Surveying the vast landscape of as-yet unarchived post-Biblical Jewish discursive traditions, Zunz says, "Turning now to the lever for lifting this mass of material, we come upon language . . . for language alone is capable of removing the veil of the past; it alone can prepare minds for the future."

Although specifically associated here by Zunz with philology—as it was three decades later by Zecharias Frankel with respect to history and Judaistic *Wissenschaft* itself[35]—his trope of *Hebel* (lever) sounds like many a panegyric to the role commonly assigned to the university as the institution fundamentally dedicated to *Bildung*, or the formation of intellectual character. In this respect, Zunz, although situated entirely outside the Universität of his time (just as *Bildung*, as emancipatory concept, was originally located by Mendelssohn *outside* institutional structures), envisions a prototype for Jewish Studies entirely in synch with the Enlightenment view of academe as the seat of national culture from which it derives its legitimating idea.

After Kant and fellow Prussian Wilhelm von Humboldt, the university itself aspires to being a kind of lever for the force it can productively exert on both individual minds and statist subjects. It is precisely there, ideally, that we learn with Georg Simmel, as in this chapter's epigraph, that "along with the fact that we have boundaries always and everywhere, so also we are boundaries" (1). This was Bakhtin's belief, as well. The human person is *interpersonal*. The institutions s/he is responsible for creating, like that devoted to scholarship and teaching, proceeds likewise.

"The university, what an idea! It is a relatively recent idea. We have yet to escape it. . . ." So muses Jacques Derrida at the beginning of "*Mochlos*, or the Conflict of the Faculties," his trenchant reflection on Kant delivered at Columbia University in 1980 for the centenary of the founding of its graduate school. The sentiment is meant to chime with Kant's own pronouncement—Derrida calls it "the birthday of the modern university in general"—in the innocent-seeming origin-story from the opening of

Der Streit der Fakultäten, in which Kant adjudges the modern research university *kein übeler Einfall* (not a bad idea).[36]

While the university in the Kantian account is ostensibly well anchored in reason, its autonomous and self-authorizing foundations, says Derrida (and as Kant himself perhaps half-suspects), turn out to be neither: Its vaunted autonomy is "conferred and limited," its authorization is answerable to or mediated by outside forces, and its guild of free-thinking scholars are more aptly identified as *Instrumente der Regierung* (instruments of governance). A genealogy that begins with Kant and continues with Hegel's *Philosophy of Right,* Nietzsche's *Twilight of the Idols,* and Heidegger's *Letter on Humanism* stands behind Derrida's meditation on modernity's never entirely resolved affiliation with tradition, bearing directly on a discourse about the humanities.

In concluding those reflections on a quasi-somber note, Derrida announces, "I break off brusquely. The university is about to close. It is very late—too late for this Kantian discourse is perhaps what I meant to say" (112). Late—but no less answerable to a founding call of responsibility: a "profession of faith, a commitment, a promise, an assumed responsibility, all that calls not upon discourses of knowledge but upon performative discourses that produce the event they speak of" ("Future," 17). If the "relatively recent" idea of the university arrives already late, what, then, shall we make of the even more belated academic pursuit—unknown to Kant, emergent for Derrida—that, in the twentieth century, came to be called "Jewish Studies"?

In many respects, the twenty-first-century American version of Kant's university appears far removed from the internal conflict his 1798 treatise stages between the insurgent "lower" faculty of philosophy and the traditionally dominant, "higher" professional ranks of theology, law, and medicine. Moreover, the intellectual climate in Prussia after the death of Frederick the Great—in particular, the Religious Edict and Censorship Commission directly inimical to Kant's own intellectual purposes—bears only a slight resemblance to the now mostly monetary and civic pressures faced by the contemporary division of Kant's university, where the instantiation of his lower faculty now chiefly resides. All modern university "faculties" equitably share and uphold as first principle the autonomy Kant assigns to the province of post-Enlightenment moral philosophy, "wo die Vernuft öffentlich zu sprechen berechtigt sein müss" (where reason is authorized to speak out publicly).[37]

And so verily, the moment at which Derrida addresses the university's post-Kantian legatees is late. That is to say, this moment when he is speaking comes well after the foundational moment when the university was instituted, established, and invested. And yet, because that event of founding, as Derrida puts it, "can never be comprehended merely within the logic it founds," and "can never be a university event" (*Mochlos*, 109), we always stand in frictional relation to it: *hors pouvoir*.[38] It therefore summons us, the professoriate, students, and administrative agents, to a founding call of responsibility for its effects, an accountability to the "performative discourses that produce the event they speak of."

While no claim is being made here for Jewish Studies itself as the (or even *a*) future of the humanities, the Venn diagram it represents for their necessary co-implication gestures "beyond any interfaculty or interdepartmental limits, beyond the limits of an institution and the political places of its inscription" (110). Calculated merely in chronometric terms, the seam it marks between tradition and the (putatively) post-traditional under academic aegis is unique. This would be my strong reading of Jewish Studies.

Derrida elects to defer the significance of his essay's initially mystifying title to this conclusion. I will place it in the foreground. *Mochlos* is Greek for "lever"—for example, the μοχλός or stake that Odysseus uses to dispatch Polyphemos, or Archimedes's famous assertion that, with it, he could move the world (δῶς μοι πᾶ στῶ καὶ τὰν γᾶν κινάσω). Like its sister contrivances, the wedge or incline plane that transfers energy over longer distances, a lever is also intrinsically "a device designed to deceive": "The lever is a simple machine. Its design copies the human arm; it is an artificial arm. Its technology is probably as old as the species homo sapiens, perhaps even older. And this machine, this design, this art, this technology is intended to cheat gravity, to fool the laws of nature and, by means of deception, to escape our natural circumstances through the strategic exploitation of a law of nature."[39] Exploiting those same circumstances, the skeletomuscular system of the human body constitutes its own set of levers. (For, what did Max Nordau's *Muskeljudentum* envision if not Jewish bodies enhanced by the cultivation of stronger and more agile corporeal levers?)

Derrida's own examples consist of "a wooden beam, a lever for displacing a boat, a wedge for opening or closing a door," all prosaic, entirely applicable expedients. Signifying "something . . . to lean on for forcing and displacing" (110), *mochlos* serves him as an object-image for capturing the modern research university's potential to mobilize cultural traditions both old and new. It also suggests to him the capacity for applying leverage to that institution itself; for the university is "not merely a few walls or some outer structures surrounding ... the freedom of our work; it is also and already the structure of our interpretation" (102).

What if we imagine JS put to similar effect: as applying institutional, inter-discursive leverage, something to lean on for forcing and displacing? Can an academic pursuit render itself a (not so) simple machine? Derrida's leaves his own use of *mochlos* tantalizingly figurative. An evolving stage of humanities practice, "the Humanities of tomorrow," within the governing structures of "the university without condition" in the double sense of unconditioned and under-sponsored, is merely projected. This book endeavors to get more life out of the metaphor, however, by pressing it into further service. Aptly enough, the university itself affords a hinge between the classical vocabulary of engineering and the discourse of postcontemporary critique.

Cantilevering Kant's parliamentary and juridical vocabulary for the conflict of faculties, Derrida suggests that in order to be poised for an evolving discourse of university responsibility, academic institutions will require some kind of "support [*hypomochlion*] for a leap toward another foundational place."[40] For our purposes, we can, with Timothy Bahti, refer this question of leverage to the humanities' crisis, or state of "injury," in an essay that pushes off both Derrida and the passing allusion by Kant to his body's lateral weakness. (Kant footnotes it with reference to Prussian infantrymen trained to start an attack by using the left foot as a *hypomochlion* for the right.)

For a body-wide (or bilateral) "injury within the 'humanities,'" Bahti's suggested therapy would require that "each bit of historical knowledge, each occasion for its articulation and transmission, should become the occasion for inquiry into its methodology and teleology." That twinning of internal and external accounting itself provides the fulcrum: "Only when the two sides lever, each against the other, will the humanistic corpus academicus begin to creak and wheeze with a newfound health, perhaps even approaching a joyful science."[41]

Kant's and Derrida's rhetorical field of reference consists largely of those domains in which surefootedness or stance allow for the possibility of leverage.[42] Thus, "[w]hen one asks how to be oriented in history, morality, or politics, the most serious discords and decisions have to do less often with ends, it seems to me, than levers" (110). *Mutatis mutandis*, such mechanics of force and movement also correspond to the probing, expository spirit of both Kant's philosophical imperative and the rhetorical-performative discourse associated with Derridean critique (which, as Stathis Gourgouris avouches, means more than merely judging things as they are, but rather, altering things, changing what they are).⁴³ Like the university structures that enable it, academic discourse generates performative possibilities for its own *mochlos*.

Derrida's assertion immediately above recalls a similar observation by the poet Robert Frost—also offered in a college setting, as it happens—that, lacking the knowledge or skill to manipulate "figurative values . . . [y]ou are not safe with science; you are not safe in history."⁴⁴ As irony would have it, history itself—as disciplinary practice—legitimates David Myers's argument for an "applied Jewish Studies," with the disciplinary study of history exercising the leverage.⁴⁵ But this is leverage in a non-provocative, almost self-evident sense: "scholarly work that sheds light on issues of contemporary relevance." Social scientists apply the lever of historical knowledge "to illuminate contemporary debates of widespread significance."

Although Myers strategically quotes Leopold Zunz and lays claim to the historicist legacy of *Wissenchaft des Judentums* (in his capacity as an important scholar of that very tradition), this does not, obviously, signify leverage in either Zunz-Frankel or Derridean senses. Nor, more immediately, does it conform to how I wish to sustain and extend the metaphor within these pages. "Applied Jewish Studies" necessarily assumes some externally positioned *hypomochlion*, mirroring the mission of the magazine in which Myers's essay appears, expressly designed to bridge the gap between a Center for Advanced Judaic Studies and the general public.

I prefer to think of leverage differently. Its action captures movement on at least two axes: how Jewish Studies orients itself, content in relation to aspect; and how it fits inside or cuts across disciplinary enterprises like history or religious studies. If, as Leslie Morris has suggested, JS should preoccupy the humanities the way Venice haunts Marco Polo's imagination in Italo Calvino's *Invisible Cities*—"always implicit, present in its absence"—and if it cannot quite claim the role of standard-bearer, then its potential efficacy as a force for/of displacement may be more than merely figurative, an especially kinetic instance of the logic Derrida isolates. Where, for instance, should the JS-lever be most powerfully applied? What will be the ratio of input and output forces, of effort versus load or resistance? When opportunities for shifting the university's foundational ground become possible, says Derrida, "we might say that the difficulty will consist, as always, in determining the best lever, what the Greeks would call the best *mochlos*" (112), a mechanism perennially at work in the university's production of knowledge.

JS as Metaphor: Calvino and R. Akiva

It may well be interjected (with prejudices sustained) from some of the more traditional precincts of Jewish Studies: *Mochlos*? The best lever? Calvino and Derrida? What does any of this have to do with, say, the history of Judaism? Morris's *PMLA* article from 2010 already demurred at ascribing some paradigm-shifting power to JS, and stopped well short of promoting it to the front ranks of a transdisciplinary cavalry-charge. And for the purposes of argument, alternate cities conjured by Calvino, which mirror, invert, or multiply themselves, might have an equally strong claim on refracting the *internal* terrain of JS. (For Jewish Venice, we recall, also bequeaths to us the word, and institution of, *ghetto*.)

Why not Ersilia, the trading city of differentially connective filaments, "spiderwebs of intricate relationships seeking a form" (76)? Or Despina, "a border city between two deserts" (17), that, depending on which of two ways it is approached, is perceived by the camel-driver in the shape of a ship and by the sailor in the shape of a camel. Or Eutropia, whose inhabitants regularly transpose their daily lives, trades, domiciles by taking up new residence in "the next city, which is there waiting for them, empty and good as new" (64).

If Calvino's Venice oscillates between presence and absence, these other specimen-cities materially displace themselves from within and without. This is not to say that Jewish Studies is unique within the landscape of academic topoi in lending itself to such fantasies of transposition and perspectival displacement. Nevertheless, with perhaps more optimism than Bill Readings, Morris asks whether a transdisciplinary "thinking in Jewish" might translate into a critical Jewish Studies, a "new variation of an imagined academic community and of the humanities as a wider terrain in which we might find spaces of the imaginary where Jewishness is constituted in ever-changing and contradictory forms" (765).

Those forms, one should note, are neither necessarily nor exclusively Jewish. Since the very question of the tribal haunts JS—who teaches, what is taught, and to whom, or professor, topic, and student—the non-Judaic and non-Jewish, institutionally speaking, will always be impinging upon the "Jewish" in Jewish Studies. Indeed, Levinas stands as the exemplary instance of a figure now multiply claimed by (or at least pivotal for) third- and even fourth-wave readerships beyond the exclusively Jewish. Amidst such pluralized reception, does his proper academic home belong entirely to Jewish Studies? Or can those bounds themselves be made more medial and shared? To put it another way, what is the JS stake in the conversation about a transnational and multicultural, global, hemispheric, and postcolonial world literature? What is the concomitant stake of that conversation in Jewish Studies itself?

Mobilizing metaphors from literary scholars like Robert Alter and David Roskies, Morris reaffirms the signal capacity of JS to "ventilate the tradition" and serve as "cultural echo-chamber" (771). Yet, such metaphors also mark the hinge between institutional ecology and the various ecologies of knowledge where JS is often tenuously located in its bureaucratic aspects: program, institute, center, and department. The same would apply to "leverage," which has a preconstituted meaning in respect to JS, once private benefactors, foundations, and advocacy groups both on and off campus are factored into the equation (a dynamic that recalls Myers's formulation of "applied JS," albeit otherwise leveraged). Against such alternately bureaucratized and extramural background, I want to take the conceit of *mochlos* one step further by asking whether it might be used, so to speak, isometrically—to frictionalize JS itself.

In other words, such leverage could not only be exerted externally—that is, with JS in dynamic relation to the academic humanities broadly construed or through its disposition by bureaucratic structures from above—but it should also produce internal effects within the (shifting) methodological and ideological bounds of Jewish Studies. Still, as it might bear on such a pluralized structure of academic inquiry, what Derrida calls the "conflict between several strategies of political *mochlos*" makes an insistent demand: Can a JS that has been traditionally configured as static mass (for example, the sheer longevity and gravitas of its subject, its uniquely configured "profession of faith") be reimagined as applied torque?

We will let rabbinic literature have the last word on leverage before we change figures and continue the inquiry in the next chapter. An origin story about R. Akiva likens his vigor and skill with Torah to a stonecutter chipping tiny stones from a mountainside to uproot the whole. Coming upon a large boulder and undeterred by either it or protestations that an entire palisade cannot be thus displaced, Akiva crawls under the boulder, pries it loose—his axe serving as lever—and flings it into the Jordan, saying: "This is not your place—that is!"[46] On the modern campus/*Kampfplatz* where such *midrash* might circulate across the internal divisions of JS and even beyond its borders, mythic exploit will certainly avail. Yet, even small shifts in terrain—as in the rabbinic tradition itself—are more likely to be facilitated by the exertion of collective ingenuity and institutional will.

INTERCHAPTER II

The Dialectics of Ownership

"Your Jewish Studies is not our Jewish Studies." Unpacking my academic library in some humbler version of Walter Benjamin's famous self-accounting, thus was I welcomed to a private college by a standard-bearing member of its academic Jewish Studies faculty. "Guilds and their vicissitudes," I'm sure I reflected to myself, softening the edginess with obliging humor. As the great Jewish satirist Victor Borge used to say, "It's your language; I'm just trying to use it." Promptly filed away as a mordant piece of *khoyzek makhn* (Yid. for "verbal hazing"), I deemed it good-natured but not ill-omened—nothing, say, on the order of *"lasciate ogne speranza, voi ch'intrate,"* signposting the Dark Wood.

And yet exactly that warning had been invoked by Max Weber about the risks inherent in an academic career devoted to *Wissenschaft* in his 1918 essay, "Science as Vocation":

> Hence academic life is a mad hazard. If the young scholar asks for my advice with regard to habilitation, the responsibility of encouraging him can hardly be borne. If he is a Jew, of course one says *lasciate ogni speranza* . . . Naturally, one always receives the answer: "Of course, I

live only for my calling." Yet, I have found that only a few men could endure this situation without coming to grief.¹

Whatever Dantean funnel might have lain ahead, the encounter related above proved not to be unique. Sometime later, I was introduced to a revealing distinction proffered by another scholar of Judaism: "soft Jewish Studies"—literary, cultural, anthropological—versus "hard"—philological and historicist in method, Judeo-scientistic in bent. A facile opposition, obviously, it all too readily inverts: for example, porous JS versus congealed JS. "Hardists" presumably would see little point to a "theoretical introduction" to the field, because the field, whether instantiated as late Antiquity, rabbinics, or medieval history, and so forth, simply goes about its disciplinary business. "Softists," conversely, wish to see a return on their investment in critique. As before, however, rigid and hierarchical dichotomization was the lesson. One might as well have said, "premodern versus (post)modern" or "religious versus secular"—as if disciplinary knowledge were not bound up with the problem of modernity and the secular in the first place!

Musing on the first instance brings to mind Walter Benjamin's 1931 essay, "Ich packe meine Bibliothek aus: Eine Rede über das Sammeln."² Unpacking his own library yet again, he confesses that he cannot march up and down the ranks of his books *um im Beisein freundlicher Hörer ihnen die Parade abzunehmen*, "to pass them in review before a friendly audience," because they still lie uncrated around him; his mood, he says, is not elegiac but rather expectant, corresponding to the collector's necessarily tensed sensibility. If Benjamin's audience comprised the readers his essay addresses and before whom he proceeds to unpack himself, mine was present in the room with me, for my library was now on public (or at least, peer) display.

Benjamin calls collectors, *Physiognomiker der Dingwelt*, or "the physiognomists of the world of objects" who, once they step into the magic circle of acquisition, become readers of their newly owned objects' provenance, the whole background for which becomes "a magic encyclopedia whose quintessence is the object's fate." Speaking of book collectors' "very mysterious relationship with ownership" as the stuff of childlike *Bezauberung*, or "enchantment," he explains that the Latin saying *habent sua fata libelli* possesses special significance for the collector in whose hands a book both materializes and rematerializes.

He stylizes acquisition as a matter of books' "rebirth" and "renewal." Acquiring a book rescues and can even free it: "To a book collector, you see, *die wahre Freiheit aller Bücher irgendwo auf seinen Regalen,* "the true freedom of all books is somewhere on his shelves." Ultimately, the most distinguished trait of a collection will be its *Vererbarkeit* or "transmissibility," for the real fate of books is bound up essentially with their ownership, a complicated notion in the essay, at the very least. "Ownership is the most intimate relationship one can have to objects" which, more than coming alive through their collector, *er selber ist es, der in ihnen wohnt,* "it is he who lives in them."

These are lofty thoughts, and they deserve to be unpacked in their own right. Say, for example, that one imagines one's role not as collector or owner but rather as custodian or caretaker. What if the true freedom of all books lies in various pairs of hands rather than on collectors' shelves? Might transmissibility happen as much through dispossession as possession?[3] Benjamin's essay suggests this much, self-critically, in its closing gesture which speaks of having erected a building made of books into which Benjamin will go "to disappear inside, as is only fitting."[4] And admittedly, the question of ownership, albeit as a disciplinary concern, bears centrally on my own concerns here, where books-as-objects yield to other kinds of hard and fast containers: methodologies, training, academic loyalties, and institutional cultures.

In this recollected case, whatever magic/demoniac circle I may have just entered across the threshold of a new office, a human face confronted me alongside the furrowed scrutiny it cast upon the books I happened to be shelving at the time. If not a Benjaminian moment, a Levinasian one, perhaps. But still not quite. I was looking at a face that was keenly peering (askance) at my books.

The books themselves were what one might expect, plus a few curios procured from Manhattan's bygone Fourth Avenue used bookshops (including a first edition of Herbert Asbury's *Gangs of New York,* in which I take particular delight). Rather, they divided into standard categories of fiction, poetry, languages, nonfiction, and so forth. Years earlier, when I taught Giuseppe Tomasi di Lampedusa's historical novel *Il Gattopardo* in an undergraduate class on the European novel, I learned that the author's villa in Palermo maintained separate libraries on two different levels for volumes of history and literature, respectively, two subjects in which the famous Sicilian author was formidably well versed.[5] From then on, I liked the idea of organizing my books from my own comparatively miniscule office library in this fashion—two tiers, set apart but facing each other.

Consequently, I singled out "Jewish books" as such, further divided into *sefarim* (classical sources in Hebrew, many of them gilt and leather-bound), and university-press books by contemporary scholars of Jewish philosophy and literary studies. Most tellingly for the audience in my office, some featured classical Jewish sources *under the gaze of contemporary theory*. This was also the shelf on which philosophers like Rosenzweig and Levinas neighbored their counterparts in sociology (Simmel), psychoanalysis (Freud), music theory (Copeland), and intellectual history (Y. H. Yerushalmi, Simon Rawidowicz, Moshe Idel, Eric Santner). I always savored Rosenzweig's dismay at learning that his *Star of Redemption* would be placed as a "Jewish book" on the same shelf with the typical sort of gift books chosen for a *bar mitzvah*.

Moreover, since I routinely taught in conjunction several modern Jewish literatures, figures like Henry Roth and S. Y. Agnon, Yankev Glatshteyn and Bruno Schulz, Isaac Babel and Ben Katchor, Ronit Matalon and Moacyr Scliar, Walter Mosley and Mezz Mezzrow, and the non-Jewish Borges and Achmat Dangor would have to rub shoulders on the same shelf or two—a prototypical, Jewishly inflected "ensemble of cultures."[6] (Although they sound like two more of Calvino's cities, "fasolia" and "dafina"—coalescent, slow-cooked Sephardic stews—would figure the recipe for interfusion at work here.)

With an admixture of such authors already thus on view and the more unblended *sefarim* still packed in their boxes, it was the pungent batch of theoretically leveraged "Jewish Studies" books that elicited the admonition about "your" Jewish Studies versus "ours." That was a boundary crossed only at one's peril and by *mekubalim* (acolytes) alone—especially in the eyes of a JS program designed to produce a certain teleological type of Jewish student.

As an invited speaker, Philip Roth had experienced his own battle (so he called it) in these precincts decades before, at a symposium where fellow panelist and fiction writer Ralph Ellison was obliged to come to his defense when put on his heels by his audience of co-religionists. I was being made aware that whatever guild membership in JS I could claim to possess—at least insofar as it is customarily practiced in centers, departments, and programs in colleges and universities outside the confines of this more sectarian institution—needed to be kept, in the idiom of Ralph Ellison's *Invisible Man*, "on the lower frequencies."[7]

Since that day over a decade ago when I unpacked my library, the practice of Jewish Studies on the national landscape has, very much like the humanities, experienced the latest installment of an anxiety (left to vibrate on the lower frequencies) about its aims, its procedures, and its status vis-à-vis neighboring programs of disciplinary and interdisciplinary research.

The next chapter contrives a set of atypical harmonics for JS in order to make those frequencies just a bit more audible, for at bottom, the matter of resonating comes down to a matter of (re)naming.

"Make each place as if it had just been made, already old, but new again from naming it,"[8] intones Ellison's Caribbean *semblable*, the late Derek Walcott, near the end of the book purporting to be his last. Subscribing to similar counsel myself, I would submit that it also rather pertinently describes Scholem's counterhistorical incentive for a post-*Wissenschaft* JS, as it does Walter Benjamin's poetics more generally, which just happen to form our connecting links to Chapter 2.

CHAPTER 2

Jewish Studies and the Pitchfork

> Not to find one's way in a city may well be uninteresting and banal. It requires nothing more. But to lose oneself in a city—as one loses oneself in a forest—that calls for quite a different schooling
>
> —WALTER BENJAMIN, *One-Way Street*

The epigraph from Benjamin is enlisted with a particular audience in mind: practitioners anchored in the archive and the Science of Judaism, for whom the business of JS comes down to method. Disciplinary practice may thus always seem a far more compelling desideratum for its work than any notional desire to shift the terms of debate to the matter of *community*. I explain that ambition in some detail in this chapter, with particular reference to postmodern philosophy: for it, too, will call for quite a different schooling and, accordingly, a new set of bearings.

As one critic has observed of Benjamin's complicated stance toward traversing cities and texts, the reward can be a "clarifying violence . . . the lack of mastery that leaves one open to the shock of an unexpected encounter."[1] In what follows, I hope to mediate that legitimate surprise by conceding that JS and its protocols are traditionally anchored where they have been for entirely plausible, if self-reproducing, reasons.

What may look like calculated destabilization on my part—using the prism of lyric poetry, for example—becomes the occasion for leaping toward another foundational place; or, Talmudically speaking, standing on one foot. Indeed, that celebrated image for learning Torah will be enlisted as one of several heuristic figures, along with outside voice and opening hand, in a third constellar series following upon those in the foregoing chapters that seeks to reimagine a Jewish Studies à venir.

Outside Suggestion: Harpham

As a sometime-shadowy supplement, academic Jewish Studies already lives, in part, a kind of prosthetic counterlife, hinged or grafted onto practices both academically prior (history of religion, philology) and immediately contemporary (visual culture, women's studies, ethnic studies). Yet, at the same time, its institutional history and sheer variety accord it an autonomy it has yet to work through fully or critically. In asking, for instance, how it might be placed in conversation with outside voices, consider the colloquy across a range of venues—scholarly journals, institutional whitepapers, general interest books, and the public press—accumulating around the humanities, frequently depicted in a state of decline or crisis, and regularly troubled about its own use-value.

From the vantage of National Humanities Center director Geoffrey Galt Harpham, "crisis" describes how the humanities necessarily subsists, given its own complicated modern genealogy from classical-biblical to statist to post-traditional. "Crisis" describes both its origins and its future, a constitutive condition that must nevertheless be understood "as its strength, not its weakness," even when the center of gravity for humanities practice seems to have shifted away from the humanities proper to other avenues for research like economics or politics or theories of mind.[2] As we recall from the introduction, that one sector of the university enacts a crisis of institutional legitimation merely serves the whole. "Skepticism about the forms of knowledge is itself a form of knowledge" (Menand, 92).

Regarding such forms of knowledge and their legitimation for the academic study of Judaism, *Wissenschaft des Judentums* represented an intellectual discourse and legacy historically parallel yet significantly oblique to both the Kantian-Nietszchean-post-Nietszchean conversation about the modern university and the nineteenth-century hegemony of philology. So, too, JS in the twentieth and twenty-first centuries runs both uncannily alongside (mirroring, echoing) but also transverse to an ongoing discourse about the humanities as something other than *Geisteswissenschaften*, *sciences humaines*, and arts and letters, that bears a distinctly American cultural imprint. Any interchange between JS and the humanities—as respective enterprises in dialogue with "crisis"—counts also as a drama about alterity, about what comes from outside as already, at least in part, residing within.

For an analogy, then, consider the anecdote that begins Harpham's *The Humanities and the Dream of America*. While delivering a public lecture on "The Humanities in America" in Istanbul—an Eastern city famously linked to that characteristic discourse of the West through such figures as émigré philologists Leo Spitzer and Eric Auerbach—Harpham is suddenly interrupted by "the passionate wail of the *azzan*." "What, exactly, is the protocol," he asks, "when you are addressing a public audience and the air is pierced by a call to prayer?" Of this uncanny visitation together with its aleatory gift of "outsideness," he confides:

> [A]rrested by the appearance of an aesthetic form—a voice coming not just from outside the room but from a long cultural religious tradition that was decisively "outside" my own—I had been shocked into an apprehension of otherness, thrown back on my uncertain resources, forced to make a judgment about values, challenged in my self-sufficiency, enriched, and perhaps even, eventually, made more tolerant and wise. It was as if "the humanities" themselves were carried on the breeze that brought the sound of that voice.[3]

Being *arrested* in such fashion and then seizing on the fortuitously timed intervention as a prompt for standing back and surveying the entire enterprise in its specifically American context recalls Bercovitch's opening maneuver in *Rites of Assent* and Kun's concerted listening to the shofar in *Audiotopia*. (And to stretch the anecdote's applicability accordingly, one does wonder whether it would yield the same insight if, with a change in topography and religious adherence, the sonic interference had originated from the din of a *ḥeder* or a *beit midrash*, or as *ḥazanut* carried outside, say, Jerusalem's Western Wall.)[4]

But to redirect Harpham's point more practicably to our own interests here, even if considered (as it must be) quite otherwise than a metonymic call to prayer, where does "outside" lie for Jewish Studies? What constructively interrupts it? Which unforeseen antiphonies might it occasion? How might it impinge upon the problem of institutional inside and outside itself, or as Derrida puts it in "The Future of the Profession," "the very limit, *between the inside and the outside*, notably the border of the university itself, and within it, of the Humanities" (23).

What, in short, will count for JS as enabling outside suggestion, rendering the field productively strange to itself and the humanities in order to clarify or generate interface with larger institutional contexts? If millennial JS boasts an intrinsically dialogical character, superimposing an optimistic contemporary face on an ambivalence (Scholem would say "contradictoriness") is already discernible for its *Wissenschaftler* progenitors. As the institution of the university now undergoes those late-century shifts chronicled by a number of recent books, JS, *faute de mieux*, discloses latent resources of negative capability in the midst of continuing Kantian *Streit*.

These include what Derrida's vision of the new Humanities calls "the history of 'professing,' of the 'profession,' and of the professoriat," which, as "professions of faith" (and as distinct from those more market-driven ambitions now coded as "professionalization"), are peculiarly relevant for Jewish-and-Judaic construed as academic practices. A decade or so ago, for example, religion scholar Susannah Heschel asked whether, in response to the ascendancy of multiculturalism, "Jewish studies as a field can revitalize the radicalism that inspired its early development in the nineteenth century."[5] Heschel dubbed this future-oriented agenda, "Jewish Studies as Counter History," building on historian David Biale's trope of "counter-tradition" in his account of Gershom Scholem's innovations.[6] Extending the trope even further, *Jewish Studies as Counterlife* asks how that gesture of countering can be pivoted even more reflexively.

JS: Proselyte on One Foot? Lupton-Reinhard and Bill Readings

"Traditional law," says Derrida, as he introduces the trope of *mochlos*, "should therefore provide, on its own foundational soil, a support for another leap or founding . . . of 'taking the call on one foot' *(prenant appel sur un pied)* as it is said in French" (110). Or, as it is said in Mishnaic Hebrew in the service of a rather different legal tradition, "*al regel aḥat.*" All but irresistible, Derrida's play with this French expression thus calls to mind the well-known Talmudic story about Hillel, Shammai, and a potential convert (b. *Shabbat* 31a), who says to each rabbi, *gaireni al menat she'telamdeni et kol ha-torah kulah ke'she-ani omed al regel aḥat* (convert me on condition that you can teach me the entire Torah while I stand on one foot).[7]

Although swiftly rejected by Shammai and ultimately accepted by Hillel; although Shammai's response—"he pushed him away with a builder's cubit" *(emet ha-binyan,* lit. "truth of building")—strikes more harshly than Hillel's—"what is hateful to you do not do to your neighbor; the rest is commentary, go and study it"; and although Hillel's position prevails as the one actually endorsed by the *Bavli*: despite these sundry surface disparities, the two modes of response could be read as possibly converging on one salient point.

If we read liberally, that is against the grain of a by-now conventional dichotomy, Shammai's choice of a measuring rod for a cudgel might just have been intended for concrete effect and Zen-like immediacy, as if to say, "*this* ruler [or truth] in my hand can only plan or refine a structure, the actual construction of which requires both building materials and human labor."[8] That "the rest is commentary," in Hillel's lapidary phrase—that is, what is now required after the force of ethical commandment is an infinite labor of study whose "building materials" enable sound interpretive argument—would, by this reading, convey merely a more sensitive rendition of the identical rebuke. For, toiling in reinscription is the freedom that Levinas, inspired by the Mishna, terms "difficult," a responsibility that *both* Shammai's and Hillel's responses differentially inscribe.

At least, that might be the sort of deconstructive reading Derrida himself might have appreciated, since a potential proselyte's decision to learn Torah from two opposed schools or disciplinary bents creates the opportunity for thinking a divide produced through *différance*. Derrida elsewhere calls it *travailler le cadre* or "working the frame": giving the framing element—the limit between inside and outside—"work to do."[9] Such an approach becomes even more plausible when, as Raphael Jospe (building on Mordechai Kaplan) suggests, "While I stand on one foot" (על רגל אחת) may be a bilingual pun if רגל is understood as the Latin *regula*, rather than literally as the Hebrew word for "foot."[10]

Whereas Shammai dismisses the Gentile with his builder's cubit, "Hillel welcomed the challenge and employed his *regula* (= מדה = rule, ruler, or rod) to bring him to the Torah" (45). Rather fortuitously for us here, the proviso or stipulation the proselyte proposes each time—his *al menat* or "on condition"—could not cut more perfectly athwart Derrida's own stipulation for the university's *non-conditionality*: that it answer only to an overriding principle of truth and responsibility.

At any rate, this aggadic tale counts as one of the most frequently cited of all rabbinic texts amid a welter of contexts, many homiletic and popular, and others more scholarly. Not so surprisingly, we even find it grounding an online statement of purpose by two comparative literature scholars, Kenneth Reinhard and Julia Lupton, to describe the future of Jewish Studies in a secular university. Self-acknowledged latecomers (like Bercovitch and Kun after a fashion), they speak for a group of scholars who "have entered the arena of Jewish studies at moments of crisis or transformation in their lives and careers, finding in it a way of reorienting and reinvigorating their prior training in literature, philosophy, history, or sociology."[11]

Likewise, they select out as part of their intended readership, students who

> come to the field from a variety of intellectual and personal backgrounds, often bringing with them the tools of history, literary criticism, or philosophy, a reawakened sense of ethnic identity cross-fertilized by contacts with other groups, or a young adult's growing awareness of both the resources and the limitations of the classic Hebrew School education.

Consequently, they identify where properly, in their opinion, JS would be best "located" vis-à-vis the university's *Kampfplatz* and campus: "'between' culture and philosophy, between the resources of historicism and the promise of theory," just as "[i]n its essence, Judaism is neither culture nor philosophy, but rather shuttles between them, taking shape in the flight from both."

Their manifesto reads cannily about such in-betweeness and is sufficiently painstaking to provide further exegesis for another go-round of the Hillel/Shammai/proselyte drama in which the condition for entry into the faith becomes the (no-longer ritually relevant) desire to become a *kohen gadol* (high priest). A complicating "difference-in-identity" and "identity-in-difference" underwrites Reinhard and Lupton's explanation of a certain dialectic of distance and proximity here as "the distance at the heart of the interior, which makes Jew and gentile, king and convert, equally 'neighbors' before the law."

Rhetorically speaking, though, I think the most intriguing, transpositional moment in the piece occurs when JS becomes personified, as it were, neo-Talmudically, "play[ing] the role of the proselyte before the gates of the secular university, impatiently requesting access to a sphere of knowledge constructed according to a different set of standards and values and demanding recognition as a full and equal member of the multi-cultural conversation." With such a demand, we have obviously traveled some distance from Leopold Zunz leveraging participation in a rather differently configured conversation nearly two centuries ago.

While Lupton and Reinhard's allegorical reframing of the story respects Shammai's suspicions insofar as they expose JS's ambiguous institutional standing—outsider-as-insider, the dissonance between "object" (*Judentums*) and "method" (*Wissenschaft*)—they do not ultimately subscribe to the double-reading I proposed almost incidentally above. Instead, well versed as they may be in deconstructivist interpretation, their *nimshal* (in the language of *midrash*, or referent-in-reality) turns out to be surprisingly conventional, as it envisions two opposing sentries, and receptions, at the gates of Jewish Studies, one visage glowering, the other welcoming:

> Shammai is a disciplinarian who guards the rigorous and uncompromising nature of the field from intellectual trespass, literally upholding standards with his curmudgeonly measuring stick. Hillel is the interdisciplinarian who meets halfway the student trained in the liberal traditions of the secular university in order to induct him or her into the exegetical habits of Jewish learning.

After a staging of JS and a Judaism that shuttles between the poles of culture and philosophy, one cannot help but be struck here by the wholly customary Shammai/Hillel dichotomy recast now as hard JS versus soft JS, "curmudgeonly disciplinarity redeemed by evolved interdisciplinarity."[12] And yet, just as Derrida claims that foundational university structures nevertheless allow for "a support for another leap or founding," one enabling the other, so a capacity to learn (or transmit) Jewish discursive traditions on one foot should allow sufficient maneuvering room for "taking the call" on that same (or the other) foot.

In other words, wouldn't a strict "either/or" schema (Hillel versus Shammai) *fall short* of the more diacritical possibilities of "and/and/and/and/and" (that is, Hillel/Shammai read *otherwise*)? Does interdisciplinary Hillel "correct for" disciplinary Shammai? Besides, the x factor of disciplinary libido doesn't guarantee that the interdisciplines are wholly immune to its effects either. A more programmatically interdisciplinary Jewish Studies has characterized the field since before the Boyarins called for a "New Jewish Studies" in 1997; and yet its status as an institutional force—at a level beyond the discipline bridging units, departments, and programs—remains ambiguous to this day, still subject to structural and ideological vicissitudes; still, that is, largely unleveraged.

Lupton and Reinhard teach in the University of California system, and their stated commitment to the modern, secular, public university locates the identical object of Bill Readings's extended critique in *The University in Ruins*, completed five years before their manifesto was published in 1999. Hillel/ Shammai was probably not an antinomy familiar to him. On the other hand, he may well have known Levinas's "Means of Identification," in either French original (1963) or English translation (1990). He would almost certainly have endorsed the link it draws between the projects of state and university as coextensive institutions of modernity, dedicated to "the project of the historical development, affirmation, and inculcation of national culture" (6).

By speculating on an "institution [that] has outlived itself," however, Readings takes a significant step beyond Levinas whose early professional decades spent outside the French university system—he almost reached the age of sixty before he held a formal professorship—may well have instilled a healthy skepticism. In doing so, he can be said to have reformulated the duel of pedagogic styles allegorized for JS by Lupton-Reinhard, transcending an internal impasse of uncompromising rigor versus liberality, the better to position Jewish Studies against a horizon for new humanities.

In a particularly eloquent moment from the later chapters of his book, Readings stresses the role of addressivity over autonomy, "the fact that we [both faculty and students] never know to whom our words may speak" (156). Autonomy, contrariwise, "holds out the impossible imagination of subjective self-identity: I will no longer be torn up, divided from myself by responsibilities to others" (186). "The minimal condition of pedagogy" must therefore be ethical, a question of justice over and above criteria of truth or knowledge.

That condition—which we could also align with Derrida's insistence on the university's "unconditional freedom to question and to assert" (202)—arises as an initial and abiding respect, an infinite attention to otherness. Such "otherness," it's important to add, does not necessarily express itself through identity markers, which Levinas has already inventoried for us as so many "signs, attributes, contents, qualities, and values." "There is some other in the classroom," says Readings, "and it has many names: culture, thought, desire, energy, tradition, the event, the immemorial, the sublime" (182). This is not something that can be known in advance, calculated as the measure of one's responsibility.

Drawing from Nancy, Lyotard, and Agamben, Readings calls this version of dwelling in the ruins, "a community of *dissensus*," dedicated not to the accomplished self-understanding of autonomy and achieved *Bildung* or to "communicational consensus," but rather to making "heteronomy, its differences, more complex" (190). In place of both autonomous disciplinarity and unifying interdisciplinarity, Readings proposes a "shifting disciplinary structure that holds open the question of whether and how thoughts fit together" (191), which he elsewhere names a "network of obligations."

This utopian vision sums up Readings's project, which, in the negatively expressed version of the *comme si*, also takes this form: "It is no longer possible to think of the politics of the university as if the institution were a simple tool or instrument that should be turned to other ends" (145). We might parse this as marking a terminological shift from a discourse of disciplines to one, rather, of "knowledge ecologies," where the *ecological* suggests an alternative framework for realm, milieu, or world.[13]

From Aiming to Opening Hand: Seamus Heaney

As with my passing allusion to Derek Walcott in the previous chapter, let me pronounce and leverage that shift unexpectedly—for a book about Jewish Studies—by turning to a short lyric by Walcott's peer, the late Irish poet Seamus Heaney. Entitled "The Pitchfork" from his 1991 collection *Seeing Things*, it entertains the vision of a simple tool or instrument turned to other ends, and readers, I trust, will indulge this interlude and the detour into close reading that follows.

> Of all implements, the pitchfork was the one
> That came near to an imagined perfection:
> When he tightened his raised hand and aimed with it,
> It felt like a javelin, accurate and light.
>
> So whether he played the warrior or the athlete
> Or worked in earnest in the chaff and sweat,
> He loved its grain of tapering, dark-flecked ash
> Grown satiny from its own natural polish.
>
> Riveted steel, turned timber, burnish, grain,
> Smoothness, straightness, roundness, length and sheen.
> Sweat-cured, sharpened, balanced, tested, fitted.
> The springiness, the clip and dart of it.
>
> And then when he thought of probes that reached the farthest,
> He would see the shaft of a pitchfork sailing past
> Evenly, imperturbably through space,
> Its prongs starlit and absolutely soundless—
>
> But has learned at last to follow that simple lead
> Past its own aim, out to an other side
> Where perfection—or nearness to it—is imagined
> Not in the aiming but the opening hand.[14]

Not an expressly religious person (as trappings go), Heaney was bound at most by tribal loyalties to Catholic Ireland. Befitting an internationally recognized poet, his work has been translated into languages as far afield as Hebrew (though not Yiddish, as far as I know). He greatly admired Osip and Nadezhda Mandel'shtam, traded occasional quips with Robert Pinsky, and was a frequent interlocutor for and occasional translator of his fellow laureate Joseph Brodsky—who, as it happens, descended from the twelfth-century tosafist and *paytan* (composer of liturgical poems), Yosef ben Yitzḥak Bekhor Shor of Orleans. Beyond those small facts and perhaps a few relevant others, there was nothing remotely Jewish about either his affinities or the content of poetry. "Aiming and opening" does not, in other words, appear to know about Shammai/Hillel.

So why invoke him in this context? For two reasons: because his poem provides an aspirational image for my topic, which directly concerns how an "aiming" might be reimagined as an "opening"; and because the text's internal commitment to an "other side" models the very attention to Otherness I wish to project for a Jewish Studies–to-come—as a set of probes that reach elsewhere.

In Heaney's poem, the pitchfork becomes weaponized (in an interview, the poet calls it a "missile");[15] at the very least, it is prized more for how far and well it can be flung mock-heroically than for the agrarian operations—"chaff and sweat"—for which it was designed. It is made of ash, the traditional material for crafting spears. While the sharpness of the pitchfork rates only incidentally alongside its aerodynamic repurposing—"it felt like a javelin"—Heaney is too at home in the heritage of English words not to know that the "pitch" in pitchfork already connotes a kind of throwing.[16] Its conversion to trident thus takes place no more than one or two degrees removed in object-kinship.

In contrast to the preceding four stanzas that almost fetishize prowess-by-hand, the final stanza's figure "is meant to be an image of unclenching and generosity," Heaney says, quoting Czeslaw Milosz's verse, "Open the clenched fist of the past."[17] At one level, the poem can be taken as an allegory of the poet's manual labor of the pen and his craft's reciprocities, the dialectic of restraint and release, limit and sublimity, writing and being read. At another, it both savors and exposes the exercise of male exploit.

Conceivably, it may even have at the back of its mind Keat's posthumous fragment, "This Living Hand," in which we see the poet "dream through his hand, a sign of dexterity, the capable movement of a capable imagination . . . the lure of the partially whole."[18] (Keats was one of Heaney's acknowledged influences.) For whether it's a matter of grasping a pitchfork or letting it go, imagined perfection in Heaney's lyric is approached more than actually achieved.[19] In typical modernist fashion, like Robert Frost's or Patrick Kavanaugh's poetry of rural life, "The Pitchfork" exploits the prosaic to explore the metaphysical. Much like "A Stove Lid for W. H. Auden" from the 2006 collection *District and Circle*, in which the titular object replaces the shield of Achilles, the homely—"hell-mouth stopper, flat earth disc"—has the capacity to reflect "the mass and majesty of the world."

How differently is the image of a pitchfork rendered in a scabrous moment from a poem much farther afield, albeit solidly within the precincts of Jewish Studies: "On Leaving Saragossa" by the eleventh-century Andalusian poet Shlomo ben Yehudah Ibn Gabirol. Unlike the pacific tenor of Heaney's wistful self-critique, this canonical Jewish poet vigorously, even peevishly defends his (Jewishly familiar) academicism: "They quarrel with all my teachings and talk/ As though I were speaking Greek/ 'Speak,' they carp, 'as the people speak/ And we'll know what you have to say.' / And now I'll break them like dirt or straw/ My tongue's pitchfork thrust into their hay" (or in the intricately rhyming original, "*Daber sefat am v'nishma/ki zeh lešon ashḳeloni"/Atah adikam k'mo tit/ki ḳilshoni leshoni*).[20]

I want to make the point here, in a specifically academic arena—the world of Jewish Studies—of foregrounding *not* (as might be expected) Ibn Gabirol's ornate medieval Hebrew and the sharpness of his tongue's pitchfork, but rather as glimpsed through Heaney's signature demotic, a more exemplary pitchfork "grown satiny from its own natural polish." *Not*, that is, the co-religionist Jewish poet's elaborate set-to of plain speech versus scholarly idiolect, but rather the outside-the-fold Irish poet's more helpful distinction between the aiming and the opening hand; between tool mastery and relaxation of grasp; between muscular exploit here, and somehow reaching past aim, grip, and control there, to the "other side" where something more nearly perfect can be achieved. Such are the dividends to be reaped by outside suggestion.

If, "to have an outside, to listen for what comes from outside" (as Levinas commends), the Jewish discursive tradition[21] corresponds to the signal property of "knowledge [*connaissance*, "as it is said in French"] or Torah" (or *Wissenschaft*, for that matter), then the same propensity might reasonably be extended to the academic bounds of Jewish Studies. Indeed, the very dissonance Levinas himself underscores in "Means of identification" between the givenness of Jewish identity on the one hand, and the university's habits of critique on the other, marks the salutary cleavage between Jewish Studies and "Judaism."

For our purposes in the inquiry, then, suppose that the clenched and aimed pitchfork figures the pen craft of *disciplinarity*. It does not demand too much of a rhetorical stretch, since in the poem "the physical arc of a pitchfork extended in the imagination," as one eminent critic insists, already stands for "our immaterial extrapolations of the material."[22] Accordingly, let it also be retrofitted for the kind of intellectual labor performed with clip and dart by those field hands known as academicians.

Let it further embody the far probing and mastery of field that the German language calls *Wissenschaft*—as for example, *Wissenschaft des Judentums*. In his zealous youth, Gershom Scholem tells us that he longed for a *Wissenschaft* that was "cruel to its practitioners" who, in turn, "struggled with the Satan of irresponsible dilettantism" by becoming exacting "specialists and masters of one trade," that is, master disciplinarians.[23]

Why, it may be interjected, does the analogy even suggest itself? It could be the nominalizing suffix "*schaft*" (shaft), which, though not cognate with our English "shaft," certainly sounds like that word. Or quite possibly, it could be the thoroughgoing instrumentalism of the scholarly enterprise, the archival deployment of it—a sturdy, long-handled archivist's implement assigned to the hard work of piercing, lifting, and aggregating material. (While Heaney and Ibn Gabirol each emphasize the pitchfork flung or thrust by hand or by tongue, its basic function makes it technically a lever of the third class.) At any rate, as the lever suggests a potential reorientation of and for JS, so the pitchfork (migrated from Heaney's poem to the precincts of JS) captures *Wissenschaft* and disciplinarity at their most pronged and labor-intensive.

Contrastively, the unclenching hand—*in the process of* opening before being already opened—I now wish to associate with the ideal of "community," most specifically in Readings's sense, but also in parallel with formulations developed by Jean-Luc Nancy and Giorgio Agamben, and explained in the next section.[24] Derrida helps also. At the beginning of his early essay on Emmanuel Levinas, Derrida describes philosophy as community—specifically, "a community of the question." The ramifications he develops readily transpose themselves to an aspirational take on Jewish Studies: "a community of initiative . . . but also a community in which the question has not yet found the language it has decided to seek, is not yet sure of its own possibility within the community. A community of the question about the possibility of the question."[25]

Levinas's own insight from one of his Talmudic readings, "As Old as the World," makes a parallel point about the semi-circular structure of the Sanhedrin in Second Temple Jerusalem: "The 'dialogue,' as they say today, was never interrupted, nor did it get lost in an impersonal dialectic. It was an assembly of faces and not a joint stock company."[26] Tropes, as Heaney, Walcott, Ibn Gabirol, and Levinas alike understand, wield expressive power of their own. In the remaining portion of this chapter, this partly tropological, partly pragmatic question of community will round out our foundational framing of JS as "a problem to itself."

JS: Community and Exemplarity, Agamben and Jean-Luc Nancy

Even if it had a predetermined answer when asked from a non-neutral vantage, the last of the four questions from our introduction about belonging and fit, about "housing" JS, may have seemed sensible at a historical juncture when an academic home was neither given nor legitimated. As the late sociologist Paul Ritterband and scholar of Jewish education Harold Wechsler have narrated this history, JS scholars had to borrow from Peter to pay Paul by establishing their bona fides with a parent discipline and then making their mark in the field of Jewish scholarship.[27] By the 1960s, the age of "Semitics" departments had waned.[28] When JS programs began to populate the university, disciplinary hegemony, faculty appointments, and endowments all contributed to decisions about campus location. Nevertheless, exactly where JS "belonged" remained a highly contingent determination.

The "counter" in JS-as-counterlife introduces possibilities of the reestablished or the disestablished aslant the preestablished. This is also a matter of place and location—the situatedness of JS as a special instance of a modern intellectual pursuit both with and against the grain. For its roughly two centuries as an institutional enterprise, the "what" and the "how" of JS (the evolving status of its knowledge base alongside determinations of method) have remained the recurrent standard of self-definition. Both the "where" and the "whose" (location or ownership among its various institutional stakeholders) have tended to take more heteronomous and contingent shape.

These questions presuppose decisions about community. In concluding these two preliminary chapters and setting up those to follow, I want now to elaborate the question of community introduced through Heaney's image of the opening hand in the somewhat different terms developed by philosophers Giorgio Agamben and Jean-Luc Nancy. I turn to Agamben first because his thought, not otherwise Jewishly inflected, makes pivotal, albeit unexpected, contact with Judaism's source tradition in a way that epitomizes "outside suggestion." We might go so far as to deem it a "gift" to Jewish Studies in an almost perfectly Derridean sense: It does not appear as such, nor will it be recompensed accordingly.[29] Like the muezzin's *adhan* in Harpham's anecdote, it provides another instance of pure gratuity.

We might think of Jewish Studies, in turn, as an institutional embodiment of the "exemplary" proposed by Agamben in a number of texts, including *Homo Sacer*, *The Coming Community*, and the lecture "What Is a Paradigm?": "one singularity among others, which, however, stands for each of them and serves them all" and "an element of the set withdrawn from it by means of the exhibition of its belonging to it."[30] Needless to say, this special sense of "the example" overshoots the mark of how academic programs in Jewish Studies commonly understand their own mission. Nor does it explain how JS is typically regarded elsewhere within academe and its guilds or even outside by extradisciplinary constituencies. It will serve us yet, however.

For Agamben, the exemplary (or paradigmatic, from Gr. *para-deigma*, like Ger. *Bei-spiel*) identifies a space "always beside itself," signaling paratactic possibility (and/and/and), the yet-to-come, apposition, and adjacency.[31] To that degree, it parallels the self-neighboring quality Readings ascribes to the university as the very structure of and for our thought: "The University is where thought takes place beside thought, where thinking is a shared process without identity or unity. Thought beside itself perhaps. The University's ruins offer us an institution in which the incomplete and interminable nature of the pedagogic relation can remind us that 'thinking together' is a dissensual process" (192).

This itself should count as a rather grandiose claim to be staked for JS. And yet, I make it here by intentionally drawing a frame around my subject and inviting us to regard it thus *as* framed—withdrawing, exhibiting it—as an example of the demarcation of intellectual topics, rhetorical habits and dispositions, and analytical methods which secure for academic knowledge practices their place on a campus or *Kampfplatz*. Other JS scholars have applied this exemplary construct in relation to "the Jew" as a discursive and political category.[32] I look instead toward Jewish Studies itself as an academic–social field whose preestablished borders between a (given or centrifugal) inside and a (displaced or distanced) outside all but compel us to think *paradigmatically* about it.

The "example" for Agamben also gestures toward Walter Benjamin, whose epigraph to this chapter models a relationship to the known and bounded that nevertheless allows for productive (self-)displacement, something prefigured in his early essays on childhood education.[33] How might an early inculcation into a communitarian spirit (which Benjamin calls "ethical" and "religious") be sustained within that augmented vehicle for *Bildung*, the university, whose self-evident claims to cultural authority themselves no longer persuade on their own? I have already deferred to

Bill Readings's answer, which centers on the scene of teaching as a reframing of university politics. Improbably enough, Agamben provides a parallel speculation with an example drawn from rabbinic literature.

"Shekinah," the penultimate chapter of *The Coming Community*, describes the condition of postmodernity and its politics as that of an "experiment in language" or *experimentum linguae*. What Agamben means is that we are now forced up against the condition of language itself, "not this or that content of language . . . not this or that proposition, but the very fact that one speaks" (82). Only those, he says, who bring language itself to language "will be the first citizens of a community with neither presuppositions nor a State. . . . Like Rabbi Akiba, they will enter the paradise of language and leave unharmed." Agamben refers here to an arresting Talmudic passage (*Tosefta Ḥagigah* 2:2, *Ḥagigah* 14b in the *Bavli*) in which four Tannaitic figures visit the "orchard" of Paradise: R. Ben Azzai "glimpsed at the Divine Presence and died"; R. Ben Zoma "was harmed" (lost his mind); Aḥer (R. Elisha ben Abuya) "chopped down the shoots of saplings" (became a heretic); and R. Akiva "came out safely."[34]

His authorial purposes for making it notwithstanding, the allusion here and in the related essay, "*Pardes*: The Writing of Potentiality," gesture toward the academic restaging of Jewish discursive traditions. Fusing the Kabbalistic interpretation of the passage with his own postmodern proclivities,[35] Agamben concentrates on the figure of Aḥer, whose actions typify for him our very modern plight of communicative alienation, an "uprooting of all peoples from their vital dwelling in language."[36] For just that reason, "the era in which we live is also that in which for the first time it is possible for human beings to experience their own linguistic being— not this or that content of language, but language *itself* . . . the very fact that one speaks" (82). *La potenza*—the materialization of a collective linguistic possibility, of "bringing language to language"—names the utopian force here, one that possesses its own Judaic bona fides.

This is also the meaning of Aḥer for Agamben: "one singularity among others, which, however, stands for each of them and serves them all." We are all "post-adhesive" selves now, Agamben might say, *pace* Levinas, who do not so much merge into a commonly shared condition of belonging but rather "co-belong" in a "community without presuppositions," where each of us stands at a threshold, exposed to all the others. "Go to the threshold," he counsels. "Do not remain the subject of your properties and faculties, do not stay beneath them; rather, go with them, in them, beyond them" (99). Wholly conditioned by university discourse, instructions such as these do not, however, specifically *address* the university and its citizens. Yet, that is exactly the force, the *potenza*, I wish to extend to them here in direct relation to questions of discipline, field, and knowledge practice as threshold entities.

Reading his ongoing work on political theology, one becomes struck by Agamben's periodic allusions to rabbinic literature and medieval Jewish texts, to which, whatever (often extreme) liberty he may take with them, I respond in kind by seizing on them as a prompt: JS, so to speak, by accident. "*Pardes*," then, also writes *interdiscursivity*. Talmud scholar Moulie Vidas's own appeal to Agamben in his study of the Talmud's formation as "the transformation of traditions into quotations" may help us here. "The breaking of tradition does not at all mean the devaluation of the past: It is, rather, likely that only now the past can reveal itself with a weight and an influence it never had before" (a statement whose own force I would extend to the many illustrations of its substance over the course of this book).[37]

Agamben's politically charged community-without-unity is one whose members, while they may share a basic existential or biopolitical reality, are not subsumed within an encompassing *corps-d'état*—their shared institutional project, so to speak—but rather traffic in finitudes. If we now narrow this Talmudically underwritten politics to the theater of the university and its intellectual culture, what might it thus tell us about disciplinary identity as either still bounded and separate (the warrant for its libidinal energies), or alternatively, something more possibly communitarian? Simply put for the purposes of this frankly condensed analysis, the virtue of Agamben's notion of co-belonging lies in the fact that its "singularities"—like so many self-contained disciplinary knowledges and practices—stand mutually *exposed*.

This happens to mark the point at which Agamben's poetics of community maps efficaciously onto the lineaments of Jean-Luc Nancy's.[38] In *La communauté désoeuvrée*, Nancy uses the term *partagé* to express the idea of a sharing in community that occurs at the point of division or separation. "In place of communion," Nancy hastens to add, "there is communication,"[39] one singularity or finitude "exposed" to others, like speech itself. Community is given to us, he says—"a gift to be renewed and communicated . . . not a work to be done and produced" (35)—and presents us with a task, unfinalizable and always incomplete. It is necessarily, if utopically, shareable and communicable. Far from that which eludes, evades, or "essentially escapes," that which "takes place beyond or prior to itself," community for Nancy is present and concrete, "in the efficacy of relation, proximity, contact."[40]

Even if Nancy does not evince an interest in Jewish thought *per se* similar to Agamben's,[41] his ethical vocabulary for a community not based on a bipolarity of same-other feels especially apt for the contemporaneous reimagined landscape for humanities practice as we have seen sketched. The "in-common," "being-with," "becoming worldly," "singular-plural" describes a post-Levinasian interpersonal scene, a *politics of community* "where I rub shoulders or stand shoulder to shoulder with the other"[42]— something like the fingers of an opening hand. Typically speaking, collegial relations tend, if anything, to be *over*-personalized: sublimated, libidinal, acted out, *face à face*, as Levinas would say, even "in-your-face." The political criterion here signifies, rather: adjacency, neighboring, the *community* of scholars (and their disciplines).

If Nancy's intellectual cohort removes him from the pragmatic realities impinging upon the contemporary American university, his immediate concerns, which are political and historical, do not. An "original community" in the sense of a *Gemeinschaft*, whose loss and fictive origin Nancy analyzes in his early work, dovetails with the eroded and now nostalgic immanentist construct whose demise Readings tracks in *The University in Ruins*. "Being together" in the service of a transformative cultural ideal by which the State cultivates its citizens is no longer how the university addresses either its various internal constituencies or its many topics and "sciences." In the preface to *The Inoperative Community*, Nancy explains that the prepositions for "in-common" and "being-with" lose their force to the extent that any community reifies itself as preconstituted. Loss has constituted it *ab initio*.

The Humanities might be thought of as one such community aggregated as a "single thing." It thrives on a kind of high-minded stigmergy: traces left by one field or its practitioners that stimulate further efforts on the part of others for collective gain.[43] In an article about Nancy's political philosophy, and with a nod to an earlier intellectual tradition embodied by legal philosopher Otto von Gierke and sociologist Ernst Tönnies, Robert Bernasconi observes that "nostalgia for community perhaps began as nostalgia for the medieval guilds, rather than as nostalgia for the Greek *polis*" (16).[44] And the line from those guilds as the very type of a "lost community" to the Humboldtian university which may once have imagined itself a "project of fusion" is neither a long nor very tortuous one.

Back to the Sources

Slightly less than a decade before Nancy wrote *La communauté désoeuvrée* (1983) and an equivalent interval since the inception of the Association for Jewish Studies (1969), the following foundational principles for Jewish Studies were proposed by a member of the profession in good standing:

> First: We, the academic profession, must recognize that "Jewish Studies" comprises data and not a method. . . . The nature of the data may vary from demographic statistics to mystical texts but its status as data . . . material studied within the rubric of "Jewish Studies" . . . does not vary. "Jewish Studies" is a data-field.
>
> Second: Given the data-field, we, the academic profession, must decide what method(s) we will use on the data. . . . Having identified the disciplines, one must then identify the academic departments practicing those disciplines.
>
> There is, however, an additional question: Is there one discipline which is particularly apt for the data-field of "Jewish Studies?"[45]

The specific answer to that third, frankly loaded and crowning question rates secondarily in importance relative to the way in which the premises are rhetorically posed. Not to keep readers in suspense, the (predetermined) answer is "religious studies." As to the framing, the stuff of JS is evidently just that: *stuff*, content, material, or in this argument's favored term, "data" for which the proper kit, container, repository, or archive remains the only "real" question at issue. When we keep in mind that the traditionally religious form of Jewish learning, *Talmud Torah*, is positioned as the argument's foil, in tandem with its repeated recourse to the phrase "academic profession," Derrida's notion of community as profession-of-faith feels peculiarly cautionary.

Yet, clearly, with such a proto-manifesto, we find ourselves well in advance of a portrait JS as an assembly of faces over and above a joint stock company—as is only fair, given the decade in which it was penned, that is, just slightly before that moment when Derrida remarks on the lateness of the moment in the university's own biography. The political question of community, let alone "the community of the question," simply does not factor into an argument whose topographic agenda postulates the most suitable departmental or disciplinary location for JS.

Self-limited by disciplinarity's aiming hand, a plainly pragmatic question about belonging, as I said earlier, also feels ever so colored (haunted?) by a perennial concern with Jews themselves and their place in the world. Similarly, even when the argument seeks to transcend an invidious dichotomy between religious or secular modes and instruments of education, it still identifies a circumscribed group of practitioners and pupils.

A more ecologically capacious, less defensive and tribal sense of Jewish Studies (disciplinarily understood) awaits a subsequent horizon for university campus and *Kampfplatz*. From that angle, at its own delimited level of stakes and stakeholding, the pathos of Jewish Studies constitutes merely a large-scale institutional pathos writ smaller amidst the ascendance of management culture.[46] A Jewish Studies–to-come can only gain by thinking the problem of its community in terms other than these, as a matter of self-leverage, of placements and displacements from within as well as without.

As to Nancy's and Agamben's admittedly idealized adumbrations of community and their immediate relevance for JS: precisely because they're politically derived, and precisely because they seek to introduce a tension between singular and some ostensibly common, unified project in whose name they speak (like "*crescat scientia*"), they map revealingly onto the university structures and the sociology of knowledge.

From Nancy's standpoint and notwithstanding the Foucauldian view that they function solely as "techniques for assuring the ordering of human multiplicities,"[47] academic disciplines will appear as "finitudes" on account of their intrinsic drive toward boundedness. As such, at least potentially, they stand mutually self-exposed, a matter more of selfhood, so to speak, than mere libido. At the same time, they also, self-evidently and perhaps unceasingly, embody *work*, endeavor, industry, and vocation. In Nancy's lexicon, a community, by contrast is *désoeuvrée*—"at loose ends," or as his translator renders it, "unworked"—because it happens alongside designed or producible outcomes, within "a network of obligations that the individual cannot master," as Bill Readings contends.

> The community is not organic in that its members do not share an immanent identity to be revealed; the community is not directed toward the production of a universal subject of history, to the cultural realization of an essential human nature. Rather, singularities ("I's" not egos, as Nancy puts it) variously occupy the positions of speaker and listener.
>
> This seems particularly important in the context of thinking about the University because it is noteworthy how often intellectuals tend to forget about the position of the listener in favor of worrying solely about the speaking position or position of enunciation. (185)

In respect to Readings's desiderata, an "alertness to otherness" and (with specific reference to Kant) *"Achtung* [or] initial respect," our immediate question becomes this: What might the *formal content* of JS have to do with formulations such as these, as Readings and I both adapt Nancy's ideas to the conditions of professing, with singularities connected within a particular university community, and with that community itself (JS) embedded in larger—or tangent to other—ones?

As a very recent example, take Sergey Dolgopolski's characterization of Talmudic discourse as a *techne* or praxis specific to a bounded speech community. If Agamben illustrates a postmodernism that makes incidental contact with the classical Jewish textual tradition, Dolgopolski exemplifies the kind of JS scholar, who reads that tradition *together* with, or inflected by, the likes of Agamben.

His most recent book, *Other Others: The Political after the Talmud* (2017), is intended to address a double effacement: "the omission of the political from the study of the Talmud and the omission of the tradition of the Talmud from current thinking about the political" (7). As to the latter, Dolgopolski develops a careful analysis of an "interpersonal encounter which is no longer intersubjective" (30), where personhood, or *interpersonality*, lends itself to a staging across a set of discursive scenes. Such speech encounters are fundamentally *positional* in expression, somewhat like a modalized game of chess (a favored metaphor of Bercovitch as well as Wittgenstein). Dolgopolski's is *dancing*.

> The interpersonal thinking displayed in the [two] Talmuds does not begin from, does not end up with, and does not necessarily include thinking subjects interacting with other thinking subjects, as the notion of intersubjectivity would require. Instead, individuals take part in a dance of thinking that consists of a to-and-fro, strophe and antistrophe, refutation and counterrefutation performed vis-a-vis a tradition, a recorded text of the past around which the dance is unfolding. What is more, the same dance is assumed to have taken place in the tradition itself and in the recorded text (31).

If Agamben's and Nancy's opening-hand-like pictures of community lend themselves to a vision of the university just short of utopian or messianic, I make no such claim for this rendition of the Talmud, postmodernistically inflected as it may be here. A "dance of refutation and counterrefutation" probably does not best mirror a Jewish Studies already populated by constitutionally disputatious folk. What such an account *does* help us to say is that if Talmudic discourse plausibly reorients a postmodern conversation about the political as a "discipline of remembering" (10), then that very collocation of discourses (a different sort of choreography) models a new, *interdiscursive* (versus either "interpersonal" *or* interdisciplinary) platform for enacting JS.[48] The epilogue to this book mounts such a performance in earnest.

It also offers a rather different perspective on communication than the defective images of ritualized community we find in the two animal fables by Kafka which accompanied our induction into the inquiry of the book: The lecture-circuit of sending and receiving in "A Report to an Academy" and *"die reigenmäßigen Verbindungen"* as the canine narrator of "Investigations of a Dog" conjures the endlessly circular dance of self-enclosure. It's probably also salutary to recall the frank confession that Kafka's dog makes toward the conclusion of his protracted narrative of investigation when he belatedly admits "my incapacity for scientific investigation [*Wissenschaft*], my limited powers of thought, my bad memory, but above all my inability to keep my scientific aim continuously before my eyes" (315).

Whether conceived as the vehicle for Jewish *Wissenschaft* or in the spirit of ethno-cultural Jewish identity, the knowledge practices of JS—its "data field"—do not automatically constitute a *Gemeinschaft*, even when some desired method like "interdisciplinarity" functions as a kind of letter of transit. Thus, Nancy will distinguish between *individual* ("closed off from all community") and *singular* ("a priori *sharing* of singularities") from the perspective of which "community is nothing but this exposition" (27).

This, it seems to me, offers a compelling model for a Jewish Studies–to-come. Necessarily self-encumbered and still poised *at the verge of community*, that consortium would exchange a social economy of bond or communion for the communicative politics of *partage*, at once an interruption and a sharing-at-the-boundary among its constituent parties and with its university others.

To conclude this chapter on that note, I want to finally, and very briefly, highlight the pitchfork motif again—already set in (tenuous) dialogue between poets Seamus Heaney and Ibn Gabirol—through an even more compressed (and improbable) dialogue. As before, a claim is not being made for some internal warrant in the Jewish discursive tradition to do so. There is none. Rather, I myself want to enact for Jewish Studies the operation whereby an *aiming* (a specific text from within its specific context) transforms into *opening* (that text lined across boundaries, both diachronic and generic) with another.

As it happens, two other allusions to a pitchfork nest within two vastly different genres across the breadth of the Jewish discursive tradition: one from the far past (Talmud) and the other from the near present (Hebrew modernist fiction). I will not have been the first to think these two super-genres together, at least within the precincts of JS.[49] But if my pairing of Heaney and Ibn Gabirol has at least provocatively conveyed the virtue of "outside suggestion" by modeling JS in dialogue with voices from beyond its putative borders, I want to close this chapter by means of a willfully forced *internal* dialogue between two discursive traditions inside it.

1.

א"ר יצחק מפני מה היו אבותינו עקורים מפני שהקב"ה מתאוה לתפלתן של
צדיקים א"ר יצחק למה נמשלה תפלתן של צדיקים כעתר מה עתר זה מהפך התבואה
ממקום למקום כך תפלתן של צדיקים מהפכת מדותיו של הקב"ה ממדת רגזנות למדת
רחמנות

[Rabbi Yitzḥak said: For what reason were our forefathers initially infertile? Because the Holy One, Blessed be He, desires the prayers of the righteous, and He therefore wanted them to pray for children. Similarly,] Rabbi Yitzḥak said: Why are the prayers of the righteous compared to a pitchfork [*eter*], as in the verse: "And He let Himself be entreated [*vaye'ater*]"? This indicates that just as this pitchfork turns over produce from one place to another, so the prayer of the righteous turns over the attributes of the Holy One, Blessed be He, from the attribute of rage to the attribute of mercy. (*Yevamot* 64a and *Sukkah* 14a)

2.

For the sake of two things, had Menaḥem come from Motza to Jerusalem to buy himself a new pitchfork and to exchange one tractate of the Talmud for another. . . . And his success in these two matters exceeded his expectations. The pitchfork could be mended and he didn't have to spend his money on a new one, and since that was the case, he could get himself a new tractate and keep the old one.

SHMU'EL YOSEF AGNON, *T'mol Shilshom*[50]

Quite conveniently for our engineered juxtaposition, Menaḥem here is perhaps the lone figure in Agnon's novel of pre-State Palestine to mediate successfully between tradition and modernity. As to the Talmudic comparison, in addition to the obvious justification on account of its particular metaphor, its virtue (generalizable to much of rabbinic literature, as we have seen previously) lies in the poetics of similitude, reflecting on why one thing compares to another through the vehicle of homophony. While it is not exactly what Agamben means by co-experiencing language's being, it does exemplify a decidedly language-conscious mentality.

To what end may one of these things be compared with the other (paraphrasing the rhetoric of *midrash*)? Let us simply say that thus different source-pitchforks improbably align by being made interdiscursive. In the Talmud, reversals (lit. turning over) in the soil predict reversals enabled by the human soul, which lays claim to transformative possibility and its surprise. In the novel, through the latency of now-disencumbered hands, hand-tool and Talmud can anticipate restored and augmented integrity, as needed. Mended pitchforks enable tractates to multiply, the prosaic and the consecrated mutually reinforcing each other. Let that stand as one provident formula for a Jewish Studies–to-come.

INTERCHAPTER III

"Past its own aim, out to another side"

Does the pitchfork betoken phallocentricism? Heaney's own text leaves that particular subtext fairly undisguised, what with the tool's "smoothness, straightness, roundness, length and sheen." Yet readerly discernment would seem to dictate that poet, speaker, or both have already recognized the fact right along with us.[1] Like the poem itself, my own predilections seek very obviously to transcend weaponized prongs in favor of its preferred image, the opening hand. I pose the question earnestly, however, since it surfaced in a roundtable discussion of the Association for Jewish Studies where I hazarded some preliminary meditations on some of what would become this book's repertoire of tropes, among them both the pitchfork and the lever.

As plausibly phallic objects, when taken together they introduce, at the very least, the risk of an unintentionally masculinist imagery, a sensitivity to which has been exigent for some time but seems especially so as I conclude these pages. At the same time, such contingencies of communication, from well-meaning sender to well-meaning yet differently situated receiver, could also be referred to a redemptive Bakhtinianism: Every word is half someone else's. We could similarly appeal to the wise direction of

Bill Readings, whose observation about the abyssal space of reading (and hearing) I quote in my preface: the fact that we never know to whom our words may speak.

And yet, I want to revisit the question here—not in order to definitively resolve what remains, I think, an open question of whether tropes such as these betray a gender bias in speaking *about* Jewish Studies. Rather, I do so because the question pivots us to both the graver and more immediately answerable one of whether or not *Jewish Studies itself* betrays a gender bias, as has been convincingly propounded in a recent article by Susannah Heschel and Sarah Imhoff. The authors ask how it is possible that a new 850-page book about Hasidism, a decade-long collaborative effort by eight eminent scholars in multiple fields, does not include a single female contributor, a lacuna perhaps even more glaring for having been ignored in the book's reviews.[2]

Heschel and Imhoff explain that, far from exceptional, such disproportionality is a regular feature of both edited books and journal editorial boards. Exclusions such as these not only negatively impinge upon individual women scholars' careers and opportunities, but they also damage the field in its self-understanding as well as in the eyes of an ever more diversified academic citizenry. Meta-historically considered, the bias becomes even more sharply etched:

> The extraordinary irony is that the field of Jewish studies struggled since the early 19th century for its place at the academic table. Jewish studies scholarship is still too often ignored within the academic world and treated by colleagues precisely the way women are treated within Jewish studies.

Allowing that such inequity may well not be deliberate—indeed, the scandal is its very inadvertency—the authors conclude their article with suggestions for redress by means of easily adopted practices in gender parity that would alter prevailing norms for conference organization, publishing edited volumes, and grant funding.

By this point in my own book, the relevance of such critique should be obvious. For sundry genealogical reasons, conventionally anchored JS remains subject to any number of torsions that entangle blindness and insight. Beyond reprehending its continued gender bias—by no means, the field's only imbalance—one can only defer to such practical mechanisms for remedy as those advocated by progressivists like Heschel and Imhoff. Of course, the significance of a feminist critique goes far beyond issues that putatively pertain to women. Feminism acts as an intellectual lever exerting a force that then pries open nearly every aspect of Jewish discursive traditions. That would be the virtue of leverage in the sense I have argued made already indispensable to the academy at large.

For my purposes here, though, let me return again to the less gender-neutral metaphor of the pitchfork. As I revisit, too, the critical term applied to it in the roundtable mentioned previously, I find myself haunted not by its adjectival component but rather its nominal: "centrism." After all, doesn't the question of "the center" cut to the heart of my avowedly quixotic/messianic project: to decenter JS, centrifugalize it, displace it from its own inwardness, and maybe even more importantly, *to move outside it in order to repopulate its interior*?

Messianic or not, the move is frankly midrashic in a loose sense, a venturing out that nevertheless remains bounded. This, it seemed to me, was the superadded import of the verse in Heaney's poem, "past its own aim, out to another side."

Accordingly, as Chapter 1 sets up a contrast between (grasped) pitchfork and opening hand, the one an image for clenched disciplinarity, the other for community, so here at the end of Chapter 2, I want to suggest another level of meaning that accounts more closely for the pitchfork's actual structure, that doesn't so much collapse a distinction between the grasping and unclenching as correlate these actions.

One obvious risk the implement courts is *reification*, when pitchfork-wielding, for example, reduces to the functionality of the tool itself; or, on a strictly rhetorical plane, becomes the almost impersonal agent for fieldwork.[3] Another is the ruthlessness to which we saw Scholem lay critical claim, where scholars concentrate their energy in *the grasp* of knowledge and its *comprehensive* transmission. A little less obviously but more after my own imaginative inclinations, the shape of a pitchfork mimics the human hand that grasps it, almost like a prosthesis, its prongs doubling for protruding fingers. All that is lacking is an opposable thumb (as on the goad) to superimpose a pitchfork onto an opening hand.

The organizing opposition in Heaney's poem actually depends on the persistence of the hand throughout all its figurations, from tightening/raising/aiming to relaxation of grip. In guarding against reifications of the disciplinary, I would therefore wish here to recall insights from Chapter 1 about the continuous logic connecting disciplinarity to its putative opposite or corrective. I would also recycle my own image of *vectoring* or bending disciplinary aim. One doesn't have to fantasize about "getting beyond" disciplinarity to believe in creative possibilities for redirecting its energies. Finally, we should note that a pitchfork counts as a lever of the third class;

just as a hinged door, the manipulation of a boundary, epitomizes a lever of the second.

To revert to it a final time, the suffix "*schaft*" in *Wissenschaft*, as in *Gemeinschaft*, *Nachbarschaft*, or *Botschaft*, may convey a hint of subliminally sexualized imagery to the ears of some English speakers. It is, however, cognate with our English "ship," which connotes status, condition, shape, or form. *Wissenschaft* is (scholarly) knowledge-ship. Yet, it is that very move from "shaft" to "*schaft*," from aiming to opening, that the next two chapters consider in respect to two very different intellectual figures. For each, however, the same repositioning of the current state of JS hovers in the background: "past its own aim, out to another side."

CHAPTER 3

Mochlos or *Makhlokes*: JS and the Humanities

> I esteem my colleagues as I do my own self, I esteem them for two things: because they are able to find perfect felicity in specialized knowledge and because they are not apt to commit physical murder.
>
> —VLADIMIR NABOKOV, *Bend Sinister*

More personalized and less thematic than the previous two, this chapter and the next concentrate on a figure who inherited *Wissenschaft des Judentums*' "scientific" reframing of the Jewish for better or worse. If Chapters 1 and 2 were more rhetorically tessellated and theoretical in tone, then Chapters 3 and 4 deliberately enflesh their subject, the better to bear out an earlier formulation about JS as a lived institutional poetics. The sentence from Nabokov in the epigraph is spoken by the dystopian novel's protagonist, philosopher Adam Krug, whose tragic fate interlaces the professorial, personal, and political at maximal cost. A limited case for intellectual integrity under the threat of state tyranny, its pathos bears but obliquely on the legacy of Franz Rosenzweig in Chapter 4 and of Jacob Neusner in this chapter. Yet, insofar as this crucial matter of collegial esteem typifies the profession's highest aspirations, which Krug connects to both pacific restraint and "felicity in specialized knowledge" as two (albeit wildly different) markers of the academic, I let the remark in the epigraph—anything but "an obscure quip"[1]—stand over this chapter and hover in the background of the next.

"My tongue's pitchfork thrust into their hay":
Neusner Agonistes

As if channeling Franz Kafka's "Gemeinschaft," the late, illustrious, surpassingly prolific rabbinics scholar Jacob Neusner penned the following in an editorial for Indianapolis's *Jewish Post and Opinion* on December 2, 1987:

> Just now, Geoffrey Hartman, professor of English at Yale, distinguished literary critic but mere enthusiast and parvenu in "Jewish studies," interviewed in the *Jerusalem Post*, stated that since "paganism" has any number of representatives at Yale, so should "Judaism." He was referring to the Classics department (!) and to the Jewish studies program, housed in Yale's Department of Religious Studies (even though not a single Jewish studies professor is in the field and discipline of religious studies or even pretends to be). He further maintained, so it was reported, that every Yale student should be required to study a page of the Talmud. As a Talmud specialist in the field of religious studies, I wonder whatever for. And as a professor in the discipline of religious studies, I never before thought of myself as the counterpart and opposite—whether in advocacy or mere inquiry—to my honorable colleagues in the Classics department. We teach about a religion, we work out an analytical program of inquiry. We do not advocate the religion(s) about which we teach. That is the work of chaplains. We are not chaplains there to persuade Jews to "be Jewish"—nor are our colleagues in Greek and Latin expected to go out and kill goats.

The content of this excerpt will establish many of the points this chapter addresses: the proper "home" for JS, the porosity of its borders vis-à-vis its parallel or intersecting pursuits in the Humanities, disciplinary vocation, and collegial sensibility. Listed as such, however, they remain entirely neutral categories. But obviously, their valence in the passage above betrays a distinct rhetorical impress. The story behind the rhetoric, the story of Neusner's professional affinities and disaffiliations, underpins this chapter's title and its purview, helping to explain why the overriding question for JS involves much more than where, topologically speaking, it "belongs."

If the *ḥavruta*-style of learning in the traditional *beit midrash* transacts itself in mildly adversarial fashion, the academy boasts the analogous component of critique, its Isocratic legacy. Both systems ideally counterbalance collegiality (*ḥavruta*'s root meaning is "friendship") against hermeneutic rigor and accountability to one another. A facing partner sits opposite in the one case; "rich argument of an analytical and propositional character," as Neusner (from the same editorial) describes the collective process of knowledge-exchange in the academy, prevails in the other. The question then becomes not how these two modes compare (a distinction Neusner himself often introduces), but rather what the fine balance is within each between fellow-feeling and conflict. How does each thus reside, self-encumbered or not, in the world?

In the remainder of the article, "advocacy" teaching of the sort professed by literary scholars like Geoffrey Hartman contrasts sharply with its counterpart in religious studies, which, for Neusner, epitomizes scholarship at its most disinterested. Either one opts for "the ethnic reading of ethnic studies (with heavy emphasis, of course, on 'Holocaust studies')," favored by the kind of academicians who "meet in their segregated learned society, the Association for Jewish Studies [where] anything Jewish goes onto the agenda, mixed together with everything else Jewish"—a pseudo-scholarly chulent Neusner derides as "ghetto babble." Or, simply and more properly, one staunchly adheres to and defends *the academic*. Mutual exclusivity defines their discord.

"But there is considerable reason of hope," Neusner opines, "because the new humanities are engaged in a bitter battle for the soul of the fields as they live in universities. The case of Jewish or Judaic studies (what you call it makes no difference to me) is suggestive. Jewish or Judaic Studies have split into two camps, and they are at war with one another." The metaphor of combat is no accident.

Homo Academicus Judaicus-Americanus

As is frequently the case for this remarkable scholar, valuable insights, courageous skepticism, lively demurral, and a laudable investment in scholarship *lishmah* (for its own sake)—as the rabbis call selfless devotion to the Torah—intermix in Neusner's writing with an almost reflexive need to see such conflicts as zero-sum games, attended by a combativeness that makes fellowship, let alone fellow-feeling, elusive.

The shortcomings in these think-pieces matter as much rhetorically as they do disciplinarily. Consequently, it is not unreasonable to surmise that the limits of Neusner's language in such polemics mean the limits of his conceptual world. Where Wittgenstein (whom I paraphrase here) once likened his own philosophical style to "poetic composition,"[2] Neusner's discourse defaults onto a testy and reproachful "Jewish rhetoric" all its own.

By the criterion of quantity of scholarship alone, however, few colleagues deserve the title *homo academicus* more than Jacob Neusner, author and editor of one thousand books on Judaism, interfaith dialogue, American Jewry's relation to Zionism and the Holocaust, and Jewish Studies in the humanities. His authorized biography rightly names him an "American Jewish iconoclast," which describes his relation to communal bodies as well as intellectual trends.[3] He produced a body of work staggering in its quantity. He mentored more than one generation of rabbinics scholars, a "legacy of learning," for which he has been justly celebrated.[4]

Neusner's academic perfectionism, which admirer and fellow rabbinics scholar Roger Brooks credits to Neusner's desire for "self-transcendence"[5] but which was also solidly rooted in professionalized selfhood, establishes the model for JS that I take up in this chapter. As such, the figure of Neusner and the figure of Franz Rosenzweig in Chapter 4 compose a study in contrasts. Advocates for Jewish education (albeit from radically different perspectives and cultural contexts), they conduct parallel "reports to the academy" in a small body of essays, making each the other's counterfoil, both of them serving as differential lenses for refracting the state of modern JS.

I make Neusner my exclusive focus here because, while specializing in discrete content areas within the study of religion, he spoke often and polemically as an exponent of Jewish Studies *in specific relation to the humanities*. That makes him truly exceptional.[6] His biographer claims for his lasting legacy the courage to "force Judaism into larger conversations,"[7] contemning its parochialization outside the university, where, as an object of research, it can be secularized in the best sense. And yet, the flip side of that very radicalism parsed the Jewish-and-Judaic in notably exclusivist terms. Institutionally speaking, his liberalism and his dogmatism ran in parallel as each other's secret sharers.

Like the Talmudic authorities cited in his book *The Idea of Purity in Ancient Judaism* (1973), Neusner held forth on what was genuine and what was spurious, what was unalloyed and what was confounded. He drew the boundaries for the vocation he practiced as stringently as the textual sources and traditions he traced as a historian. The determinative difference between analyzing those ancient texts and espousing this modern field, however, lay between disciplinary rigor on one hand, and ideological fervor on the other—however the latter may have understood itself to be premised on the former.

Neusner was not one to hinge the vexed, too easily oppositional divide between secular and religious, Jewish and Judaic, within an institutional domain where such dichotomy presents a continuing intellectual problem: the *Kampfplatz* on which rests the university's "communitary structure" or *Gemeinschaft*. The groves of academe appeared to function for him as *Kampflatz*, pure and simple.

To recall Kafka's "Fellowship" (*Gemeinschaft*): "There was a time, of course, when the five of us did not know one another, either, and it could be said that we still don't know one another, but what is possible and can be tolerated by the five of us is not possible and cannot be tolerated with this sixth one." In real academic life, among Israeli scholars for example, Neusner was initially regarded as that "sixth one," just as he reciprocally relegated them to more or less the same category (eventually modulated with a younger generation).[8]

A comparable dynamic prevailed for an *agon* Neusner routinely enacted with single individuals, university collectives, and entire institutions. Kafka's confiding spokesman estranges himself through the act of narration itself, yet will insist on common cause: "but here we are together and will remain together; a new combination, however, we do not want." Neusner never estranged himself that self-consciously. But membership and estrangement, insider and outsider, pure and impure, ghetto babble and true scholarship, "my" JS and "yours," established the limits within which he chose to exercise his scholarly ethos.

As iconoclastic as he may have been, he nonetheless donned the mantle of forensic heir to a "science" of Judaism[9] while pronouncing on the "Judaic" *tout court*, which is why the editorial on the ethnicizing of strictly intellectual priorities begins on this sober-sided note: "We in the academy can make no compromises in our commitment to the academic disciplines that govern all academic teaching and scholarship."

On the off chance Neusner was familiar with Seamus Heaney's writing, he might have known the double meaning Heaney assigned to the trope in his essay of the same name, "Government of the Tongue," which signifies at once the "jurisdiction of achieved form" through the exercise of a self-validating authorial will and, at the same time, "a *denial* of the tongue's autonomy and permission," a self-silencing very near the medieval-monastic sense of "discipline."[10] For *government*, in short, implies something both willed and imposed.[11]

To assert, as Neusner does, that it is the academic disciplines that *govern* all academic teaching and scholarship is to intimate, if only inadvertently, this double sense, a mutual granting of power that also proclaims an autonomous assertion of sovereignty. Yet, the paradox remains unaccounted for in his otherwise perspicacious writings on this subject. As we have already had occasion to note in this book, the "academic disciplines" constitute an epistemic social field as much as a set of putatively pristine intellectual pursuits. Sociologist Pierre Bourdieu called academicians so many "constructed individuals," sharply observing that, "[in] a general fashion, the progression of academic disciplines within each faculty corresponds to the substitution of an academic necessity which is socially arbitrary for a social necessity which is academically arbitrary (and culturally arbitrary)."[12]

This central dynamic of power and knowledge, and of the latter's dependency on norm and hierarchy within the academy's *habitus*, marks a constitutive feature of university life that, a decade after Bourdieu's book, Dominick LaCapra, reflecting on the founding ideal of *objectivism* for the profession of historians, regards as fundamentally transferential—something that can be either "acted out" or else "critically worked through" (48). In the case of Neusner's writings on the humanities, the former tended to preside.

The impetus for his 1987 editorial was what he felt to be the pollution of knowledge by politics; and yet, the precedent of Mishnaic sagacity notwithstanding, we should not forget Garber's aperçu that purity is always another name for impurity. To that degree, the intersocial world of the academy stands a world away from the Talmud. Thus, a well-known passage from the same Tractate (b. Ḥagigah 3b), cited in my preface, speaks about the Sages, "some pronouncing unclean and others pronouncing clean, some prohibiting and others permitting, some disqualifying and others declaring fit." Likewise,

חָתְכוּ חֻלְיוֹת וְנָתַן חֹל בֵּין חֻלְיָא לְחֻלְיָא, רַבִּי אֱלִיעֶזֶר מְטַהֵר, וַחֲכָמִים מְטַמְּאִין. זֶה תַּנּוּרוֹ שֶׁל עַכְנַאי. יוֹרוֹת הָעַרְבִיִּין שֶׁהוּא חוֹפֵר בָּאָרֶץ וְטָח בְּטִיט, אִם יָכוֹל הַטִּיחַ לַעֲמוֹד בִּפְנֵי עַצְמוֹ, טָמֵא. וְאִם לָאו, טָהוֹר. וְזֶה תַּנּוּרוֹ שֶׁל בֶּן דִּינַאי:

> If an oven is cut into rings, and sand is placed between the rings, Rabbi Eliezer says it is pure. But the sages say it is susceptible to impurity. This is the oven of Akhnai. Arabian vats, which are holes dug in the ground and plastered with clay—if the plastering can stand by itself it is susceptible to impurity; otherwise, it is not susceptible. This is the oven of Ben Dinai.
>
> —משנה כלים ה י MISHNAH *Kelim* 5:10

These legal guidelines are subsequently elaborated in a well-known and complex rabbinic story about dividing lines both object-related and interpersonal, called *tanur shel* (oven of) *Akhnai*.[13] In the sections on Neusner's writings that follow, I will try, accordingly, to tease out, from behind a surface screed about the Judaic as distinct from the ethnic, a precritical reification of disciplinarity as if it were a kind of oven, made of both intrinsic and interposed elements (like plaster and sand). Or else, in Heaney's equally useful metaphor, as a kind of controlling device or engine attachment: the centrifugal governor of academic intellectual life. I emphasize, however, that it is solely this bounded dimension of Neusner's titanic (and in spirit, noble) output that I subject to vigorous critique. While it shares features with other spheres of his scholarship, those do not enter into consideration here.

Tarbut ha-maḥloḳet

Neusner's intellectual pedigree was as notable as his learning was formidable. Despite a paucity of early Jewish education, he was fortunate in his apprenticeship to come within the orbit of mid-century luminaries at several elite institutions: Harry Wolfson, Saul Leiberman, Salo Baron, Abraham Joshua Heschel, and Morton Smith. Yet, interpersonally and interdiscursively, the theater or literary genre that is academia seems to have selected him out as his own singular fusion of Kafka and Roth, suspended between the drama of counterlife and a continual series of reports to the academy.[14]

A recent Festschrift like *A Legacy of Learning* (2014) attests to Neusner's continuing influence among a subsequent generation of scholars, on display in essays by Shaul Magid and Elliot Wolfson. Encomia upon his recent passing in 2016 in one way or another capture the impact he had on field, discipline, and scholarship. Yet the polemical and sometimes needlessly caustic tone of his editorializing voice survives him, as well. Ethnoculturally speaking, he fairly exuded *maḥloḳet*, in its academic mode a peculiarly Jewish compound of ruction and irascibility.[15]

Makhlokes (Ashkenazi spelling, the better to chime with *mochlos*), connotes "dissensus," "separation," "faction," "squabble," and "dispute"—not unlike Ger. "*Streit*" in Kant's *Der Streit der Facultäten*. A more vernacular rendering would be "squabble." Its trilateral root חלק *HLK* can signify either "to divide" or "to be smooth, slippery, viscous."[16] Talmudic discourse is structured around the dynamics of *maḥloḳet*, that "dance between refutation and counter-refutation" which manifests a peculiarly Jewish rhetorical style.

As reasoned debate, it also suggests a quintessential *academic* ritual, although as philosopher Marc-Alain Ouaknin observes, "In *Makhloqet*, reconciliation is not sought . . . we would have to talk of an open dialectic, since no synthesis, no third term, cancels out the contradiction" (84). At the same time, "[i]ncessant destabilization . . . that resists synchronization, making way for a sojourn in infinity" (85) was probably not what the "Science of Judaism" originally had in mind; nor, really, is it what Neusner's massive *oeuvre* ultimately embodies.

And yet, aside from the vivacity of its mark *in* his work and in response to his colleagues, *makhlokes* in its near homonymity with Derrida's *mochlos* poses a question of considerable relevance for our purposes in this book and for Neusner as spokesman for Jewish Studies. Wherever it may properly "belong," how *does* JS position itself with respect to the academic humanities? As a mode of leverage? Or, at a node of energetic conflict and contestation?

Perhaps contestation *is* the very mode of leverage that Jewish Studies models (a parallel to which we encounter next when we revisit Timothy Bahti). Whether Neusner would have endorsed such a position is a matter for speculation. Nevertheless, the problem here is one we've seen before, since JS at this post-traditional juncture boasts too variegated and multiple a topography to reduce so readily to the dynamics of (originally religio-legal) disputation.

Still, Neusner's analysis of a *maḥloket* internal to JS prompts further reflection. His critique of identity politics as partial catalyst for the proliferation of new JS programs of study on American university campuses in the 1970s was prescient, honed over several essays and addresses published in those years and the following decade. He was no mean author of manifestos, either. Yet, despite the then concurrent infusion of French thought into the American academy, Neusner's scholarly contributions never quite caught the wind of post-structuralism or cultural studies.[17]

That inattention was only abetted by a proprietary attachment to the study of religion—"the quintessential form of humanistic learning," in his view[18]—and more specifically, rabbinic Judaism. Despite important ecumenicist contributions and work that offers genuine sociological and theological insight into the place of Judaism on the American scene, in respect to the post-traditional spirit of contemporary humanities practices, his approach now appears singularly anachronistic, however passionately and intelligently argued then.[19] Neusner's "new humanities," as he also liked to call them, were not Derrida's, although each writer coincided with the other in real time.[20]

Iconoclastic by temperament, Neusner was nevertheless resolutely pledged to the guild ethos of the academic social field, a privileged sensibility hard to mistake in both his essayistic and occasional writings. His pieces on JS and the humanities form a distinct and consistent genre within Neusner's body of work whose aggregate illocutionary force is that of standard bearing. For this chapter, I draw from several of these in addition to editorials like the one with which we began and an article review with which we conclude.

In the spirit of *tarbut ha-maḥloket* (the rabbinic culture of dissensus), Neusner's voice here is sounded in counterpoint to those associated with an academic speech genre outside his own *dalet amot* (the Mishnaic delimitation of personal domain). One suspects he would have heard such voices as Derrida's, Bahti's, or Bourdieu's as only contributing a "dissonant note" and a "dissident chord" to his consistent refrain: as produced through spurious or superfluous disciplinary harmony.[21]

I should anticipate a sensible objection. Neusner's work continues to be read diligently albeit not uncritically within the circles of his several fields of specialization: rabbinics, the religion of ancient Israel, and Judaic theology. These constitute his sounding board, his proper acoustic space. Why devote space, then, to more ephemeral and occasional pieces such as these? In truth, the precedent represented by this segment of his oeuvre only inadvertently becomes a foil for me because within JS it simply has few (if any) peers.

Given this author's own declared proclivities, then, a contrapuntal approach might seek justifications both Levinasian—that is, the pressure of exteriority, of the Other on the selfsame—and Bakhtinian, because "[d]iscourse lives, as it were, beyond itself . . . on the boundary between its own context and another, alien, context."[22] In what follows, I endeavor to proceed in just this spirit through a series of constructed colloquies between Neusner and contrasting figures (Derrida, Readings, Bahti, Hartman, Boyarin) who espouse the academic vocation with similar faith but quite different hopes.

Affirming and Performing

A purely practical aspect of an appeal to Neusner's "outside" is shown by the parallel conversation about the future of the modern university and the state of the humanities conducted by several of the thinkers already marshaled in the book. Although Neusner sought common cause with ideologues like Allan Bloom, William Bennett, and Dinesh d'Souza, opposition might well have made truer friendship. While Neusner was fighting an *arrière-garde* action against theory (among other suspects), some very smart theorists were propounding uncommonly wise things about the current state of humanities practice—which is where, fittingly enough, Neusner wished back then to place JS.

It makes for a sobering but also enlightening experience, for example, to peruse a book like *Reaffirming Higher Education* (one of several that Neusner cowrote with his son Noam) in light of Jacques Derrida's essay on the "University without Condition," in which the rhetoric of "affirmativity" sounds so much more robust and less sloganeering. Derrida's prose certainly betrays its liabilities. But despite excess convolutions and appositions, what we don't find there are sentences that speak of "the demise of departments of English brought about by 'lit. crit.' [sic]" (9).

Would the proper names "religious studies" or "rabbinics" or "medieval hermeneutics" ever lend themselves to such trivializing vernacular, even despite having incurred a certain degree of disciplinary contamination by the postmodern? And as to demise, the chronicle of that particular death foretold has yet to be inscribed in obituary fashion. English departments seem to have survived well into their "after theory" moment, with the apparatus of lit crit still intact. Kant's image of Prussian infantry on the attack (redeployed by Derrida and mentioned in the first chapter) might be hyperbolic here in respect to a quasi-militarized left or right—but only slightly. At any rate, Neusner felt that he needed to mount a robust defense as he contemplated JS's two "warring camps."

A trenchant reflection on academia's culture wars of the time, Timothy Bahti's essay "The Injured University" (introduced in Chapter 1) speaks hauntingly to the kind of left/right university politics that would become one of Neusner's idées fixes. Its central motif of *injury* feels peculiarly apt where Neusner is concerned, as well. Making extended use of Kafka's "Conversation with the Supplicant," Bahti interprets the story as an allegory of the *failure* into which defenses so vigorously mounted by oppositional figures like Neusner commonly collapse, readily "falling into reversals of opposition and projections of identification" (64). "Where would leverage, or opposition, then be?" Bahti asks.

Neusner himself seems to intuit at least part of this cautionary lesson when he frankly concedes that if the humanities have become refashioned in the new academy, it bodes only well since any knowledge practice that remains static ceases to function optimally. Yet the case of JS in Neusner's severe diagnosis, at the same time, demonstrates *precisely* the weakness in the new humanities, which, like Immanuel Kant's infirm and cramp-plagued left side, will consequently need *pari passu* to be righted by the strength and vitality of classical disciplinarity.

As I have already ventured my own refashioning of the lever-motif in that same vein, alongside lever-and-fulcrum (which suggests an effectual economy of force), Bahti teases out the congruent metaphor of injury, drawn from his own personal experience as a patient diagnosed with a collapsed left lung, from which he extrapolates the following three lessons:

> Balance between left and right can be disturbed from the outside, or from the surrounding context, such that one side usurps the functioning and ultimately the place of the other. . . .
> Leverage can occur between left and right horizontally as well as vertically; lying down as well as standing up; in the injured as well as in the healthy body—but always, as with all leverage, where the one side or position of strength is "weakened," so that the weak one might be strengthened (68).
> Symmetrical injuries that allow for no reversals or leverage are often the fatal kind (76).

The academy represents a fundamentally *conflicted* body. Yet, Bahti's concerns reinscribe Neusner's inside a different discourse entirely. If the university is ailing, if it requires some corrective to its corpus, then the malady may very well not lie in one "side" or the other, but rather *bilaterally*, as an infirmity afflicting the whole, suggesting "not dramatically but analytically, that the modern university is injured" (69). In line with deconstructive criticism, injury and imbalance should be understood to inhere within the university's structure, its body politic, *to begin with*.

Balance, leverage, "optimal health" may simply amount to some of its more elusive qualities, which is why the therapy or cure of interdisciplinarity often appears merely cosmetic. Furthermore, imbalance and injury may well generate the *wrong* kind of leverage. While it may superficially resemble Neusner's grievance, the double move that Bahti conducts for the discipline of philosophy "with respect to other faculties around it [as well as] an internal division within the philosophy faculty or what it has come to mean today" even now reads so much more compellingly because its scaffolding is analytic and diacritical rather than dramatic-diagnostic.

I spend some time with theoretical discourse like this because its careful attention to rhetorical detail and textual exegesis should so obviously remind JS of its traditionally native procedures, even if the critical language feels somehow uncomfortably "foreign." This reminds us of Harpham's self-interruptive lesson in humanities talk. To tell the institutional story of Jewish Studies—say, as scholars Gerald Graff, Deidre Lynch, and Robert Scholes narrate for English, or Peter Novick for History—should now mean listening to just this kind of theoretically informed forensic narrative, one unavailable to Neusner when he sought to anatomize the vulnerabilities (disabilities, infirmities?) JS came to embody for him, as we saw Scholem do a generation before, vis-à-vis *Wissenschaft des Judentums*.

The same applies to the story of the humanistic disciplines themselves. When Louis Menand observes that "the seeds of the undoing of the old disciplinary models were already present in the models themselves," whose very "artificiality . . . made an implosion inevitable" (81), we begin to glimpse that,

> the more rigidly a discipline's borders are enforced and the more autonomy it claims, the more vulnerable it is to subversion. Either the premises on which the discipline rests can be extended ad absurdum, or it can be shown that the discipline is suppressing some relevant aspect of its subject matter (and this suppressed aspect usually turns out, in the new dispensation, to be what was secretly driving everything all along). (81)

Solely as a rabbinics scholar bridging the generations of Saul Lieberman before him and of Daniel Boyarin afterward, Neusner well knew this inevitable refashioning of disciplinary practice and discourse. If "lit crit" seemed to signal the demise of English, it is really only because the field "became a kind of broker of exchanges between specific disciplinary languages as they tried to reconfigure themselves in order to participate in the opening up of new domains of interrogation and make interdisciplinary dialogue possible."[23]

What make the humanities really "new" are not additions to the canon of fields (for example, the "interdisciplines"), but rather a division-wide propensity to interrogate boundaries. Within the bounds of Jewish Studies as presently constituted, Zachary Braiterman thus wonders aloud, "Whose fault is it that Jewish thought and philosophy writ small and Jewish Studies writ large remain a minor literature if not, in parts great or small, our own?"[24]

In respect to his sustained polemic about JS and the humanities, the very historicism Neusner demanded of himself as a scholar never makes an entrance on the stage of this more generalized arena of his thought. Again, a critical discourse that ran parallel to Neusner's helps us see the aporia. Not only, as we learn from Louis Menand, does academic disciplinarity belong to "an episode in the history and division of labor," but the disciplines themselves have been "constructed at a particular historical moment," a forty-five year period (1870–1915) that represented "the big bang of American higher education."[25]

But also—according now to Jacques Derrida—if the history, norms, and "deontology" of fields can still remain obscure to those who most strenuously profess them, then how much more *rhetorically* discernible can the effects of such selective perception can be (even more glaringly obvious for a scholar whose métier was the history, norms, and "deontology" of his own field)?

> The approach I am advocating here is often felt by certain guardians of the "humanities" or of the positive sciences as a threat... For the principle of reason may have obscurantist and nihilist effects. They can be seen more or less everywhere, in Europe and in America among those who believe they are defending philosophy, literature and the humanities against these new modes of questioning that are also a new relation to language and tradition, a new affirmation, and new ways of taking responsibility. (147)

Sacvan Bercovitch has already introduced for us the comparable point: When interpretive frames come into conflict, for example, when the empirical "facts" of philology, history, and textualism vie with the hermeneutical (and more anachronistically, the belletristic and moral) "values" of literary study, or when both become forced into conjunction under the auspices of some supra-disciplinary construct (like "English"), it is at just that juncture that they most *especially* invite critique and leverage.

The relevant point to make here, in appealing to theorists who stand outside the boundaries of JS yet offer a broader perspective on disciplinary knowledge and practices, is that in turning a critically acute eye on much larger university structures like "the humanities" or "interdisciplinarity" or "the marketplace of ideas," they reveal themselves as unusually capable of addressing large meta-questions about the university. They seem to *read* them, as if the university were itself an epic poem or novel. Neusner needed to have performed something similar, especially grounded as he was in the unique discursive corpus of the Talmud.

Even more pertinently than personality or discipline-driven reasons, the limitation on display follows from the particular speech-genre Neusner chose for himself and the cultural moment that embeds and inflects it. Although *performed* with a vengeance, his was not a deeply theorized position. Nor was it really understood *performatively* (as Derrida uses that term), even if one elaboration of what that means would appear to fit Neusner's prodigious authoring to a tee: "by producing events, for example by writing, and by giving rise to singular *oeuvres* (which up until now has been the purview of neither the classical nor the modern Humanities)"[26]

The aim of *Reaffirming Higher Education*, which was written in in the 1980s when Neusner was a member of the National Councils on the Humanities and Arts and a political cohort that included Irving Kristol and Lynne Cheney, was to disentangle what he understood to be learning or pure scholarship from the misdirections of "special pleading," universals from the improperly imported localities of cultures, and intellectual truth from the adulterations of the personal and the political.

However, the question that presumably drives the book's passion, the one that Derrida asks so pointedly—"What relation is there between professing and working? In the university? In the humanities?"—takes the form of these flat and utilitarian chapter headings: "Who Should Teach in a University? What Should Universities Teach? Who Should Go to College? What Is at Stake on Campus?"

Readers will look in vain for evidence of what Francis Oakley calls the "tensions which have wracked [liberal education] for centuries" in Neusner's reaffirmative agenda (which, yet again, must count as a particularly glaring lacuna for a scholar of historical traditions). When he pauses to reflect on the change wrought by the new humanities, his definition of humanistic inquiry correlates two fundamental elements: intellectual power ("clear thinking, lucid and simple expression, cogent and connected argument") and imagination (the thing "we teach, that thing which sets us apart" as professors).

In the vein of J. S. Mill's *Autobiography*, as rendered in third person, Neusner adds a personal aside. After recording a litany of professional wounds and woes incurred along the way,[27] he tells us that he sought to correct for a certain cognitive habit—the tendency to rely wholly on "the rational intellect" and "mind," by learning "to appreciate the experiences of the heart," a sensibility he attributes to "the resources of the humanists."[28] Assuredly, the existential gain to an enlarged selfhood, through "imagination and sensibility, our capacity to appreciate and respond to the being of humanity" (84) cannot be gainsaid here. And by this much, one must concede, Neusner interrogated his own place in the academy.

Remaining intact and unmodified, however, is the lopsided platform on disciplinarity. Thus, rabbinics scholars are like mathematicians, perceiving "the enduring patterns of relationship and relation." One looks to humanists, contrariwise, to provide the superaddition of "feeling and emotion," in order "to feel with Othello, to weep with Achilles, to admire the heroism and be awed at the nobility of Socrates." It betrays a strange bifurcation, perhaps not uncommon for traditionalist JS scholars but eerily reminiscent of the traditionally gendered opposition reproduced within modern JS between Hebrew on one hand, and Yiddish on the other.[29]

Even if we credit an emended professorial ethos, a coaxing of rationality in closer affiliation with Mill's Romanticist "cultivation of feelings," it is fascinating to watch how Derrida repositions on such a radically different footing than Neusner's, a shared commitment to "classicism, which is the conviction we in the humanities espouse and profess" (85).

> *Grammaticum se professus*, Cicero tells us in the *Tusculanes* (2, 12), is to give oneself out to be a grammarian, a master of grammar. It is neither necessarily to be this or that nor even to be a competent expert; it is to promise to be, to pledge oneself to be that on one's word. *Philosophiam prefiter* is to profess philosophy: not simply to be a philosopher, to practice or teach philosophy in some pertinent fashion, but to pledge oneself, with a public promise, to devote oneself publicly, to give oneself over to philosophy, to bear witness, or even to fight for it. . . . Because the act of professing is a performative speech act and because the event that it is or produces depends only on this linguistic promise, its proximity to the fable, to fabulation, and to fiction, to the "as if," will always be formidable.

Neusner's lecture on the occasion of receiving an honorary degree from the University of Bologna on its 900th anniversary offers a telling instance of this slide in professing from promise to fabulation. Comparing the University and the Talmud, he constructs a rather odd analogy between the premodern Jewish intellectual canon and the institutional structure of the higher learning as he understood it. Talmud and university both exemplify a canonical tradition "meant to comprise and compose: everything put together, all at once, in a cogent way, in a single intelligible statement."[30]

Put aside the Talmud's defining hallmarks of multifariousness, heterogeneity, and polyvocality that militate against homogenizing synthesis. Put aside also the Judaic source tradition's discursive resistance to monism, metalanguage, and unifying systematicity of statement, seriously complicating an intentional fallacy that regards it as "a singular instance of what it means for learning to come together into a single system of understanding, for facts to yield a rationality, and for data all together and all at once to make sense." More consequently, imputing to the Talmud and university a totalizing will toward unifying intelligibility fails to do justice to either in its most expansive, diacritical sense.

What Neusner describes here is what Bill Readings calls the administration and autonomy of knowledge, the production of sovereign subjects in the doubled sense of person and argument. It is the difference between a monologic model of communication (Saussure) and a dialogistic one (Bakhtin), which, as it happens, probably becomes no less salient for a compelling account of Talmudic discourse than it does for the discourse of the university.[31] Likewise, Neusner's aspiration for a "theory of the whole, all together and all at once" (138) anachronistically misconceives the university no less than it does the Talmud. On this point at least, Neusner's rabbinics scholarship and his philosophy of education revealingly converge.

"To master and demystify"

In a posthumous series of lectures quite outside of Neusner's affinities, both political and temperamental, Edward Said identifies an alternate connotation for the term "canon," derived not from texts but from music, which recalls his earlier, more familiar concept of "contrapuntal reading" from *Culture and Imperialism*.

> The other [sense of "canon"] is a musical one, canon as a contrapuntal form employing numerous voices in usually strict imitation of each other, a form, in other words, expressing motion, playfulness, discovery, and, in the rhetorical sense, invention. Viewed in this way, the canonical humanities, far from being a rigid tablet of fixed rules and monuments bullying us from the past . . . will always remain open to changing combinations of sense and signification; every reading and interpretation of a canonical work, reanimates it in the present, furnishes an occasion for rereading, allows the modern and the new to be situated together in a broad historical field whose usefulness is that it shows us history as an agonistic process still being made, rather than finished and settled once and for all.[32]

Said establishes this point in the context of explaining how, in the wake of a much more "demographically mixed" world, "the whole concept of national identity needs to be revised" (24). Ideologically driven arguments about a "positive American identitarian unanimity" almost always lose their persuasive intellectual force, however much they may hit their mark emotionally.

Neusner would never have denied the sheer answerable fact of heterogeneity, of course, especially as an American Jew. But his purism about the special confines of academia—the object of Bill Readings's critique, the site for Derrida's affirmatory profession of faith, the broad historical field for Said's canonical humanities—insisted on a cordon around scholarship and learning to keep at bay the *intellectual* threat posed by a staging of identity that he felt belonged elsewhere.

If, surprisingly, Said did not earn Neusner's wrath in print, his fellow practitioner Geoffrey Hartman did, through the intemperate persiflage to which we have already been made privy.[33] Rather than let Hartman remain under the cloud of "mere enthusiast and *parvenu*" (where by Neusner's lights, I would doubtless belong as well), however, it feels right to defer to him at this juncture on the literary critic's task, the essence of which, he believes, is to make readers "formally aware" of literature's enlivening bewilderments, upon which he expatiates in respect to terrain adjacent to Neusner's:

> In biblical hermeneutics there was often a conflict between regarding Scripture as *analogical*, or written in the language of men, accommodated to human understanding; and *anagogical*, or taking the mind out of itself, inspiring it until it appeared "beside itself." The question is whether we must insist on the one or the other: on the resolvable strangeness or the unresolvable otherness. Could we not say there must be a willingness to receive figurative language? To receive is not to accept; between these, as between active and passive, critical thinking takes place, makes its place. We cannot solve, a priori, the issue of strange or other; we can only deal with it in the mode of "resonance" that writing is. We rewrite the figure, in commentary or fiction, we elaborate it in a revisionary way.[34]

Neusner's charge against Hartman that, as a literature scholar, he "understands teaching as a mode of advocacy" may miss its intended mark but inadvertently confirms that such pedagogy begins with a baseline *advocacy* for the texts taught. But in addition to advocating hermeneutically on behalf of literary works, as an emissary for readers with their own letters of transit in hand (which is not quite what Neusner meant), Hartman captures the commentator's vocation as a matter of "disconcerting responsibility" and "answerable style."[35]

I did not select the passage from Hartman at random, obviously. The literary examples he considers in this essay are drawn from Milton, Yeats, Wordsworth, Hegel, and Kleist, with additional reference to "the Ancient Classics and Scripture." In his final paragraph, he speaks of the theoretical reorientation of the field in the 1970s and 1980s as betokening a "philosophical criticism," whereby "philosophy and the study of art can join forces once more [and] . . . might evolve leading to the mutual recognition of these separated institutions" (41).

The path from biblical hermeneutics to *midrash*[36] to Yeats and Kleist was only possible for Hartman because he took the step of thinking *interdiscursively* about texts and their reading procedures as well as disciplinary knowledges like poetry and philosophy. Like Readings, albeit in the more localized scene of teaching a literature classroom, Hartman felt his vocation to be the custodianship of otherness and the instructive staging of bewilderment, which he called a "criticism in the wilderness," and which "proposes a type of analysis that has renounced the ambition to master or demystify its subject (text, psyche) by technocratic, predictive, or authoritarian formulas" (41).

In these respects, Neusner would seem to represent Hartman's professorial anti-type. Disciplinary boundaries were prima facie what demarcated for him the division of labor in the humanities. If indeterminacy lurked anywhere within the rabbinic literary corpus, it was scholarship's duty to demystify it. Moreover, whether or not Neusner's distinctive scholarly innovation, his literary-structuralist "documentary hypothesis" for rabbinic literature, proved to be sound, it discloses a telling investment in the worldviews of authorships and the monological boundaries of a single work.[37]

His vast output about this discursive tradition alone reads as one gigantic jurisdiction of its canonical boundaries. No wonder, then, that Neusner's own writing was suffused with that sense of *droit moral*,[38] which also seemed to govern his territorial definition of JS in its authorized standard version as "the study of Judaism under the auspices of the academic study of religion" and its corresponding community of scholars and acolytes. That a similar case can be made about History as the rightful anchor and disciplinary home for JS merely underscores the proprietary (and libidinal) conviction at work here.

Returning to the 1987 editorial at the beginning of this chapter, one notes the exclusionary positioning of Hartman outside the bounds of JS proper, signaled by the disparaging open quotation marks around "Holocaust studies" (which Neusner conflates with the popular mythologization thereof) and the dismissive diction of "ethnic reading of ethnic studies," where "ethnic," for Neusner, appears to denote any instance of Jewish cultural production beyond classical Judaic sources.[39] While his stated concern is "the case of Jewish or Judaic studies (what you call it makes no difference to me)"—although it most certainly does, to me[40]—he takes the core to be a contemporary reinscription of the Science of Judaism *outside and other than yeshiva.*

The framing essays for *New Humanities and Academic Disciplines: The Case of Jewish Studies* (1984) make this position clear: the academicizing of Judaism's "sacred sciences" as "an accepted subject of study" (xvi). In distinguishing between the knowledge practices of the university on the one hand, and seminaries and *yeshivot* on the other, he takes pains to emphasize how disciplines are predicated on differences in methodology.

Kafka's "Gemeinschaft" makes itself felt yet again, since one community of method bears little resemblance to the other (although for the teaching of Judaism, exclusivism remains central to each). This organizing particularity, say, of sociology or economics (Neusner's examples), means that any specific datum comes under the sway of an organizing analytical procedure, and by that *tendenz*, "the particular is forced to serve as an exemplification of the general" (xix).

Neusner performs an interesting move here. The very next sentences say, "What is specific turns outward to address issues of general concern. What is private becomes public. What is arcane gains intelligibility. That is what we mean by a university, a place in which we speak of universals, asking the same thing about everything." Disciplines, for Neusner, constitute the guarantor of those shared neo-Aristotelian protocols of knowledge acquisition and transmission. (Yet, at the Lyceum itself, Aristotle was still marked as a *metic*.)

Neusner acknowledges the paradox of Jewish Studies scholars who, in being called academicians, must therefore "stand outside the community of Judaism" (xxi), although the percentage of religiously self-identified JS scholars of Bible, Talmud, and Jewish history largely moots that argument in 2017. (Moreover, bestriding a divide between religious Jewish education and secular higher education, as many scholars of Judaism do, does not typically impinge upon their colleagues in, say, literary studies.

"We Jewish professors of Jewish learning are like our field. We fall within no frame of available norms. People do not know what to make of us. We are authorities without responsibility, leaders without a constituency. We speak but no one said we might. And none can silence us" (xxi). While those scholars may teach sacred texts (again, assuming that JS is coextensive with the study of Judaism), Neusner argues, they teach them in the same institutionally sanctioned fashion as any text might be taught in a university. And thus symmetrically, from that other side, as he wrote in "Jewish Studies and the New Humanities," "If we claim right of entry, ours is the burden of presenting a valid ticket of admission" (99).

It should be obvious that such exceptionalism reveals itself to be haunted by both the spectral legacy of *Wissenschaft des Judentums*—whose exponents, had they been fully enfranchised like their twentieth-century American-Jewish counterpart, might have voiced very similar sentiments—*and* the shadow of the dramatic contrast between Jewish religious education and the university's Enlightenment values of "criticism, judgment, the exercise of reasoned taste." But what may appear less so is the subtle parallelism between a strictly rationalist rhetoric of specificity, generality, intelligibility, and universality and a communal one of private and public.

The methodical, coherence-bestowing function of disciplinarity parallels the nonsectarian, unifying dimension of the university as public space—the reduction of personal identity to a series of signs, attributes, and so forth, that, according to Levinas, express the Academy's *mentalité*. This is consistent with Neusner's secularist, anti-tribal imperative that distinguishes between a "segregational" or "separatist" faction within Jewish Studies programs dedicated to the "ethnic" or identitarian, and the "integrative" or assimilationist, which simply embodies fidelity to disinterested reason as a scholar and pedagogue. The valences of these terms obviously fan out in directions unintended by Neusner or are at least left unacknowledged—in addition to hearkening back, for our purposes here, to satire and allegory as contrastive modes of discursive thought.

Neusner stressed this distinction in essay after essay, editorial after editorial. His report of ethnic studies' imminent death—African American Studies in particular—was greatly exaggerated. But it was evidently crucial for him to square the advent of the "new humanities," or in current academic parlance, pedagogies of minority difference, with the more legitimate humanistic value of *disciplinary* difference. The entities that Roderick Ferguson understands to be a set of *interdisciplines*—Women's and Queer Studies, ethno-racial or cultural discourses of identity formation and subject position[41]—Neusner defines as enclaves, traps of "an-other-than academic character": the reductionist, involuted distortion of disciplinary specificity.

> The crisis of ethnic studies in the academy is because the ethnics have ignored the disciplines of the academy and because the academy has conspired in the segregation of the new humanities. So, the issue is clearly drawn: "us" vs. "them," or a shared and public discourse, open to all qualified members of the academic world, upon issues of common intelligibility, discourse vastly enriched by the particular record of a distinctive social group, whether defined by gender or ethnicity.

At the same time, however, Neusner was principled enough to argue that "Black studies are too important to be left only to the blacks, and (as a non-Jewish doctoral student of mine said) Jewish studies only to the Jews. . . ." It appears to be the academic *privatization* of difference that so exercised him, which he took to mean a wholly illegitimate smuggling of politics into the universalist space of research and teaching—an anxiety neutered, for example, by the flourishing of essential fieldwork in Jewish ethnomusicology.[42] Also to his credit, he stops short of the kind of rhetoric that got Saul Bellow into such trouble when he asked, "Who is the Tolstoy of the Zulus? The Proust of the Papuans?"[43]

But he stumbles rhetorically anyway, in characterizing his "new humanities" as the diminished intellectual capital of "insiders teaching private things to insiders," such that Bellow's question can now be re-accented to betoken egalitarianism rather than seeming superiority: "Where was the Jewish Aquinas or Plato, the Black Shakespeare, the Catholic equivalent to the Reformation that everyone studies with such admiration?"[44]

Unlike its classically grounded predecessor, an ethnicized humanities "lay[s] no important claim on the university" for the same reason that "scholarship by its nature pays no attention to claims of privacy" (94).[45] Like many American Jewish intellectuals who over-generalize their own good fortune across racial and cultural divides, Neusner wrong-foots similar terrain when, in the course of lamenting "the tragedy of black studies," he magnanimously esteems his counterpart while repressing the special and systemic features of discrimination that continue to be experienced by African Americans.[46]

Intriguingly, where Neusner sees subversion, "a realm of private discourse" and "a new ghetto," a proponent of pedagogies of minority difference like Ferguson sees containment, with the crescendo of the interdisciplines signaling merely one stage in an ongoing process of recalibrated institutional recognition: "Institutions are the outcome and locations of imagined communities, with interpretive modes representing the brick and mortar of those imaginations" (16).

That foregrounding of interpretivity over disciplinarity takes us back to the realm of literary studies. Speculating on a post-Neuserian, postmodern trade-off between a liberal-pluralist yet guarded readerly will—with antennae scanning for whether a given text matches the self's particulars or not—and the demands of otherness imposed by any literary text, Renaissance scholar Barry Weller proposes a very different analysis of segregation and its discontents:

> If we avoid a condition of educational segregation, in which readers read only the texts to which their multiple subject positions give them access and a claim, all other texts become—not altogether inappropriately—a ground of intellectual and emotional warfare, where the designs of alien subjects on the subjectivity of the reader must be disputed.... And yet one obligation of a teacher may well be to disrupt or at least complicate this pleasure of self-communion, not in the name of reinscribing readers in a symbolic order that diminishes the worth of their separate identities, but in the name of pleasure, a realm in which I paradoxically anticipate that self-loss will enlarge the range of self-discoveries.[47]

The counterposition with which Weller sympathizes in this instructive *maḥloket* would defend the need to read more narrowly for self-recognition (a condition of group solidarity) as legitimately empowering. For my part, I merely want to highlight how much more nuanced and less dichotomous a model of reading practices is being advocated here. And indeed, Weller frames the problematic as a matter of *reading practices or postures* in the first place as opposed to systems of rationality and intellection.

Transposed to the boundaries or obligations of criticism, a similarly dialectical spirit underpins Hartman's thesis about a new kind of performative critical writing (ca. the 1970s in France and somewhat later for American academics) through which the reading of literary texts and a report of that reading interlace, troubling the hard-and-fast distinction between one practice and another. Hartman observes that "in philosophy there is less of a distinction between primary and secondary literature: ask a philosopher what he does and he will answer 'philosophy.' It could be argued, in the same spirit, that what a literary critic does is literature" (20).

Even if the performative-theoretical moment that Hartman celebrates has waned, an argument for the necessary interpenetration of discourses needs no elaborate defense in 2018. But Hartman's moment in the academic scene is also Neusner's, and we should mark how differently they invoke even a discourse held in common:

> [Hartman, on the critic's staging of textual bewilderment:] Books are our second Fall, the reenactment of a seduction that is also a coming to knowledge. The innermost hope they inspire may be the one Heinrich von Kleist expressed: only by eating a second time of the tree of knowledge will we regain paradise. (21)

[Neusner, on the scholar's commitment to critical reason and method:] Insofar as we claim to know the difference between good and bad, we act like God, and appropriately so, created as we are in God's image. When we give up that claim and treat one opinion as no better than any other, when we make things up as we go along and call it truth or learning, we are no longer like God. (xxv)

Where Hartman lays claim to a quasi-Blakean commitment to human fallibility—that is, the fool growing wise in the persistence of his folly, Neusner's veneration of scholarly rectitude trades upon an almost too lofty analogy. That "books are our second Fall," however, is simply to acknowledge the pathos of *Wissenschaft*—something to which Rosenzweig painfully attests in the next chapter and Neusner, in somewhat stranger fashion, elucidates in the next section.

Ruins, According to Neusner and Readings

Not quite what Harold Bloom had in mind when he imported Andrew Marvell's phrase as title for *Ruin the Sacred Truths*, still Neusner's suggestion of a fall from a more paradisal state puts one in mind again of Bill Readings. Readings—a British-born professor of Comparative Literature who taught in Quebec after leaving Syracuse University—shares none of Neusner's obeisance to a (formulaically) Cartesian model which locks both knowledges and disciplines into place rather than taking advantage of their loosening as an "opportunity for the installation of disciplinarity as a *permanent question*" (177).[48]

For Neusner, a hierarchy of disciplines as the rational grouping of knowledges truly "governs all academic teaching and scholarship." In the case of Jewish Studies, that structure should be tripartite, and the question of belonging is easily resolved: "'Judaica,' appropriately belongs in a department of religious studies, 'Hebrew studies' or Hebraica in a department of Near Eastern Languages, and 'Jewish studies' pursued from a historical or sociological perspective in a department of history or sociology or anthropology."[49]

Neusner specifies but two modes of Jewish learning retooled for the Academy: "concentration in Hebrew languages and literatures for Near Eastern or comparative literature departments, and in the history of Judaism for departments of religious studies," the latter identifying the "particular point at which a specialist in Jewish studies most nearly approximates the university's needs" (25). For a specialist in modern Jewish thought or contemporary Jewish philosophy, Neusner saw "no role"; likewise, he saw "a limited space for the Jewish historian *as such* in a history department" (7).

Modern Jewish literatures in languages other than Hebrew, Jewish cultural studies, Holocaust studies, Jewish discursive traditions in tandem with some non-Jewish component or counterpart, visual arts, or any other knowledge practice that came under the heading of "ethnic" for Neusner earn no mention whatsoever. But what is included or excluded in a prospective JS program in Neusner's estimation concerns me less than a rigid apportioning of disciplinary labor, an equally rigid separation of the disciplines themselves, and a rigid equation of discipline *with* knowledge, abstracted from its sociology. Iconoclasm or not, this is disciplinary libido with a vengeance.

Compare Readings's evocation of the scene of teaching, so different from Neusner's framework for the same intellectual space:

> In the classroom, Thought intervenes as a third term alongside speaker and addressee that undoes the presumption to autonomy, be it the autonomy of professors, of students, or of a body of knowledge (a tradition or a science). Thought names a differend; it is a name over which arguments take place, arguments that occur in heterogeneous idioms. Most important, this third term does not resolve arguments; it does not provide a metalanguage that can translate all other idioms into its own so that their dispute can be settled, their claims arranged and evaluated on a homogeneous scale. As a name, Thought does not *circulate*; it waits upon our response. (161)

Very roughly, this recalls, within Neusner's demesne, the "dance" of Talmudic discourse we saw sketched earlier, which, however—and I emphasize this point—departs as much from Neusner's critical vocabulary as Readings's Lyotardian notion of the *differend*.

Contrariwise, Neusner's stance appears absolutely uncompromising in its absolutist, custodial "oversight"—certainly, one long-legitimated approach to what Readings would have us see now as the province of ruin. For Neusner, too, "[o]urs is the task of remembering, recapitulating, reenacting." And yet, as he acknowledges, "that leads us to the word 're-mind.' Ours is the task of reminding, in a very odd sense of the word, that is to regain mind. We form the links in the great chain of learning" (*Reaffirming*, 158–159).

"Thought" versus "(re-)mind." In one rhetoric, the *horizon* and the vigilance required to prevent slippage of trans-referential name into commodified idea; in the other, a doctrine, an idealization which, like "excellence," functions as the *simulacrum* of an idea. On the one side, a "network of obligations." On the other, "links in the chain of learning," upon which Neusner insists, all the work of previous generations depends. Finally, the postcontemporary challenge of the *differend* over against the unsurrendered classicism or "recapitulation of received knowledge" (160).

But since my aim here is not to fall into the binary trap of *maḥloḳet*, that is, Neusner "versus" Hartman/Readings/Lyotard, I want to take Neusner as seriously as possible in reconceiving JS *in the context of* humanistic inquiry. In this chapter's concluding section, therefore, I take up the essay that casts a bright light on the human process of intellection itself, but in almost tragic guise. If the scholar's voice seems to acquire the tonalities of Kohelet the preacher in the Neusner excerpt we will read, so Rosenzweig's sufferings in the last decade of his life bestowed upon him, in others' eyes, the patina of a saint. Yet, the differences are stark.

Neusner Ecclesiastes

"'Being Jewish' and Studying about Judaism" stands apart from Neusner's other lectures on the subject. It mounts nothing less than an epistemology of the specialized intellectual labor called academic. The lecture strikes a remarkably chastened, maybe even melancholy note amidst its pronounced didacticism, considering its occasion, which was the inauguration of a highly ranked institution's new chair in Judaic Studies. Nominally a meditation on the limitations of normative and descriptive approaches to the academic study of religion, which need not be seen as debasing or misrepresenting the experientially sacred, Neusner's true argument, it appears, concerns the way both approaches "replicate a profound flaw in the humanities in general, a flaw which derives from the modes by which our minds grasp and respond to reality" (2).

Echoing the subjunctively wishful liturgy of the Passover *Haggadah*, Neusner writes, "[E]ven if we danced, sang, burned incense, or spent our fifty minutes with our students reciting Psalms, even if all our students were Jews and we were all rabbis, we still should not have entered into the realities both interpreted and created by these merely-intellectual processes" (12). Intellectualization—the wording of the world and its realia, the preference for static system over immanent dynamism—is another name for human fallibility, an enduring problem "because the thing described and interpreted comes to us from intellectuals, and because we ourselves are intellectuals" (16).

Neusner refers at various points to philosophers, including those "in the guise of" anthropologists and of historians, but some time spent with Wittgenstein or even Rosenzweig might mitigate the force of the pessimism here. Especially Wittgenstein, who avoided the corner into which Neusner paints himself by speaking rather in terms of *Sprachspielen* and of "leading words back [*zuruckfiihren*] from their metaphysical to their everyday use."[50]

Readers will also recall that in "Shekinah," the penultimate chapter of *The Coming Community*, Giorgio Agamben reads the famous aggadic story about the "Four Who Entered *Pardes*," a creative appropriation that I restyled as an unintended "gift to JS." Neusner's far more stoical and didactic lecture ends with its own treatment of rabbinic narrative, the equally famous "myth of Talmudic Judaism" (16) recorded in Tractate b. *Menaḥot* 29b, when Moses is transported from Heaven to the backmost of eight rows in R. Akiva's Tannaitic academy.

אמר רב יהודה אמר רב

Rabbi Yehuda said, "Rav said,

בשעה שעלה משה למרום מצאו להקב"ה שיושב וקושר כתרים לאותיות אמר לפניו

'When Moshe ascended to the heavens, he found the Holy One, Blessed be He, sitting and attaching crowns to the letters. He said before Him,

רבש"ע מי מעכב על ידך

'Master of the Universe! Who is staying your hand?'

אמר לו

He said to him,

אדם אחד יש שעתיד להיות בסוף כמה דורות ועקיבא בן יוסף שמו שעתיד לדרוש על כל קוץ וקוץ תילין תילין של הלכות

'After many generations, there will be a man, and Akiva the son of Yosef is his name, who will expound on each and every crown, piles and piles of laws.'

אמר לפניו

He said before Him,

רבש"ע הראהו לי

'Master of the Universe! Show him to me.'

אמר לו

He said to him,

חזור לאחורך

'Turn around.'

הלך וישב בסוף שמונה שורות ולא היה יודע מה הן אומרים תשש כחו

He went and sat at the end of eight rows [of students in Rabbi Akiva's Beit Midrash], and he did not know what they were talking [about]. He grew upset.

כיון שהגיע לדבר אחד אמרו לו תלמידיו

As soon as he got to one [other] thing, his students said to him,

רבי מנין לך

'Our teacher, from where do you learn this?'

אמר להן

He said to them,

הלכה למשה מסיני

'It is a law [that was taught] to Moshe at Sinai.'

נתיישבה דעתו

He calmed down.

חזר ובא לפני הקב"ה אמר לפניו

He returned and came before the Holy One, Blessed be He, and said before Him,

רבונו של עולם יש לך אדם כזה ואתה נותן תורה ע"י

'Master of the Universe! You have a man like this, and You are giving the Torah through me?'

אמר לו

He said to Him,

שתוק כך עלה במחשבה לפני

'Be silent. This is what I have decided.'

אמר לפניו

He said before Him,

רבונו של עולם הראיתני תורתו הראני שכרו אמר לו

'Master of the Universe! You have shown me his Torah; show me his reward.' He said to him,

חזור [לאחורך] חזר לאחוריו ראה ששוקלין בשרו במקולין אמר לפניו

'Turn around.' He turned around, and saw that they were tearing his skin with iron combs. He said before Him,

רבש"ע זו תורה וזו שכרה

'Master of the Universe! That is Torah, and that is its reward?!'

א"ל

He said to him,

שתוק כך עלה במחשבה לפני

'Be silent. This is what I have decided.'"

To modern eyes familiar with literary fictions about time travel and many a contemporary film, this narrative of teleportation conveys an undeniable uncanniness. Within the Judaic commentarial corpus, as a story that fuses important theological questions about the continuity of revelation and of theodicy, it has enjoyed a long and rich tradition of readings. Many of these focus on its particulars of form, the literary dimension of rabbinic literature, which Neusner's relentlessly historicist concerns tended to skirt.[51]

Because they speak particularly to Neusner's ideological self-positioning, I would single out two of these, by Laurence L. Edwards and Neusner's recurrent foil, Daniel Boyarin.[52] I cite the one because it parallels my own point that "[o]ur text seems to invite dialogue with recent thinkers who are often associated with the discourse of postmodernity" (430), and the other, because it performs a similar service by invoking Mikhail Bakhtin.

In his 2009 book *Socrates and the Fat Rabbis*, Boyarin reads the story as a *menippea* of the sort associated with Lucian, the second-century CE Greek satirist, about whom Boyarin's (and Neusner's) mentor Saul Lieberman avowed, "Lucian holds the keys to the Talmud" (24).[53] Allowing that the conceit about interpreting the *kotzim* (serifs) seems to suggest a caricatured model of *midrash*—as if to say that Akiva's interpretive brand can also lend itself to critique[54]—Boyarin says this about the Biblical Moses, a figure initially perplexed, subsequently relieved, and finally silenced in an epiphany that pictures to him his post-Biblical practitioners, the rabbis:

> It will be seen that a sharp challenge is being offered to rabbinic authority here. "Moses" would represent on this account a more rational, logically based read of the Torah while Rabbi Akiva represents a kind of theurgical or mystical reading. The turn against the rational, the logical is what motivates the Menippean satire, for it is the inadequacy of Moses's intellection to understand and make sense of the Torah and the world that is at issue. In this sense, it is "Moses" who is being satirized: the rationality of his practices of understanding his own words is being challenged, and with this, rabbinic rationality is itself being queried. (240)

Before I turn to Neusner's account of the story below, let me just offer here a suggestion that whatever else it may be doing, the rabbinic story seems to decenter *makhlokes*, maybe even creating a space for *mochlos* (which Boyarin would read as the interpretively liberating space of satire). If the ingredients of *maḥloket* include intellectual parity and mutual self-confidence, this *midrash* posits a radical knowledge gap between Moses and Akiva but also a strange chiasmus between their respective levels of knowledge and authority.

What I like particularly about this "inside narrative" from the classical source tradition is its *sidelining* of conflict and dissensus for other kinds of combinatorial accountability. While he comes to no such conclusion himself, Neusner agrees in one respect with Boyarin by adjudging the story a self-critical fiction about epistemological opacity, "a philosophical formulation of the inadequacy of human knowledge and the existence of a reality that transcends reason" (234). But any convergence ends there.

In its capacity as Menippean satire, Boyarin understands b. *Menaḥot* 29b as "a *mise en abyme* for the whole Talmud," a paradigmatic story where assertion and denial of tradition and of interpretive mastery coexist in the same plurivocalic space yet at the same time precisely *within* the context of the surrounding Mishnaic discussion about halakhic exactitude. Rabbis, like Lucian's philosophers, are thus assigned a kind of tragicomic status here. Their work of professing, as Derrida would say, simply fails to make good on its pledge. This would seem to be Neusner's conclusion also, keeping in mind that he made no pretense of being a philosopher, even while insistently aligned with the pole of the rational and logical.

But where Boyarin sees satire, Neusner discerns a solemn rebuke to the aspirations of those he calls "intellectuals." Boyarin, however—while embedding the story within its Mishnaic context—truncates it by not considering (or even reproducing) its coda about theodicy. In other words, the story functionally works as Menippea only up until a decisive point, whereupon it considers the matter of reward-as-punishment, which Boyarin does not address. For Neusner, who does not adduce the immediate discussion in the *mishna*, *that* exigency—"show me his reward"—remains as central as the continuity of revelation—"you have shown me his Torah."

It is strange enough that Neusner insists that the reader's subject position in the Talmudic text should be identified with Akiva (who is martyred), not Moses (who is merely silenced), which makes sense only formally. As a character, it is the bumbling and overwhelmed Moses who probably elicits most readers' sympathy. But Neusner extends the fate of silencing to academicians, too, as their "just punishment." Poetic justice (of a sort) requires that those specialized "intellectuals" who permanently oscillate between the poles of *hubris* and humility, of wishing to transcend the truth of revelation as known historically to Moses, should be transcended in turn by "the limitations of thought itself" (22).

Had Kohelet's rhetoric conformed to a modern day academic-scholastic speech genre rather than that of Near Eastern wisdom literature, he might have sounded something like Neusner himself, as he reads out the story's manifest drama of anxiety pacified but abruptly recoded as pathos:

> For the limited capacities of intellectuals, studying religion begins in the use of language for the purpose of study, both to contain and create reality. And reality cannot, in the nature of things, find whole and permanent place within language.... In that wry and ironic fact is to be located the apologia for our infirmities and incapacities of our intellect: in mind we indeed construct flawed reality corresponding to flawed reality outside. (19–20)

In Neusner's understanding, a question about Moses versus Akiva, about legacy and belatedness, traces a reflexive line that aims directly at rabbinic intellectuals—Levinas's *"docteurs de Talmud"*—and, after them, the rabbinics scholar in the modern academy, "who sees his [sic] own contribution to be one of worth, yet who is also constrained to locate that contribution within the processes of tradition" (21). Even if, with rabbinics scholar Azzan Yadin-Israel, we read b. *Menaḥot* 29b against a Second Temple background (attenuated in Tannaitic literature but resurgent in the *Bavli*) as an instance of a more general textual motif, the decline of the prophet and the elevation of the interpreter,[55] Neusner's extension to the modern scholar-*clerc* feels forced.

When we recall that this essay's title plays "being Jewish" (identity) against "studying about Judaism" (scholarship), and that its main argument seems to be a qualified defense of the academic study of religion, the lachrymose conclusion becomes only more puzzling. It certainly strikes a very different chord—minor, diminished, dissonant—than Neusner's other essays about JS and the humanities, which why I choose to focus on it here.

On the model of apophatic theology (both religious and secular),[56] we could call these reflections on the "ineffable tragedy of the mind's incapacity to do its work" (22) *negative epistemology*. As our intellectual vocation, says Neusner, obstructs the ratiocinative process of description, so our philosophical bent compromises the success of our interpretations. "Mind cannot transcend its own participation within the human condition. We cannot be more than we are. That is why God tells us, through death, to be silent: Ask no more, risk no more, think no more" (22).

Unless this is Menippean satire—which it so clearly is not—Neusner's lecture may well have left its original audience in 1977 fairly baffled. If JS readers of Agamben's gloss on b. *Ḥagigah* 14b felt similarly positioned at the end of Chapter 2, I would simply propose: Does that reading, slanted toward avowedly postmodern concerns, come across as so much more gratuitous than Neusner's—skewed, we might even say, by his own positionality as a rabbinics scholar? Intriguingly enough, whereas Agamben exploits a Talmudic text (as he reads it) about self-separation in order to open up a space for a discourse about community, Neusner edifyingly cites one in to render a verdict about evolved academicism, and sharpen the divide between one tribal modality ("being Jewish") and another ("studying Judaism").

"Don't let the sun go down on your grievances"

Apropos of "our intellectual vocation," Max Weber's essay, "Wissenschaft als Beruf" (a paradigm for the kind of speculations Neusner assays in his talk), concludes with a somewhat different verdict about knowledge "organized in special disciplines." After extensively reviewing the external conditions grounding academic pursuit in German and American universities, and internal motivators like "enthusiasm" and "personality," Weber equates *Wissenschaft* first and foremost with *vocation*. It neither approximates "the gift of grace of seers and prophets dispensing sacred values and revelations, nor does it partake of the contemplation of sages and philosophers about the meaning of the universe."[57] Through it, human finitude actively comes to terms with its historical sociology.

In the academicized milieu of "intellectual rationalization," any metaphysical rapprochement with the world and its features is now rendered either inapposite or obsolete (as we saw Levinas reaffirm in "Means of Identification"), for Weber's organizing theme is the "disenchantment of the world" (134) in—and as—secular modernity. It's not surprising, then, that at moments his pronouncements draw nigh to Neusner's. He celebrates the fact that both the *Wissenschaftler* and his work will always be surpassed by subsequent practitioners and advancements. He juxtaposes *Wissenschaft* with religious belief. He ends by quoting the Edomite watchman's song in Isaiah 21 (earlier in the essay, he invokes Plato's allegory of the cave in the *Republic* and Tolstoy).

Rather differently than Neusner, however, Weber acknowledges the *Wissenschaft's* conditionality within a political and economic world that underwrites academic pursuits, where individual scientist and system, moreover, will always be at odds with each other.[58] As one research scientist has suggested, the pressure of such contingent forces explains the cryptic last word of Weber's essay: "the external ideology that is bound to science itself, always and everywhere: this is Weber's 'demon.'"[59] So then, what good is *Wissenschaft*, given its inability to answer transcendental questions or promulgate transcendental values?

Ideally inculcated, the practice of intellectual scholarship is just that: *practices* that, even with their suppositional character intact, fuse character and action through ratiocinative choice, amounting to its own intrinsic "value." For, "Ladies and gentlemen," Weber declaims, "[i]n the field of science only he who is devoted solely to the work at hand has 'personality'" (137). Exceeding "the question of man's *calling* for science" (134), vocation takes its place in the largest human arena, "within the total life of humanity" (134), where one is "called" in and by modernity.[60]

Decades later, this modernist, secularized, delimited view of scholarship was refined for a contemporary professoriate in literary and cultural studies by Bruce Robbins, who insisted that in the absence of "an ultimate judge," a debate over legitimations "becomes more self-conscious, more troubled, more dramatic" such that "the persistence of this debate within one's work" (26) is what identifies the very mark of a "secular vocation." In other words, the curtain of negative epistemology to which we saw Neusner resign himself parts here to reveal a divergent dedication to vocational conscience: debating legitimation as the very exercise of academic discourse, a grappling, in public view, with Weber's "demon."

Synthesizing Weberian circumspection and Robbins's insistence on critique—and clearly at odds with Neusner's wistful, sometimes somber tone—Geoffrey Galt Harpham parses the secular vocation as the enlivening gap between mind and words because "in the humanistic text, even 'the facts' are humanized and must be grasped mind to mind as well as mind to object, and this difficult process exercises both the intellect and the imagination" (36). To recognize the immeasurable yet insistent otherness of others may be humanism's most profound gift.

Harpham pens these words at a decidedly different cultural moment than Neusner's. But more differentiates their positions than the thirty-year difference spanning the culture wars that witnessed the flourishing of various difference-based programs in the Academy loosely organized under the banner of cultural studies. Where Harpham historicizes the humanities, pitching his story from the vantage point of a literary scholar, Neusner appeals to a model of free-standing scholarly pursuit, such that the Jewish source tradition in all its rich permutation becomes a kind of an analogue to the fifty-two volume "Great Books of the Western World." For Weber, Robbins, and Harpham alike, no scholarly pursuit "stands free"—a property, and positive value, inhering in its primary mandate to interrogate.

An accompanying response to Neusner's lecture from the newly installed Chair entitled "Judaic Studies: An Exercise in the Humanities" stressed a more self-evidently given, grandiose, and less emergent version of Harpham's perspective, wherein what epitomizes the humanities (or its stand-in, JS as the study of religion) is the circular mandate "to teach the human in whatever is being taught" (28). Perhaps more significant than any such non-(*adhan*)-interrupted claim for JS, however, is how eerily the academicism recalls both the crypto-theology and universalizing apologetics of *Wissenschaft des Judentums* made so dubious by Buber, Scholem, and Kurzweil in the generations to follow, informed by a distinctly enterprising American-Jewishness.

In its rejection of Leopold Zunz's formal request to the Prussian ministry for a professorship in the history of Judaism, the Berlin faculty committee insisted that "If Jewish history and literature desires to become an independent and respected field at the university, it has to prove and legitimate itself by way of quiet and solid advance." Slightly more than a hundred years later, the cultural conditions for such rejectionism have altered substantially. Yet, even while Neusner dismisses the political impulse to cultivate a Jewish academic space that would ingather Jews on campus, *legitimation*, the self-evidence of masterly scholarship in the history of religion, still drives all of Neusner's polemics about the proper place and purpose of Jewish Studies as humanistic pursuit.

A late piece by Neusner responding to an essay of personal reflections by Zachary Braiterman about teaching two courses, "Judaism and the Holocaust" and "American Judaism: Thought and Culture," in a Catholic university system could not be blunter in its castigation of JS as anything but the history of Judaism "under the auspices of the academic study of religion."[61] Nor could it be any more ad hominem in its signature distillation of *makhlokes* through its liberal use of animadversion. (The specific ecumenical character of Braiterman's situation would not have escaped Neusner's attention, to its likely disparagement as well.)

In his thoughtfully conceived essay, Braiterman references Gershom Scholem, Wassily Kandinsky, and maybe most relevantly, Eugen Rosenstock-Huessy and Franz Rosenzweig; all remain unreferenced in Neusner's critique. Braiterman's students at Santa Clara read, among other authors, Abraham Cahan, Nathan Glazer, Abraham Joshua Heschel and Mordecai Kaplan, Cynthia Ozick and Judith Plaskow, and James Baldwin

JS and the Humanities

and Henry Louis Gates Jr. Likewise undignified with citation, not one of them makes it into Neusner's derisory appraisal of the memoir, whose essential heresy entails constructing just such a catalog of "ethnic" Jewish (and non-Jewish) figures, thus signaling yet again the entirely wrong turn for JS.

In his rejoinder, Braiterman equitably remarks, "Professor Neusner must surely have confused my essay for something else."[62] Sadly, or maybe just fittingly, the very same sentiment could be said to encapsulate Neusner's own consistent polemic against Jewish Studies' institutional proliferation since the 1960s: that is, a confusion for the real and more authentic thing, for indeed, the obsessive refrain hearkens directly back to the editorial about Geoffrey Hartman in 1987, with which this chapter begins. However, such contumely may have reflected, for Neusner, very real social and political impingements on the twentieth-century university (and those on him), twenty-first-century Jewish Studies, it is fair to say, deserves a different brand of advocacy.

Collectively, then, Neusner's essays on JS and the humanities do not readily provide the *mochlos* he must have imagined for them. Within his vast chain of utterances, they make for less than durable links; indeed, *linkage* describes both their intellectual mandate and their ideological deficit. In recirculating unreconstructed pieties about the privileged intellectual space reserved for the university and its disciplinary practices, they evade the meta-disciplinary gain assigned by Marc-Alain Ouaknin to *maḥloket* at its dialogical best, a "thinking that resists synchronization." While they may pinpoint the moment when JS has matured sufficiently to speak authoritatively about itself, they also calculatedly miss the mark. Affirm and perform they do; but only precritically; the ember of their assorted grievances glows long past sunset.

At the same time, and almost alone among his peers, Neusner reflected conscientiously and repeatedly on the relationship between JS and its university others that this book seeks to re-interrogate. If only he had allowed himself more latitude for historicizing and theorizing the humanities, he might not have fallen back onto reactionary positions that read now as signaling their own wrong turn.

Neusner was a scholar of rare ambition, undeniable rigor, and perspicacity. But *as a disciplinarian*, his pitchfork was decidedly more Ibn Gabirol–thrust than Heaney-flung. Even while he acknowledged the modification, over time, of a foundational canon of texts, he was far less accommodating of a postcanonical approach to boundaries and practices, which calls for a different kind of intellectual temperament.

In the next chapter, therefore, we leave the confines of the university to consider what a para-academic structure for Jewishly infused knowledge practices looks like elsewhere and otherwise, through the counter-personage of Franz Rosenzweig. He, too, was a conscientious reader of Ecclesiastes, though the lessons he took away speak in markedly different accents—a duality already inscribed in the verse that reads, *et l'hashlikh avanim, v'et kenos avanim* ([there is] a time to scatter stones and a time to gather stones together).

INTERCHAPTER IV

Speaking of JS; and Its Vicissitudes

Speaking of JS to JS can be hit or miss. Two occasions on which I was asked to do so offer instructive lessons. The first talk was pitched to a composite audience of colleagues in Jewish Studies and literary studies. Such conditions of "bilingualism" stand out most starkly at institutions where an affiliative history bridging two distinct constituencies remains only emergent. The presentation was built on the central figure of reading as a tactile practice: books as the felt objects of palpable hands in relation to interpretive will and the rabbinic tradition, more specifically, where the question also intersects intriguingly with criteria for canonicity.

The latitude for sources and references was rather wide: Talmudic discussions of *tum'at yadayim*, the capacity for certain objects to transmit impurity to the hands; an extended passage from *Die Ausgewanderten* by the late writer W. G. Sebald; citations from Jean-Luc Nancy and Maurice Merleau-Ponty, Helen Keller, and Dickens; the engraved parapets that enclose the September 11th memorial in New York City, Levinas's Talmudic readings.

The manifest burden of the talk was hermeneutic, but so was the performative bridging of differing textual traditions and respective audiences.

What lent itself to being more or less synthesizable or amenable to juxtaposition *within* the talk, however, proved more challenging in regard to the intramural conversation it was designed to elicit, since whatever bridge the presentation was intended to model depended in part upon two-way traffic. In this case, "JS" elements and "non-JS" elements seemed content to hail each other politely across a divide.

Some years after, I gave a keynote address for a small conference assembled by a JS program whose disciplinary bias tilts unremarkably toward history and the study of religion, its whole (not atypically) somewhat less than the sum of its contentedly monadic parts. For this second presentation, the task in some part involved *constituting* an audience addressed in the context of the broader humanities. The conference's organizing topic nominally envisioned an alternative to the inward gaze that continues to drive so much scholarship and conditions so many structural choices for Jewish Studies generally.

If I say that for my own contribution I took inspiration from the Yiddish pioneers Mendele Moykher Sforim and Sholem Aleichem, whose challenge was to bring a readership into being for the fiction they sought to peddle, then the parallel endeavor of marshaling an audience represented a distinct task of its own. Marshaling an audience, *constituting* it, really, in the context of the broader humanities, was the real perlocutionary challenge.

Yet, as a more contemporary comedic Jewish sensibility has memorably tied success to the routine coup of just "showing up," so, too, even when JS programs as a joint stock company make a point of looking outward in order to reap the benefit of transactional exchange, they still depend internally on the robust investment of shareholders. If conjuring an assembly of faces will always necessitate a certain idealism, so the attempt was underscored in this instance when the first query after the talk was over began by preemptively disavowing any particular esteem for Levinas.

The plain lesson to deduce here is structural, however. The specific details of such campus rituals, which answer to any number of contingencies, matter less than the vicissitudes of JS programs, more widely: how they are positioned, staffed, and directed; what "desire lines" do or don't open out onto other habitats in academic ecology; what the promise is of critical mass; and what the differential effects of professing and professionalization are in the face of the profession's irrevocably altered economics. While one of the two programs more closely approximated a "concentration model" (prioritizing a certain chronological period, geographical focus, or methodological thrust), both stood in evident need of bridges to the wider humanities.

It may not be insignificant that the histories of the encompassing institutions were imprinted with a strong focus on Christian religious training. As is typical for such campuses, once their divinity schools opened up intellectually to other religious traditions, it was primarily through religious studies that "the Jewish" came to be studied in its own right. On the other side of a potential viaduct to and from JS, when "the Jewish" finds itself subject to an economy of neighboring, if not competing minority-multicultural discourses, the problem of connectivity may only be compounded (particularly so if the department in question approximates the kind of profile on which the 2009 MLA symposium, cited in the introduction, was premised).[1]

The personal discovery gleaned from these experiences sharpened in relief not only Derrida's point that "one of the tasks to come of the Humanities would be, *ad infinitum*, to think and know their own history ... the history of the concepts that, by constructing them, instituted the disciplines and were coextensive with them" (49–50). It also brought home the salient fact that unlike the average English, French, or History department, Jewish Studies programs are disciplinarily variform. Indeed, it counts as a reasonable question whether there is such a thing as an average JS program, since each answers to the most contingent of institutional forces—a lottery of research scholars, appointment, donor, student body, local Jewish community, and leadership.

The vignettes sketched by this interchapter do not therefore presuppose every JS program, however or wherever constituted, or even some generalized template for JS, with optimal intellectual range and depth at one end and something more idiosyncratic at the other. In describing two very particular constellations of JS, however, they do make a virtue of the accidental as opening a window onto the normative.

In the cases related above, JS was left largely autonomous to the degree that units other than the given affiliations in History or Religion—Literary Studies, Philosophy, other area studies programs, to take the relevant instances—remained disinvested in it, with boundaries serving effectively as dividing lines. The result? A quite modern (as opposed to Aristotelian) sense of "either/or," where one term doesn't simply negate or logically exclude the other so much as preserve it while hollowing it out from within[2]— that is, Jewish Studies registered, "hailed"—but at a discreet (even neutered) distance, and a far cry from Roth's multiplicative "and/and/and/and/and."

Which brings us back to Kafka. "I was stiff and cold," begins a parable from 1916/17 entitled "Die Brücke" about the mode of connection that is metaphoricity (*Gleichnis*):

> I was a bridge, I lay over a ravine. My toes on one side, my fingers clutching the other, I had clamped myself fast into the crumbling clay. The tails of my coat fluttered at my sides. Far below brawled the icy trout stream. No tourist strayed to this impassable height, the bridge was not yet traced on any map. So I lay and waited; I could only wait. Without falling, no bridge, once spanned, can cease to be a bridge.

The parable predicts its swiftly dramatized denouement. Just before collapsing after being crossed by a pedestrian for the first time, the newly actualized bridge exclaims, "Und ich drehte mich um, ihn zu sehen.—Brücke dreht sich um!" (And I turned around so as to see him. A bridge to turn around!) Granted, this would seem to entail something more like double-jointedness than leverage.

But still: If JS warrants conduits of several sorts, certainly at less impassable heights, it might itself function as that brand of uncommon bridge that can *turn or be turned around*. Without, that is, surrendering fatefully to the doom that awaits Kafka's: "I already began to fall, I fell and in a moment I was torn and transpierced by the sharp rocks which had always gazed up at me so peacefully from the rushing water." In the next chapter, we investigate one celebrated attempt to construct, stabilize, and realize a thoroughfare of that sort: *Brücke dreht sich um*.

CHAPTER 4

Bildungsheld or *Pícaro*, Canon and List: A Heterotopology for JS

> It is necessary for [a person] to free himself from those stupid claims which would impose Juda-"ism" on him as a canon of definite, circumscribed "Jewish duties" (vulgar Orthodoxy), or "Jewish tasks" (vulgar Zionism), or—God forbid—"Jewish ideas" (vulgar liberalism). . . . All recipes, whether Zionist (with their Jewish tasks), Orthodox (with their Jewish duties), or liberal (with their Jewish ideas), produce caricatures of people that become more ridiculous the more closely the recipes are followed. And a caricature of a man is also a caricature of a Jew; for as a Jew, one cannot separate the one from the other.
>
> —FRANZ ROSENZWEIG, "Bildung und Kein Ende," *On Jewish Learning*

Afterlives: Rosenzweig and Lehrhaus

The epigraph above comes from an essay by Rosenzweig that speaks to the heart of our concerns in this chapter. It was written in 1920, the same year that the institutionally weary thinker launched his Freies Jüdisches Lehrhaus, a new initiative in adult education for his co-religionists in Frankfurt. It opened one month into the Jewish new year of 5681 and lasted a decade.

Words carry with them the places they have been, and "Lehrhaus" happens to be particularly well traveled. But as such, one of Rosenzweig's animating beliefs for its realization lay in its essential *transportability*: "what is possible more or less everywhere."[1] As we shall see, *place* figured almost as prominently in Rosenzweig's thought as *time*, and especially so for language, intrinsically transportable: as terrain, as border, as *topos*. Thus, *Lehrhaus*, German for "House of Study," which itself translates *beit midrash*, a term of more ancient Hebrew provenance, possesses an energetic iterative afterlife.[2]

It was Rosenzweig's original choice for formalizing a program of amateur adult education, whose ideal pedagogue, in his view, would be a composite of *schülerhafte Lehrern*, "masters and at the same time pupils."³ Freiburg, Karlsruhe, Köln, Mannheim, Munich, Stuttgart, and Wiesbaden all saw the establishment of Lehrhäuser in the 1920s and 1930s.⁴ While Hochschulen in Berlin and Breslau (also formally designated as "Freien Jüdischen") preceded Rosenzweig's by one year; they were established in a very different, quasi-academic configuration.

The term "Lehrhaus" was subsequently reclaimed by Hermann Levin Goldschmidt for the understandably different post-Shoah institute he established in Zurich from 1951 to 1962. In the Netherlands, in addition to specifically Jewish *Leerhuizen*, the brand has become popular among groups that promote interfaith dialogue. More recently in 2005, Ephraim Meir of Bar-Ilan University authored a prospectus for a "Jewish House of Study in Kassel inspired by Franz Rosenzweig's Frankfurt Lehrhaus." Finally, as transposed to the United States in 1974 with intentional fidelity to the legacy of Rosenzweig's school for Jewish learning, the nondenominational community-based Lehrhaus Judaica continues to thrive in Berkeley, California.

In light of this genealogy for a concept that continues to find new homes, this chapter will dwell on the *Stichwort* (keyword) of "Lehrhaus" itself by reflecting on the spatial and ideological alternative to the university it originally embodied. There, a program parallel to what we know as academic Jewish Studies was practiced but conceived deliberately as an intellectual counterlife to *Wissenschaft des Judentums*.

On analogy with the preference to speak of zero-article "Talmud" rather than "the Talmud" (the better to capture its quality of *techne* and discursive practice), so we might likewise speak of *Lehrhaus*, unmodified by the definite article. What might seem the central question of whether it could be imported into academic space is subordinate to its utility as an analytical *mochlos*. This, for example, is how I read Rosenzweig's conceit in his introductory piece on the Lehrhaus about its teacher-scholars as *"Chorführer des Chors des Fragenden"* (choir leaders for the choir that asks questions).

At the time of this book's completion, a Google search for the terms "Franz Rosenzweig" and "Lehrhaus," yielded the following four results in descending order: (1) "Franz Rosenzweig and the Founding of the Lehrhaus"; (2) "The Frankfort Lehrhaus" (N. N. Glatzer); (3) "Franz Rosenzweig" (Stanford Encyclopedia of Philosophy); and (4) "A Prayer at the Grave of Franz Rosenzweig." If one were to search solely for the term

"Lehrhaus," the website that sponsors this fourth search result, www.thelehrhaus.com, will be the very first to appear, owing to a canny choice of domain name and keyword. (The domain name, "lehrhaus.com"—without presumption of the definite article—appears still for sale.)

The web page connected with the site features a brief elegiac reflection at Rosenzweig's gravesite in Frankfurt am Main. Its point of departure, and return, is the philosopher's *teshuva* experience in the Potsdamer Brücke Synagogue in 1913, which marked his commitment to Jewish practice on the near verge of conversion to Christianity. The elegy begins with a quotation about the Ashkenazic custom of visiting the graves of the righteous from the Talmudist, *posek* (decisor), and leader of the Jewish communities of Germany, Austria, and Bohemia, Yaakov ben Moshe Levi Moelin (ca. 1365–1427), better known as the MaHaRIL.

It concludes with the author's own affecting prayer, couched in traditional liturgical fashion, prefaced by the following sentences invoking Rosenzweig in context of the then newly launched web forum: "Perhaps, then, *Moreinu* Rosenzweig—and despite his deprecation of his own accomplishments in traditional Jewish learning, he has taught us all—would smile at the idea of reciting a prayer for the success of this new venture at his grave. After all, Maharil, the hero of Ashkenazic custom, was part and parcel of that treasure trove that *Moreinu* Rosenzweig inherited."[5]

The smile thus surmised might also be elicited by the decision to refer to Rosenzweig as "Moreinu" (our teacher), a conventional Orthodox honorific addressed chiefly to pulpit Rabbis or learned Jews of great stature, but "among German Jews," as the author himself notes, "given to a learned layman who has exhibited mastery of halakhic texts." "Rosenzweig was indeed awarded this title" (paraphrasing Nahum N. Glatzer's biography), "though he did not publicize this fact during his lifetime."

Biographically considered, and especially in light of his tragic and fatal illness, the figure of Rosenzweig certainly invites pietistic reception. He received as much from Glatzer, one of his closest acolytes and biographer. But as intellectual historian Peter E. Gordon has observed, "The God Rosenzweig affirmed in his philosophy was post-Nietzschean [and] whatever else it was; Rosenzweig's philosophy was hardly an affirmation of piety in the customary sense."[6] Even less helpfully for this website's sectarian purposes, "the more Rosenzweig is made available for open-ended inquiry, the less usable he may be for purposes of Jewish self-affirmation" (42).

Benevolent sanguinity as to Rosenzweig's postmortem might also express itself at the decision to begin this online article with authorizing footnoted references to a medieval Torah authority—not because Rosenzweig might not have been aware of or even have referenced the MaHaRIL. His work, to quote Gordon again, "was the very embodiment of philosophical syncretism" (2), for better and for worse. No, rather, because the decision locates the article within a distinctive speech-genre practiced in academic and para-academic publications by diversely credentialed Modern (or Centrist) Orthodox American Jews.

But maybe of all inducements, a smile from the conjured figure of Franz Rosenzweig, might let itself slip *most* knowingly (perhaps even a little satirically), at something labeled "thelehrhaus.com." How, he might wonder, did his vision for an alternative adult education program for German Jews with little or no history of Jewish learning find itself transposed to a forum on the World Wide Web? For there, he would encounter scholarly articles on the likes of Rav Soloveitchik and Rav Kook, text culture, personal refections, and cultural criticism designed primarily for the institutionally self-organized community of American Modern Orthodoxy, whose frequent subject—less an expression of creedalism than credentialism—tends to be its own denominational self.[7]

The gravesite reflection, as far as one can determine, constitutes the sole instance on the website that indicates "this exciting new project [is] named for Rosenzweig's adult education initiative, Lehrhaus." For American Jewry, the hagiographic stage in Rosenzweig's reception marked by Glatzer's biography and translations, even if it may have reflected postwar assimilationist anxiety, also meant claiming him as an exemplary quasi-religious figure for "private self-affirmation in a pluralistic public sphere."[8]

In Will Herberg's phrase, Rosenzweig charted "a third way" between Orthodoxy and Modernism—notwithstanding footnotes to the web article establishing his bona fides for ritual practice. Moreover, as neo-Hasidic thinker Rav Shagar (Shimon Gershon Rosenberg) remarks, to the extent that Orthodoxy "can be perceived as a mirror image of modernity, hopelessly enmeshed in it," each falls short of promising some synthetic "grand narrative."[9] Postmodernity, in other words, will have its due, which is the burden of this chapter's conclusion.

In short, if one had to imagine a genial mien for the tutelary genius of Rosenzweig, it is because he would have to struggle to recognize his intellectual legacy—non-specialist, non-rabbinical, non-polemical, non-apologetic, universalist in content and spirit—transposed to this denominationally canted, digitally friendly form. Does that mean that Franz Rosenzweig's dialogical thinking stands in inimical relation to intellectual and relational possibilities facilitated by the World Wide Web? Of course not. Visit www.sefaria.org, "A Living Library of Jewish Texts

Online," gaze for a moment at the mesmerizing calligraphic loop on its home page of the first words of the Torah being engraved on parchment, peruse its astonishing archive of Hebrew and Aramaic sources and commentary, and you will see conjured the regenerative, modernizing spirit of Franz Rosenzweig.

Rather, it means more restrictively, that whatever Rosenzweig envisioned for his Freies Jüdisches Lehrhaus does not necessarily ensure against the vagaries of translation. The website, in an obvious sense, differs from the university (Derrida's point about "topology"); yet, it is also just as obviously parasitic on it in a way that Rosenzweig's vision for his Lehrhaus was designed to eschew. Each element in the proper name he chose contributes its own tonal cast. The qualifying adjectives "Freies" and "Jüdisches" redirect the noun "Lehrhaus," each in turn; the first half of the noun phrase oscillates between "study" and "instruction," and the second enframes it, so to speak, in a space of habitation and dwelling, anticipating Heidegger by a good two decades.

This was the same Franz Rosenzweig who, in explaining the famous two-word, capitalized conclusion to his magnum opus, *The Star of Redemption*, "*INS LEBEN*," referred it to two plateaus in his own everyday life: marriage to Edith Hahn and the founding of the Freies Jüdisches Lehrhaus.[10] The "Leben" in Lehrhaus was Rosenzweig's rejuvenating antidote to mummified tradition and sclerotic practice, with *Wissenschaft des Judentums* positioned on one side and neo-Orthodoxy on the other. This was the same organizationally unbound Franz Rosenzweig, several generations removed from the Haskalah but still its self-aware legatee, who, in his open letter to Martin Buber, averred "Nichts Jüdisches ist mir fremd"—a German-Jewish refashioning of Terence's famous dictum, "Homo sum, humani nihil a me alienum puto."[11]

Heterotopology

My business in this chapter concerns itself only glancingly with a web-based effort intended to rebrand Rosenzweig's differently constituted institute. I adduce it here only to pinpoint its remarkable illustration of well-intentioned, aspirational, yet still proprietary cultural transposition, blending the enterprisingly American and Modern Orthodox under the aegis of a not-at-all American, programmatically un-Orthodox, and historically resonant proper name.

As to whether Rosenzweig's Lehrhaus might be reconstructed within the university's walls, historian Herbert Strauss has keenly isolated the

Rosenzweigian model as a compound of "highly intellectual irrationalism and personalism."[12] That it originated for German Jewry with "the potential disassociatedness of Jewish existence in the modern national state" after the Great War rather complicates its transferability to Jewish educational needs that lie considerably beyond Weimar.

Surveying the dissimilar landscape for the inculcation of academic Jewish Studies on American campuses, Strauss questioned whether its "level of secure, communicable, and verifiable knowledge" could reasonably accommodate the subjectivism of Rosenzweig's pedagogical brand. His verdict: "The religious basis that rendered the Lehrhaus unique cannot and should not be recreated under college circumstances even if the gifted and dedicated teachers would be available that characterized Rosenzweig's Lehrhaus" (28).

While this might seem to return us to Jacob Neusner's impassioned critique in the previous chapter, we should still at this early stage of analysis wish to know more about what specifically contributed to that defining uniqueness. In a 1920 letter to Eduard Strauss, Rosenzweig captured the "Science of Judaism" as lying "outside the student, and he must enter it and make himself at home in it" (68). What alternate home for Jewish learning itself might therefore be established *extramurally*? If Lehrhaus stands to university as *beit midrash* does to Temple—not so much a reconstitution or replacement as a reorientation, less an afterlife than an alteration—perhaps a vocabulary that has succeeded Rosenzweig's but is not therefore incompatible with it, may help us begin. I propose the nontraditional but still expedient term, "heterotopia."

Coined by Michel Foucault as a complement to "utopia" in his lecture "Des Espace Autres: Hétérotopies," a year after his original (and rather different) working out of the concept in the preface to *Les Mots et Les Choses*,[13] heterotopias can be many things. Foucault lists six overarching principles for them; at bottom, though, the term connotes a "contestation of space," *contre-emplacements* or counter-sites, in which the spaces we typically inhabit "are simultaneously represented, contested, and inverted" (24). Foucault's metaphor that rather audaciously explains the concept is the mirror. As a utopia, "the mirror is a placeless place" in which "I see myself where I am not, in an unreal, virtual space that opens up behind the surface."

> But it is also a heterotopia insofar as the mirror does exist in reality, where it exerts a sort of counteraction on the position that I occupy. From the standpoint of the mirror I discover my absence from the place where I am since I see myself over there. Starting from this gaze

that is, as it were, directed toward me ... I come back toward myself; I begin again to direct my eyes toward myself and to reconstitute myself there where I am. (24)

For some, this prose epitomizes the dense intellectualism of a figure George Steiner dubbed "the mandarin of the hour."[14] And yet, the notion readily lends itself to the purposes of this chapter, which are, quite simply, to ponder a counter-site for Jewish Studies outside the academy—that is, situated otherwise from within. Where the previous chapter staged the space Jewish Studies already occupies in the person of Jacob Neusner, this one uses a late episode in the career of Franz Rosenzweig to diagram "a counteraction on th[at] position." Thus dialectically personified, "inside" and "outside" allow us, once again, to think the place of JS.[15]

But why, skeptically minded readers may wonder, would terminology like "heterotopia" even need to be imported into its conventional discursive space in the first place? It is perhaps a question to refer to heterodox Torah scholar Rabbi Shimon Gershon Rosenberg, who (in specific connection with Rosenzweig, no less) wrote, "The Torah is the heterotopic space in which the Jew resides,"[16] altered or othered space being thus ascribed to a prototypically Judaic category.

More immediately, though: Why can't Jewish Studies simply reside where it does, undisplaced, unreconstructed, unmirrored, unaltered, at home? In fact, however, it was Rosenzweig's own intellectual disenchantment with the academy that prompted him to look into the mirror, and then look outside academic boundaries to reimagine the location of Jewish culture, and possibly exert leverage on it and one's habitation within it. We therefore turn to that decision.

From Akademie to Lehrhaus

Franz Rosenzweig was born in the same year that Leopold Zunz died. His own premature death forty-three years later coincided with Salo Wittmayer Baron's appointment as the Miller Professor of Jewish History, Literature, and Institutions at Columbia University and the incorporation of the American Academy for Jewish Research. We thus mark three periods in the history of Jewish scholarship, as well as a cultural shift between Europe and the United States, conspicuously bridged by the historico-theological enterprise of *Wissenschaft des Judentums*.

The story of the Freies Jüdisches Lehrhaus was first narrated to an English audience by Glatzer in his book, *Franz Rosenzweig: His Life and*

Thought, first published in 1953, and much expanded in an article three years later.[17] As we learn from Glatzer and from more recent accounts by Michael Brenner and Leora Batnitzky, earlier precedents for Rosenzweig's plan for a new kind of Jewish education can already be found in the 1916/17 programs, "Volksschule und Reichsschule" (focused on reforming the German school system) and "Zeit ist's: Gedanken über das jüdische Bildungsproblem des Augenblicks" (which proposed a curriculum and infrastructure for Jewish primary and secondary education).[18]

"Zeit ist's," formally an open letter to philosophy professor (and later *Geheimrat*) Hermann Cohen, represented a kind of report on/to the academy which laid out Rosenzweig's vision for a community-sponsored "Akademie für die Wissenschaft des Judentums," to be supervised by a core of theologically trained but also critically sophisticated teacher-scholars. Such a hybrid required new pedagogical training, resources for which were not readily available.[19] Its promulgation by Rosenzweig (and Cohen, who died in 1918), owes its rationale, very simply, to the exclusionary practices of the German university system that had still made no place for a disciplinary component in Jewish Studies.

In fact, an "Academy for Judaism-Science" *was* established in Berlin, though no longer in any real accord with the original spirit of the Cohen-Rosenzweig initiative.[20] Glatzer notes that "its function . . . was the execution of . . . scholarly projects and the publication of results of individual research. The turn to the purely historical . . . prompted Rosenzweig, its initiator, to look to other ways of realizing his idea of a renaissance of Jewish learning" (107). In other words, an alternative to methodologically driven disciplinarity was eventually replaced by a research institute (*eine reinwissenschaftliche Anstalt*) conforming to conventional German academic standards of unity and coherence, dedicated to the historicist legacy of *Wissenschaft des Judentums* in the very way Rosenzweig wished to revise and redirect for a rejuvenated modern Judaism (while continuing that institution's characteristically religious thrust).

Intellectualism of the university sort could serve as only a means to an end: a revitalized Jewish identity and a revivified Jewish learning. By that point and not without psychological cost, Rosenzweig had sufficiently deinstitutionalized himself. In cultural historian Eric Santner's words, he "clearly began to experience the entire academic enterprise as a defense against the exigencies of being in the midst of life, the forms of answerability he was coming to associate with it."[21]

He wished no longer to incur the fate of the academic philosopher rendered as a spinning top in Kafka's short text, "Der Kreisel," which

Santner also connects with Rosenzweig's evolving post-academic persona (118): "So long as he could catch the top while it was spinning, he was happy, but only for a moment; then he threw it to the ground and walked away." If Kafka's philosopher "believed that the understanding of any detail, that of a spinning top, for instance, was sufficient for the understanding of all things," Rosenzweig had far loftier aims. In abandoning the university and its structures, he chose *Gestalt* over *Figur*, a star rather than a spinning top, the overlapping triangles (*Dreiecke*) of the *Magen David*.

The *Akademie für die Wissenschaft des Judentums* was not without accomplishment, publishing valuable editions of Hermann Cohen's writings as well as Moses Mendelssohn's. It steadfastly supported the work of Gershom Scholem, then a young scholar based in Jerusalem just beginning his research into the texts of Jewish mysticism. It sponsored the scholarship of Eastern European researchers and cultivated an interest in Jewish cultural legacies beyond the German-Jewish in an intellectual trend known as "dissimilation" (Myers, 159). But, the topological place it assumed was simply not the Jewish intellectual heterotopia Rosenzweig imagined, which he also wished to differentiate from both the standard Jewish *Volkshochshule Bewegung* (adult education movement) and its German counterpart.[22]

House as Counterspace

In Foucault's taxonomy, heterotopic space entails several criteria. Among these, a heterotopia can be reckoned as outside all other places; it can coincide with "slices in time" and with apertures that simultaneously function as barricades; it can juxtapose several incompatible spaces within itself. Two of Foucault's examples, the cemetery (a sort of counter-city displaced to the urban frontier, which at the same time marks a heterochrony between ongoing life and its surcease) and the garden (a microcosm and macrocosm in one), clearly indicate that heterotopias rename (and reframe) extant places.

As we gauge Rosenzweig's vision for a different sort of Jewish education, its heterotopic (and heterochronous) aspects emerge into view. "This movement," writes Rosenzweig, "would begin with its own bare beginnings, which would be simply a space to speak in and time in which to speak" (68). Shortly thereafter, he writes,

> In the very speaking space and at the same speaking time that the students are found, the teachers will be discovered as well. And perhaps the same person will be discovered at the same speaking time

as a master and a student. Indeed, whether he is suitable as a teacher is entirely certain only once this occurs. The precondition for this to occur is that the speaking space is a single room, without a waiting room. The speaking time must be "public." Whoever comes waits in the speaking space itself. He waits until the moment arrives from him to enter into the conversation. The consultation [*Sprechstunde*] turns into a conversation. Those who find each other here and want to continue their conversation in private may arrange for an appointment. The speaking time brings together everyone with everyone. For it unites everyone with everyone with respect to that which everyone has in common with everyone: the consciousness, however germinating, however hidden, to be a Jewish human being. That, following this, he can come together with others, that he can wish together with others, this will become his encounter [*Erlebnis*] even if his wish should remain unfulfilled.[23]

This "time," this "space," and this "consultation" all cluster around human dialogue.[24] In truth, Rosenzweig's "movement" might as well have been named *Sprechhaus*. The Lehrhaus, among its several innovations, some realized, some not, fell midway between a *schule* and a *haus*. It aspired to be "an existential meeting place," in historian Martin Jay's telling formulation.[25] Not a solitary hut or cabin, like Martin Heidegger's in Todtnauberg in the Black Forest, or Ludwig Wittgenstein's in Skjolden and Connemara, or Walter Gropius's in Berlin.

Nor a communal synagogue, and not really even a *beit midrash*,[26] but rather a collective, para-institutional space. One will search in vain for a street address or plaque marking the original site of the Lehrhaus in Frankfurt, since it had none. True to its heterotopic structure, "courses and lectures were offered in rented halls and private homes, rather than in a central building."

Its faculty, almost all of them "nonprofessional Jews," included a biochemist, a physician, an archaeologist, an educator, and a lawyer. What it housed, beside its assemblage of teachers and learners, was not calcified *Wissenschaft des Judentums*, not academical "Jewish Studies," but rather *Neues Lernen*, "new learning": classical Jewish learning dialogically practiced by amateur Jews alienated from tradition, on whose behalf Rosenzweig nevertheless "granted assimilation a dialectical dignity."[27] At least, that was Rosenzweig's vision for it.

Mostly, it appears from the preceding passage, what he envisioned for his learning heterotopia was that it would catalyze and define by desire, to "wish together with others." This, to use Zachary Braiterman's apt terminology, was the shape of revelation it was designed both to inspire and embody. Lehrhaus-and-Bauhaus as "quintessentially modern spaces" (186) might be one way to encapsulate Braiterman's analysis here, which juxtaposes topological themes in Buber's and Rosenzweig's writing with the aesthetic movements concurrent with them in Weimar.

> Just as the members of the Bauhaus looked forward to the salubrious effect of modern design upon industrial society, the Lehrhaus worked for the renewal of a Jewish person redeemed from the limiting confines of pre-modern ghetto life, the rigid sectarian space of creedal confession, the narrow notion of essential teachings, and rigid legal borders separating Jewish and non-Jewish. (187)

Along with Braiterman's point here about Lehrhaus-as–alternative space, the allusion to the Jewish ghetto reinscribes Foucauldian criteria for heterotopia, whose oppositional power mirrors back our own through a productively distorting lens. To take Foucault's own example, cemeteries also demarcate where beings "reside," where they neighbor and crowd each other between and across transit lines or "streets," and where their opposites, the living, decide just where their space will be located, subject as it will become, to regular incursions from without.

Likewise, in Braiterman's schema, reconceiving already inhabited space liberates it. If the university signifies "not merely a few walls or some outer structures surrounding . . . the freedom of our work . . . but also and already the structure of our interpretation" (Derrida), then the space which houses the Judaic past in the midst of, and infused by, modernity exemplifies heterotopia at its most transformative.

Institutional space, in this sense, is diacritical or relational. Cities are represented, contested, and inverted by cemeteries—or, for that matter, by brothels and fairgrounds (two of Foucault's other examples), and, in the more historically Jewish example, a ghetto. So is a university by a Lehrhaus. "How to maintain, as an open border, the difference upon which identity depends?" (168): Braiterman's question sums up Rosenzweig's evolving thought about the bounded Jewish space (ghetto, clique, text) in relation to all that it counterposes. For a cluster of German-Jewish figures—Rosenzweig, Buber, Freud, Kafka, and Benjamin, most prominently—the borderline that brought Jews and Jewish culture into adjacency with an outside was a desire line all its own, and vice versa.[28]

Nevertheless, as Braiterman quickly adds, relative to the Bauhaus's successful expatriation of its ideas and even its personnel to Harvard and Chicago, Rosenzweig's new House of Study failed even on its own terms:

internecine friction between the very constituencies it sought to merge (its own intellectual *Gemeinschaft* and the larger Jewish population of Frankfurt); study groups that never achieved critical mass; Rosenzweig's inscrutability and revisions of the curriculum;[29] and his increasing infirmity from symptoms of ALS and eventual replacement by Rudolf Hallo (although he continued as *spiritus rector* until Buber assumed that position).[30]

Perhaps most ironically, as time went on more of its registrants were Gentiles than Jews, demographics that evidently frustrated the founder's aspirations such that he eventually adjudged the Frankfurt Lehrhaus, "a great Potemkin village with very little behind it."[31] The same space that promised wider thoroughfares and desire lines for Jewish self-identity became an increasingly narrowed circle, lasting only six years before it was disbanded.[32]

"A new sort of learning"

How well did it succeed, then, on those same terms? First, as to its entire name, "Freies" connoted both fully open inquiry and fully open registration. In the 1923 essay he wrote for Buber, "Die Bauleute: Über das Gesetz" ("The Builders: Concerning the Law"), Rosenzweig praises Buber's transposition of "the vast subject matter of learning": "Teaching begins where the subject matter ceases to be subject matter and changes into inner power" (76). The much shorter draft for his address that would inaugurate the Lehrhaus (given the title "Neues Lernen" by the editor of the 1937 edition of his *Kleinere Schriften*) speaks of "learning in reverse order," from the midst of life back into the Torah, from periphery to center.

The recommended method was *Dialogik* over against *Vorlesung* (lecture). The actual roster of teachers, in-house as well as visiting, for its ninety courses and 182 study groups over its six-year lifespan included figures as disparate as Rabbi Nehemia Anton Nobel, Martin Buber, Leo Strauss, Bertha Pappenheim, and even S. Y. Agnon, among notable figures less well known today. Several reasons for its untimely demise are ventured by Glatzer and others—among them finances, administrative strife, and the ultimately failed German-Jewish symbiosis.

Maybe the most pertinent and telling judgment for our purposes, however, was rendered by scholar of German-Jewish thought Alfred Jospe, who, like Herbert Strauss, lamented its "over-intellectualized" tenor, which (once again) does not make it an "adequate model" for transposition to late-twentieth-century American Jewish life.[33] According to this view, what Lehrhaus (the thing, not the word) can't or doesn't do well is *travel*.

Reading Jospe, one would not realize how programmatically Rosenzweig himself sought to differentiate the "intellectual transmission" (Jospe's phrase) embodied by Rosenzweig's Lehrhaus, its teachers, and study groups not only from the contemporaneous *Volkshochschule* (both Jewish and German), but also from his own rejected precedent of an *Akademie für die Wissenschaft des Judentums*. As befits the would-be physician for whom biomedical metaphors came naturally, his 1921 pamphlet *Understanding the Sick and the Healthy* goes so far as to diagnose the patient afflicted with the disease of philosophy—as if he had developed vertigo after chasing too many tops.

"A sense of at-homeness in Judaism and the Jewish community," says Jospe, "is generated not only through study but also through having significant models, through human contacts, [through a focus on] perennial questions." (83). The dichotomy quite misses Rosenzweig's point, however much it may italicize the historical and cultural differences between Jewish Weimar and Jewish District of Columbia. Aslant the deficiencies of Orthodoxy, Zionism, and liberal assimilationism (the primary modes of expression for Weimar Jewry), and the Hobson's choice between academy and *Wissenschaft des Judentums*, Rosenzweig pursued what his Austrian contemporary Robert Musil called "the uninvented third possibility."[34] The core of his program for a *Neues Lernen* forms the oft-quoted core of the Lehrhaus address:

> This is a new sort of learning. A learning for which—in these days—he is the most apt who brings with him the maximum of what is alien. That is to say, not the man specializing in Jewish matters; or, if he happens to be such a specialist, he will succeed, not in the capacity of a specialist, but only as one who, too, is alienated, as one who is groping his way home. It is not a matter of pointing out relations between what is Jewish and what is non-Jewish. There has been enough of that. It is not a matter of apologetics, but rather of finding the way back into the heart of our life. (99)

While Jospe speaks of "at-homeness in Judaism" (the very property Jacob Neusner wished to subordinate to the claims of intellectual vocation), Rosenzweig plants his flag in the heterotopic and dialectical space of *Entfremdung* (alienness) through which it is possible to become both *Enfremdete* and *Heimsuchende/ Heimkehrende* at the same time (shades of Kafka and, not to mention, Bercovitch and Kun).

As scholar of religion Michael Zank observes, his was a "spiritualist Judaism that was an oddity even among the many odd phenomena of the so-called German Jewish renaissance"[35] Rosenzweig's stated goal, in the concluding sentence of the Lehrhaus address, is *Erinnerung*, a *teshuva* of reclaimed interiority: "Turn into yourself, return home to your innermost self and to your innermost life" (102). Yet, such innerness was to be facilitated through outside suggestion—not didacticism, not academicism, not historicism—but rather, dialogical learning.

The stated goal fell somewhere between qualified success and temporary reprieve. At its heart, we find the engine of desire: the conscious displacement of professionalized academic culture with a reoriented commitment to *Bildung* as "liveliness," as a "wishing together with others." This production of desire appears absolutely essential to Rosenzweig: "For because of its uniting the many a common wish, even if unfulfilled, is as alive as a lecture is dead that was [merely] mentioned in a course listing [without ever taking place]" (238).

Zweistromland; or, "Between Two Streams"

When, in "Bildung und Kein Ende," Rosenzweig writes, "Lehrer muss hier sein, wer 'wünschen kann'" (He who can desire/wish must be the teacher here), the quotation marks almost certainly function in parallel to those in other sentences, like "lehren kann" (can teach) "offentlich" (public), or "kehre um" (turns around). Let us just pretend, though, that Rosenzweig is surreptitiously channeling Goethe, who was a dominant presence in much of his writing.[36]

> Windfahne [nach der eiten Seite]
> Gesellschaft, wie man wünschen kann:
> Wahrhaftig lauter Bräute!
> Und Junggesellen, Mann für Mann,
> Die hoffnungsvollsten Leute!

> A Weather-Vane [swinging to one side]
> Society, as one would like it done:
> True pure brides along the slope!
> And young fellows, one for one,
> People quite brimful of hope!

Faust I (ll. 4295–8)[37]

It is an admitted stretch. Yet, if "desire" or "wish" resonates deeply across the tapestry of Goethe's text, we also recall that the subtitle for Rosenzweig's essay is "Wünsche zum jüdischen Bildungsproblem des

Augenblicks, insbesondere zur Volkshochschulfrage" (Wishes concerning the *Bildungsproblem* of the moment, especially concerning the question of adult education). The essay's epigram, *"Wünsche sind die Boten des Vertrauens,"* is repeated later in the text in the same paragraph in which Rosenzweig connects teaching with desire. The lexeme shimmers in his prose:

> And wishes are the messengers of confidence. Wishes that find each other: human beings that find each other: Jewish human beings. Let us then attempt to create what they desire. Very modestly this, too. For who knows whether such wishes—real grown wishes rather than wishes artificially produced according to a schema of *Bildung*—can find their fulfillment. But he who understands to hearken to the voice of such real wishes will then perhaps also understand to point them in the way that they desire. This will be the most difficult part. For the teacher who can meet such grown wishes must no longer be a teacher according to any schema; he must be much more and much less: he must be a master at the same time that he is a student. It is not at all sufficient for him to "know" himself, nor that he "can teach." He must have an entirely different "skill": he must himself be able—to wish. Here, the teacher must be someone who "can wish." (237)

Goethe's *Gesellschaft* (at least when the weather vane rotates in one direction) takes the form of happy marriage: "as one would like it done."[38] For Rosenzweig, *Gemeinschaft*—a term that crescendos toward the end of "Zeit ist's"—marries teacher to the scene of teaching. In the grammar of *"wünschen kann"* we're also reminded of Marjorie Garber's insight about disciplinarity structured as a desire, with an asymptotic relation to its own ego-ideal. To that end Rosenzweig aspired mightily, beyond what the limits of the practical and social realities of 1920s bourgeois Frankfurt permitted if the Lehrhaus was to function as veritable counter-site and *contre-emplacement*.

Rosenzweig's "Bildung und kein Ende" and the "Lehrhaus address" imagine a space other-than-university, other-than-*Akademie*, that would simultaneously represent and invert the knowledge practices we customarily associate with precisely those institutions (to which, in the contemporary circles of strictly Jewish education, we might also add *yeshiva* and *kollel*). His distinctive brand of Dilthey-inspired *Lebensphilosophie* and *Erfahrende philosophie*[39] was meant deliberately to ventilate those spaces, retaining their emphasis on *Bildung* without end, while eschewing their machineries and ideology of self-production.

Expanding on Goldschmidt's analysis, however, Martin Kavka suggests that the Lehrhaus's mirror effect may have ultimately been more reflective than contestatory:

> The spatial metaphors of Rosenzweig's discourse about the Lehrhaus are metaphors in which there is some alteration of the self: "from the periphery back to the center," "groping one's way home," "finding the way back into the heart of our life." [T]he rhetoric of ending in a different place than one began—center, heart, home, but not the margins—suggests that the foreign content that is brought into the Lehrhaus either disappears or is somehow transfigured in the act of learning. The student does not move the periphery to the center; the student herself ends up moving elsewhere. (5)

Even if the classical sources, together with the professors who transmit them, bespeak a seeming sovereignty of "tradition," knowledge in Lehrhaus did not conform to the administered entity it signifies within the conventional topology of university and academy. Glatzer attributes its distinctiveness to an institution constructed "in a time of transition" which will have terminated when the new learning was fully internalized. "The Builders," written halfway through its six-year duration, however, suggests that its heterotopic spirit will continue as long as the event of teaching only commences when "subject matter ceases to be subject matter and changes into inner power" (76).

Like the decentered and decentering scene of teaching evoked by Bill Readings, Lehrhaus represents "a radical form of dialogue" (154), where the teacher, like his or her dialogic partners, assumes the role of *rhetor* rather than self-authorizing *magister*, and where the pedagogical goal lies otherwise than with "mimetic identity: either as replication of the professor or as replication of a place in the system" (158). Instead, Readings's authorizing condition for pedagogical practice becomes "an infinite attention to the other." Ideally, a Lehrhaus "other" would designate both learner-interlocutor (or colleague, for that matter) and source-text.

In an eerie fore-echo of Readings, three years after drafting his address upon the opening of the Lehrhaus, Rosenzweig writes in his letter to Buber (a sentence omitted in Glatzer's translation), "the teaching itself is nothing knowable, it is only my and your and our knowledge." As Geoffrey Harpham has argued for the transitive meaning of "ethics," so Lehrhaus (as praxis, *mentalité*) similarly names "a mutual stimulation of theory and example" and thus represents "a fundamental instance of the relation of consciousness to life." Harpham calls ethics "a matrix, a hub from which various discourses, terms, concepts, energies fan out," which does not so much "solve problems as structure them."[40] Lehrhaus could be said to function likewise as an alternative configuration for Jewish texts, teachers, students, and particulars.

In writings such as "Das Neues Denken" (1925) that accompanied the gradual decline of both the Lehrhaus and his own bodily autonomy, Rosenzweig sought to clarify some of the obscurity in *The Star of Redemption* (whose aim, he insisted, was "anti-mystical but not anti-intellectual"[41]), while reformulating the more heuristic elements in the essays on Jewish learning. According to Willi Goetschel, the Lehrhaus concretized for Rosenzweig a "philosophy of the standpoint."[42] In short, it gave him leverage, a *mochlos* whereby to "rethink philosophy from the outside in" and to "rethink the practices of learning and teaching as forms of an emancipatory and self-empowering experience in general" (68–69). And that brings us back to the question of cultivation that German names *Bildung*.

Bildung *and* Büchermachens

In his open letter to the chemist Eduard Strauss, Rosenzweig, so preoccupied with wishes and desiring, characterizes his cultural moment as "obsessed with *Bildung* and suffocated by it." The opening paragraph (excised by Glatzer in his English translation) reads as follows:

> When, three years ago, I directed my call to our great teacher Hermann Cohen, who has since passed away, that it was 'time' for something fundamental to happen in Jewish education on German soil, I concluded with the words: the vital Jewish question of the moment is the Jewish problem of *Bildung*, on all levels and in all forms. The moment has passed, [but] the problem has remained. (229)

What exactly is this "Jüdische Bildungsproblem"? Could it be the Jewish appropriation of something more genealogically German than Jewish? Or else, perhaps the way *Bildung* has taken (or lost) shape with specific regard to Jewish textual practice?

Rosenzweig surely knew that *Bildung* signified an emancipatory concept originally located by the Jewish Mendelssohn outside institutional frameworks like the academy. He was also likely familiar with how greatly Rabbi Samson Raphael Hirsch, his co-religionist from a generation earlier in Frankfurt am Main, extolled the Schillerian properties of *Bildung* as already rooted in Torah.[43]

Although Judaism's connatural analogue to *Bildung* would be something more like חינוך (education, inauguration), the formative process at his own cultural moment, which is Rosenzweig's topic in his essay on *Bildung*, entails a gap between otherwise synchronous elements: the intellectual or merely bookish on the one hand, and the spiritual or enlivening on the other.

As he contemplates the extant structures for Jewish education in his milieu, it is the latter element he isolates when he writes, "the living force is missing that would bring the endless bookworld of *Bildung* to its end and from which alone it could therefore take its living, bookless, beginning: the centerpoint and point of germination for the Jewish life of the Jewish human being" (237). That idealized form of *Bildung* differs as much from the Jewish *Bildung* known as *Wissenschaft des Judentums* as it does from neo-Orthodox and Zionist alternatives. Michael Zank explains:

> To Rosenzweig, Judaism no longer exists as the unifying whole of Jewish life that was once constituted by the unity of Jewish law, Jewish home and Jewish ritual (*Kultus*). Second, the elite institution of *Wissenschaft* he sees as too much under the spell of German academic culture, running after the latest intellectual trends and methods instead of seeking to ground itself philosophically in the sources of Judaism. Furthermore, *Wissenschaft* seems to him to belong under the general heading of the "making of books," a pursuit devoted to the examination of the past which is a necessary but insufficient condition for Jewish life. (240)

Where his own contribution to *Bildung* and *des Büchermachens* was concerned, he could seem ambiguous, however. In the preface to *The New Thinking*, for instance, Rosenzweig expresses some dismay over the reception—the "social misapprehension" as he calls it—of *Der Stern der Erlösung* as a "Jewish book."[44] But then, Rosenzweig, in both his person and in his work, exemplified the kind of irrefragable German-Jewish merger detailed in Michael Brenner's book about Weimar Jewry, in which seemingly authentic Jewish elements (including Rosenzweig's model of Bible translation) were fused with a very German genealogy of cultural formation.[45]

Whatever its nature, the problem of *Bildung* appears to be a function more of time than of space. The "living moment" (*Augenblick*), is bordered by two realms of the making of books, of *Bildung*, and "in these there is no end to the making of books." Enquiry, instruction (*Belehrung*), and science (*Wissenschaft*) are limitless. It is the fire of the *Augenblick*, however, that illuminates the way to the future and makes the past visible. "It is only out of the spirit of the moment, free of letters, that the worlds bordering on it, the world of research and the world of teaching, that science and education derive strength and life" (231–232). Contrariwise, *the place* in which such spirit of the moment was crystalized, which Rosenzweig wished to see constellated as *erlebnis* (experience, encounter) for fellow Jews alienated from their collective past and trepidatious about their cultural future, was the Lehrhaus.

I have taken recourse to Goethe and Rabbi Samson (Hirsch) in this chapter because I want to pivot strongly here back to Bill Readings's conception of *Bildung* as the modern academy's pedagogical engine and rationale. Its genealogy is traced by Readings in German Idealist philosophy—from Kant, through Schiller and Fichte, Schelling and Schleiermacher, and finally Humboldt, whose 1810 template produced the University of Berlin as institutional prototype and from whom Readings extracts the following fusion of *Bildung*'s dual aims: "The principle of culture embodied in the University fuses the advancement of objective science (cultural knowledge) with subjective spiritual and moral training (cultivation)" (66).

From Rosenzweig's perspective on Jewish learning, or education (not quite the same thing), *Bildung* signified cleavage, not a fusion: a splitting between *Bildung* and *Wissenschaft*, and a divergence of history and purpose between Jewish and German expressions of *Bildung*, however they might coincide or overlap.[46] If, as I postulated earlier, *The University in Ruins* can be read as if it had had Jewish Studies (if not the Jewish) in mind, Readings's account opens a gap into which we could imagine the figure of Rosenzweig stepping,[47] when he speaks of "the time of pedagogy, the chronotope within which the order or knowledge can be established as a spatial system" (68).

> The time of *Bildung* effectively expresses the idea of absolute science, since it is both a single moment and an eternity. . . . As Schleiermacher points out, the time of University is in fact but a single moment, the moment of the awakening of the idea of knowledge, when the subject is both conscious of reason and conscious of itself as rational. This single moment is also an eternity since, as Fichte insists, the rational ordering of time allows the infinite multiplication of time. It is above all the time of teaching that allows the German idealists to propose the University as the model for an institution in which the present could fuse past tradition and future ambition into a unified idea of culture. (67–68)

There is no end to instruction, says Rosenzweig in echo of Ecclesiastes, in the "endless bookworld of *Bildung*" we know as the university in all its Fichtean, Schleiermachian, Humboldtian glory. But contrastively, Rosenzweig also imagines a "living, bookless, beginning" for *Bildung* as "the centerpoint and point of germination for the Jewish life of the Jewish human being." This would be the Lehrhaus in all its idealized, heterotopic splendor. Whereas the German Idealist legacy for the University of Culture bequeaths a chronotope for teaching as both instant and amaranthine, the past, present, and future all unified in and by *Bildung*, in Rosenzweig's more Judeo-centric view, "life stands between two times, namely, the moment [*Augenblick*] between past and future."

"Emancipated German Jewry," Rosenzweig insists, "lacks a platform of Jewish life where the bookless present would be able to receive its due." Once again, the heterotopia of Lehrhaus offers itself as that platform. The "time of *Bildung*," if we can now merge Rosenzweig with Readings, that temporality of the living moment outside the university's walls, may be bookless but it is thoroughly and immersively textual, expressively and transactionally hermeneutic.

If, according to Readings, the Humboldtian university—the *old* university, on the model of Rosenzweig's contrast of an Old Learning to his New Learning—marks the site of communicative transparency, of self-unveiling by teacher and student alike united into one corporate body, the Lehrhaus-University traffics in the infinite attention to otherness: necessarily, generatively opaque. Retrieving Schleiermacher toward the end of his book, Readings cites his counterintuitive praise of the *ex cathedra* lecture in the prototypical German university, which, although it diverges from Lehrhaus's putative self-concept for pedagogy, does exhibit certain resonance with the way the Judaic hermeneutic reveres the revelatory power of text. "It awakens the idea of intellectual community in its hearers and enacts the process of knowledge rather than transmitting knowledge as a product" (123).

Of course, Lehrhaus was designed to proceed according to the rather different logic of *dialogue* (even if Rosenzweig's own contributions to it consisted of impenetrable lectures). In our own time and place, the "expressive claim for revelation," as Readings calls it, has been replaced now by the newer, transactional waves of consensus (Jürgen Habermas), interpretive community (Stanley Fish), and conflict-as-conversation (Gerald Graff). But as for *Bildung*, Readings sees no place for it anymore as the university's means and end; in its post-historical dereferentialized state, rather, it "opens a space in which we can think the notions of communication and community differently" (124), where something other than *Bildung*, in league with *Wissensschaft*, should preside.

Our particular interest here, however, lies with a "Jewish problem of *Bildung*," in Rosenzweig's phrase, which would seem to betoken something more particularized. In order to locate it more accurately, we'll need another slight detour, via certain texts about learning and teaching, by Martin Heidegger, who also merits a not insignificant allusion in Readings's book.[48]

However radically their paths diverged after Rosenzweig's death, a kinship between the two thinkers is discernible against the background of Weimar Modernism that Peter Gordon calls "philosophical expressionism," an epiphenomenon of the "crisis of academic and neo-Idealist philosophy at the beginning of the 1920s."[49] Gordon does not devote any attention to Rosenzweig's Lehrhaus project. Nor does he explore the ramifications of *Bildung* in the essays with which we are concerned here. Yet, it is around this term, and more broadly the aims of pedagogy, that Heidegger and Rosenzweig share a particularly strong, perhaps surprising affinity.

Bildung, *Dwelling*, *Thinking*

First, let it be acknowledged that neither Hebrew nor English possesses a strict equivalent for the German term *Bildung*, and it probably best serves each as a calque. Semantically, the word signifies both the process of learning and its product. In a 1942 essay on Plato's το σπήλαιον (cave allegory), Heidegger connects it directly with Greek παιδεία, which, while it connotes "a movement of passage[,] does not lend itself to being translated."[50] Over against the nineteenth-century "misinterpretation" and even anchoring the post-traditional use of the term by Readings et alia, Heidegger projects a back-formation, as it were. His παιδεία-*Bildung* amounts to a kind of leverage, "turning around" and "reorienting" the person through its effects, as Heidegger reads and amplifies Plato, "leading us to the place of our essential being and accustoming us" (167).

Moreover, in line with the stage-model of Plato's narrative, whose culmination is a now-unshackled and cognitively enfranchised "return to the cave," Heidegger moves from the state of being "formed" or "impressed" to the formation that is teaching. (In Plato, of course, the sacrificial exponent of such formation is Socrates.) Pivoting back to Rosenzweig, we might say that Heidegger's reading of the cave confers upon it the educational virtues—aspirations, obligations, efficacy—of a "Lehrhaus." Almost.

In the first lecture of the series, *Was Heisst Denken* ("What Is Called Thinking") from 1954, Heidegger ponders,

> Why is teaching more difficult than learning? Not because the teacher must have a larger store of information, and have it always ready. Teaching is more difficult than learning because what teaching calls for is this: to let learn. The real teacher, in fact, lets nothing else be learned than learning. The teacher is ahead of his apprentices in this alone, that he has still far more to learn than they—he has to learn to let them learn. The teacher must be capable of being more teachable than his apprentices.[51]

But this is late Heidegger, almost three decades after Rosenzweig's death, despite the affinities it appears to show with "the new learning." At an earlier stage roughly parallel for both philosophers, as Rosenzweig confronted his fellow German-Jews' *Bildungsproblem*, so Heidegger opined on his fellow-students' *Bildungsfrage*, the name for a debate on educational philosophy that goes back to early German idealism, and continues in Nietzsche and Weber.[52] In an article he wrote in 1911, while still a student at Freiburg, the ontologically coded answer to it that Heidegger proposes is *Eigenentwicklung* (the unfolding of that which is one's own), which, as Iain Thompson interprets it, means "yoking pedagogical reform to ontological questioning, the evolving core of Heidegger's mature philosophical thought."[53]

As if—and I emphasize the conditional—in rebuke of the 1920s Rosenzweig (at this point in time drafting his soon-to-be-disavowed dissertation on Hegel and the state), then-aspiring theologian Martin Heidegger pens a critique of then-current subjectivist philosophical trends in the conservative journal *Der Akademiker*. It encourages the art of "getting hold of oneself," of "unfolding that what is one's own," a proto-ontological questioning that will serve students as the most efficacious grounding for their individual solutions to the *Bildungsfrage*.

Crystallized in *Being and Time* (1927), Heidegger's own thinking on a "re-ontologized" German University was formalized in his remarks on his "new concept" of unified *Wissenschaft* in his now infamous Rectoral Address of 1933, "Die Selbstbehauptung der Deutschen Universität" (The Self-Assertion of the German University), in which science becomes "the innermost determining center of all of popular and national existence."[54]

Clearly, with such radically *volklich* formulations, we have left Max Weber's more modest endorsement of *Wissenschaft* as a calling quite behind;

moreover, they make the intrinsically Jewish project that begins with Zunz's and Eduard Gans's 1819 *Verein für Kultur und Wissenschaft der Juden* seem hopelessly naive, and worse, archaic in the very midst of their proto-modernist aspirations. In "Mochlos," Derrida considers Heidgger's Rectoral Address "the last great discourse in which the Western university tries to ponder its essence and its destination in terms of responsibility, with a stable reference to the one idea of knowledge, technology, the state and the nation" (88)—a claim Readings takes up in connection with French philosopher Gérard Granel. As such, it, too, failed even more spectacularly.

In Derrida's view and despite its manifest flaws, Heidegger's vision for a new kind of university nevertheless conceived "a more essential responsibility, one which, before having to answer for knowledge, power, or something or other determinate . . . must first respond to being, for the call of being, and must ponder this coresponsibility." That call, Heidegger's *Seinsfrage*, overwrites the question of education (*Bildung*-as-παιδεία) along with all others. And here is where Rosenzweig reenters the picture.

The Place of Lehrhaus

All this appears only remotely pertinent to Lehrhaus, of course—so distant from it as to be all but irreconcilable with Rosenzweig's conception of a place of learning located outside the university and Jewishly heterotopic in relation to it. Through the lens of the Lehrhaus, however, we might see both German higher education's *Bildungsfrage* and modern Jewry's *Bildungsproblem* reflected in the image of the Lehrhaus teacher-scholars as *Chorführer des Chors des Fragenden*, returning us to Heidegger's later insights about learning and teaching.

Yet, here we discern Rosenzweig's great innovation, and the distinction Lehrhaus (in theory, at least) marks from the entire *Bildung* tradition. For German Idealists, through Nietzsche and even the later Heidegger's claim of *"echte Bildung,"* formation/education remains largely the process of self-realization, even when the self at issue is a national/cultural subject-to-be. *Bildung* is actually *Selbst-Bildung*[55]—not entirely solipsistic, since some Other (for example, teacher, beauty, knowledge, culture) is needed, yet still premised on acquisition and appropriation.

Can a process of *Bildung* be transacted that somehow escapes the various economies (institutional, pedagogical, cultural) that inscribe it? Need an alternative to a conventional sense of (self-) *Bildung* conform to a reform of education as dramatic as Heidegger's substitution of "ontological questioning" for metaphysics? Finally, could *Bildung* migrate elsewhere, to some other "genre," so to speak?

Lehrhaus, at its aspirational best, can be understood as answering the first two questions; I reserve consideration of the last for the chapter's end. Rosenzweig's modernized *beit midrash* instituted a dialogically modeled sociality where rabbinical authority had once dominated; it proposed a Jewish "wholeness" to redress the various fragmentations that beset Rosenzweig and his co-religionists, especially in their capacity of prospective learners (pedagogue and pupil both) answerable to the dual claims of tradition and secular modernity.

He seems to have had two images of *Bildung* in mind in his essay: the humanist version fostered by institutions yet sometimes compromised by the politics of socialization (like Socratic *maieutics*), and the kind that awaits dialogical reformulation. As to the first, while his dismay does not correspond to that registered by Adorno forty years later in his essay on postwar "*sozialisierte halbBildung*," the concept of "half-education" might well describe the unintended consequences of *Wissenschaft des Judentums* and historicist academicism.[56] Rosenzweig's plan for the second, optative version, the *Bildung* of "*Wünsche*," was modest, if elusive:

> The unlimited refuses to be organized. What is farthest [*das Fernste*] can be captured only by the nearest [*der Nächste*], by every respective nearest of every single moment. Every plan is here wrong to begin with because it is—a plan. For the highest is impossible to plan. In relation to it, everything rests, indeed, on being ready. We can offer the Jewish human being in us, that we mean, only our readiness [*Bereitsein*] and nothing else. Only the slightest push of the will; even the word "will" contains almost too much; really only that very slight tug that we exert when, in a confused world, we say to ourselves, "we Jews," and thus accept that infinite bondsmanship [*Bürgschaft*] for the first time that is meant by the ancient saying which lets every Jew be the bondsman [*Bürge*] of every other Jew. Nothing else is presupposed but this simple decision, to say it once that "nothing Jewish is alien to me"—this too hardly a decision but barely a "small push" [*kleiner Ruck*], a looking around and looking within oneself. What the individual will see, who is to predict? (235)

I think the truly important note is struck here by the idea of *Bürgschaft* as the modest opposing force and applied leverage to the more propulsive *Wissenschaft*. *Bürgschaft* translates the halakhic idea of cosigning or inter-responsibility, '*arevut*.[57] But it also recalls our image of an opening hand that replaces an aiming hand, which Rosenzweig captures in the productively "empty forms of readiness that allow something to happen, merely 'space and time.' Really nothing but this: a speaking space [*Sprechraum*], a speaking time [*Sprechzeit*]" (384).

This would be Rosenzweig's countermove to Heidegger, had they ever compared notes as philosophers of education (or played chess). Instead of *Eigenentwicklung*, we find *Bürgschaft*; co-responsibility of a shared intellectual enterprise, a "looking around oneself," takes the place of "an unfolding of one's own." Yet at the same time, and unlike the self-convinced Heidegger, Rosenzweig recognizes keenly how airy all this seems: "I already hear the voices that say: 'how vague, how indeterminate, how foggy'"—particularly in the context of the Weimar Jewish cultural "renaissance." Zank adroitly captures its marketplace of ideas:

> In the 1920s one could study Karaism and other deviant movements in Jewish history with the secular, assimilated sociologist Leo Löwenthal, hear Leo Strauss lecture on Spinoza or read cabbalistica with Gerhard Scholem; one could join the Zionist student corporation "Saronia" and help in their recruitment efforts, take walks with Agnon and Bialik, listen to the sermons of Nehemia Nobel, seek therapy at the "Thorapeuticum" of Frieda Reichmann in nearby Heidelberg, or visit Martin Buber in Heppenheim at the Bergstrasse. Or one could do all of the above. For despite all the noise of the internal debates, the young people who constituted this elite were in the end voracious for everything that was equally Jewish and non-trivial. (240)

Lehrhaus necessarily competed for attention from within this urban economy, and in Zank's laconic appraisal of the scene, "Naturally, not everyone felt attracted by this new Jewish pietism, and some stayed away" (240). At its peak (1922–1923), enrollment exceeded eleven hundred students, greater than 10 percent of Frankfurt's adult Jewish population, a truly impressive figure. Rosenzweig's death, administrative exigencies, and the tide of events soon to overtake Jewish Weimar ensured, however, a limited realization.

Even so, it can be argued that the Lehrhaus possessed "the curious property," as Foucault describes heterotopia in general, "of being in relation with all the other sites, but in such a way as to suspect, neutralize, or invert the set of relations that they happen to designate, mirror, or reflect" (24). Certainly, this was its intent vis-à-vis the German University of its time. And as we have seen, it bequeathed a healthy, fructifying afterlife, as well. Rosenzweig envisioned an alternative to academicized Jewish learning, "non-specialist, non-rabbinical, non-polemical, non-apologetic" (Glatzer, 117), realizable wherever a desire for Jewish *Bildung* in some oblique relationship to the university might manifest itself. Even Foucault's concept gets us only so far.

One obvious reason that Lehrhaus resists importation to and appropriation by the university lies in its teleological thrust—exactly what Neusner so vehemently wished modern JS expressly to disavow if it was to justify itself as academic inquiry. Rosenzweig conceived it as a means to deepen and enliven an etiolated Jewish identity he ascribed to his fellow German-Jews, having been one of them himself less than a decade previous.

A goal is laid out in the strongest possible terms in "Zeit Ist's," where Jewish knowledge must be allotted its own time and space, its own world to "possess" (29). *Bildung* may lead Germans into other civilizations, which share the same "spiritual space"—Winckelmann and Schopenhauer demonstrate as much—but Jewish space remains fully heterotopic, constituted as its own "sphere," whether or not *Bildung* is understood to serve as a conduit through which Jewish knowledge gets "smuggled."[58]

At any rate, as a fascinating (and certainly unintended) revision of the less evolved 1916 essay where Rosenzweig expresses his belief that "the classroom must remain the ante-room leading to the synagogue and of participation in its service" (20), in "Bildung und Kein Ende," he imagines the Lehrhaus taking shape as "a single room [but] without a waiting room" (238). Instead of a teleology from the secular to the religious, or a spatial transit from the secular-pedagogical to the Jewish-liturgical, Rosenzweig now envisions a discursive chronotope, through which its special features, *Sprechraum, Sprechzeit, Sprechsaal, Sprechstunde*, and most of all, *der Wunsch*, would take expressive, palpable shape.

"For who knows whether such wishes—real grown wishes rather than wishes artificially produced according to a schema of *Bildung*—can find their fulfillment?" (237). Rosenzweig doesn't know—indeed, in a 1923 letter to Rudolf Hallo, he confesses that no one views the Lehrhaus more skeptically than he does—but he certainly *desires*. Consequently, he tried to emplace such desiring at the core of his project, for teachers and students alike. The "new learning" was as much, if not more so, a *new teaching*—in keeping with the semantic thrust of the proper name "Lehrhaus."

If for no other reason than this, Lehrhaus fails the test of admission that would allow it to take up residence within the university's walls. Even though, as more recent critics of Readings claim, "the production of national subjects under the guise of research into and inculcation of culture"

(89) no longer commonly define its mission, the fact remains on a salaried echelon that "until professors are produced in a different way, the structure of academic knowledge production and dissemination is unlikely to change significantly" (Menand, 121). Certainly as regards JS, it is a point whose consequences cannot be overstated.

Canon and List

Beyond the pedagogical spirit Rosenzweig wished to create, and however much it sought to differentiate itself from the guild structures of university scholarship, how exactly did the Lehrhaus curriculum compare to its counterpart in a modern Jewish Studies program? Glatzer devotes half of his essay on the Lehrhaus to a meticulous tabulation of the 108 courses (lectures, seminars, study groups) over its six-year tenure: 42 introductory courses in the Hebrew language and the basic books; 40 seminars in the Hebrew Bible; 30 courses in Talmudic-midrashic literature; 25 in Jewish history; 14 in Medieval Hebrew literature; 15 courses in liturgy and prayer; 30 courses in theology, mysticism, and comparative literature; 6 courses in Modern Hebrew and Yiddish literature; these were "subjects of a general nature ... discussions of the Jewish spirit (difficult to define), special assemblies and lectures, and meetings arranged for the youth" (119).[59]

Other than a trend away from Jewish history in line with Rosenzweig's own anti-historicist predilection and allowing for a relative paucity of courses in what we would now call "cultural studies," the inventory previously listed would not be out of place in any JS program in the contemporary university that tilts toward engagement with the classical texts of Judaism.

The Freies Jüdisches Lehrhaus struck a balance between the canonical and a somewhat more oblique approach to sources and precedents, which, after literature scholar Jacques Lezra, we might call "reading for the list."[60] If canonical reading obeys "an immanent principle of structure derivable, if at all, from the totality of the list," a reading follows the logic of texts "as they present themselves to us, rumored, accidentally, contingently" (163). Reading for the list "opens the experience of reading to the accidents of contiguity and of circumstance."

Perhaps the most revealing account of the Lehrhaus in this respect belongs to Gershom Scholem, who contrasts his painstaking analysis in small seminars of "mystical, apocalyptic, and narrative sources—the kind most likely to inspire pneumatic exegeses," but also as far as the Judaic canon was then construed, almost entirely the stuff of "list" (rumored, accidental, contingent)—with the lecture-performances of Eduard Strauss on grand and encompassing themes, "a pure case of a Jewish pietist," whose "listeners were spellbound as though they were held by a magic circle."[61]

Three years earlier, in a letter to his cousin Rudolf Ehrenberg that contains his *Urzelle* ["Germ Cell"] *des Stern der Erlösung*, Rosenzweig expressed an impassioned commitment to the midst of life, to *Mitten am Leben*: "Only from the center does there arise a bounded home in an unbounded world, a patch of ground between four tent pegs, that can be posted farther and farther out" (57). The Lehrhaus, as we have read, was imagined contrariwise: from the periphery to the center. Each of these bounded terrains, life and Lehrhaus, understood itself in heterotopic distinction to the space of the university—a canonical space, a space of *Wissenschaft*-as-aiming hand, an endless bookworld.

Rosenzweig's Lever

"There is much in Rosenzweig that is well beyond retrieval," writes Zank (245). In addition to his force of personality and religiosity, what distinguished the Lehrhaus as bearing the defining impress of Rosenzweig's signature was, on a far more tragic note, his seven-year struggle with neurodegenerative disease, paralleling its brief six-year span under his leadership. In his biography, Glatzer describes the artificial mechanics of communication to which Rosenzweig had to adjust, once he succumbed to almost total paralysis. Even thus compromised, however, he was still able to co-translate the Pentateuch in addition to seven more books of the Bible, complete his annotated translation of Yehudah Ha-Levi, and compose essays on various subjects—his own prodigious *Bildungsheld*.

> In the spring of 1923, a typewriter was bought to facilitate communication; the construction of this machine was such that the person working it had only to move a simple lever over a disk containing all the characters until the point indicated the desired character and, at the same time, one pressed a single key to make the imprint. At first, Rosenzweig was able to operate the machine by himself, but later on he had to point out the characters with his left hand. Arm and hand were supported in a sling hanging from a bar next to the sick man. The key was operated by someone else, usually by Edith. Eventually, his ability to indicate the characters lessened, so that they had to be ascertained by guesswork. . . . In order to facilitate this work it was

necessary to use a second disk and lever, attached by means of a connecting rod to the lever manipulated by the patient; the helper then read from the second disk what the patient had indicated on the first. (140)

Yes, the "lever" here denotes simply the hand-size projecting piece for operating a small machine rather than the kinds of examples Derrida enlisted to illustrate his usage of *mochlos*: "a wooden beam, a lever for displacing a boat, a wedge for opening or closing a door, something, in short, to lean on for forcing and displacing." And yet, I would like to propose, the same mechanical principle applies. At first blush, such an analogy appears perhaps unseemly. Rosenzweig's body is paralyzed; his communicative need is exigent in the extreme. If it was "very late, too late for this Kantian discourse," as Derrida conducted it, it was even later for Rosenzweig as he coped with the relentless degeneration of all his body's muscles and the inexorable extinguishing of motor neurons.

But let us recall from the previous chapter Timothy Bahti's reinscription of the leverage motif in relation *not* to "a well-positioned, upright body," but rather to a weakened or even incapacitated body, a casualty of imbalance, but also thus positioned for the work of forcing and displacing. Injury, in this counter-normative case, can become the very condition of leverage. Rosenzweig no longer presided over the Lehrhaus in his severely debilitated state. Yet in the six years left to him, he was still producing penetratingly erudite essays on a range of subjects dear to him: the continued relevance of Lehrhaus for Jewish learning, translation (for example, "Neuhebräisch? Anlässlich der Übersetzung von Spinozas Ethik"), "The New Thinking," and Jewish election and the authority of Jewish law as elaborated in the 1924 text addressed to his colleagues known as "the Lehrhaus letter."

But I conflate two categories of leverage, do I not? There is, first, the discrete mechanical operation performed by Rosenzweig, or on his personal behalf, as a matter of therapeutic or prosthetic necessity—which some might say sustains the merely clever (even forced) connection with "lever." And there is the intellectual leverage attaching to Rosenzweig's work and its effects—for our purposes here, the pedagogical innovations of Lehrhaus—a means of production which post-traditional theorists like Derrida and Bahti connect to larger institutional structures and forces. The first category, obviously, ceases to be relevant with the final stage of Rosenzweig's terminal illness. That lever did its work. With the second category, we enter the realm I conjured at the beginning of this chapter,

Rosenzweig's and his Lehrhaus's afterlife. Exactly what kind of leverage does it afford us now?

Getting Out of Lehrhaus

In his lengthy letter to Rudolf Hallo in 1922 about its short history, Rosenzweig wrote, "It is one of the tasks of the director to help those who have really gone through the Lehrhaus to get out of it again and to stand on their own Jewish legs in doing and learning" (118). This represents a crucial pivoting point to a parallel aspiration (articulated or not) for Jewish Studies in the contemporary academy, which also hearkens back to Timothy Bahti's lessons about leverage and balance.

What could standing on one's own ("Jewish") legs mean for the Jewish Studies aspirant (including the limit-case of one who may well not be Jewish)? What might it mean to be a well-balanced student of JS, someone who can either leverage it or him/herself act as a lever? What it might mean to really go through the university "to get out of it again?" Short of nonmatriculation or simply quitting, does that indicate a constructive possibility? What, if anything, does this say to faculty who, presumably, stay on until circumstances force them to leave? And finally, what does a desire for *Ausweg* (like Rotpeter's) look like here?

Unlike both Rosenzweig and Neusner, I make no claim in these pages to speak cross-generationally. My intended audience, at least primarily, consists of *schülerhafte Lehrern*, readers of both Rosenzweig and Kafka, whether they call JS their home or not. An answer to these questions, though, might begin with the example introduced by Michael Zank in the concluding section to his translation-commentary of "Bildung und kein Ende," which he calls "Analogies: Textual reasoning and the <<email>> moment of Jewish *Bildung*."

Seemingly bringing us full circle (though still quite some way from the web-based thelehrhaus.com), Zank explains this "email moment" as ". . . no more than a (virtual) space and a (virtual) time, utilizing a new medium to allow for openness, unplanned spontaneity, anonymity and equality between students and masters where neither title nor affiliation were to matter, where specialist and non-specialist, and specialists of different sorts, were to be able to meet, lurk, listen and—mail" (243).

In the spirit of Lehrhaus, thus was inaugurated "The Postmodern Jewish Philosophy Bitnetwork," evolving into the *Journal of Textual Reasoning* (*JTR*), a regularly published online journal and a continuing series of discussions. Most pertinent for our concerns here, "TR was based on the attempt to generate a conversation among individuals who do not usually inhabit the same spiritual universe, namely, philologists and philosophers" (243). As the cross-disciplinarity sought to achieve its moments of encounter while grounding them in a textual canon, so the rhetoric of discussion was designed to permit "an unheard-of liberality in regard to difference and an unprecedented latitude in regard to the tentative and undefined" (245).

A useful example from the journal's original issue (1.1, 2002) is Aryeh Cohen's essay, "Why Textual Reasoning?," which reads a Talmudic narrative (b. *Bava Batra* 7b) recounted in the context of a discussion of neighborly relations and the obligations of citizenship. The prophet Elijah makes a brief appearance there to decry the otherwise laudable erection of a gatehouse because it either has no door or is locked; or, as medieval commentators suggest, because it "buffers the voice" of fellow citizens on the other side of its boundary. "One might read Elijah," Cohen creatively suggests, "as the intervention of theory."[62] Thus construed and sharpened in respect to the boundaries of JS, the question for the gatehouse becomes: How to enter into relations with what lies beyond? How to think JS within and outside its statutory *dalet amot*?

This—as one intervention of theory—may be as close as Lehrhaus can insinuate itself into the academic province of modern Jewish Studies. If much in Rosenzweig remains beyond retrieval, we still recall that like a theoretically attuned Elijah, (s)he "who understands to hearken to the voice of such real wishes will then perhaps also understand to point them in the way that they desire." A kind of open gatehouse, then, Lehrhaus also offers a platform to "get out" of the university while still remaining inside it.

Happily, upsetting "everything that organizes the places defining it, namely, the territory of its fields and its disciplinary frontiers as well as its places of discussion . . . the communitary structure of its 'campus,'" as Derrida envisioned a "politics of the virtual," does not seem to have been the conscious aim of the original *Textual Reasoning* participants anyway, even if what is most radically upset by the virtual academy is "the topology of the event, the experience of the singular taking place" (13).

The topology of the event—or its heterotoplogy, should we wish to sustain such terminology in relation to Lehrhaus—returns us to Rosenzweig's place and moment, as we acknowledge that the envisioned Lehrhaus-like structure of the *JTR*, like the original vision for Lehrhaus itself, was designed to apply a certain leverage to the university. To be sure, its conversations could only be conducted by academicians and apprentice-academics, many affiliated with preeminent institutions of Jewish scholarship, in much the same way that Rosenzweig's initiative could not help but mold itself through the speech-genres acquired by its university-educated pedagogues, even if most of them were not learned Jews. And indeed, since its formal inception in 2001, the journal has coalesced into a distinctive but by no means unique niche for a certain post-contemporary Rosenzweigian sensibility *within* the academy.⁶³

Perhaps, finally, that elucidates the very heterotopic lesson to be gleaned here. If nothing else, Lehrhaus might be held up to Jewish Studies currently practiced as a productively distorting mirror. This, I believe, is what Rosenzweig has in mind in the closing sentences of "Bildung und kein Ende," where he plainly confesses the utopian aspect of Lehrhaus:

> But the odd few may perhaps also wish: "how nice," and merely question doubtfully, "if only it existed." And with their doubt, I agree. They should doubt. But they should come. They should test whether "it exists." For that it exists is due to these ones, and only due to these ones. It is due to their power to wish, their urge to ask, their courage to doubt. The students and masters are found among these ones. These ones should come. If they fail to come then, of course, ancient Ecclesiastes will be proven right again also for our generation—and there will be no end to the making of books. (229)

If the postmodern philosophy bitnetwork of the 1990s and its email moment of Jewish *Bildung* offered one scenario of "getting out of Lehrhaus," remaining within it—that is, within its sensibility, its imaginative space—would require something of this *wishing and doubting presence.*

Rosenzweig is obviously speaking about his own intended audience, the Jewish adult population of Weimar that seeks to be Jewishly educated. But—like my thought experiment with Goethe—what if the aforementioned passage might also be mobilized in the direction of the current standard-bearers of JS themselves, including those thoroughly convinced and self-satisfied, after Neusner's fashion, about its disciplinary authority? What if, in Rosenzweig's sense of the term, they desired differently? What if JS itself presented an occasion for the intervention of theory?

On Conjunction: "the and" before "and/and/and/and/and"

Rosenzweig's thought offers several thematic leitmotifs or hooks, such as the geometry of star or circle, election/chosenness, threshold and gate. German Studies scholar David Groiser focuses on another of these "conceptual figures," "*Das Und*," which he renders, "the idea of a conjunctive relationship between two terms, which interanimate each other without ever being reducible one to the other" (270). Cataloging various ways in which such conjunctive logic informs Rosenzweig's philosophy, Groiser includes: the symbiotic relation between disparate cultural elements, such as the German-Jewish linkage so crucial to 1920s Weimar; "Jewish thinking itself" as a kind of negative capability or "coexistence of contraries"; and the dual or symmetrical pull of influences, each dignified in the same measure as the other, what Rosenzweig called being "between two streams."

Most important, *language* amounts to the "organon of relation, the bridging or splicing mechanism par excellence." Applying a little leverage to this last component, we discover the grammatical possibilities of "and" itself, which in the words of another Rosenzweig scholar, "functions asymmetrically, as a movement from an origin to an end that is not reversible."[64] In "Das Neues Denken," conjunction doesn't merely indicate connection, but rather progression.

As glossed by Rav Shagar, it signifies "the keystone that supports the entire edifice and imbues it with meaning."[65] As a supplementary theme to this chapter, however, it obviously relates directly to the standing question of Jewish Studies and its Other(s). Syntactically hinging the "Jewish" in Jewish Studies to some proper-named confederate shows how Jewish Studies names itself relationally at the level of phrasal adjacency. For what is JS, if not coordinating conjunction—a grammatical *mise-en-scène* in which to observe it in action?

Rosenzweig almost certainly knew that the Hebrew letter "*vav*" ו signifies, aptly enough, a "hook." Both consonant and vowel, it also often acts as a coordinating conjunction, usually unpointed or vowelless. Depending on context, it will signify: *and, or, nor, but, although, if, then, since, even*. Biblical Hebrew grammar, however, distinguishes between two primary syntactic uses of the letter at the beginning of words: (1) the paratactic *vav ha-ḥibur* ("conjunctive *vav*"), which translates as "and"—as in the American university mottos (in Hebrew), *Or v'emet* and *Torah u'madda*; and (2) the temporalizing *vav hahipukh* ("consecutive *vav*") which indicates preterit or future consequence of actions, inverting the aspect of the verb in the word it prefixes from either imperfect to perfect or perfect to imperfect. (Properly speaking, the first *vav* counts as a true conjunction, whereas the second *vav* amounts to a verb-construction, a marker for a change in tenses used primarily to denote consecution.)

In the spirit of Rosenzweig's *das Und*, one question for JS, then, would be whether its conjunctions—those academic practices to which it conjoins, affiliates, or neighbors itself—leave room for movement beyond mere adjacency. Such intuition about syntax of joining prompted Levinas to wonder whether *conjunctive "and"* in Rosenzweig's own thought more properly signified *prepositional "for"*; as in, "for-the-other." To make a more intentional case for relation means projecting a Jewish Studies that aspires beyond the exclusively Jewish and the administratively routine, athwart insularities and chauvinisms of several kinds.

Another, on the model of the two *vavim* in Biblical Hebrew, would ask whether JS merely connects its various properties, or more imaginatively, it possesses some temporalizing effect, a change, as it were, in tense—say, from perfect to imperfect, leaving open the possibility of possibility, of uncompleted action. Keeping in mind that Hebrew *hipukh* means "turn over," as in "reversal," but also as in "somersault" or "roll," JS stages the coordination of conjuncts as something more syntactically flexible, even calisthenic, its *Bildungsheld*-aspirant also something of an agile *pícaro*.

That is the prospect to which we turn in our next and final chapter, where "heterotopia" becomes the space of juxtaposition, a rapprochement between the discursively premodern and the postmodern. If, says Levinas, research takes form as a question because the project of knowing is itself placed intersubjectively *in* question,[66] then "rapprochement"—*Wissenschaft*'s interspace—is where method discovers, or enacts, community.

INTERCHAPTER V

Bildung and Built-ins

Hebrew school from the childhood years in New York City. Dickens and Tolkien, the social protests of 1968, experienced at eleven years of age in the Bronx. In the 1970s, liberal arts college, where mentors in music theory and composition and, later, literary studies, were teaching. Friendship with peers and teachers who were adolescents at the time of the Rosenberg affair, a vision, dazzling for a newcomer, of a fellowship that professes the Humanities and of a vocation to which one can attach oneself by spirit and heart as much as by training. A stay in the 1980s on the West Coast, and an apprenticeship in teaching composition. Harvard, Stanley Cavell. The theoretical *corps d'élite* at sessions of the Center for Literary and Cultural Studies. The intellectual and anti-intellectualist refinement of various graduate educators and their generous friendship, gained after a longueur in commercial transport. Thesis for the Doctor of Philosophy Degree in 1992. Ongoing communication with colleagues, occasional visits to David Weiss Halivni, the prestigious—and magnanimous—teacher of source-and-form criticism in Talmud. Interim director of a Jewish Studies program. Periodic conferences on narrative, philosophy, and

Jewish texts. Professorships at two universities, and lectureship at Université Sorbonne Nouvelle, Institute de Monde Anglophone, and elsewhere. This disparate inventory is a biography.

Keen readers might recognize the "disparate inventory" above as a pasquinade of the first paragraph in the standard English translation of Emmanuel Levinas's concluding essay to *Difficult Freedom*, "Signature" (1965/76).[1] I've elected the Levinasian harmonics or accents here because they are so conspicuously anti-memoiristic—as if the entire point were to avoid uttering the first-person pronoun in the first place. As with Kafka's hunger artist, one has to admire Levinas's rhetorical fasting here. Just as his inventory styles, itself a biography and not an autobiography, so that very polarity readily reverses itself, that is, "this biography is a disparate inventory."

My own experiment, in double-voiced mimicry above, could likewise be regarded in the fashion of an anti-Bildungsroman, for tucked into the middle of its selective details and elisions, a trace of a modest stint administering a Jewish Studies program in a public university can be discerned. The point of the allusion to Levinas's "signature" in this final interchapter is to inventory some of the features of this brief tenure while de-subjectifying the narrative as much as possible.

Repeated attempts had been made over a span of some time to configure a Jewish Studies major at this institution. In partial question about which knowledge practice should primarily constitute "the Jewish," planning for its formalization circled as much around disciplinary bent and language—modernism versus antiquity, Hebrew/Aramaic versus Yiddish—as anything else.

Once a space opened to propose a new initiative aimed at coordinating faculty from various departments and fashioning a curriculum that could exploit the full range of teaching interests, a double-pronged major was proposed. It was anchored by two diachronically structured tracks: one oriented toward Jewish modernity, the other toward classical sources and the history of Judaism. While the decision may have reproduced some of the large-scale divisions within the field, a bargain was nevertheless struck.

As for many of its peers, a programming component exhibited the program's public face, a lecture series across divisions, and disciplines designed, in part, to hinge JS to other campus units and model community. Shortly thereafter, a grant for a full-fledged Center was submitted to a philanthropic foundation that makes such campus centers one of its donative priorities; customarily for such initiatives, a mix of junior and senior appointments (some of them dual, a common feature in JS programs) to fill teaching and research gaps required robust financial support. Ultimately, the Center was established, its workings administered, and a brief induction into ad interim management concluded.

This *kleine geschichte* is, by no means, exceptional. Scholarship and faculty recruitment, student demand and demographics, administrative oversight, and Jewish philanthropy all coalesce according to no one rule or standard. The JS curriculum that eventually emerged agreeably occupies its institutional niche, with strengths in certain areas, and gaps in others. Of such contingently structured programs and the effort to build them, *kein Ende*. Yet, if there is such a thing as a Platonic ideal for Jewish Studies programs, not unlike its peers, this one evinces a disparate inventory with corresponding biography, each mutually determining.

Every JS program possesses an origin story, and that history will often determine the eventual shape it not only assumes, but it does so effectively, as even an informal survey of such programs can clarify. How otherwise to explain the rich and strange phenomenon of Jewish Studies at the City College in New York, the vast majority of whose majors (95 percent) do not claim Jewish heritage?[2] Or its opposite number in homogeneity at the College of Charleston in South Carolina, with its "unique threefold model of academics, community outreach, and student life"[3]—"ethnically" underwritten (as Jacob Neusner would say) in prototypical fashion?

As we've seen, Andrew Bush, in his theoretical introduction to JS, likens the field to environmentalism, "a political and scientific movement that envisions and supports the balanced interaction of mixed elements whose boundaries, in principle, may be infinitely expanded" (10). Yet, ecologies of knowledge are never isomorphic with the institutional ecology that embeds them, even if the one ultimately depends on the other for sustainability. Another effective metaphor for JS, then, might be topography, or as this chapter has preferred, topology. If criticism (from formalist to political) is charged with exposing the uncanny of reading, then other terrain may be equally susceptible to such interpretive operations.

Shall we take, for instance, *the uncanny* of JS, a recurrent, maybe even inherent, component in its "disparate inventory?" Subsequent to the administrative stint described previously, toward the end of a panel in one year's AJS conference, an audience member and quondam associate in that initiative approached the dais to murmur, "we'll continue this over e-mail." Either in regard to the presentation I had just given or to the (interrupted) institutional association, the susurration remained in suspense. Protracted still, it awakens in me now a consciousness of the conditional that haunts so much of JS as a twice-fashioned creature of the academy.

Call it an <<e-mail>> moment of Jewish *Bildung* yet to come, for which Rosenzweig's epigram quoted several times in this chapter, "*Wünsche sind die boten des vertrauens*," augurs a clarifying counterweight. There is hope for it yet, and maybe for us, too. One religion professor interprets the maxim as expressing the Jewish educator's quasi-messianic confidence that "to find [and] recognize each other as in the same position is the beginning of thinking that one's desires and wishes can really be fulfilled."[4] Likewise in this chapter's context, I remain persuaded of the power of adjusted sights, the difference between "real grown wishes" and those "artificially produced" by institutional fiat: built-in. Whatever else it may portend, a powerful commitment to the theory and practice of Lehrhaus adroitly, courageously, and inventively balances realism against redemptive faith.

CHAPTER 5

Ventilating the Tradition: Rashbam and the Coen Brothers

> The more passionately thought denies its conditionality for the sake of the unconditional, the more unconsciously, and so calamitously, it is delivered up to the world. Even its own impossibility it must at last comprehend for the sake of the possible.
>
> —THEODOR ADORNO, *Minima Moralia*

At the annual conference of the Association of Jewish Studies in 2010, an 8:30 a.m. session on the final day—not quite a barn-burner in the general schedule—was unexpectedly well attended. It featured a symposium on the Coen Brothers' 2009 film, *A Serious Man*. The presentations—by specialists in Modern Hebrew Literature, Anthropology, Jewish Cultural History, Holocaust Studies, and Minority Rights—made their way into the *AJS Review* one year later (two years after the film's release). According to the editors' introduction, "the essays exemplify the range of resources in Jewish studies for analyzing contemporary culture."[1] In the aggregate, they comprise what Jacob Neusner disparaged most about the AJS, "the ethnic reading of ethnic studies." Their self-understood aim, however, portended something else: the interdisciplinary future of JS.

The speculative inquiry that follows in this final chapter takes the additional step of positioning this postcontemporary version of Jewish Studies athwart a more *Wissenschaftlich* model, as reflected by the bulk of research articles on religious culture and intellectual history published in the *AJS Review*, *Jewish Quarterly Review*, and the like. What I wish to do is make this particular symposium's topic "speak" across a scholarly gulf to academic knowledge practices at a formally far remove.

While *A Serious Man* (*ASM*) may channel the Book of Job, include both Hebrew words and subtitled Yiddish (each embedded in inset stories), and feature Jewish ritual practices, the critical commentary the film has received tends—unsurprisingly—not to concern itself with narrative/representational strategies either in the Torah or medieval rabbinic commentary. My book leaps headlong into that breach.

Such conjunction at first blush may seem forced, even gratuitous. Yet, it is choreographed this way not only because of the author's interdiscursive predilections for "contiguity" among quite separate, even distant regions within the landed property of JS. The dialogism staged here also derives its warrant from a critical intertext shared by both film and Biblical story-and-commentary. Contrapuntal strategies of narrative poetics underwrite the "letters of transit," as I termed them in my introduction, that facilitates an otherwise impeded passage between them.

More plainly put, premodern and postmodern methods of narrative—or, as this chapter will term them, *renarration* and *denarration*—offer twin foci and hermeneutical points of contact as I envision dialogic possibilities for JS, even beyond the "conversation across disciplinary boundaries" modeled for the field by the AJS symposium.

Although I don't develop the meta-point in detail, renarration and denarration might similarly speak to the story of JS itself and its subsequent tellings. A renarrated text repeats itself; a denarrated text undoes itself, but perhaps only then to reframe what it has disembedded. Between the two, lies Adorno's conditionality (so echoic of Bercovitch's hermeneutics of nontranscendence), the particular dimension of JS this book has taken pains to adduce.

Let me only acknowledge that for a book whose introduction spoke of a "lived institutional poetics," the readings ventured here, forcing secular and religious, sacred and profane, premodern and postmodern—possible/impossible?—against each other, seek to demonstrate the kind of affirmatory posture heretofore described as a "profession of faith." As counterlife but also academic report, we thus enter a certain kind of malleable Jewish terrain—"a space of continuous, perilous, and exuberant inscriptive and reinscriptive performance."[2]

It parallels that heterotopic space inhering in a specifically Judaic context, which Israeli religious writer Rav Shagar, seeking to reconcile halakhic faith with postmodernism (and with Franz Rosenzweig, Slavoj Žižek, and the Maharal all in mind), has called *the remainder*. "[H]uman creative works are never brought forth ex nihilo," he writes, "but are always adaptations of elements from earlier works, which is why every such creation can be deconstructed and then reconstructed differently."[3]

Less grandiosely but no less rooted in Jewish discursive tradition, I would defer in a final prefatory gesture to the precedent furnished by avant-garde Yiddish poet Itsik Manger (Czernowitz-born contemporary of our cover illustrator, Yosl Cutler), to whose singular discursive interface between vernacular and holy, between *mame-loshn* and *loshn-koydesh*, he assigned the perfect portmanteau: *literatoyre*, "literature-Torah." As a testament to the "component awareness"[4] of Jewish languages (their self-consciousness as linguistic hybrids), and his fusion of Yiddish idiom and Biblical-Hebraic source material, Manger's modernist innovation opens the door for *dybbuk-dibeks* of the postmodern sort, which we shall glimpse next.

Countertexts; or Literatoyre

Picking up where the AJS symposium left off, we begin post-Biblically with an excerpt drawn from the Coens' *A Serious Man*. Our speaker is hapless protagonist Lawrence ("Larry") Gopnik, addressing his college physics class in 1960s Minnesota. The "dead cat" refers to the famous thought experiment about the principle of quantum superposition known as "Schrödinger's paradox":

> You understand the dead cat? But . . . you . . . you can't really understand the physics without understanding the math. The math tells how it really works. That's the real thing; the stories I give you in class are just illustrative; they're like, fables, say, to help give you a picture. An imperfect model. I mean—even I don't understand the dead cat. The math is how it really works.[5]

For those familiar with the film, if not the physics, stand-alone fables in its diegesis seem to promise something illustrative: "these are signs, tokens," as one of the film's characters genially remarks. In fact, narrative is revealed by film's end to be a deeply imperfect communicative medium. The more permutations or iterations of story introduced, the more telling and the more pervasive the imperfection.[6]

Even a label for the general concept seems variable: first "stories," then, "fables," then "pictures," whereas, the math, "the real thing," just stays *the math*. Math is apodictic, deeply true, an account of how things really work. Story—or more accurately, story*telling*—marks a deviation from transparency and reliability alike, the progressively complicating interplay of *fabula* and *syuzhet*, story and discourse.[7] Math describes how "it really works"; storytelling, dubious enterprise that it is, at best approximates, at worst, misleads.

Here, from a vastly different textual universe, is a second passage, both more concise and less ambiguous: "The servant then related to Isaac all that he had done" (Gen 24:66), a verse that marks the conclusion of a biblical chapter conspicuous for its inset and iterative storytelling, which is revealed to be anything but a dubious or misleading enterprise. The more repetition and permutation in this case, the more consolidated and successfully self-interpreting the content and the more unambiguous its takeaway lessons. Illustrative stories, fables to help give a picture: these *are* the real thing.

It is probably fair to say that a chapter from the Book of Genesis composed around the tenth century BCE and a twenty-first-century film by the Coen brothers share contiguous space in an encompassing Jewish discursive tradition by only the most maximalist criterion. To word that disclaimer as a question: Can an inset triad of similarly narrated accounts—call them "renarrations"—of Rebekah's betrothal to Isaac be meaningfully juxtaposed with the narrative collapse—call it "denarration"—of certain interpolated shaggy dog stories in *A Serious Man*, with an eye on the understory in each?[8]

To take just a small anticipatory example: If the "signs and tokens" alluded to by Sy Ableman (the agent of *de*-marriage in *A Serious Man*) proliferate and merely confuse, in the episode from Genesis 24 that narrates the search undertaken by Abraham's servant for Isaac's prospective spouse, such signifiers function, rather, as proofs and guarantees. The contrast not only explains the juxtaposition, but also enables us to ask a question about Jewish discursive tradition.

With a nod to Talal Asad, the editors of *Jewish Studies at the Crossroads of Anthropology and History* argue that such a notion "takes us beyond a limited corpus of foundational texts and instead focuses our attention on the processes through which *every* Jewish text potentially participates in the creation of a canon and the modes of authority associated with it" (15). Despite the italicized modifier of "*every* text," certain limits are presupposed by this flexible framework, which is still referred to the functional utility of canonicity and its authorizing gestures. Thus, "beyond a limited foundational corpus" applies nominally to textual heterogeneity lying just outside the borders of the biblical and rabbinic canon, that is, hagiographic or paraliturgical discourse, artifacts like gravesites and amulets, and ritual practices such as pilgrimage.

And yet, because a Jewish discursive tradition, as the editors acknowledge, "only *partly* . . . makes reference to a set of foundational texts," I wish to test the plasticity of the concept in relation to both different kinds of "Jewish texts" (one foundational, the other not) and different kinds of interpretive and guild practices that lay claim to them, while stopping short of appealing to one, all-encompassing canon. To hearken back to our introduction, the juxtapositional magic I propose to work here proceeds satirically than allegorically.

Plasticity (and its dialectical opposite, rupture) are signaled by the prologue to *ASM*, whose *mise-en-scène* (a *shtetl*), language (Yiddish), and denarrating ambiguity preface the film without truly introducing it. In echo of the essay-volume above, my analyses take place at a neighboring crossroads: foundational Jewish narrative and the American Jewish postmodern. That said, I should be clear about what I intend. Mine will *not* be an exercise in reading the Bible through postmodern eyes. Many such studies already dot the critical landscape.

Rather, I want to situate *ASM* as its own instance of what we might playfully call postmodern wisdom literature while at the same time using some of its features as a countertext for Genesis 24, somewhere between explanatory foil and anti-gloss. In so doing, I follow the lead of the concluding affidavit in the film's credits, assuring its audience, "No Jews were harmed in the making of this motion picture," but which nevertheless failed to mollify a certain subset of viewers and critics, alike.

Harm of a more generalized sort may have been inflicted on their expectations for narrative coherence. Gaps, freighted background, and seemingly redundant retellings notwithstanding, narrative coherence is something the Bible, traditionally interpreted, models with magisterial authority. Adapting a narratological term, I deploy "the renarrated" to describe such apparent redundancy in the form of prominent *display texts*—the Pentateuch's twice- and even thrice-told tales.

Its obverse in the Coen Brother film—also the stuff of display text—is "the denarrated," a term with some currency in specifically postmodern narratology. As such, it expresses the proprietary and self-authorizing function of narration in the first place, which *renarration* in a foundational text all the more artfully and authoritatively affirms. Furthermore, it shows us what the *drama* of *reading* looks like when applied to ideological literature of both foundational and anti-foundational sorts.[9]

Denarrating episodes in *ASM* track marital collapse at the same time as they perform narrative collapse: both marriage (as one archetype *for* plot) and storytelling fail to cohere, becoming co-implicated in that very breakdown. The renarrating moments in Genesis 24, by contrast, invest storytelling and endogamy with the highest significance as foundational structures that are also co-dependent: the originary crossroads that is law-and-narrative. The betrothal we see in Genesis 24 becomes at once a protracted narrationally self-conscious *story* at the same time as it functions, in the words of one recent study, "as a significant and uncontested resource for rabbinic marriage law."[10]

By contrast, in *A Serious Man*, legal, narrative, and marital structures alike retain their ritual function, certainly, but appear to forego the coherence entirely. That the film incorporates a subplot about Larry Gopnik's pending tenure decision—also ritualized—merely adds the perfect institutional supplement of *secular vocation* to that list, and partially explains my fondness for *ASM* in the first place.

Within the archetypal human realm envisioned by Genesis, we can ascribe to that same nexus of binding structures exactly the force of the apodictic "math" so vaunted by Larry Gopnik; that is, the meta-narrative design of life, death, espousal, and procreation. In Gopnik's classroom vernacular, that would be how providential human pairing and its issue "really work." If biblical stories in a plain sense function illustratively—like, fables, say, to help provide a picture—they also lend themselves to the applications and modeling of *nomos*—law, custom, norm.[11] I therefore pivot to the Bible itself now, and an interpretive apparatus associated with the traditional focus on classical sources that defines mainstream Jewish Studies.

Renarration in Genesis 24

A particularly evocative, almost self-contained instance of renarrating is exhibited in the Torah portion known according to Masoretic division as *Ḥayei Sarah* or "the life of Sarah," which begins, counterintuitively perhaps, with the verse that records her death. It proceeds to the economic arrangements for her burial in Ḥevron and after an elaborate, ritualized account of her son's betrothal to Rebekah, concludes with this eloquently simple verse about generational progression and surrogacy, "And Isaac brought her to the tent of Sarah his mother, and he took Rebekah, and she became his wife, and he loved her. And Isaac was comforted for his mother" (24:67). In between, the story which introduces Rebekah as Isaac's future wife is told three times. It is the *ritualized* feature of the narrated narrating here—a matter of giving and reading signs—that I highlight under the name "renarration."[12]

A fuller summary of the plot would go as follows: The matriarch Sarah dies at age 127 and is buried in the Cave of *Maḥpeḥlah*, which Abraham purchases in a public and rhetorically elaborate sale from Efron the Hittite. Abraham then delegates his servant (whom the *midrashim* identify as Eliezer)[13] to find a wife for Isaac not from the daughters of the Canaanites among whom he dwells but by journeying to his land and birthplace. He is sent to Haran, and at the village well in the city of Naḥor in Aram Naharayim, he petitions God for a sign: When the women approach the well, the woman who replies to his request for water, "drink, and I will also give your camels to drink" shall be the one destined for his master's son.

Rebekah, the daughter of Abraham's nephew Betuel, appears and performs according to this anticipated script; the servant is thereupon invited to their home, where he repeats the story of the day's events to Betuel and Rebekah's brother, Laban. Rebekah returns with Eliezer to Canaan, where they encounter Isaac praying in the field. The betrothed both "look up" at each other, and the espousal is sealed. Chapter 25 begins when Abraham takes a new wife, fathers six more sons (with Isaac as his sole designated heir), dies at age 175, and is buried beside Sarah by Isaac and Ishmael.

This arcing of lineage is brilliantly illuminated by literary scholar/social theorist Elaine Scarry, whose *The Body in Pain: The Making and Unmaking of the World* describes the play of "list and story," a binary perfectly captured by the Hebrew word *toldot*, which connotes both "generations" and "chronicles" (or "accounts"). "The link between the two kinds of passage—list and story—is clear and open, requiring no explication, for many of the stories have as their overt subject some aspect of the successful bringing forth of children." Scarry's first example, appositely enough, is Genesis 24:

> Each of the two [*list* and *story*] contains within itself what is withheld from view in the other: the men and women in the stories contain within their bodies not the singular children specified in the narrative, but the tiers and tiers of offspring contained in the lists; so, in turn, the formal tiering in the lists conceals what only becomes manifest in the stories, the extremity of physical and imaginative work required of human continuity and connection.[14]

Narrative and marriage mutually depend on the reliability of providential signifiers, which in turn justifies the process of renarration itself—a story first *prefigured* (in the form of the servant's petition—his "plotting"—for a successful outcome, 12–15); then *figured* (the plot's eventuation as witnessed by the servant, 15–27); and lastly *refigured* (that plot now retold intradiegetically as the narrated past to Lavan and Betuel, Rebekah's brother and father, 34–39). Not only is the chapter "unique in the amount of quoted speech it contains," says Bible scholar George W. Savran, but "[t]his controlling voice is all the more remarkable in light of the servant's anonymity and relative passivity," the more convincingly to show the workings of Providence.[15]

Classical rabbinic commentaries emphasize the very same ideological thrust. The union of Rebekah and Isaac counts as paradigmatic in the Pentateuch on several grounds.[16] It represents the sole ancestral marriage in the Book of Genesis that does not involve concubinage; it establishes a precedent for endogamous union, with husband and wife as essential prototypes: the virginal *Rivka* and the circumcised *Yitzḥak*. It also supplies rabbinic tradition with source material for several marital legal principles, for example, prohibited union with an orphan or minor against her will. The hinge between narrative and law—as blended, layered, or interpenetrating genres—is just how Judaic tradition correlates the written and oral law in an ongoing process of commentary and codification, a point often missed by approaches premised exclusively on narrative poetics.

As a special instance of the Bible's intentional "structures of repetition,"[17] renarration affirms the promissory story-arc of betrothal in the act of textually re-producing it. Reproduction at the textual level serves reproductivity as the very thrust of narrative design. Whether the particular structure of repetition here suggests a unifying compositional technique—the juncture where poetics joins hands with classical rabbinic exegesis—I'd prefer to leave an open question. This is only partly because repetition also happens to provide the historical-critical method with one of its most telling indicators of diachrony—the documentary aggregation and source redaction over time of the Biblical corpus.[18]

But even apart from assumptions or conclusions about design, specific formulae in Biblical narrative introduce hermeneutic opportunities or *solicitations* (Levinas's word). For example, prefiguring Elaine Scarry by almost ten centuries, the twelfth-century Northern French exegete Rashbam reads the many iterations in Genesis of story-compacted-into list, economically expressed as *toldot*, as Moses's personal scribal redaction, the "narrative introduction" that lays the literary ground for an ensuing exegetical reception of the Exodus story and the large scale of outline of the Jewish legal system.[19]

Such literary formalism will be expressed in a more strictly historicist terms a century later by Naḥmanides in a famous synchronic principle—*ma'aseh avot siman le-banim*, "the acts of the fathers become imitated signs for their children."[20] In other words, the Torah programmatically builds in narrative repetition as historical modeling, a training in the tradition's internal coherence. For Genesis 24, I want to encourage the application of this idea to the act of reading itself, cognizant, of course, that "reading" has its history across a diachronic and cultural range of various phenomenological practices.[21] The story of Rebekah's betrothal at the level of form trains readers in an ethics of narrative procedures, a programmatic behavior-by-proxy. This is the Biblical text's under- or meta-narrative—the story, one could say, of reading its discourse.

On the matter of verbatim repetition and what critic Robert Alter calls the "slow, stately progress" of the betrothal type–scene,[22] eleventh-century commentator Rashi quotes a *midrash* that typifies the Rabbis' hermeneutic of generosity: "Rabbi Aḥa said: 'The mere conversation of the slaves of the Patriarchs' household is more important than the Torah of the [Patriarchs'] descendants, for the chapter of Eliezer is repeated, whereas many important principles of the Law are derived only from a slight indication.'"[23] The thirteenth-century commentator Ḥizkuni and the fifteenth-century commentary of Yitzhak ben Moses Arama make related points about the seemingly surplus repetition as the Torah's compliment to Eliezer for demonstrating his wisdom and acumen, which includes the discrepancies discernible only to readers.

Some medieval and post-medieval commentators proceed on the assumption of the Bible's omnisignificance; every textual "particle" matters, including those that bespeak variations in iterated material, whether in grammar, syntax, or orthography. We could call such omnisignificance the Torah's own, illimitable version of "signs and tokens." For example, R. Baḥya ben Asher (thirteenth–fourteenth century) points out that the phrase for "well," *ein hamayim*, is repeated three times, with varied syntax in each renarration; "we need to understand the precise reason for each of these nuances," he says.[24] The entire type-scene at the well, as we know from the servant himself, is premised upon some "sign" that he can read; *hakrei na lefanai hayom*, "let it chance before me this day," he says portentously in v 12, and the commentaries devote enormous attention to this pivotal idea of *mikra* or "happenstance."[25]

Even the graphic text at this point is assigned a rare and meaningful sign, according to the Masoretic cantillation tradition that indicates how the Torah (otherwise lacking *nikud* or vowel points, in scroll form), should be chanted, vocalized, and accented.[26] The most baroquely ornate of all such notations (*ta'amei ha-mikra*), that sign is called *shalshelet*, meaning "chain of three," and marks one of only seven such usages in Tanakh (four in the Pentateuch—additionally emphasized in this verse by a caesura or *psik taʿama*).²⁷ In appearance, this cantillation note looks like a piece of Rotini, sounds like a warble of around thirty ascending and descending notes chanted in triplets, and is found directly above "and he said," which introduces the servant's prayer for a providential outcome. Omnisignificantly, its duration is taken to signify the servant's lengthy contemplation.²⁸

Exegesis of this sort ensures that any and every textual feature—lexical, syntactic, orthographic (Hebrew *taʾam* means the "taste" or "sense," but also "reason")—participates in an overall semantics requiring minute construal. The medieval Spanish *peshat* school associated with Naḥmanides and R. Abraham Ibn Ezra, on the other hand, consigns differences in repeated content to an unremarkable norm of Biblical narrative style.²⁹ For example, according to twelfth-century R. David Kimḥi (the Radak) on Genesis 24, "And when these matters are repeated, there occurs variation in wording, but the sense is the same (*yesh bahem shinui milot, aval ha-taʿam eḥad*). For this is the norm of Scripture (*minhag ha-katuv*) with repetition: it preserves the sense, but not the exact wording."³⁰

Chiefly, however, and following the lead of Bible scholar Adele Berlin in not wishing to conflate exegetical sense-making with poetics,³¹ I want to read the element of renarration, rather, as a hermeneutic opportunity, an invitation to construe narrative form in the service of what we might, playfully, call "higher reading," with the servant himself as a kind of allegorized, faded figure for the act itself. Narrative critic Meir Sternberg is quick to note, however:

> The servant is not a "reader" in the sense that we are. Like all figural interpreters, he directly confronts a world that we receive through the artful mediation of an artful teller and text. He exercises interpretation on a world of objects; we, on a web of words that projects such a world. (141)

It is there, and only there, on the surface of that web that the play of verbal cues and echoes and its deeply serious moral theater and mime, is made known in the act of reading.

Directly after a highly ritualized play of similarly staged cues and echoes in chapter 23, the patriarch turns to his servant and assigns him a task, whose directions happen also to contain a story-kernel. In turn, the servant constructs that kernel into an imaginative plot, witnesses its enactment as detailed in the diegesis, and then renarrates the whole sequence himself in public. The speech acts about burial and payment in chapter 23, politically charged as they are, prepare the performative ground, if only by contrast, for the set-pieces of renarration to follow.³² A number of other correspondences, especially the back-and-forth permutations of the verb roots *shin.mem.ayin* ("listen") and *aleph.zayin.nun* ("hear"), connect these ostensibly separate episodes within a larger narrative arc of intentional tellings and retellings.

Because a set of display texts is thereby so prominently staged in Genesis 24, reading as its own reflexive staging (or restaging) is thrown into that much higher relief. The critical language I deploy here obviously comports with modern scholarship on Biblical narrative poetics. It has a rabbinic precedent, however. Rabbi Samuel ben Meir, better known by his acronym רשב"ם (Rashbam), grandson of Rashi and preeminent exponent of the then-radically new *peshat* school of "contextual exegesis" developed by the French Tosafists in the eleventh and twelfth centuries, coined a number of terms—a rudimentary critical vocabulary—for a more self-consciously literary (rather than strictly homiletic or legalistic) reading of the Biblical corpus. As both means and end, the practice of reading *peshuto shel mikra* (according to Scripture's plain sense), seeks to account for just the sort of arcing story structures foregrounded here.³³

A related term in Rashbam's critical vocabulary is *derekh ha-mikra* [the way of scripture]—what we moderns would call "poetics"—notably on display in the Bible's *kefel lashon* (double expression), its penchant for parallelisms and patterned rhetorical doublings, about which he will observe, *derekh ha-mikra'ot likpol et ha'devarim* (it is the way of Scripture to double its words).³⁴ Another pair of terms are *maskilim* (intellectuals) and *ohave sekhel* (lovers of reason); or as we might express these same constructs in more contemporary critical idiom, "authorial audience" and "interpretive community."

The most salient family of terms, in particular regard to the renarrations of Genesis 24, orbits around the root *kuf.daled.mem* (meaning both "precede" and "advance"). Signifying "anticipatory information," Rashbam's terminology denotes those proleptic units both large and small that depend on a technique familiar to students of literary modernism. Hannah Liss explains: "In Rashbam's view, entire narrative blocks, thus, turn into literary anticipations.... In this, Rashbam's approach reveals an 'aesthetic of reception,' a sort of 'reader-response,' meant for an intellectual and well-educated reader who considers the Torah a piece of literature, composed according to literary standards."³⁵ Also geared toward modeling or training, obviously, such literary sophistication also seems to understand the act of reading, even of sacred text, as a performative hermeneutic.

Repetition functions as a well-known staple of Biblical discourse, on particular display in Genesis—at lexical or phrasal levels, as the scribal technique of *Weideraufnahme*, as recounted story or dual reporting, as motivic parallelism, as quoted or reiterated speech, at the largest structural levels of genre or discursive unit.[36] Certain famous recapitulations—for example, Pharaoh's dreams told and retold in Genesis, the confirmation of instructions for building the *Mishkan* (Tabernacle) in Exodus, Balak's and Balaam's injunctions and proclamation in Numbers—will always elicit commentary from reading communities of all sorts. The traditional rabbinic name for the entire book of Deuteronomy, the quintessential Mosaic example of renarration, is *Mishneh Torah*, or "the Torah twice-told."[37]

I single out Genesis 24 for its remarkable correspondence between textual shape and narrative ethos, where redundancy of content and recurrence of form serve an overarching design that correlates promise with fulfillment. Similarly, it exhibits the performance of story with "the half-embodied state of moral theater and mime in which one person devotes himself to being someone other than who he is," as Scarry underscores Eliezer's agency on behalf of both his master, Abraham, and Isaac, his heir.

This is the surrogacy required to facilitate marital union across the distance between Haran in northern Mesopotamia and Kiryat Arba in Canaan. According to a famous image associated with critic Georges Poulet, the practice of reading also facilitates a kind of surrogacy,[38] producing its own deeply serious form of theater and mime. With the faded figure of Abraham's servant-narrator in Genesis 24—first recessed, then very much center-stage as first anticipator and then recapitulator—we become especially cognizant of our own proxy-role as bystander and stand-in on the plane of reading.

At some level, then—ethical, affective, cognitive, enactive—this renarration, this *shalshelet* of the "thrice-told," gestures in our direction through the act of lending ourselves to the text before us. As the "thrice *fold*," The Book of Ecclesiastes knows such braided structure ("The three-fold cord shall not quickly come undone" 4:12) as *haḥut hameshulash*: the sturdiness of triplicate form. It also plays a role in that other famous discourse of wisdom literature, the Book of Job.

Both of these books happen to be the Biblical texts that most prominently inform *A Serious Man* as a kind of mythic underwriting, not unlike the way the rabbinic citation—"Receive with simplicity everything that happens to you," Rashi on Deuteronomy 18:13—commencing the film seems intended to stand over it.[39] The Coens are nothing if not liberal with homage, with their own penchant for intertexts and genre tributes, and I will therefore take the "Rashi" as privileging the very commentarial tradition I want to adduce here.[40] And with that, I turn to the Coens' film, with its own more disconcertingly embodied state of moral theater and mime, and the puzzling feature of its various denarrating structures.

The Denarrations of A Serious Man

The term "*de*narration" was coined by narrative theorist Brian Richardson[41] with specific reference to postmodern and late modern narrative texts that appear to undo themselves by calling into question or subsequently falsifying statements in the discourse. As such, for Richardson, it clusters around a set of techniques and structures under the general heading of "unnatural narrative." These include unnatural time-spaces and chronotopes, unnatural narrators and storytelling scenarios, and unnatural framing devices.[42]

Strictly speaking, the examples from the Coen brothers' film that I enlist denarrate less by outright denial or discursive contradiction than by means of discontinuous diegesis or the shaggy dog story, whose effect is comparably antimimetic.[43] Denarrating performances amount to artifacts of self-consumption. If one of the cardinal principles of rabbinic exegesis that smooths out textual protrusions, as reformulated by Bernard Levinson as "there is neither redundancy nor contradiction in the Torah,"[44] then the Coens revel in both: redundancy for redundancy's sake, contradiction as both an epistemological and metaphysical norm.[45]

More plaintively articulated by Larry Gopnik while in despair at God's inscrutability, "Why does he make us feel the questions if he's not going to give us any answers?" (88)—for which Gopnik, in concluding one of his physics classes, also provides the denarrating chime, "The Uncertainty Principle. It proves we can't ever really know . . . what's going on. So it shouldn't bother you. Not being able to figure anything out. Although you will be responsible for this on the mid-term" (98).

And if the all-but-inscrutable classroom math merely provides a proof for unknowability, one might as well count on what Gopnik's non-physicist brother calls "The Mentaculus," a minutely scribbled "probability map of the universe," which nevertheless boasts the practical virtue of exploiting math for remunerative ends. No "Schrödinger's paradox" this: The unemployed brother's back-room gambling pays real dividends—at least until he's taken into custody.[46]

I began by invoking *ASM* as a post-biblical source; "Biblically-inspired" would have been more accurate, in a spirit similar to the film's opening title-card that purportedly cites Rashi. At one point in the plot, Larry's friend Mimi tells him, "It's not always easy deciphering what God is trying to tell you. But it's not something you have to figure out for yourself. We're Jews. We've got that well of tradition to draw on to help us understand. When we're puzzled, we have all the stories that have been handed down from people who had the same problems."

Narrative had better compensate, given the inscrutability of God's doings in the film, along with the structural waywardness of human institutions—Larry's family, his university, his son's Hebrew school, the synagogue he attends—perhaps best instanced in the film by two attorneys, one of whom, Solomon Schlutz of *Siegelson, Schlutz* collapses just as he is about to provide the solution for Larry's property-line issues; while the other, the very reputable Ron Meshbesher, like God Himself, never actually makes an appearance while nevertheless charging a hefty retainer, "payable upon receipt."[47]

Like its countertexts, the Book of Job and Genesis 24, *ASM* flirts with triplicate form, an extremely loose version of *shalshelet* or *haḥut hameshulash*. Three consultations with Rabbis as would-be dispensers of advice for Larry Gopnik's purgatorial travails mark diegetic breaks in the story, each announced by title cards: "the first Rabbi" (Ginsler) "the second Rabbi" (Nachtner), and finally, "Marshak" (the aged, distracted, and utterly anachronistic rabbi emeritus). The last of these reconnoiters does not produce an actual encounter, leaving Larry Gopnik to feel the questions again without the solace of answers.

But that absence is compensated by the extended space given to the movie's similarly Old World—if not otherworldly—seven-minute prologue in Yiddish about Reb Groshkover, a possible *dibek* (malevolent possessing spirit), played by the late star of Yiddish theater and television Fyvush Finkel, who visits the house of a *shtetl* couple and is or is not fatally stabbed in the process. To take the allegorical step, we could say that the displaced Minnesota Jewish community of this film remains nevertheless haunted by dybbuks whose language, and whose discursive tradition *in all its pointed renarration*, they no longer share. This would also be the link, in my strong reading, between the Yiddish of the prologue and the Bar Mitzvah Hebrew chanted in a teenager's cracking voiced and under the influence of a just-smoked joint late in the film. Any cultural patrimony, from *shtetl* or Bible, remains equally at a distance—*partes extra partes*, in Jean-Luc Nancy's patois.

"The import of this parable is cryptic to the point of inscrutability, making it a perfect introduction to the rest of the movie," wrote one critic[48]—

although another essayist astutely suggests that its antechamber structure merely underscores Jews' exterior relation to the places they inhabit, including suburban America.[49] Whether or not that's the case, the aspect ratio happens to change at this point from 1.37:1 to 1.85:1. The film, as readers may know, received mixed notices from reviewers who either applauded or derided it.

"As a piece of moviemaking craft, 'A Serious Man' is fascinating," wrote *The New Yorker*'s David Denby. "[I]n every other way, it's intolerable."[50] "Too Jewish," signifying both praise and lamentation, was a familiar appraisal. As if affirming my original, maximalist claim about Jewish discursive tradition (which, conveniently enough, *within* that tradition, is known as *shalshelet kabbalah* or "chain of reception"), another reviewer observed acutely, "The Coens may play around with that tradition, they may disparage it or mock it. But they are irrevocably a part of it, and that's all to the good."[51]

This is especially the case in the three inset episodes in which Gopnik seeks advice from his synagogue's three rabbis. The first of these amounts to pure bathos, with the junior rabbi's admonition to Larry to change his perspective if he has "the feeling of losing track of Hashem" (despite the many real and substantial woes Larry has come to be advised about) and, therefore, to "just look at that parking lot, [with] these autos and such."

With the next of these exchanges, "The Second Rabbi," we fully enter the domain of the denarrated, the very exemplar of the Jewish shaggy dog, which Rabbi Nachtner introduces by asking rhetorically, "How does God speak to us?" As his perfectly pitched narrative performance continues, we learn about the dentist Lee Sussman who, while "making a plaster mold for corrective bridge work" discovers "something engraved on the inside of the patient's lower incisors," the Hebrew letters that spell *Hoshieni* (Help me, save me). "This in a goy's mouth, Larry."

> Sussman goes home. Can Sussman eat? Sussman can't eat. Can Sussman sleep? Sussman can't sleep. Sussman looks at the molds of his other patients, goy and Jew alike, seeking other messages. He finds none. He looks in his own mouth. Nothing. He looks in his wife's mouth. Nothing. But Sussman is an educated man. Not the world's greatest sage, maybe, no Rabbi Marshak, but he knows a thing or two from the Zohar and the Kabbalah. He knows that every Hebrew letter has its numeric equivalent. 8-4-5-4-4-7-3. Seven digits . . . a phone number, maybe? "Hello? Do you know a goy named Kraus, Russell Kraus?" "Who?"

The dentist anticipates Larry himself, appealing to Rabbi Nachtner for some answer. Is it a sign? Is he supposed to be helping this Gentile? Or people more generally? "Is the answer in Kabbalah? In Torah? Or is there even a question? Tell me, Rabbi, what can such a sign mean?" A studied pause ensues in the storytelling, upon which Larry seizes to enact (repeat) the identical supplicatory role, to which Rabbi Nachtner responds with only more patter and platitudes—"Helping others . . . couldn't hurt." Frustrated in the face of apparent indifference to a definitive answer, Larry says, "It sounds like you don't know anything! Why even tell me the story?" Patronizingly, Rabbi Nachtner offers, "These questions that are bothering you, Larry—maybe they're like a toothache. We feel them for a while, then they go away."

> LG: I don't want it to just go away! I want an answer!
> RN: Sure! We all want the answer! But Hashem doesn't owe us the answer, Larry. Hashem doesn't owe us anything. The obligation runs the other way.
> LG: Why does he make us feel the questions if he's not gonna give us any answers?
> RN: He hasn't told me.
> LG: And . . . what happened to the goy?
> RN: The goy? Who cares?

Recall now the comforting words of Larry's friend, Mimi Nudell: "When we're puzzled we have all the stories that have been handed down from people who had the same problems." The metalepsis[52] related by Rabbi Nachter is quintessential denarration; the lack of any discernible narrative point—"The goy? Who cares?"—is of a piece with a borsch-belt rendition that merely compounds the uncertainty Larry vainly hopes to parse: "First I should tell you, then I shouldn't!" *Discours* and *récit* alike make his teeth hurt. The fable also corresponds to the "fakelore" (Jeffrey Shandler's neologism) in the *shtetl*-based prologue to the film, which entirely fabricates a Yiddish original for dialogue composed in English.

Shandler calls the Jewish storytelling on display in *ASM* a "definitional practice," with the film serving part and parcel as "an example of this storytelling practice in itself" (353) through whose "cultural markers," Jewishness signifies also ambivalence.

> The stories in *A Serious Man* mark these interrogations of the supernal as a Jewish practice, not simply by dint of cultural markers (use of Yiddish, portrayal of synagogue life, references to the Book of Job),

but also by enacting the telling and listening to them as communally constitutive activities. They are as much about affirming Jewish peoplehood, history, and cultural literacy as they are about contemplating the supernal. Like the characters' various efforts to explain the uncanny, this affirmation of Jewishness is double-edged: The community takes itself very seriously, and yet is often ridiculous. (352)

Evidently, the definitional instability of communicative-communal practices inside the film was doubled in the process of making it, recounted in Riv-Ellen Prell's essay about the film's reception among the local Minneapolis Jewish community. For a rehearsal of the Bar Mitzvah scene in which a Torah Scroll is raised—the signal in an actual service for the congregation to demonstrate their reverence by rising—the congregant-extras stood up without being cued to do so by director Joel Coen, who promptly directed them to sit back down. "What was the great illusion, then, in the confusion of reality for representation—the filmmaker who saw the Torah as a prop, or the extras who took the scene for a Torah service?" (371).

In introducing the film's proposition of unresolvability or misdirection as the governing property of narrative—certainly, its chief vicissitude—I mentioned that even the nomenclature wobbles: first "stories," then, "fables," then "pictures," whereas, the math just stays "the math." "The teeth don't tell," says Rabbi Nachtner. But Rabbi Nachtner assuredly tells, and his garden (path) variety storytelling leaves Larry Gopnik no wiser—if anything, visibly pained—even if the film's audience, and fans of Jewishly-tinged denarration generally, are at the very least entertained.

In a subsequent scene, Larry's divorce lawyer and friend Don Milgram asks him whether he's "seen the rabbi," meaning the ensconced sage Marshak, "a very wise" but also a "very old" man. When Larry explains that he's seen Nachtner instead, shrugging in reply to whether he was helpful at all, Milgram says, "What—did he tell you about the goy's teeth? You should talk to Marshak."

By this point the stuff of cliché, the self-consuming patter of the denarrated becomes all the more reinforced by being *re*narrated. When the same Rabbi Nachtner delivers a eulogy for Sy Ableman, the recently deceased paramour of Larry's wife who may have also attempted to sabotage Larry's tenure case, he intones, Book-of-Ecclesiastically:

> *Olam ha-bah* is in the soul of this community which nurtured Sy Ableman and to which Sy Ableman now returns. That's right, he returns. Because he still inspires us, Ableman returns. Because his

memory instructs us, Ableman returns. Because his thoughts illuminate our days and ways, Sy Ableman returns. The frivolous man may vanish without a ripple but Sy Ableman? Sy Ableman was a serious man." (89)

Nachtner's earlier exhortation, "A *tzadik*—who knows, maybe even a *lamed vovnik*—a man beloved by all, a man who despised the frivolous; could such a serious man simply disappear?" recasts Sy Ableman almost in the image of Job. And yet what we have actually seen of him in the film—his unctuousness, pomposity, manipulativeness, pretension (in a dream Larry has him misdescribe mathematics, when it's actually politics, as "the art of the possible")—exposes Rabbi Nachtner's panegyric as one more instance of denarration, more performatively insidious than the practiced *shtick* of "The Goy's teeth" because it bears the pronouncement of the pulpit.

ASM may actually constitute the only example of "the storytelling idiom of dramatic filmmaking for the American public" (Shandler, 355) in which we are witness not only to the Torah being chanted in synagogue but the Torah portion itself practiced at home by the prospective *Bar Mitzvah*. And yet, how is that shown to us? Without actually following the Hebrew text in some form or other (the screenplay later describes an open Torah scroll from Danny's perspective as "a swarm of Hebrew letters"), Larry's son repeatedly lifts the phonograph needle in order to pause a recording of it which he can then memorize, almost as if it were Jefferson Airplane's "Somebody to Love," the song to which he listens hypnotically on his transistor radio. Reiterated, replayed—but in this moment at least, technologically *dis*narrated. Welcome to the American Jewish postmodern.

And that brings us, by way of final contrast, back to the Jewish premodern and the brief verse from the end of Genesis 24. I have referred to the renarration in this episode as "triplicate." But this is not technically correct. In verse 66, directly after we are told that Rebekah covers herself upon seeing Isaac and before Isaac brings her to his mother's tent, the narrator inserts one last stage direction for Abraham's servant before he disappears entirely from the Biblical text: "The servant then related to Isaac all that he had done." On this verse, the Radak elaborates, "He did so during the time it took to reach Abraham's house after Isaac had met them" (presumably, it took a while, with the nesting of renarrations intact). At any rate, here at the end of chapter 24, not only does the recounting refer to something outside *our* hearing and reading, it represents a *fourth* iteration of the meeting at the well, encapsulated in the laconic *kol hadevarim asher asah* (all he had done).

I have referred to both of these narrative examples, so different from each other and yet improbably associated through the contrast, as "display texts." Either ethnographically or socio-culturally, each italicizes narrative performance, staging it in both its iterative or self-canceling modes as a "definitional practice" within the long arc of a Jewish discursive tradition. In Genesis 24, displaying a text reinvests it with tellability. In *ASM*, displaying a text disenchants it, brought home materially in the Bar Mitzvah scene where the *yad* or pointer on an open Torah scroll fails to isolate the correct passage and must be dragged down a few inches to the cringe-inducing, over-amplified sound of parchment-scraping, and where the same scroll elicits an incongruously muttered "Jesus Christ" from the congregant being publically honored with lifting it but unprepared for its weight. (That last mismatched has already been prefigured in a short scene between Danny and his sister when the latter barges into his room while he is practicing his Torah portion and accuses him of stealing twenty dollars from out of her drawer, to which he responds "Studying Torah! Asshole!")

This public ritual of displayed text, comically subverted in the film, echoes a powerfully compressed Biblical trope, on pronounced display in Genesis—indeed, it occurs in chapter 24—whose decidedly different effect and syntactical-semantic function receive particular attention from modern scholars.[53] The deictic idiom "and behold" or in Hebrew, *ve-hinei*, as in the verse when the servant sees Rebekah for the first time—*vayehi hu terem kilah ledaber* (He had not yet finished speaking), *vehineh Rivkah yotzet* (and *behold* Rebekah came out) (24:15)—and again when Isaac comes upon her—*vayisa einav vayar ve-hinei gmalim baim* (And he raised his eyes and saw, and behold camels were coming)—typically signals either a change in perspective from narrator to character (for example, Gen 22:13, the binding of Isaac) or, in the words of the Rashbam on Gen 25:24, "whenever the Torah speaks about something new"[54] such as an entirely new personage or narrative setting.

On Rashbam's use of the idiom, Hannah Liss observes, "Rashbam's commentary takes a narrative course on its own, which opens up new fictional realms, outside the biblical-rabbinic discourse. Exegesis becomes narration, a (re-)telling of 'old-new' stories."[55] The idea here is that Rashbam's own tracking of Biblical narrative understands itself as renarration—not in the strict sense I've been using, but rather in the service of disclosing the story that takes shape hermeneutically on the plane of reading. Renarration signifies redundancy, of course, but, Biblically (and exegetically) modeled, it also speaks a kind of reenchantment, as if the act of telling becomes reinvested with conjuring power when conspicuously reenacted—the very opposite of Rabbi Nachtner's latest recitation of "the Goy's Teeth."

Let's say, then, that the power of the fourth iteration in Genesis 24:66 lies in its modesty and elected silence after the display work, the conjuration of the thrice-told. And *A Serious Man*? Beyond the return of Danny Gopnik's transistor radio to him, the film's ending resolves few of its subplots, leaves the affiliations between physics, morality, and *yidishkayt* unclear, and moreover, introduces entirely new ambiguities in the very last minutes. Is Larry seriously, perhaps mortally ill when his physician phones him to come in so that they can discuss the X-rays, insisting pointedly that, "I think we'd be more comfortable in person. Can you come in? Now. Now is good. I've cleared some time now?" (The "now" thrice-told.)

Is there some connection to be drawn between these medical results and "unjust test results" of which his Korean student Clive had originally complained? Should we thus impute causality to the fact that Larry's office phone rings almost simultaneously with his decision to override his teacher's scruples by replacing the "F" next to Clive's name in his grade-book with a passing "C-" grade, and keep the bribe-money Clive mysteriously deposited with him? Does the funnel cloud in the middle distance, as word of a tornado approaching Danny's Hebrew school mobilizes the students toward shelter, presage imminent disaster? And are we meant to connect the final shot of that cloud to the culminating shot in the film's prologue in which Reb Groshkover "staggers out into the moaning wind and snow to be swallowed by the night [as] the wife and husband stare at the door banging in the wind?" Or to Danny's radio earpiece, through whose aperture the film proper begins?

Where do we stand vis-à-vis the intersubjective culture-clash (as Clive's father terms the "misunderstanding" between his son and Larry Gopnik) of one person's insistence on the one hand, that "I know about my actions" (Clive) and the other's equally insistent but most probably inaccurate belief on the other, "I can interpret. I know what you meant me to understand" (Larry)? Is the denarrating parable of "The Goy's Teeth" any more or less vacuously symbolic than the recurring motif of being unable to get reception for a particularly inane 1960s television show, epitomized by the line, "*F Troop* is still fuzzy?"

Such questions are, of course, quite beside the point since the film keeps both its several secrets and its indeterminacy. In Allen Redmon's formulation, the film is not a code to be broken but a text to be assembled (132). It is left to spectators to construct its (satirical) syntax accordingly. In that choice, the film's audience becomes so many "discretionary constructivists," a term Redmon borrows from film philosopher Berys Gaut.

Viewers of *ASM* are, in short, quite differently positioned than Larry Gopnik, so fatefully plagued by the curse of *seriousness*, the Coens' twist on what psychologist Victor Frankl, in the Jewish generation proceeding that of the movie's time-period (after the Holocaust he survived but whose absence in the film one also marks), famously named "man's search for meaning." That is a hermeneutic quest *ASM* fairly sterilizes. If, as Rabbi Nachtner says, it's not God who owes us an answer but the other way around, then it's quite possible to be in a similar relation to a film like *A Serious Man*.[56]

Above, I spoke of the drama of reading in relation to both of the texts I've examined here, the denarrational as well as the renarrational sort. But I also maintained that denarration paradoxically affirms normative styles of narration, in particular those associated with a foundational text like the Bible. That claim certainly seems to suggest that where the latter sketches narrative "positivity," that is, plenitude and an ultimately redemptive omnisignificance; denarration, by contrast, inclines almost necessarily toward a correspondingly "negative" or skeptical pole, conducing to an omnignificance where the meaningful is . . . just anyone's guess.

At worst, meaningfulness remains suspended—and the "worst" here merely signifies instructively frustrated desire; at best, as Derrida might say, it is a meaningfulness-to-come. In that vein, therefore, I want here to invoke the non-dybbuk but revenant-like figure of Walter Benjamin, who, when he cast a retrospective look upon the past and detected a "secret protocol [*Verabredung*] between the generations of the past and that of our own," ascribed to his and every modern generation, "a weak messianic power."[57]

If every "time of the now" (*Jetzeit*) is "shot through with chips of Messianic time," then tradition will always make claim on the present in some redemptive, revolutionizing fashion, a potentiality no less true for specifically *discursive* traditions. Thus, in his 1916 essay "On Language as Such and on the Language of Man," in an aside on the "use-value" of Biblical discourse, Benjamin disclaims any textual appeal to "revealed truth." He points, rather, to "the discovery of what emerges of itself from the biblical text with regard to the nature of language," for which purpose, he says, "the Bible is only *initially* indispensable."

Obviously, even in its subliminal biblicality, *ASM* makes no such appeal, neither "presupposing language as an ultimate reality," nor demonstrating any fundamental concern with language *as such*, what Benjamin calls "the fundamental linguistic facts." If anything, it exalts a distinctly American Jewish vernacular, while beginning, cryptically, in Yiddish. As Clive's father suggests to Gopnik just as inscrutably after a circular conversation about culture clash and defamation, mysteries sometimes demand simple resignation—a directive the film itself more or less addresses to its own audience.

> LG: It doesn't make sense. Either he left the money or he didn't.
> CF: Please. Accept the mystery.
> LG: You can't have it both ways!
> CF: Why not?[58]

Having it both ways—the cat is both alive and dead—fairly defines the parameters of postmodern wisdom literature, a matter sometimes constructively left to interpreters' discretionary constructivism (a phrase, incidentally, that parallels the vocabulary of modern Biblical criticism in specific regard to textual gap and/or redundancy). The upshot of Benjamin's essay (unpublished in his lifetime) is that human language always renarrates an ostensibly pure language of divine speech that, by dint of its sacrality, has the effect of denarrating our own, pulling us in both directions: "First I should, then I shouldn't."

Does the Coens' film do something similar? While it may not be as modest as Genesis 24:26, *ASM* concludes with unexplained mystery: a threatening tornado (Joban whirlwind?), a possibly life-threatening illness, a blurring of contingency and causality. Upon accomplishing the conjuration and display-work of *its* various denarrations is, *ASM* leaves us with this distinguishing and wholly familiar feature: It makes us *feel* the questions even though it's not going to give us any answers. And feeling the questions might not be such a bad thing, after all; nor is it an inconsiderable effect of the film's contructivist postmodernism.

Such rhetoric of ambiguity also jibes with what Eric Santner regards as "a distinctly modern notion of *revelation*, perhaps even one that is distinctly Kafkan," a surplus of address over meaning, or as Scholem expressed it in correspondence with Benjamin, *validity without actual significance*.[59] As Santner notes, Scholem's idea has by now become all but doctrinal in the commentarial discourse of postmodernism. He himself repeatedly cites Žižek, Agamben,[60] and Derrida, as central figures for that moment, along with Scholem, Kafka, and especially Benjamin; their presence in contemporary Jewish Studies as exemplified by Santer's characteristic synthesis of contiguous fields is by now unremarkable.

More to the point perhaps, they are all creatively at home prowling around biblical texts (as Kafka says people "prowl around" the mount in the parable "Der Berg Sinai"). Even Žižek pronounces the Book of Job, *ASM*'s hypotext, "the first critique of ideology."[61] If some of them stop short of providing definitive answers, they are all similarly insistent about feeling, and having us feel, the questions, too. Which, then, supplies the film's truer gloss: Job or Žižek? You can't have it both ways. But, as an exercise in interdiscursive arbitrage—moving assets between two exchanges while holding seats on both[62]—why not?

"Ich könnte mir einen anderen Abraham"

Until now, I have sought to construct a tale of two Jewish Studies as mostly parallel academic practices, while hoping that they might fruitfully converge in a JS-to-come—with two very different hermeneuticist readerships within JS thereby converging as well. Although this chapter has presented a dialogue between premodern and postmodern voices, its metadiscursive experiment aims for something beyond simply underscoring that chronological difference. Narrative poetics offers a *hypomochlion* by which the renarrations of Genesis 24 get to "speak to" the denarrations of *ASM*, and vice versa, creating two voices inflected toward each other, made proximate.

If one looks back at the program for the 2010 annual conference of the Association for Jewish Studies, one discovers that at the same time as the *ASM* session was scheduled, members could also choose to attend sessions on the following topics: "Jewish Cyberculture," "On the Relevance of Yiddish in the Academy," "Jewish Activism in Mid-Twentieth-Century France and the Colonies," "A Comparative Look at Argentine and American Jewry, 1960s–1970s," "Interreligious Relationships in Medieval and Early Modern Times," "Living and Constructing Crypto-Jewish identities," "Medieval Kabbalah and Creative Contribution," "Redaction, Ideology, and Theology in Rabbinic Literature," "Israel and Diaspora(s): Convergences and Divergences," and "Missionaries and Modernity."

In time-space, this is what Jewish Studies now looks like *grosso modo*: a screenshot or cache of a multidisicplinary field that at the time of this book's writing has become almost paradigmatic in the academy for its topical richness and polyphonic diversity. A very long way, in other words, from Gershom Scholem's "Reflections on Modern Jewish Studies," whose bitter critique of *Wissenschaft des Judentums* and its legacy we sampled earlier in this book. Scholem's alternative model for the newer Jewish Studies (ca.

1944) was his own subversive reclamation of the uncanny or demonic aspects of Judaism as recorded by a medieval textual tradition long ignored by Judaic-scientists and their heirs. *ASM* represents something even more subversive for a successor version of JS unimagined by Scholem: American-suburban, Yiddish-ghostly, multiethnic, *visnshaft*-as-*postmodern*.

To retrieve Benjamin and conclude, sacred text and its canonization may serve as the point of departure, "only *initially* indispensible," for revelation in linguistic being *tout court*. And while Benjamin seems to leave the implications for post-biblical language, specifically, the discourse of modernity, to speak for themselves; and while I would not go as far as to ascribe to a post-canonical hermeneutic of Jewish Studies (*not*-philology, *not* history, *not*-source text) the "weak messianic forces" that, according to Benjamin, interrupt and redemptively fissure the continuity of history in its canonical form; a claim for the interface between canonical Jewish textual practice and the multiform practice(s) of contemporary Jewish Studies is still worth staking.

In another one of his "semitic" parables, Kafka wrote, "Ich könnte mir einen anderen Abraham": I can conceive of a different Abraham for myself—a non-heroic Abraham, a comic or at least laughable Abraham, an unsure Abraham, a Gopnik-like Abraham, an Abraham who fears he will transform into Don Quixote. The parable ends as follows:

> It is as if, at the end of the year, when the best student was solemnly about to receive a prize, the worst student rose in the expectant stillness and came forward from his dirty desk in the last row because he had made a mistake of hearing, and the whole class burst out laughing. And perhaps he had made no mistake at all, his name really was called, it having been the teacher's intention to make the rewarding of the best student at the same time a punishment for the worst one.

This reads like a scene from the Coens' movie, like the Hebrew School framing its opening and closing moments. As Derrida glosses Kafka's text, the other Abraham models a certain truth for its hearer-readers: "that anyone responding to the call must continue to doubt, to continue to ask whether he has heard right, whether there is an original misunderstanding."[63] (We might think, also, of Neusner's Moses.)

That there should be more than one Abraham, that Abraham can signify or generate alternate Abrahams, is not only "the most threatened Jewish thought," says Derrida, "but also the most vertiginously, most intimately Jewish one that I know to this day" (35). It also tells a tale of two (or more than one) Jewish Studies. Even if *nobody* understands the dead cat—underscoring "originary misunderstanding" as the very ethos of *ASM*—I believe something like these twin virtues of Jewish vertigo and Jewish intimacy trace a tangent (not continuity but contiguity) between the world of ritual renarration in foundational scripture and the denarrating world of the Coen Brothers' film.

And for those who prowl around Jewish discursive traditions—philologist-historians and cineastes (for the Coens, film scholar Jeffrey Adams prefers the term "epicureans"), *Wissenschaftler* and post-classical alike—"none comes straight down a broad, newly made, smooth road that does its own part in making one's strides long and swifter."[64] Indeed, maybe like Wittgenstein (who enjoyed going to movies), "we want to walk: so we need *friction*. Back to the rough ground!"[65] Answerability as interrogativity.

As Gerald Bruns has formulated the concept of satire in terms adaptable for JS and the mysterious finale of *ASM* alike, "It would not be too much to say that the earth [the primordial] is satirical with respect to the world [the human] precisely because its resistance is the world's limit and finitude, its situatedness or belonging-ness to history, its exposure to contingency."[66] And so finally, to redirect Larry Gopnik's question away from the lofty heights of divinity where it hangs suspended to such ground as the very condition of JS itself: feeling the question in absence of any positivistic answers may just have to suffice. If JS programs do not already lack for a Sy Abelman or a Nachtner in their rosters, they need their Gopniks and dybbuks, too.

EPILOGUE

Knotted thread, middle game: an *envoi*

> A historian who takes this as his point of departure stops telling the sequence of events like the beads of a rosary. Instead, he grasps the constellation which his own era has formed with a definite earlier one. Thus, he establishes a conception of the present as the "time of the now" which is shot through with chips of Messianic time.
>
> —WALTER BENJAMIN

The institution that *embodies* the mentality associated with acts of adhesion, we have been told, is the university. According to Levinas's formulation, analyzing and weighing oneself up defines the intellectual habits and sociopolitics of university life. All that we have said in this book about disciplinary frames of mind would seem to fall under the same rubric: one elects, believes in (gets stuck to?) a knowledge practice. Sociologists, musicologists, and evolutionary biologists represent creatures of *adhesion* in respect to the sciences they practice. So do humanists and *Wissenschaftler* of whichever pursuit.

When I broached the term "adhesion" in this book's introduction, I recast Levinas's rather disparaging frame of reference more positively in terms of "elective affinity" and "affiliative relation." The former, in the sense we associate with eighteenth-century chemistry (creatively refashioned by Goethe, and Max Weber after him, for the sphere of human relations), is a semantic neighbor of "adhesion," since it meant the property by which chemical substances become compounded.[1] In its modern usage, chemical affinity explains how certain atoms or molecules aggregate or bond with others of dissimilar composition—as Primo Levi well understood—a material correlate, so to speak, to chips of Messianic time.

In the culture of the university, acts of adhesion *elect* an affinity, choose, and create an affiliative relation to it. Edward Said's famous (and less than fully clarified) distinction between filiative (natal) and affliative (elective) relations at times suggests a progression—like the movement from *Gemeinschaft* to *Gesellschaft*, or nature to culture—and at other times, resembles something more dialectical or oscillating. According to David Shumway, the Saidian implication that affiliative choice transcends "the persistence of instinct" is itself chastened by the fact "that all those relations Said calls affiliations are internalized, where they function on the model of filiation."[2] The acts of adhesion we perform in the academy can aim at or be motivated by exteriority, but they never fully escape certain tribal, and as Garber reminds us, libidinal energies. Or in Shumway's compact formula, "Disciplinary identification is affiliative, but as identification it is also filial."

"Means of Identification" serves Levinas as a phrase for the "credentialing" of Jewish identity—as if such a thing were even necessary. Like Rosenzewig, he presumes a baseline *"kleiner Ruck"* [slight tug] by which one pre-adheres. Yet, it would seem to be so in a contemporary world where all identities—personal, social, professional, ethno-cultural, and so forth—can be reduced to "a series of signs, attributes, contents, qualities, and values." Disciplinary identity validates itself no differently, of course. And it explains why JS so often itself reduces to a series of guild-based signs, attributes, contents, qualities, and values that adhere to, or affiliate with, each other in the aggregate only loosely—non-elective affinities for which "Jewish Studies" serves merely as an artificial container.

In the introduction, I wondered aloud whether academicians could be said legitimately to "profess Jewish Studies." Inasmuch as Jewish historians identify primarily *as* historians, and rabbinics scholars likewise, as well as all the other small classes within the nominally encompassing proper class of JS that do not practicably feel any more strongly consolidated by being thus encompassed; inasmuch as all such disciplinary identities redraw the contours of a question about where JS belongs (external leverage) to one about their own intrinsic belonging under its auspices (internal leverage); inasmuch as the conditioned nature of institutionality lays itself barer than usual at the present time in our polity: "Jewish Studies" typifies what Bill Readings would recognize as an *administered* structure.

Affiliation lies at the core of Jewish Studies–as-counterlife, knitting together the various threads I have unspooled in this chapter and all the others. It describes the architectonics of the enterprise and explains its topographic history and evolution. It captures the intramural pathos of Jacob Neusner. It shadows the construction of the portable heterotopia by the alternately disaffiliated-reaffiliated Franz Rosenzweig. It decodes the grammar of conjunction whereby Jewish Studies makes common cause with assemblages across a shared boundary. Finally, it bespeaks the conjunctive syntax of and/and/and/and/and, for as readers of Philip Roth know well, perhaps nothing problematizes the self-evidence of "affiliation" more than "Jewishness."

Yet, if large-scale, variegated pursuits like Jewish Studies offer a wide field for affiliation as exercised by individual practitioners, it makes less sense to speak of the field itself as exercising, enmeshed in, or resisting affiliation. Or does it? A provisional answer can be found in the way two contributions to an essay-volume on academic affiliation, depart from the realm of the biographical (affiliations acquired, multiplied, abandoned) to some other platform for connectivity.

One reminds us that Roland Barthes spoke of a literary work being "caught up in a process of filiation," with the implication that "the Text is affiliative," producing set of connective articulations[3]—much like Dan Miron's "contiguity" or Dominick LaCapra's "articulatory practices." The other defines affiliation (as anticipated by my own metaphor above) as "threadedness: as in a filament joining concepts, thinkers, histories in . . . an alternative kinship, a loosely flexible lineage,"[4] which, evidently unknown to the author, echoes one of Levinas's more compelling metaphors about the generative interruption of discourse, *le fil renoué*, the re-tied, knotted thread[5]—so very different from continuity's beaded rosary.

As we conclude, could we not reasonably coax the figure in the direction of JS itself as a threaded and knotted project? The question of affiliation then becomes interpersonal, dialogically speaking, rather than merely personal, a matter of disciplinary identity. Aslant Levinas's assertion that one "just is a Jew," that Jewishness constitutes a given "means of identification," we have also learned that "identity" defined as categoricalness, as ascription, as legibility, as datum or textual attribute, misrepresents what more accurately should be acknowledged as a "project, produced in the institutionally bound activity of reading and deferred through an assemblage of metonymic recognitions."[6]

If Jewish identity is so assiduously policed by JS practices and scholars, then that disposition speaks rather for its elusiveness, the fact that it cannot be readily fixed. Archived, certainly. Secured: not quite. "What this country really needs is a good five-cent synthesis,"[7] quips Saul Bellow's valetudinarian *Bildungsheld*, Moses Herzog. For its part, however, Jewish Studies will probably not count as a dependable arena in which to circulate or be regulated by such synthesis, cut-rate or not—especially as market forces increasingly transform the deep structure of academia. What it can boast, however, are rich possibilities for affiliation on multiple levels and in diverse senses—something Bellow's perplexed protagonist rehearses in his many dealings, reveries, and offhand reports to the academy.

Although he intends it for quite different ends than I am postulating here, the memorable excursus on the 1966 Western, "The Ambiguities of *The Professionals*" by the decidedly non-Herzogian cultural theorist and Jewish academic Bruce Robbins[8] comes to mind at this concluding juncture. Speculating about the "comforting site where the spectator's confidence" across the range of various specialized characters that are viewed "can be total," Robbins writes,

> Is this because the narrower the activity, we believe, the greater the possibility of mastering it? More likely, it is because the specialized characters join together to form a team, a whole greater than the sum of its parts, and it is this whole, rather than any of the parts, that is most strongly identified with. Their heroics are harmonized; their individual expertises are vividly individualized only in order to be as vividly assimilated to a shared goal. . . . Membership in the collectivity is defined by a partial, peculiar transcendence of self. Individuality persists but only in the form of specialization; any self-interest at odds with or separable from the common interest of the group is effaced.[9]

As an allegory of academic specialization, this suggests a clearly different approach to self-transcendence than the one we saw espoused by Jacob Neusner in an earlier chapter. Neusner's stated ideal for his work was "to be made obsolete . . . by the greater achievements of my apprentices"[10]— as forthright a statement of filiality as one could wish for, but still quite otherwise than the affiliative economy Robbins identifies when he observes of the film that "the specialization of the 'handpicked' professionals seems by a strange economy to account for the fact that all emerge at the end alive" (30).

Specialization demands integration by group, just as the combine only makes sense as the agglomeration of multiple expertise. The analogy to academia falters, of course, when we consider that the professionals in the Lee Marvin movie are meant to be a *bande à part*, in stark opposition to civil society (which is why they resemble most their putative opposites, a regiment of Mexican guerrillas). Yet, Robbins's local analysis of "harmonized heroics" and self-transcending assimilation to a shared goal equally well describes the imagined machinery of affiliation of an academic program or unit like JS, at the lateral level where intellectual community, as the very logic of structure, is the aspect "most strongly identified with."

From this point, Robbins's ingenious reading proceeds in an alternate direction than my interests here. His model of professionalized intellectual within the academy ends up tracking closer to Edward Said than, say, Jacob Neusner or Franz Rosenzweig. Literary critics and cultural theorists epitomize his ideal specialist-professional.[11] Nevertheless, to envisage Jewish Studies affiliatively this way—on analogy with a *fil renoué* rather than, say, the "center of gravity . . . for order and intellectual community" (Neusner)—exchanges a centripetal, hierarchical structure for an "alternative kinship, a loosely flexible lineage" that recalls both Roth's formula of and/and/and/and/and as well as the weakly messianic visions of community advanced by Nancy and Agamben.

More than once, in earlier pages of this book, I referred to it as a kind of manifesto writ large. Its aim, however, has not been hard-eyed subversion.[12] Nor has it called for ambitious macro-reform.[13] Rather, it aspires modestly but still resolutely. In the conclusion to his genealogy of the interdisciplines, where, given its sheer ambition, one might expect large-scale, revolutionary recommendations, Roderick Ferguson advocates instead "small and seemingly insignificant acts [as] the basis of our alternatives."[14] For heroic agency and "will-to institutionality," Ferguson prefers a cultivation of the minor, more *picaresque* than *Bildungsroman*. "A syllabus, a job ad, a recruitment strategy, a memo, a book, an artwork, a report, an organizational plan, a protest—such are the little things that we can deploy in order to imagine critical forms of community" (232).

One can cavil: Those seem like rather trifling dividends to have reaped after such lengthy and heady theorizing. To avoid such a judgment, and because I genuinely deem it prudent, I prefer to set my sights on a middle ground between the seemingly insignificant and the Herculean, neither too unheroic as to be ultimately irrelevant nor too ostentatious as to be impracticable. I conclude the body of the book, then, with some bullet points for the swerve to which I gestured in the preface. Consider the following "action plan," then, as a small-scale fulcrum for a JS *mochlos* of the future—a (rough) guide for the (still) perplexed.

> Against the grain of specialists knowing how to speak chiefly to other specialists, I call on practitioners within a given JS program to live out the possibility evoked by Louis Menand for professors (and

graduate students, correspondingly) to be "produced in a different way." In practice that means striving to read each other's work, outside the proprietary protocols of research, in the twinned spirit of affiliative curiosity and dialogic responsibility. In short, I urge a grander bid for the *studies* in "Jewish Studies" that hearkens back to Derrida's crucial insight about the event of *founding* and an invigoratingly frictional relation to it.

Notwithstanding the circumscriptive field-specific rigors of *Wissenschaft*, such interchange and the intellectual fellowship it seeks to create could still embody "a profession of faith, a commitment, a promise, an assumed responsibility" at its most efficaciously local level. "Thought does not circulate; it waits upon our response," wrote Bill Readings. This formula bespeaks an aspiration toward a collegial dialogic more substantive than, say, interoffice memoranda or selecting the speaker for next year's flagship campus lecture—wherein "founding" signifies a power and a motivation no less exigent than funding.

If the initials "JS" aren't just to double for *joint stock*, then the intellectual company they presume should invite, rather, a Jewishly critical, richly affiliative *assembly of faces*—a coming community. In those programs with either deep benches or deep pockets that already embody this ideal, where elastically federated membership withstands management's complacent or reifying hand, the otherwise formulaic jargon of "best practices" is rightfully earned.

As to the borderlands, that terrain of the humanities and social sciences contiguous with Jewish Studies, one should wish for conduits extending from both sides. Self-sufficiency guarantees only that JS counts as merely one institutional silo among others. It counts as a reciprocally intellectual loss if neighboring or intersecting departments, tangent pedagogies of minority difference, area studies programs, and intellectual institutes and centers keep their distance from its alluvially salty, mustard-rich terrain, not to mention its unique pageant of chronotopes, languages, genres, and *Lebensformen*.

Not because they need to align themselves with another "emancipatory project." And not because an identity politics focused solely and negatively on Zionism or the State of Israel can obscure legitimate energies of emancipation. Rather, because the potential leverage and performative force of a Jewish Studies–to-come should be able to speak to the humanities at large about the history of its concepts and institutions. Too many forward-looking instances now crowd the academic book market in which the "Jewish" is left to signify either the bygone or simply, *other people's business*.

Citing Aristotle's *De Anima* in one of his university essays, Derrida contrasts a signal aspect of the human with its corresponding morphology in other species: the ability to blink. "What is terrifying about an animal with hard eyes and a dry glance is that it always sees. Man can lower the sheath, adjust the diaphragm, narrow his sight, the better to listen, remember, and learn" (132). In asking whether "the University is master of its own diaphragm," Derrida wishes to interrogate the visual depth of field on the part of its "body," the faculty (*corps professoral, corps enseignant*), to assess how well it sees "its own destination[,] that in view of which it stands its ground."

Slightly reorienting that capacity for adjusted sight, I would leave as an open question how capably, generously, and *diaphragmatically* the rest of the university "sees" Jewish Studies as a singularly multifaceted figure within its own multifaceted ground. Hard eyes and dry glances will not bestow on it the recognition it manifestly deserves. As for JS itself, one can only urge its university Others to reap the benefits that accrue to a blinking eye: listening, remembering, and learning.

Derrida's contemplation of the university's faculty as its "body should remind us not only of Kant (his persistent source in these essays), but also of his American epigone, Ralph Waldo Emerson, whose scholastic avatar "Man Thinking" we last glimpsed in this book's introduction. In his famous 1837 Phi Beta Kappa address and paean to intellectual exploit, "The American Scholar," Emerson recounts "the old fable" of One Man divided into men, "that he might be more helpful to himself; just as the hand was divided into fingers, the better to answer its end"—Heaney's opening hand, as it were, as a moral about affiliation. For this instrumental American retelling, "the fable implies that the individual, to possess himself, must sometimes return from his own labor to embrace all the other laborers."

> But unfortunately, this original unit, this fountain of power, has been so distributed to multitudes, has been so minutely subdivided and peddled out, that it is spilled into drops, and cannot be gathered. The state of society is one in which the members have suffered amputation from the trunk, and strut

about so many walking monsters—a good finger, a neck, a stomach, an elbow, but never a man.[15]

In their degenerative state, all such laborers have been collapsed into so many metonymies: "the attorney, a statute-book; the mechanic, a machine; the sailor, a rope of a ship."

Accordingly, Emerson distinguishes between the true scholar's function as "the delegated intellect," and in "the degenerative state," his reduction to a mere or derivative thinker. As the only mention of "university" in his famous essay is figurative and personified—the scholar "must be a university of knowledges"—I take the liberty of adding a supplement to Emerson's catalog of men metamorphosed into things by retrieving our figure from Chapter 1. That would be *the disciplinarian, a pitchfork*. Should s/he wish to aspire beyond mere disciplinary identity, Emerson's American Scholar, like his nineteenth-century German-Jewish counterparts in *Wissenschaft*, faces a set of new possibilities at the twenty-first-century sites of academic placement-and-displacement, centering-and-decentering.

When we remember, with Marjorie Garber, that the various recent proliferation of "studies" associated with the new humanities all depend upon a term that originally connoted *overlapping areas of interests as opposed to disciplines* (77), Jewish Studies offers a singular opportunity for cross-disciplinary "recommencement," the word that punctuates the first sentence of Emerson's address and to come full (Emersonian) circle, signals for Sacvan Bercovitch dynamic and recursive change, "resonant with alternative possibilities" (32) like a "middle game of chess."

Recommencement describes the very form of Emerson's essay, "whose rhythm and logic require us to reconceive the meaning of each of its parts" (55).[16] As Bercovitch explains some of the intricacies, chess's middle game comes to sound materially analogous to Roth's "counterlife," presented initially in the introduction as a figure for *beginning again*. "Positionality, inventiveness, and strategic combinations": these are some of its features; a middle game of chess "specializes in potentiality" (31). "Reciprocity" counts as another virtue: "a configuration of diachronic flow *and* synchronic structure that unsettles disciplinary endgames," where the strategy "is designed to mediate between ludic categories and categorical imperatives" (49).

While we should remain mindful of another of Bercovitch's provisos that such analogies work "insofar as we contextualize the game, globally as well as temporally" (41), the series of figures designed to reconceive my own subject across the range of this book's topics and chapters deserves one last superaddition: JS as *a middle-game of recommencement*, "a game of particulars, agency, predicaments, and limitations" (56).

"We in academia are part of the game plan, like it or not" (56), says Bercovitch toward the end of his essay. Surveying the terrain of the same Emerson text in the essay "Declining Decline," his late and esteemed colleague, Stanley Cavell, makes much of the caveat, "I ask not for the romantic." In respect to the work of aspiration and intellectual cultivation for the purpose of the "upbuilding of a man" (a phrase that "virtually pronounces *Bildung*"), Emerson tenders, "Here are materials strewn across the ground."[17] It is a phrase, says Cavell, "to be given the weight of, or the place of, or the power to displace, the philosophical idea of ground or foundation, a displacement which constitutes the scene or work of philosophical progress" (9).

Substitute for "philosophical" the words "humanistic" or "critical"—or for that matter, "institutional" and "interdiscursive"—and (with adjustments made) you have a signpost for Jewish Studies: that, to paraphrase Cavell's Emersonian voicing, "the [community] in its present form is a sign, representative of the [community] to be. Likewise, "*Here are materials strewn across the ground*," a possibly gnomic statement which, Cavell says, "we are invited to take in part as suggesting fragments or ruins" (8), might also suggest the specific work here before *us* now, the refashioning of the already upbuilt. And as we have already been advised, refashioning ruins within the environs of the university means dwelling within them, working without alibi.

It's there also that we meet the recommendation for the "shifting disciplinary structure that holds open the question of whether and how thoughts fit together" (Readings, 191) in the place of both autonomous disciplinarity and putatively unifying interdisciplinarity. Assuredly, this is not how the scholars of *Wissenschaft des Judentums* conceived their task; nor is it how Gershom Scholem, critiquing them, isolated "the demonic" in JS. Nor did it form part of the platform of the Association for Jewish Studies when it was formed in 1969.

And it only partially corresponds to the agenda of the "new Jewish cultural studies," the name of a then-cutting-edge book (now two decades old) when the culture wars were brand-new. If we entertain the possibility that the silent partner evoked in the phraseology of "an attention to otherness" is Emmanuel Levinas (implied as much in Readings's endnotes),[18] then reciprocal, positively estimated acts of adhesion between the university and JS may have as much to say to the institution as they do to a pluralized understanding of Jewish Studies and its dialogical possibilities.

Such possibilities have taken shape partly in this book through its orchestrated voices and contrapuntal discourses, which, to inveigle one last smile from Rosenzweig, express Derrida's "community of the question" as a *Chors des Fragenden*. In the last pages of this book, that choir-community has included not only Emerson, Readings, Levinas, Derrida, and Rosenzweig, but also the linked figures of Stanley Cavell and Sacvan Bercovitch.

Like Bercovitch and Kun in the introduction, they epitomize a category of Jewish academic that, while not formally participating in or espousing JS *per se*, provides a transferential model of crossing-over that anticipates my own very deliberate, interdiscursive experimentation in genre traversal.

In taking a position toward the structures that regulate its practices, I have projected a Jewish Studies–to-come as an exemplary occasion for institutional leverage—the support for leaping to another place. This would mark the kind of founding (Derrida) by which we also find ourselves (Cavell's Emersonian analogue). Like an America-to-come, near yet not entirely within grasp,[19] it cannot be approached alone, for "the eventual human community," says Cavell, "is between us or nowhere" (108). Where Emerson calls for a regrounded philosophy, so a different and more chromatic horizon for JS is being summoned here. Call it a recommencement.

Will a door be wedged, a wooden bean applied, a lock jimmied? That has been a wager of this report on and to a community of the question. During its composition, the ground under American feet shifted dramatically. About the tectonics of higher education and the future disposition of its shifting boundaries, one can only speculate. As to a project such as Jewish Studies, locally sited and globally tilted, a foundation underpins but does not fix the acts and performances that seek leverage there. What, then, does *JS as counterlife* finally signify?

A re-founding.[20]

NOTES

PREFACE AND ACKNOWLEDGMENTS

1. Robert Musil, *The Man without Qualities*, trans. Sophie Wilkins (New York: Alfred A. Knopf, 1995), 267.

2. Programs in the United States and Canada are the primary focus here; a consideration of their counterparts in Europe, Israel, Asia, and Latin America would require a different cultural-historical lens. The "Jewish Studies in Comparative Contexts" section in *Teaching Jewish Civilization: A Global Approach to Higher Education*, ed. Moshe Davis (New York: New York University Press, 1995), provides initial purchase.

3. Hence, the subtitle for an essay in *Tablet Magazine* about seventeenth-century jurist John Selden: "How the modern academic discipline of 'Jewish Studies' was invented in Renaissance England by the greatest Christian Hebraist of the age," December 15, 2017, www.tabletmag.com/jewish-arts-and-culture/251506/john-selden-and-restoration-of-jews-to-england.

4. Two recent, albeit contrastive, examples: Jay R. Berkovitz's *Protocols of Justice: The Pinkas of the Metz Rabbinic Court 1771–1789* (Leiden: Brill, 2016), a legitimate feat of documentary archivalism; and Hannah Pollin-Galay's *Ecologies of Witnessing: Language, Place, and Holocaust Testimony* (New Haven, Conn.: Yale University Press, 2018), a prodigious melding of oral history, genre, and the poetics of place.

5. The primacy of Jewish law as devotional study and devotional study as Jewish thought garners theoretical attention in Chaim N. Saiman, *Halakhah: The Rabbinic Idea of Law* (Princeton, N.J.: Princeton University Press, 2018).

6. Louis Menand, *The Marketplace of Ideas: Reform and Resistance in the American University* (New York: W. W. Norton & Company, 2010), 92. A perceptive appraisal of Menand's own ideas can be found in Jeffrey R. Di Leo's review, *Comparatist* 35 (May 2011): 249–254.

7. Gershom Scholem, "Reflections on Modern Jewish Studies," in *On the Possibility of Jewish Mysticism in Our Time and Other Essays*, ed. Avraham Shapira, trans. Jonathan Chipman (Philadelphia: Jewish Publication Society, 1997), 58, 63.

8. In *Happiness, Death, and the Remainder of Life* (Cambridge, Mass.: Harvard University Press, 2000), philosopher Jonathan Lear identifies "swerves" and "breaks" as two principal categories of self-disruption. Even if the latter proves the more psychically transformative—"a possibility for new possibilities" (118)—the former expresses the *reasonable perturbation* of everyday life, where "the space of reason is always and everywhere susceptible to being bent out of shape" (115).

9. Bill Readings, *The University in Ruins* (Cambridge, Mass.: Harvard University Press, 1996), 156.

10. Emmanuel Levinas, *Otherwise Than Being: Or, Beyond Essence*, trans. Alphonso Lingis (Pittsburgh, Pa.: Duquesne University Press, 1981), 171.

11. www.sefaria.org/Chagigah.3b?lang=bi.

12. www.sefaria.org/Kiddushin.29a?lang=bi. The explanation appears on page 30b in the same tractate: "Because their life may depend upon it."

INTRODUCTION

1. From the comic strip "Metamorphosis" by Eli Valley, originally published in *The Forward*, November 25, 2009, www.elivalley.com/comics/metamorphosis/.

2. A configuration coincidentally anticipated by Haeckel himself in an embryological illustration that juxtaposes the eggs of human, dog, and ape in *Die Natürliche Schöpfungsgeschichte* (Berlin: Georg Reimer, 1868), fig. 5–7, 242.

3. Sacvan Bercovitch, "The Music of America," in *The Rites of Assent: Transformations in the Symbolic Constructions of America* (New York: Routledge, 1993), 12. The essay was published separately under the title, "Investigations of an Americanist," *Journal of American History* 78 (1991): 972–987.

4. Joshua Kun, *Audiotopia: Music, Race, and America* (Berkeley: University of California Press, 2005), 12.

5. On the Jewishness of American Studies, see Jonathan Freedman, "Do American and Ethnic American Studies Have a Jewish Problem; or, When Is an Ethnic Not an Ethnic, and What Should We Do about It?" *MELUS* 37.2 (Summer 2012): 19–40.

6. First appearing in print in 1917, together with "Schakale und Araber," in the monthly magazine *Der Jude*, edited by Martin Buber.

7. In *Elizabeth Costello* (New York: Penguin Books, 2004), by J. M. Coetzee, the protagonist coordinates Kafka's two animal narrators, if only by contrast, by distinguishing Rotpeter as "not an investigator of primate behavior but a branded, marked, wounded animal presenting himself as speaking testimony to a gathering of scholars" (70). See also Coetzee's *The Lives of Animals* (Princeton, N.J.: Princeton University Press, 1999).

8. Franz Kafka, *The Complete Stories*, ed. Nahum N. Glatzer (New York: Schocken Books, 1995), 285.

9. The title phrase of Rael Meyerowitz, *Transferring to America: Jewish Interpretations of American Dreams* (Albany: State University of New York Press, 1995).

10. Philip Roth, *The Counterlife* (New York: Farrar, Straus and Giroux, 1986), 147.

11. William Gass, "Deciding to Do the Impossible," *New York Times Book Review*, January 4, 1987, 25.

12. Debra B. Shostak's phrase, from *Philip Roth: Countertexts, Counterlives* (Columbia: University of South Carolina Press, 2004), 187.

13. Emily Miller Budick, "Performing Jewish Identity in Philip Roth's *Counterlife*," in *Key Texts in American Jewish Culture*, ed. Jack Kugelmass (New Brunswick, N.J.: Rutgers University Press, 2003), 79.

14. Agata Bielik-Robson, *Jewish Cryptotheologies of Late Modernity: Philosophical Marranos* (New York: Routledge, 2014), 4.

15. "Qu'est-ce qu'une nation?," trans. Ethan Rundell (Presses-Pocket, 1992).

16. Benjamin Schreier, *The Impossible Jew: Identity and the Reconstruction of Jewish American Literary History* (New York: New York University Press, 2015).

17. Ziad Elmarsafy, "Aping the Ape: Kafka's 'Report to an Academy,'" *Studies in Twentieth-Century Literature* (1995): 159–170.

18. Dan Miron, *From Continuity to Contiguity: Toward a New Jewish Literary Thinking* (Stanford: Stanford University Press, 2010), 359.

19. Augustine, *Confessions*, Book X, ed. J. J. O'Donnell (New York: Oxford University Press, 2013), www.stoa.org/hippo/frame_entry.html.

20. Marjorie Garber, *Academic Instincts* (Princeton, N.J.: Princeton University Press, 2009), ix.

21. On this "too-much," see Lear's *Happiness*, 109–111.

22. Louis Menand, *Marketplace of Ideas: Reform and Resistance in the American University* (New York: W. W. Norton & Company, 2010), 119.

23. The title of a *New York Times* op-ed by Mark C. Taylor, April 26, 2009, sec. A23, www.nytimes.com/2009/04/27/opinion/27taylor.html. An expanded argument is conducted in the same author's *Crisis on Campus: A Bold Plan for Reforming Our Colleges and Universities* (New York: Alfred A. Knopf, 2010); see also Marc Bousquet, *How the University Works: Higher Education and the Low-Wage Nation* (New York: New York University Press, 2008).

24. Willi Goetschel, *The Discipline of Philosophy and the Invention of Modern Jewish Thought* (New York: Fordham University Press, 2013).

25. For the supplement to the supplement and margin around the margin here—i.e., the role played by gender in academic Jewish philosophy—see the excellent collection in Hava Tirosh-Samuelson, ed., *Women and Gender in Jewish Philosophy* (Bloomington: Indiana University Press, 2004).

26. The term, indicating a universalist aesthetic, became popular in art and architecture circles a decade ago. As such, it is explained in the following conversation between Armen Avanessian and Suhail Malikin in *DIS* magazine, dismagazine.com/discussion/81924/the-time-complex-postcontemporary/.

27. Jacques Derrida, *Without Alibi*, trans. Peggy Kamuf (Stanford: Stanford University Press, 2002), 202–237.

28. Scott Heller, "The New Jewish Studies: Defying Tradition and Easy Categorization," *Chronicle of Higher Education*, January 1999, A21.

29. Scott Jaschik, "The New Jewish Studies," *Inside Higher Ed*, December 21, 2005, www.insidehighered.com/news/2005/12/21/jewish.

30. The immediate context of the debate on "multiculturalism" dates these concerns by more than a decade. See Sara R. Horowitz, "The Paradox of Jewish Studies in the New Academy," in *Insider/Outsider: American Jews and Multiculturalism*, ed. David Biale et al. (Berkeley: University of California Press, 1998).

31. Yaakov Elman, "Review of Daniel Boyarin, *A Traveling Homeland: The Babylonian Talmud as Diaspora*," *AJS Review* 40.1 (April 2016): 168–171.

32. Daniel Boyarin, "Jewish Studies as Teratology: The Rabbis as Monsters," *Jewish Quarterly Review* 88.1/2 (July–October, 1997), 57–66.

33. "Michigan State University Jewish Studies Newsletter" (Spring 2006), jsp.msu.edu/wp-content/uploads/2013/03/Spring-2006-Newsletter.pdf.

34. Sergey Dolgopolski, *The Open Past: Subjectivity and Remembering in the Talmud* (New York: Fordham University Press, 2013); *What Is Talmud?* (New York: Fordham University Press, 2009); *Other Others: The Political after the Talmud* (New York: Fordham University Press, 2017); Marc Caplan, *How Strange the Change: Language, Temporality, and Narrative Form in Peripheral Modernisms* (Stanford: Stanford University Press, 2011); Zachary Braiterman, *The Shape of Revelation: Aesthetics and Modern Jewish Thought* (Stanford: Stanford University Press, 2007).

35. The latter coinage belongs to Jonathan Boyarin, from *Thinking in Jewish* (University of Chicago Press, 1996), with a new foreword at ingeveb.org/articles/yiddish-science-and-the-postmodern. As early as 1901, Martin Buber called for a "*Jüdische Wissenschaft*" alternative to a *Wissenschaft des Judentums*: "a smaller part ... embodied in what is presently called the

Science of Judaism; its greater part is in various other disciplines. And it is not a matter of creating, but one of tracing and linkage." Buber, "Jewish Scholarship: New Perspectives," in *The Jew in the Modern World: A Documentary History*, ed. Paul Mendes-Flohr and Jehuda Reinharz (New York: Oxford University Press, 2010), 214–242.

36. Andrew Bush, *Jewish Studies: A Theoretical Introduction* (New Brunswick, N.J.: Rutgers University Press, 2011), 4.

37. Ra'anan S. Boustan, Oren Kosansky, and Marina Rustow, eds., *Jewish Studies at the Crossroads of Anthropology and History: Authority, Diaspora, Tradition* (Philadelphia: University of Pennsylvania Press, 2011), 4.

38. In article form, the subject of thoughtful critique by Zachary Braiterman, "Too Jewish Studies (Response to Aaron Hughes)," *Jewish Philosophy Place* (May 8, 2014), jewishphilosophyplace.com/ 2014/05/08/ too-jewish-studies-response-to-aaron-hughes/.

39. Jonathan Boyarin, "Responsive Thinking: Cultural Studies and Jewish Historiography," in *Modern Judaism and Historical Consciousness: Identities, Encounters, Perspectives*, ed. Andreas Gotzmann and Christian Wiese (Leiden: Brill, 2007), 477–478; also, Michael Kramer's argument against the "casuistry of metonymical ethnicity" in "Race, Literary History, and the 'Jewish' Question," *Prooftexts* 21.3 (2001): 287–349.

40. Schreier, *Impossible Jew*, 11. See also Cynthia Baker, *Jew*, 65ff.

41. Susannah Heschel, "Jewish Studies Program Review" (New England: Dartmouth College Press, 2003), 3.

42. Talal Asad, *Formations of the Secular: Christianity, Islam, Modernity* (Stanford: Stanford University Press, 2003).

43. David Blumenthal, "Where Does 'Jewish Studies' Belong?," *Journal of the American Academy of Religion* 44.3 (1976): 535–546.

44. Emmanuel Levinas, *Difficult Freedom: Essays on Judaism*, trans. Seán Hand (Baltimore: Johns Hopkins University Press, 1990), 50.

45. Levinas uses the same expression in *Beyond the Verse: Talmudic Readings and Lectures*, trans. Gary D. Mole (London: Athlone Press, 1994), 119.

46. Astutely and especially apropos of the current political climate, Levinas connects the comparativist mentality to "nationalist movements" in which, he says, it "uncovers something savage."

47. Edward Said, "Secular Criticism," in *The World, the Text, and the Critic* (Cambridge, Mass.: Harvard University Press, 1983), 1–30; and Stathis Gourgouris, *Lessons in Secular Criticism* (New York: Fordham University Press, 2013), 8.

48. English translation of *Zeh Im Hapanim Elenu* by the late Israeli novelist Ronit Matalon.

49. Stefan Maechler, *The Wilkomirski Affair: A Study in Biographical Truth* (New York: Schocken Books, 2001); and Tom, Reiss, *The Orientalist: Solving the Mystery of a Strange and Dangerous Life* (New York: Random House, 2005).

50. Harvey Shapiro, *Educational Theory and Jewish Studies in Conversation: From Volozhin to Buczacz* (Lanham: Lexington Books, 2013), 16.

51. Leslie Morris, "Placing and Displacing Jewish Studies: Notes on the Future of a Field," *PMLA* 125.3 (2010): 764–773.

52. See Scott Jaschik, "The Lost Tribe," *Inside Higher Ed*, December 28, 2009, www.insidehighered.com/news/2009/12/28/jews; and the Freedman, "When Is an Ethnic Not an Ethnic."

53. Dominick LaCapra, "The University in Ruins?," *Critical Inquiry* 25.1 (Autumn 1998): 32–55. In a footnote, LaCapra (in unintended echo of Buber) emphasizes the "importance of pointing out the problem of articulation, even when significant linkages may not be found, and holding open the possibility of future linkages" (53).

54. As in the Cavell-inflected essay by Paddy Scannell, "The Life of the University," in *Making the University Matter*, ed. Barbie Zelizer (New York: Routledge: 2011), 17–22.

55. Mikhail Epstein, *The Transformative Humanities: A Manifesto* (New York: Bloomsbury, 2012).

56. Moshe Davis, ed. *Teaching Jewish Civilization: A Global Approach to Higher Education* (New York: New York University Press, 1995), 54.

57. As a present participle, the term was used by Kierkegaard and retrieved by Samuel Weber, in "The Future of the Humanities. Experimenting," *Culture Machine* 2, 2000, www.culturemachine.net/index.php/cm/article/view/311/296.

58. Giorgio Agamben, Part 3 of *Potentialities: Collected Essays in Philosophy*, trans. Daniel Heller-Roazen (Stanford: Stanford University Press, 1999), 177–240.

59. Gerald L. Bruns, *Hermeneutics Ancient and Modern* (New Haven, Conn.: Yale University Press, 1995), 204.

60. Bruns on satire as "social medium," tradition as the place that "registers" it, 208–212.

61. Cynthia Franklin, *Academic Lives: Memoir, Cultural Theory, and the University Today* (Athens: University of Georgia Press, 2009), 3.

62. Frank Lentricchia, *Ariel and the Police: Michel Foucault, William James, Wallace Stevens* (Madison: University of Wisconsin Press, 1988), 3.

63. Primo Levi, *The Periodic Table*, trans. Raymond Rosenthal (New York: Schocken Books, 1984), 34.

64. *Postfazione* to *Il processo* [*Der Prozeß*], trans. Primo Levi (Einaudi, 1983).

65. David Grossman, "Letter from Israel: Fifty Is a Dangerous Age," trans. Chaim Watzman, *New Yorker* (April 20, 1998), 56.

66. Edward A. Portnoy, "Modicut Puppet Theatre: Modernism, Satire, and Yiddish Culture," *TDR: The Drama Review* 43.3 (T 163) (Fall 1999), 115–134.

INTERCHAPTER I: *JS DAVKA*

1. Hebrew/Aramaic from a root meaning "thin" or "fine," it has several connotations in modern spoken Hebrew, including "actually," "precisely," "in spite of all." Regarding the Yiddish intensifier "*dafke*," see Jordan D. Finkin, *A Rhetorical Conversation: Jewish Discourse in Modern Yiddish Literature* (Philadelphia: University of Pennsylvania Press, 2010), 79ff.

2. The text is read to different effect by David Suchoff, *Kafka's Jewish Languages: The Hidden Openness of Tradition* (Philadelphia: University of Pennsylvania Press, 2012), 36; and Vivian Liska, *When Kafka Says We: Uncommon Communities in German-Jewish Literature* (Bloomington: Indiana University Press, 2009), 23–25.

3. The phrase belongs to Pierre Bourdieu, from the preface to the English edition of *Homo Academicus*, trans. Peter Collier (Stanford: Stanford University Press, 1988).

4. The focus, with reference to Ferdinand Tönnies, of Mark E. Blum, *Kafka's Social Discourse: An Aesthetic Search for Community* (Bethlehem, Pa.: Lehigh University Press), 2011.

5. Martin Buber, "Die Lösung," [The Watchword] Zur Programmatik der Zeitschrift, *Der Jude* 1 (1916): 1–2. Quoted in Michael Brenner, *The Renaissance of Jewish Culture in Weimar Germany* (New Haven, CT: Yale University Press, 1996), 36.

6. Franz Kafka, *Letters to Felice*, trans. James Stern (New York: Schocken, 2016), 157–158.

7. Braiterman, *Shape of Revelation*, 42.

1. JEWISH STUDIES AS LEVER

1. See the volume, *Languages of Modern Jewish Culture: Comparative Perspectives*, ed. Joshua L. Miller and Anita Norich (Ann Arbor: University of Michigan Press, 2016).

2. The main web page indicates that the site (consisting of links to academic associations, libraries, archives, Jewish Studies at universities, research institutes, and other internet resources was last updated in May 2017; the specific web page for "Jewish Studies at universities," however, was last updated in June, 2012.

3. Arnold J. Band's 1967 article for the *American Jewish Yearbook*, "Jewish Studies in American Liberal-Arts Colleges and Universities," vol.

67, 3–30, tabulates faculty according to their specializations for forty JS programs, but one indicator of many that would need to be included for any dependable and instructive statistical survey fifty years later.

4. The entry is headed by a "Cleanup" message (from September 2012) and whisk broom icon to signal that "the page reads like a promotional guide to various Judaic studies programs."

5. David Blumenthal, "Jewish Studies and Religious Studies," *Religious Education* 81.1 (Winter 1986): 29–36.

6. *Moby Dick*, chapter 89. Inasmuch as Ishmael forms the "opening hand" to Ahab's "pitchfork (a distinction I develop in the next chapter), the landscape of Melville's novel presents an intriguing space in which to consider both abstract and embodied questions of relatedness and community. See, for instance, Lisa Ann Robertson, "'Universal Thump': The Redemptive Epistemology of Touch in *Moby-Dick*," *Leviathan* 12.2 (June 2010): 5–20.

7. Judith R. Baskin's short history, "Jewish Studies in North American Colleges and Universities: Yesterday, Today, and Tomorrow," *Shofar* 32.4 (2014): 9–26, is instructive, as is the one traced by Martin Kavka in "What Does It Mean to Receive Tradition? Jewish Studies in Higher Education," *Crosscurrents* (Summer 2006): 180–197.

8. Boustan, Kosansky, and Rustow, "Anthropology, History, and the Remaking of Jewish Studies," in *Jewish Studies at the Crossroads*, 10.

9. A corrective to the standard account can be found in Frederick E. Greenspahn's "The Beginnings of Judaic Studies in American Universities," *Modern Judaism* 20 (2000): 209–225.

10. Scholem's "Reflections on Modern Jewish Studies" (*Mi-Tokh Hirhurim 'al Hokhmat Yisrael*), along with the redoubtable genealogies by Isidore Elbogen (1922) and Alexander Altmann (1957).

11. Thus, see Gerson Cohen, "An Embarrassment of Riches: Reflections on the Conditions of American Jewish Scholarship in 1969," in *The Teaching of Judaica in American Universities*, ed. Leon A. Jick (New York: Ktav Publishing, 1970).

12. See, among other sources, the articles by William Brinner, George L. Mosse, David Myers, and Martin Jay in "The Origins of Modern Jewish Studies and the Founding of the Hebrew University," *Judaism* 45 (Spring 1996): 131–163; and Ismar Schorsch, *From Text to Context: The Turn to History in Modern Judaism* (Lebanon, N.H.: University Press of New England, 2003).

13. Bryan Cheyette's essay, "Against Supersessionist Thinking: Old and New, Jews and Postcolonialism, the Ghetto and Diaspora," *Cambridge Journal of Postcolonial Literary Inquiry* 4.3 (September 2017): 424–439,

positions this problem—the "belonging" of JS—athwart certain proclivities in postcolonialist inquiry, rejoined ed. by Michael Rothberg's "For Activist Thought: A Response to Bryan Cheyette" in the same journal, Vol. 5.1 (January 2018), 115–122.

14. Gershom Scholem, *The Messianic Idea in Judaism and Other Essays on Jewish Spirituality* (New York: Schocken Books, 1971), 311.

15. The principal controversy at the first meeting of the AJS in 1969 was the nature of the relationship between a scholarly association and the larger Jewish community. See Kirsten Loveland, "The Association for Jewish Studies: A Brief History" (AJS Annual Conference, December 21, 2008), www.ajsnet.org/ajs.pdf. On Neusner and the AJS, see Aaron W. Hughes, *Jacob Neusner: An American Jewish Iconoclast* (New York: New York University Press, 2016), 119ff.

16. On this topic, see Dan Miron, *From Continuity to Contiguity: Toward a New Jewish Literary Thinking* (Stanford: Stanford University Press, 2010).

17. On "content" and "aspect," see Bush, *Theoretical Introduction*, 8–9. A selection of Scholem's poetry has been translated as *The Fullness of Time: Poems*, trans. Richard Sieburth (Jerusalem: Ibis Editions, 2003); see also *Gershom Scholem: Literatur und Rhetorik*, ed. Sigrid Weigel, Stéphane Mosès (Cologne: Bohlau, 2000). Kurzweil was a notable critic of Scholem as both legatee of the *Wissenschaft* tradition and its foremost post-assimilatory "normalizer." On a public exchange between the two in 1965, see David Myers, "The Scholem-Kurzweil Debate and Modern Jewish Historiography," *Modern Judaism* 6.3 (October 1986), 261–286.

18. Shira Wolosky, "A Jewish-American Poetics," *The Cambridge Companion to Jewish American Literature*, ed. Michael Kramer, Hanna Wirth-Nesher (Cambridge: Cambridge University Press, 2003), 250–268.

19. Heschel, "Jewish Studies Program Review," 5.

20. For example, Nicholas Royle, "Yes, Yes, the University in Ruins," *Critical Inquiry* 26.1 (Autumn 1999): 147–153; Samuel Weber, "The Future of the University: The Cutting Edge," in *Ideas of the University*, ed. Terry Smith (Sydney: Sydney University Press, 1996), 43–75; Srinivas Aravamudan,"The Character of the University," *Boundary 2* 37:1 (2010): 23–55; and Jeffrey J. Williams, "History as a Challenge to the Idea of the University," *JAC* 25.1 (2005): 55–74.

21. Bill Readings, *The University in Ruins* (Cambridge, Mass.: Harvard University Press, 1996), 168.

22. "Lyrik der Kabbalah," *Der Jude* 6.1 (1921–22): 55–69.

23. See especially in this context, Elena Makarova, Sergei Makarov, and Victor Kuperman, eds., *University Over the Abyss: The Story Behind 520*

Lecturers and 2,430 Lectures in KZ Theresienstadt 1942–1944 (Jerusalem: Verba Publishers Ltd., 2004).

24. Leslie Morris, "Placing and Displacing Jewish Studies: Notes on the Future of a Field." *PMLA* 125. 3 (May 2010): 765–776.

25. Jacques Derrida, *Without Alibi*, trans. Peggy Kamuf (Stanford: Stanford University Press, 2002), 212.

26. Derek Attridge, "The Humanities without Condition: Derrida and the Singular Oeuvre," *Arts and Humanities in Higher Education* 13.1–2 (2014): 54–61.

27. For instance, the essays collected in Patrik Svensson and David Theo Goldberg, eds., *Between Humanities and the Digital* (Cambridge, Mass.: MIT Press, 2015); and also Taylor's *Crisis on Campus*.

28. The phrase belongs to philosopher Hermann Levin Goldschmidt, the title of his seminal work *Das Vermächtnis des deutschen Judentums* (1957).

29. Willi Goetschel points out that the reified opposition between Hebrew and Greek, Athens and Jerusalem, in nineteenth-century thought "served as a displaced reiteration of the exercise of asking the question of what was modern and how to define modernity" (36).

30. Jonathan Boyarin, "Responsive Thinking: Cultural Studies and Jewish Historiography," in *Modern Judaism and Historical Consciousness: Identities, Encounters, Perspectives*, ed. Andreas Gotzmann and Christian Wiese (Leiden: Brill, 2007), 477–478.

31. For example, "Ballads of Itzik Manger," *Moment* 3.4 (1978): 44–52.

32. Specific to the discourses of JS are German-Jewish intellectual figures for whom the dialogic becomes a core concept, like Rosenzweig, Buber, and Goldschmidt. Yet, I invoke Bakhtin because the metaphors he customarily employs for it cluster around genre and discourse *per se*.

33. M. M. Bakhtin, "Response to a Question from the *Novy Mir* Editorial Staff," in *Art and Answerability: Early Philosophical Essays*, trans. Vadim Liapunov and Kenneth Brostrom (Austin: University of Texas Press, 1981), 274.

34. M. M. Bakhtin, "From Notes Made in 1970–71," in *Speech Genres and Other Late Essays*, trans. Vern W. McGee (Austin: University of Texas Press, 1986), 155.

35. His *"Einleitendes"* to *Monatsschrift für die Geschichte und Wissenschaft des Judenthums* Vol. 1 (1852) declares history to be "the most effective lever to awaken renewed interest in higher things [*das Höhere*]" (3) and *Wissenschaft des Judentums*, the religion's "most powerful lever, without which there is no Judaism" (5); cited in Michael Meyer, "Two Persistent Tensions within Wissenschaft Des Judentums," *Modern Judaism* 24.2 (May 2004), an acute survey of its exponents' religious motivation (notwithstanding the principled secularism of figures like Zunz and Steinschneider, and discernible even in Scholem).

36. Jacques Derrida, *Eyes of the University: Right to Philosophy 2*, trans. Jan Plug (Stanford: Stanford University Press, 2004), 90.

37. Immanuel Kant, *The Conflict of the Faculties*, trans. Mary J. Gregor (Norwalk, Conn.: Abaris Books, 1979), 30.

38. Compare Lear's analysis of psycho-economic "remainder" in *Happiness*: "If we think of a name as standing unproblematically for that which it names, then an *inaugural* act of naming . . . always misses its mark." (95).

39. Vilém Flusser, "On the Word Design: An Etymological Essay," trans. J. Cullars, *Design* 11.3 (Autumn 1995): 50–53.

40. Point of support or fulcrum of a lever, center of rotation of a joint, point of rest of a process.

41. Timothy Bahti, "The Injured University," in *Logomachia: The Conflict of the Faculties*, ed. Richard A. Rand (Lincoln: University of Nebraska Press, 1992), 69.

42. In respect to the question of translation (as pertinent for Derrida as for Kant), the metaphor is also used to quite beautiful effect by Nidra Poller in her translator's note to Levinas's *Humanism of the Other* (Champaign: University of Illinois Press, 2003) when she speaks of honoring the alterity of text or authorial intelligence (and one could add, knowledge practice/disciplinary tradition) by "finding one's personal point of leverage" (xlvi).

43. Stathis Gourgouris, *Lessons in Secular Criticism* (New York: Fordham University Press, 2013), 25.

44. Jacques Derrida, "Education as Poetry: A Meditative Monologue," in *The Collected Prose of Robert Frost*, ed. Mark Richardson, 2007, 106.

45. David M. Myers, "Rethinking the Jewish Nation: An Exercise in Applied Jewish Studies," *Havruta Journal* (Winter 2011): 26–33.

46. *Avot d'Rabbi Natan* Version A, chap. 6, www.sefaria.org/Avot_D'Rabbi_Natan?lang=bi.

INTERCHAPTER II: THE DIALECTICS OF OWNERSHIP

1. Max Weber, "Science as a Vocation," in *Max Weber, Essays in Sociology*, trans. H. H. Gerth and C. Wright Mills (New York: Oxford University Press, 1946), 34.

2. Walter Benjamin, "Unpacking My Library: A Talk about Book Collecting," in *Illuminations: Essays and Reflections*, ed. Hannah Arendt, trans. Harry Zohn (New York: Schocken Books, 1968), 59–67.

3. Similar kinds of questions prompt José Ángel García Landa's "Unpacking Benjamin: A Note on Walter Benjamin's 'Unpacking My Library: A Talk about Book Collecting'" (1988), www.unizar.es/departamentos/filologia_inglesa/garciala/publicaciones/benjamin.html.

4. On this point, see Joseph D. Lewandowski, "Unpacking: Walter Benjamin and His Library," *Libraries & Culture* 34.2 (Spring 1999): 151–157.

5. As described in David Gilmour's introduction to *The Siren and Selected Writings*, trans. Archibald Colquhoun, David Gilmour, and Guido Waldman (London: Harvill Press, 1995).

6. Rosenzweig's phrase, cited by Paul Mendes-Flohr, "The Jew as Cosmopolitan," in *Divided Passions: Jewish Intellectuals and the Experience of Modernity* (Detroit, Mich.: Wayne State University Press, 1991), 413–423.

7. Ralph Ellison, *Invisible Man* (New York: Vintage Books, 1995), 561.

8. Derek Walcott, *The Prodigal* (New York: Farrar, Straus and Giroux, 2004), 99.

2. JEWISH STUDIES AND THE PITCHFORK

1. Anne Golomb Hoffman, "Topographies of Reading: Agnon through Benjamin," *Prooftexts* 21.1 (Winter 2001): 74.

2. Geoffrey Galt Harpham, *The Humanities and the Dream of America* (Chicago: University of Chicago Press, 2011), 40.

3. Or, as Joseph Conrad, an author of special consequence to both Harpham and myself, expresses a similar idea in "The End of the Tether": "And our conduct after all is so much a matter of outside suggestion," in *From Youth, Heart of Darkness, the End of the Tether*, ed. Owen Knowles (Cambridge: Cambridge University Press, 2010), 237.

4. And thus, see Abigail Wood, "The Cantor and the Muezzin's Duet: Contested Soundscapes at Jerusalem's Western Wall," *Contemporary Jewry* 35.1 (April 2015): 55–72.

5. David Biale, Michael Galchinsky, and Susannah Heschel, eds., *Insider/Outsider: American Jews and Multiculturalism* (Berkeley: University of California Press, 1998), 101–116.

6. In his *Theoretical Introduction*, Bush explains the work of "counter" for JS as parallel to that of "post" in other allied fields (37).

7. The story is part of a triad within a group of six examples, all conforming to the same pattern of outcome: Shammai rejects while Hillel accepts. The organizing *sugya* (literary-analytic unit) is framed by two summary comments praising Hillel as *anvetan* (gentle person).

8. As another anecdote in the same grouping shows Shammai brandishing the builder's rod, Jeffrey L. Rubenstein speculates that Shammai must customarily carry the tool on his person, in *Rabbinic Stories*, ed. Rubenstein and Shaye J. D. Cohen (Mahwah, N.J.: Paulist Press, 2002), 291.

9. Jacques Derrida, *The Truth in Painting*, trans. Geoff Bennington and Ian McLeod (Chicago: University of Chicago Press, 1987), 12. Of this working of *paraergon*, Derrida writes that it "comes against, beside, and in

addition to the *ergon*, the work done (*fait*), the fact (*le fait*), the work, but it does not fall to one side; it touches and cooperates within the operation, from a certain outside. Neither simply outside nor simply inside. Like an accessory that one is obliged to welcome on the border, on board (*au bord, à bord*)" (45).

10. *Regula* could have been known to first-century Jews through both Greek and Latin usage, suggests Jospe in "Hillel's Rule," *Jewish Quarterly Review* 81.1/2 (July–October 1990): 45–57, explaining further that, "in addition to the metaphoric usage of 'foot' as a principle or foundation of the Torah in our story, 'standing' may also be employed metaphorically."

11. Kenneth Reinhard and Julia Reinhard Lupton, "Jewish Studies and the Secular University: Religion Between Culture and Philosophy," 1999, www.jcrt.org/archives/01.1/reinhard_lupton.html.

12. "Interdisciplinarity requires, by definition, the double work of engaging the canonical and the modes of interrogating it. Interdisciplinary training is, first, disciplinary training. It means to take the disciplinary logic to its limit in order precisely to interrogate the construction of the limit." (Gourgouris, *Lessons in Secular Criticism*, 6–7).

13. This corresponds to the culminating argument of Ronald Barnett's *Being a University* (New York: Routledge, 2014). As to knowledge ecologies themselves, Barnett poses queries like "How are forms of knowledge clustered? How do they connect with the world? And do those connections sustain relationships of reciprocity or domination and control?" (142).

14. Seamus Heaney, *Seeing Things* (London: Faber and Faber, 1991), 25. The whole collection is assessed by Henry Hart, "What Is Heaney Seeing in Seeing Things?," *Colby Quarterly* 30.1 (March 1994): 33–42; Michael Hofmann, "Dazzling Philosophy: Seeing Things by Seamus Heaney," *London Review of Books* 13.15 (15 August 1991): 14-15.

15. "A Soul on the Washing Line," *The Economist*, June 1991, www.economist.com/blogs/prospero/2013/09/poetry.

16. Heaney speaks of wanting "to turn out, to go out . . . to pitch the voice out," after his volumes *North* and *Wintering Out*, in "An Interview with James Randall," *Ploughshares* 18 (Spring 1979), www.pshares.org/issues/spring-2011/archive-interview-seamus-heaney-james-randall.

17. Seamus Heaney, "A Soul on the Washing Line: Interview with Seamus Heaney," *Economist*, June 1991.

18. "On John Keats's 'This living hand,'" *Poetry Society of America*, https://www.poetrysociety.org/psa/poetry/crossroads/old_school/on_john_keats_this_living_hand/.

19. As Eugene O'Brien, one of Heaney's shrewder critics, puts it in *Seamus Heaney Creating Irelands of the Mind* (Dublin: The Liffey Press,

2002), "Thus the 'perfection' of a 'pitchfork' is described in terms of its 'imagined perfection', and this, in turn, is described, not in terms of the object itself, but in terms of the 'opening hand' which reached out for it" (103).

20. Shlomo Ibn Gabirol, *Selected Poems of Solomon Ibn Gabirol*, trans. Peter Cole (Princeton, N.J.: Princeton University Press, 2001), 57–60.

21. Levinas, *Difficult Freedom*, 49.

22. Helen Vendler, *Seamus Heaney* (Cambridge, Mass.: Harvard University Press, 1998), 139.

23. Gershom Scholem, "Bertrachtungen eines Kabbala-Forschers," *Du* (April 1955): 64–65.

24. The concept of community for American academe is worked out in Francis Oakley's *Community of Learning: The American College and the Liberal Arts Tradition* (New York: Oxford University Press, 1992); and Mark R. Schwehn, *Exiles from Eden: Religion and the Academic Vocation in America* (New York: Oxford University Press, 1993).

25. Jacques Derrida, "Violence and Metaphysics: An Essay on the Thought of Emmanuel Levinas," in *Writing and Difference*, trans. Allan Bass (Chicago: University of Chicago Press, 1967), 80.

26. Emmanuel Levinas, *Nine Talmudic Readings*, trans. Annette Aronowicz (Bloomington: Indiana University Press, 1990), 72. In *When Kafka Says We*, Vivian Liska explains the double sense "uncommon communities": "not only unusual, as the simple meaning of the word suggests, but they are uncommon because they question the foundation of community based on identity and sameness, of 'having something in common'" (3). See also Chantal Mouffe's explanation of political community as "a discursive surface" in "Democratic Politics and the Question of Identity," in *The Identity in Question*, ed. John Rajchman (New York: Routledge, 1995), 33–46.

27. Paul Ritterband and Harold S. Wechsler, *Jewish Learning in American Universities: The First Century* (Bloomington: Indiana University Press, 1994), 214ff. See also Ira Robinson, *Translating a Tradition: Studies in American Jewish History* (Boston: Academic Studies Press, 2008).

28. In addition to Ritterband and Wechsler, see also Baruch Sperling, A. Levine, and B. Levy, *Students of the Covenant: A History of Jewish Biblical Scholarship in North America* (Atlanta: Scholars Press, 1992); and Steven J. Zipperstein, "Home Again?," *Judaism: A Quarterly Journal of Jewish Life and Thought* 44.4 (Fall 1995): 10–12.

29. Jacques Derrida, *Given Time: I. Counterfeit Money*, trans. Peggy Kamuf (Chicago: University of Chicago Press, 1992).

30. Giorgio Agamben, *The Coming Community*, trans. Michael Hardt (Minneapolis: University of Minnesota Press, 1991), 10; and "What Is a

Paradigm?," www.maxvanmanen.com/files/2014/03/Agamben-What-is-a-paradigm1.pdf, 9.

31. See Jacob Meskin and Harvey Shapiro, "'To Give an Example Is a Complex Act': Agamben's Pedagogy of the Paradigm," *Educational Philosophy and Theory* 46.4 (2014): 421–440.

32. For example, Sarah Hammerschlag, *The Figural Jew: Politics and Identity in Postwar French Thought* (Chicago: University of Chicago Press, 2010) and Cynthia Baker, *Jew* (New Brunswick, N.J.; Rutgers University Press, 2017).

33. Invoking the paradigm of the progressivist *Freie Schulgemeinde* (Free School Community)—founded by Gustave Wyneken in 1906 and attended by Benjamin as an adolescent—he suggests that early education is where "we first attain the concept of community [*Gemeinschaft*]" (110). As such, schools stand in for both family and State; their true function is catalytic rather than archival. *Walter Benjamin, Early Writings (1910–1917)*, trans. Howard Eiland et al. (Cambridge, Mass.: Harvard University Press, 2011); quoted also in Jacob Meskin and Harvey Shapiro, "'To Give an Example Is a Complex Act': Agamben's Pedagogy of the Paradigm," *Educational Philosophy and Theory* 46.4 (2014): 434.

34. The text is discussed by many modern commentators. See, for example, Alon Goshen Gottstein, expanded in *The Sinner and the Amnesiac: The Rabbinic Invention of Elisha ben Abuya and Eleazar ben Arach* (Stanford: Stanford University Press, 2005); and Jeffrey Rubenstein, "Elisha ben Abuya: Torah and the Sinful Sage (Ḥagigah 15a–b)," in *Talmudic Stories: Narrative Art, Composition, and Culture* (Baltimore: Johns Hopkins University Press, 1999), 66–104.

35. Informed especially by Guy Debord's *La société du spectacle*, trans. Ken Knabb (London: Black and Red, 2000).

36. The companion essay, "*Pardes*: The Writing of Potentiality," associates this most specifically with the deconstructive project of Jacques Derrida, whom it casts in the role of *Aḥer* (lit. "the other") himself.

37. The productively "alienating power" of quotation thus offers "a dialectical, objectifying relation to the past," which both preserves and disrupts it. See Moulie Vidas, *Tradition and the Formation of the Talmud* (Princeton, N.J.: Princeton University Press, 2014), 15; and Agamben's *The Man without Content*, trans. Georgia Albert (Stanford: Stanford University Press, 1999), 107–108.

38. The debt is explicitly on display in Giorgio Agamben, *Homo Sacer: Sovereign Power and Bare Life*, trans. Daniel Heller-Roazen (Stanford: Stanford University Press, 1998), which cites several of Nancy's texts, including *La communauté désoeuvrée*.

39. Jean-Luc Nancy, *The Inoperative Community*, trans. Peter Conner (Minneapolis: University of Minnesota Press, 1986), 28. See also by Nancy, "Of Being-in-Common," in *Community at Loose Ends*, ed. the Miami Theory Collective (Minneapolis: University of Minnesota Press, 1991), 1–12; and "Sharing Voices," in *Transforming the Hermeneutic Context*, ed. Gayle Ormiston and Alan Schrift (Albany: State University of New York Press, 1990), 211–59.

40. Jean-Luc Nancy, *The Disavowed Community*, trans. Philip Armstrong (New York: Fordham University Press, 2016), x, 78.

41. On Nancy's seeming resistance to Levinas, for example, see Daniele Rugo, *Jean-Luc Nancy and the Thinking of Otherness: Philosophy and Powers of Existence* (Bloomington: Indiana University Press, 2013).

42. Simon Critchley, "With Being-With? Notes on Jean-Luc Nancy's Rewriting of Being and Time," *Studies in Practical Philosophy* 1:1, 67.

43. Olga Cielemęcka and Monika Rogowska-Stangret, "Stigmergy as a Collective Research Practice," in *Imagine There Were no Humanities . . . Transdisciplinary Perspectives*, ed. Ines K. Ackermann, Katarzyna Chruszczewska, Ewa Róża Janion, Ágnes Máté, Natalia Obukowicz (Warsaw: Wydawnictwo DiG, 2015), 51–59.

44. "On Deconstructing Nostalgia for Community within the West: The Debate between Nancy and Blanchot," *Research in Phenomenology* 23.1 (1993): 3–21.

45. Blumenthal, "Where Does 'Jewish Studies' Belong?," 535–536.

46. Though it does not detail the advent of corporatized higher education, Theda Skocpol's book on the decline of national cross-class federated associations, *Diminished Democracy: From Membership to Management in American Civic Life* (Norman: University of Oklahoma Press, 2003), suggests some cautionary lessons for the university's own civic life in the twenty-first century. See also Benjamin Ginsberg, *The Fall of the Faculty: The Rise of the All-Administrative University and Why It Matters* (New York: Oxford University Press, 2011).

47. Michel Foucault, *Discipline and Punish: The Birth of the Prison*, trans. Alan Sheridan (New York: Vintage Books, 1995), 217.

48. A project related to Dolgopolski's in this respect is Mira Beth Wasserman, *Jews, Gentiles, and Other Animals: The Talmud after the Humanities* (Philadelphia: University of Pennsylvania Press, 2017), which uses Tractate *'Avodah Zarah* to "read" the posthumanist discourse of animal, gender, disability, and critical race studies to consider the question, "What does it mean to be human?"

49. Daniel Boyarin, "The Talmud as a Fat Rabbi: A Novel Approach," *Text and Talk* 28.5 (2008): 603–619.

50. S. Y. Agnon, *Only Yesterday*, trans. Barbara Harshav (Princeton, N.J.: Princeton University Press, 2002), 636–637.

INTERCHAPTER III: "PAST ITS OWN AIM, OUT TO ANOTHER SIDE"

1. That said, the pitchfork in this poem is very obviously an aesthetic device associated with the lyric purposes of Seamus Heaney rather than the more politically ironic ones of, say, Grant Wood. In *America Goes to College: Political Theory for the Liberal Arts* (Albany: State University of New York Press, 1997), John E. Seery devotes a chapter to "American Gothic," Wood's celebrated and elusively satirical painting of two Midwesterners with a pitchfork (the latter originally conceived as a rake) in an oeuvre routinely mined for phallic objects, for example silo, trough, plow, ear of corn.

2. Susannah Heschel and Sarah Imhoff, "Where Are All the Women in Jewish Studies?," *The Forward*, July 3, 2018, forward.com/culture/404416/where-are-all-the-women-in-jewish-studies/.

3. On this predilection, see Gerald A. Cohen, "Complete Bullshit," in *Finding Oneself in the Other*, ed. Michael Otsuka (Princeton, N.J.: Princeton University Press, 2012), an academician's response to Harry G. Frankfurt.

3. *MOCHLOS* OR *MAKHLOKES*: JS AND THE HUMANITIES

"Don't let the sun go down on your grievances" quoted from Robert Johnston, *Yip/Jump Music* (1993).

1. Vladimir Nabokov, *Bend Sinister* (New York: Vintage Books), 58.

2. Ludwig Wittgenstein, *Culture and Value*, trans. Peter Winch (Oxford: Basil Blackwell, 1980), 24e.

3. It also inadvertently conjures an unlikely linkage with fellow contrarian (and no fan of Jews) H. L. Mencken, dubbed by his biographer Marion Elizabeth Rodgers, "the American iconoclast."

4. Alan J. Avery-Peck, Bruce Chilton, William Scott Green, and Gary G. Porton, eds., *A Legacy of Learning: Essays in Honor of Jacob Neusner* (Leiden: Brill, 2014).

5. Roger Brooks, "Transcendent Education: Immortality and the Liberal Arts," in *A Legacy of Learning: Essays in Honor of Jacob Neusner*, ed. Alan J. Avery-Peck, Bruce Chilton, William Scott Green, and Gary G. Porton (Leiden: Brill, 2014), 389–399.

6. A number of recent symposia have accentuated this link; for example, "Hebrew and the Humanities: Present Tense" at the University of Washington (2016), *jewishstudies*.washington.edu/hebrew-humanities-symposium/; and "Jewish Text(s) and the College Humanities: A Symposium" at Boston University (2013), www.bu.edu/jewishstudies/jewish-texts-symposium/.

Although they share one discursive world in common, Neusner's sense of the other and Wasserman's in *Jews, Gentiles, and Other Animals* could not be at greater variance.

7. Hughes, *American Jewish Iconoclast*, 6 and 166ff. Hughes has also written a companion volume, *Jacob Neusner on Religion: The Example of Judaism* (New York: Routledge, 2016).

8. See Hughes, *American Jewish Iconoclast*, 182ff. For a particularly cogent discussion of the biography and its authorized status, see Albert I. Baumgarten's review in *Enoch Seminar* (March 4, 2017), enochseminar.org/review/12805.

9. A section on Neusner appears in Seth Schwartz, "Historiography on the Jews in the 'Talmudic Period': 70–640 CE," in *The Oxford Handbook of Jewish Studies*, ed. Martin Goodman (New York: Oxford University Press), 200479–114. Cf. Baruch Kurzweil's critique of Scholem and the "Jerusalem School" as secular, post-*Wissenschaft* claimants to the pseudo-"prophetic authority" accrues to scientifically objective historiography.

10. Seamus Heaney, *The Government of the Tongue: Selected Prose, 1978–1987* (Farrar, Straus and Giroux, 1988), 92, 96.

11. Neusner's statements on poets and poetry appear to be confined to a review he wrote of a 1998 volume, *Telling and Remembering: A Century of Jewish American Poetry*, the bulk of which, however, he dismissed as neither Jewish nor having anything to do with Judaism. See "What's Jewish about Jewish American Poetry?," *Judaism* 47:4 (1998): 487.

12. Bourdieu, *Homo Academicus*, 9. An equally powerful way to conceptualize academic social space ethnographically as both tribal and territorial is conducted by Tony Becher and Paul Trowler, *Academic Tribes and Territories: Intellectual Enquiry and the Cultures of Disciplines* (Philadelphia: Open University Press, 2001).

13. Tractate b. *Bava Metsi'a* 59b. See, most recently, the reading by Miriam Gedwiser, thelehrhaus.com (February 17, 2019).

14. Central to the arc of Neusner's embattled reputation is a posthumous review of his scholarship by his mentor at the Jewish Theological Seminary, Saul Lieberman, whose review of Neusner's *Talmud of the Land of Israel* still speaks volumes. See Lieberman, "A Tragedy or a Comedy?," *Journal of the American Oriental Society* 104.2 (April/June 1984): 315–319. From another flank of early rabbinic corpora, Neusner was the subject of sharp critique by Shaye Cohen and Daniel Boyarin, who takes him particularly to task for various contraventions of "acceptable scholarly discourse."

15. Joel Geberoff, "Talmudic Stories about Angry and Annoyed Rabbis," in *A Legacy of Learning: Essays in Honor of Jacob Neusner* (Leiden: Brill, 2014), 82–109.

16. The locus classicus in the Mishna for a distinction between kinds of *maḥloket*—*l'shem shamayim* (for the sake of heaven) and *she'lo l'shem shamayim* (not for the sake of heaven)—is found in the Tractate *Avot* 5:7. On *maḥloket* more generally, see Avi Sagi, *The Open Canon: On the Meaning of Halakhic Discourse*, trans. Batya Stein (New York: Continuum, 2007); Marc-Alain Ouaknin, *The Burnt Book: Reading the Talmud*, trans. Llewellyn Brown (Princeton, N.J.: Princeton University Press, 1995); Sergei Dolgopolski, *Political After the Talmud*; and Shaul Magid, "The Intolerance of Tolerance: *Makhloket* and Redemption in Early Hasidism," *Jewish Studies Quarterly* 8 (2001): 326–368.

17. In "Jacob Neusner as Reader of the Mishnah, Tosefta, and Halakhíc Midrash," *Henoch* XXXI (2005), 259–270, critiquing Neusner's "documentary hypothesis," Steven D. Fraade ventures the pertinent parallel between structuralist and post-structuralist schools of thought on one hand, and Neusner and "post-Neuserian" scholarship on the other. Two other articles by Judith Hauptman and David Goodblatt in the same volume provide additional context for Fraade's estimation of Neusner's mixed achievement as rabbinics scholar.

18. Jacob Neusner, "Stranger at Home: The Task of Religious Studies," *Lectures on Judaism in the Academy and in the Humanities* (Atlanta: Scholars Press, 1990), 21.

19. In another footnote from his review essay of Neusner, Boyarin writes, "It is extraordinary that Neusner wishes to make theoretical interventions in the study of 'History of Ideas' and yet makes no reference to such seminal works as Dominick LaCapra's 'Intellectual History and Critical Theory' . . . I would not carp at Neusner's adoption of an older intellectual style were it not for the fact that he himself regards all work done in other (and older) intellectual paradigms as totally useless." (456).

20. Compare, however, the contemporaneous volume by Shaye Cohen and Edward Greenstein, eds., *The State of Jewish Studies* (Detroit, Mich.: Wayne State University Press, 1990), the product of a 1986 conference under the same title held at the Jewish Theological Seminary.

21. Both phrases are from Jacob Neusner, "'Being Jewish' and Studying about Judaism" (Atlanta: Emory University, 1977), 20.

22. M. M. Bakhtin, *The Dialogic Imagination: Four Essays*, trans. Caryl Emerson and Michael Holquist (Austin: University of Texas Press, 1981), 284.

23. Stathis Gourgouris, *Lessons in Secular Criticism* (New York: Fordham University Press, 2013), 4.

24. jewishphilosophyplace.com/2014/05/08/too-jewish-studies-response-to-aaron-hughes/.

25. Louis Menand, *The Marketplace of Ideas: Reform and Resistance in the American University* (New York: W. W. Norton & Company, 2010), 97.

26. Jacques Derrida, "The Future of the Profession," in *Jacques Derrida and the Humanities: A Critical Reader*, ed. Tom Cohen (Cambridge: Cambridge University Press, 2009), 26

27. The low point in Neusner's voluminous output may well be marked by the foreword he wrote for *The Martin Luther King, Jr. Plagiarism Story* (Rockford, Ill.: Rockford Institute, 1994) by Theodore Pappas, the white supremacist editor of the ultra-right magazine *Chronicles*—left unmentioned in Hughes's biography. A crude denunciation of "political correctness" (and sadly reminiscent of the current political climate), Neusner's foreword includes, among other lamentable features, a shameful analogy between universities "strangled by affirmative action" and the persecution of Jews in Nazi Germany.

28. Jacob Neusner Noam Neusner, *Reaffirming Higher Education* (New York: Transaction, 2000), 84–85. The passage also appears (in first-person) in *How to Grade Your Professors: And Other Unexpected Advice* (Boston: Beacon Press, 1984).

29. Naomi Seidman, *A Marriage Made in Heaven: The Sexual Politics of Hebrew and Yiddish* (Berkeley: University of California Press, 1984). Evidently, Neusner was once advised by A. J. Heschel to learn Yiddish "and begin the process of studying systematically the sources of Eastern Europe" (Hughes, 80), a road apparently left untaken.

30. Jacob Neusner, "The University as Locus for the Judaic Life of the Intellect," in *Lectures on Judaism in the Academy and in the Humanities* (Atlanta: Scholars Press, 1990), 131–139.

31. For instance, Daniel Boyarin, "Talmud as a Fat Rabbi," 603–619; or Moshe Simon-Shoshan, "The Talmud as Novel: A Bakhtinian Approach to the *Bavli*," AJS Conference (Chicago, 2012).

32. Edward Said, *Humanism and Democratic Criticism* (New York: Columbia University Press, 2004), 25

33. Neusner's enmity for Hartman (and *parti pris* literary theory) also surfaced in an op-ed, where he lambasted Hartman's defense of Paul de Man, viz., "To deconstructionism, things are what you say they are. So up is down and black is white and east is west and somehow this disreputable and disgusting Nazi, de Man, has been turned into a man of conscience, no less. . . . No Jew can admire Hartman for writing this way about a vicious anti-Semite and Nazi collaborator," *The Jewish Advocate*, March 31, 1988), sec. 2, p. 2

34. Geoffrey Hartman, *Criticism in the Wilderness: The Study of Literature Today* (New Haven, Conn.: Yale University Press, 1980), 27. Hartman's

intellectual memoir, *A Scholar's Tale: Intellectual Journey of a Displaced Child of Europe* (New York: Fordham University Press, 2007), in which he relates his discovery of *midrash* under the tutelage of Nehama Leibowitz at Hebrew University, supplies a bracing corrective to Neusner's trivialization.

35. Respectively, in "The Culture of Criticism," *PMLA* 99.3 (May, 1984): 371–397 and "History-Writing as Answerable Style," *New Literary History* 2.1: "A Symposium on Literary History" (Autumn 1970): 73–83.

36. The Hartman-Budick volume *Midrash and Literature* (New Haven, Conn.: Yale University Press, 1986) was published just one year before Neusner published his own *Canon and Connection: Intertextuality in Judaism* (Lanham, Md.: University Press of America, 1987). See also "Intertextuality and the Literature of Judaism," *American Journal of Semiotics* 7.1/2 (2008): 153–182; and "The Case of James Kugel's Joking Rabbis and Other Serious Issues," in *Wrong Ways and Right Ways in the Study of Formative Judaism* (Atlanta: Scholars Press, 1988), 59–73.

37. Jacob Neusner, *Judaism, the Evidence of the Mishnah* (Chicago: University of Chicago Press, 1981); and *Rabbinic Judaism: The Documentary History of the Formative Age, 70–600 CE* (Bethesda, Md.: CDL Press, 1994). For a general introduction, see Schwartz, "Historiography on the Jews," 79–114.

38. Milan Kundera's phrase from *Testaments Betrayed: An Essay in Nine Parts*, trans. Linda Asher (London: Faber and Faber, 1995).

39. "Contexts and Constituencies: The Diverse Responsibilities of Higher Jewish Learning," the inaugural address for the guest lecture series sponsored by Dropsie University (1980–86), represents Neusner's definitive statement on what does and does not constitute JS.

40. In a brief section entitled "Jewish and Judaic," in the introduction to *Jacob Neusner on Religion: The Example of Judaism* (New York: Routledge, 2016), Hughes writes, "Neusner is quite literally defining a field at a time when none of this as clear. He is doing so, moreover, not just academically, but in the popular media for all to witness" (6), a footnote to which clarifies that "Jewish Studies" more accurately signifies the Neusnerian brand of "Judaic Studies." The problem left intact here, however, is that practitioners in fields other than the academic study of religion are thus deprived not only of their local disciplinary claim on "the Jewish," but also on the field so defined as the *complication* of boundaries rather than a proprietary delimitation of them—an even more crucial distinction for contemporary practitioners than in Neusner's day.

41. Roderick A. Ferguson, *The Reorder of Things: The University and Its Pedagogies of Minority Difference* (Minneapolis: University of Minnesota Press, 2012).

42. For example, the work of the late Amnon Shiloah or Assaf Shelleg, *Jewish Contiguities and the Soundtrack of Israeli History* (New York: Oxford University Press, 2014); and Ruth F. Davis, *Musical Exodus: Al-Andalus and Its Jewish Diasporas* (Lanham, Md.: Rowman and Littlefield, 2015).

43. "Op-Ed- Papuans and Zulus," *New York Times Book Review*, March 10, 1994, www.nytimes.com/books/00/04/23/specials/bellow-papuans.html.

44. Jacob Neusner, "Professors or Curators? Universities or Museums," The Case of Jewish Studies," in *Lectures on Judaism in the Humanities and the Academy* (Atlanta: Scholars Press, 1990), 91.

45. Since Neusner's time, of course, any number of grants and initiatives have pursued exactly this connection; for example, NEH's Crossing Borders, Making Connections: The Humanities and Ethnic Studies (2015), or Maryland Humanities' Humanities and the Legacy of Race and Ethnicity in the United States (2016).

46. Thus, Neusner will speak of "the profound human experience of blacks in America, the extraordinary record of humanity in Africa, the vast representation of society in stress both there and here—these are represented as 'for blacks only'" (990).

47. Barry Weller, "Pleasure and Self-Loss in Reading," *ADE Bulletin* 99 (Fall 1991): 8–12.

48. From LaCapra's review of Readings's book. "Here a basic distinction may need to be rethought: the distinction between the core of a discipline and its externalities or merely peripheral, parasitic elements. What is marginalized or seen as merely external is at times the larger setting in which an activity has social and cultural significance, notably including the culture of various disciplines themselves" (51).

49. Jacob Neusner, "Modes of Jewish Studies in the University," in *New Humanities and Academic Disciplines: The Case of Jewish Studies* (Eugene: Wipf and Stock, 2004), 7. Hughes rehearses this apportionment in *Jacob Neusner on Religion*, 4–6.

50. In *This New Yet Unapproachable America: Lectures After Emerson After Wittgenstein* (Albuquerque: Living Batch Press, 1989), Stanley Cavell captures this particular delusion: "I must empty out *my* contribution to words, so that language itself, as if beyond me, exclusively takes over responsibility for meaning" (57).

51. See Yonah Frankel, *Darchei HaAggadah ViHaMidrash* (Jerusalem: Givatayim, 1991) and "Hermeneutic Problems in the Study of the Aggadic Narrative," *Tarbiz* 47 (1978): 139–172; Jeffrey L. Rubenstein, "Theodicy and Torah," in *Stories of the Babylonian Talmud* (Baltimore: Johns Hopkins University Press, 2010), 182–201; Shlomo Naeh, "The Script of the Torah in

Rabbinic Thought (B): Transcription and Thorns," *Leshonenu* 71 (2010): 89–123 (Hebrew); Azzan Yadin-Israel, *Scripture and Tradition: Rabbi Akiva and the Triumph of Midrash* (Philadelphia: University of Pennsylvania Press, 2015); and Nachman Levine, "Reading Crowned Letters and Semiotic Silences in *Menahot* 29b," *Journal of Jewish Studies* 53.1 (2002): 35–48. Finally, see the introduction and chapter on Akiva in Abraham Joshua Heschel's *Heavenly Torah: as Refracted through the Generations*, ed. and trans. Gordon Tucker (London: Bloomsbury, 2006).

52. Laurence L. Edwards, "Rabbi Akiba's Crowns: Postmodern Discourse and the Cost of Rabbinic Reading," *Judaism* 49.4 (Fall 2000): 417–435; and Daniel Boyarin, *Socrates and the Fat Rabbis* (Chicago: University of Chicago Press, 2009), 233ff.

53. Barry Scott Wimpfheimer, "The Dialogical Talmud: Daniel Boyarin and Rabbinics," *Jewish Quarterly Review* 101.2 (Spring 2011): 245–254; and the review of Boyarins's book by Reuven Kiperwasser in *Jewish History* 25 (2011): 377–397. More generally, see Richard Hidary, *Rabbis and Classical Rhetoric: Sophistic Education and Oratory in the Talmud and Midrash* (Cambridge: Cambridge University Press, 2017).

54. Levine construes this element as non-satiric (9).

55. Yadin-Israel, *Scripture and Tradition*, 178ff.

56. See Michael Fagenblat's introduction to *Negative Theology as Jewish Modernity* (Bloomington: Indiana University Press, 2017).

57. Max Weber, "Science as Vocation," in *Max Weber, Essays in Sociology*, trans. and ed. H. H. Gerth and C. Wright Mills (New York: Oxford University Press, 1946), 153.

58. The companion essay to "Science as Vocation" (which should really be read in tandem) is a talk that Weber delivered at the University of Munich two years later entitled "Politik als Beruf," from *Max Weber, Essays in Sociology*, 129–157.

59. Adam Liska, "The Myth and the Meaning of Science as a Vocation," *Ultimate Reality and Meaning* 28:2 (2005), 149–164.

60. Harvey Goldman, *Max Weber and Thomas Mann: Calling and the Shaping of the Self* (Berkeley: University of California Press, 1988).

61. Jacob Neusner, "Teaching Jewish studies 'under gentile auspices' versus the academic study of religion, including Judaism: Response to Zachary Braiterman," *Religious Education* 95.1 (Winter 2000): 95–96. Braiterman's essay is entitled "Teaching Jewish Studies in a Radically Gentile Space: Some Personal Reflections," *Religious Education* 94.4 (Fall 1999): 396–409.

62. Zachary Braiterman, "Response to Jacob Neusner," *Religious Education* 95.1 (Winter 2000): 105.

INTERCHAPTER IV: SPEAKING OF JS; AND ITS VICISSITUDES

1. Both institutions were in the upper rankings of the 2009 *US News and World Report* list from which Josh Lambert drew his original data on courses, appointments, and departmental mission statements.

2. I follow the extraordinary analysis of this structure in Philip Fisher's reading of *Benito Cereno* in "Democratic Social Space: Whitman, Melville, and the Promise of American Transparency," *Representations* 24 (Fall 1988): 60–101.

4. *BILDUNGSHELD* OR *PÍCARO*, CANON AND LIST: A HETEROTOPOLOGY FOR JS

1. "Das Freie Jüdische Lehrhaus: Einleitung für eine Mitteilungsblatt," in *Der Mensch und sein Werk. Gesammelte Schriften, III: Zweistromland: Kleinere Schriften zu Glauben und Denken*, ed. Annemarie and Reinhold Mayer (Dordrecht: Martinus Nijhoff, 1984), 515.

2. The root meaning of *midrash* is "study, seek out investigate," while German *lehr* means "instruct."

3. Franz Rosenzweig, *On Jewish Learning*, ed. N. N. Glatzer (New York: Schocken Books, 1955), 69; Zank translation, 238.

4. These are treated in some detail in Michael Brenner, *The Renaissance of Jewish Culture in Weimar Germany* (New Haven, Conn.: Yale University Press, 1996).

5. Elli Fischer, "A Prayer at the Grave of Franz Rosenzweig," *Lehrhaus*, October 6, 2016, www.thelehrhaus.com/commentary-short-articles/grave-franz-rosenzweig.

6. Peter E. Gordon, "Rosenzweig Redux: The Reception of German-Jewish Thought," *Jewish Social Studies* 8.1 (Fall 2001): 17.

7. Bracketing Rosenzweig's legacy, the forum's founding statement cites, instead, an 1843 epigraph on the launching of the Philadelphia-based religious periodical, *The Occident*, explaining that "*Lehrhaus*, [then,] can trace its lineage back to the first Jewish literary revival in the United States." The criterion for the choice would appear to be denominational credentials.

8. Gordon, "Rosenzweig Redux," 16, later adding "Rosenzweig's asceticism, however, performs its most stringent resistance not against material life as such, but against any effort to find its primary meaning in the public sphere" (33).

9. Rosenberg, Shimon Gershon (Rav Shagar), "Religious Life in the Modern Age," *Faith Shattered and Restored Judaism in the Postmodern Age*, trans. Elie Leshem (Jerusalem: Maggid Books, 2017), 43.

10. 1925 letter to Martin Buber, cited in Braiterman, *Shape of Revelation*, 122ff.

11. By semi-clandestine way of the *Wissenschaftler* Shmuel David Luzzatto (1800–1865), who wrote, "Judaeus sum, judaici nihil a me alienium [sic] puto, as cited in Meir, 66.

12. Herbert A. Strauss, "A Program for Jewish Studies," in *Conference on Intellectual Policies in American Jewry*, ed. Herbert Strauss (New York: American Federation of Jews from Central Europe, Inc., 1972), 23.

13. Published shortly after Foucault's death in *Architecture, Mouvement, Continuité*, no. 5 (October 1984): 46–49. At roughly the same time (1970) Foucault's contemporary Henry Lefebvre was developing a similar, threefold taxonomy: *isotopies*, or identical space, *heterotopies*, or other spaces, and *utopias*, or non-places.

14. George Steiner, "The Mandarin of the Hour-Michel Foucault," *New York Times Book Review*, February 28, 1971, www.nytimes.com/books/00/12/17/specials/foucault-order.html.

15. As far as I am aware, the only linkage of Neusner and Rosenzweig together occurs in passing (310) in Eliot Wolfson's "Parting of the Ways That Never Parted: Judaism and Christianity in the Work of Jacob Neusner," in *A Legacy of Learning: Essays in Honor of Jacob Neusner* (Leiden: Brill, 2014), 299–317.

16. Shimon Gershon Rosenberg (Rav Shagar), "Seventy Bullocks and One Sukka: The Land of Israel, Nationalism, and Diaspora," in *Faith Shattered and Restored Judaism in the Postmodern Age*, trans. Elie Leshem (Jerusalem: Maggid Books, 2017), 187.

17. Nahum N. Glatzer, "The Frankfort Lehrhaus," *Year Book Leo Baeck Institute* 1.1 (1956): 105–122.

18. Rosenzweig composed the essay on the Macedonian front in 1917, which appeared several months later in print in the *Verlag der Neuen Jüdischen Montatshefte*.

19. See Leora Batnitzky, *Idolatry and Representation: The Philosophy of Franz Rosenzweig Reconsidered* (Princeton, N.J.: Princeton University Press, 2000), 183ff.

20. See David M. Myers, "The Fall and Rise of Jewish Historicism: The Evolution of the Akademie für die Wissenschaft des Judentums (1919–1934)," *Hebrew Union College Annual* 63 (1992): 107–144.

21. Eric Santner, *On the Psychotheology of Everyday Life: Reflections on Freud and Rosenzweig* (Chicago: University of Chicago Press, 2001), 15.

22. The affinities and divergences are traced by Glatzer, "Frankfort Lehrhaus," and Brenner, *Renaissance of Jewish Culture*, 76–78.

23. Michael Zank translation, "Of *Bildung* There Is no End," in *Textual Reasonings: Jewish Philosophy and Text Study at the End of the Twentieth Century*, ed. Peter Ochs and Nancy Levene (London: SCM Press, 2002), 238.

24. See the chapter on Rosenzweig in Efraim Meir, *Dialogical Thought and Identity: Trans-Different Religiosity in Present Day Societies* (Boston: Walter de Gruyter and Magnes, 2013), 69–79.

25. Martin Jay, "1920. The Free Jewish School Is Founded in Frankfurt am Main Under the Leadership of Franz Rosenzweig," in *Yale Companion to Jewish Writing and Thought in Germany*, ed. Sander Gilman and Jack Zipes (New Haven, Conn.: Yale University Press, 1997), 395–400.

26. The distinction between *"Lehrhaus"* and *"beit midrash"* is the subject of Martin Kavka's "Two Study-Houses: Authority in Goldschmidt and Jewish Tradition" (Zurich: Stiftung Dialogik, 2013), www.dialogik.org/wp/wp-content/uploads/2010/12/Martin-Kavka-2013.pdf.

27. Paul Mendes-Flohr, "The Freies Jüdisches Lehrhaus," in *Jüdische Kultur in Frankfurt am Main von den Anfängen bis zur Gegenwart*, ed. Karl Erich Grözinger (Vienna: Harrassowitz Verlag, 1997), 227.

28. David Suchoff's organizing idea in *Kafka's Jewish Languages: The Hidden Openness of Tradition* (Philadelphia: University of Pennsylvania Press, 2012). See also Dana Hollander, *Exemplarity and Chosenness: Rosenzweig and Derrida on the Nation of Philosophy* (Stanford: Stanford University Press, 2008).

29. As noted by both Glatzer and Zank, in articles by Ernst Simon, "Franz Rosenzweig and Jewish Education," *Conservative Judaism* 18.2 (Winter 1964): 10–24; and Alex Pomson, "Franz Rosenzweig and the Elementary School Teacher: A Midrashic Re-viewing of an Experiment in Adult Education," *Journal of Jewish Education* 71.3 (2005): 261–277.

30. I take the term from Mendes-Flohr, "Freies Jüdisches Lehrhaus," 217–230.

31. Franz Rosenzweign, "Letter to Eduard Strauss, January 28, 1926," in *Briefe und Tagebücher 1918–1929* (The Hague: Martinus Nijhoff, 1979), 1083.

32. Revived by Buber from 1933 through *Kristalnacht*, 1938.

33. Alfred Jospe, "The Frankfurt Lehrhaus: A Model for American Jewish Education?," in *To Leave Your Mark: Selections from the Writings of Alfred Jospe*, ed. Eva Jospe and Raphael Jospe (New York: Ktav Publishing, 2000), 80–83.

34. Robert Musil, *The Enthusiasts*, trans. Andre Stone (New York: Performing Arts Journal Publications, 1983), 19.

35. Michael Zank, "Franz Rosenzweig, the 1920s, and the <<e-mail>> moment of textual reasoning," in *Textual Reasonings: Jewish Philosophy and Text Study at the End of the Twentieth Century*, ed. Peter Ochs and Nancy Levene (London: SCM Press, 2002), 238.

36. See Franz Rosenzweig, *Philosophical and Theological Writings*, trans. Paul Franks and Michael Morgan (Indianapolis: Hackett Publishing

Company, 2000); and Ephraim Meir's *Dialogical Thought and Identity*, and *Differenz und Dialog* (Berlin: Waxmann, 2011).

37. Goethe, *Faust, Part One*, trans. David Luke (New York: Oxford University Press, 2008).

38. Rosenzweig uses the metaphor himself in *Das Büchlein vom Gesunden und Kranken Menschenverstand* and the essay "Die Wissenschaft von Gott," in *Zweistromland*, 641–642.

39. On these terms, see Brenner, *Renaissance of Jewish Culture*, 74–77. Zank makes the pertinent point about Rosenzweig's rhetoric that "his proposed solution is spiritual and internal, albeit not without a turn toward the biological metaphorics of Jewish 'life' (*Leben*) and the sociological metaphorics of 'community' (*Gemeinschaft*), to which he also adds the pietistic metaphorics of 'encounter' (*Erlebnis* as in *Bekehrungserlebnis*, the experience of a conversion), metaphors that were common in the rhetorics of the Jewish youth movement of the time" (241).

40. Geoffrey Galt Harpham, *Shadows of Ethics: Criticism and the Just Society* (Durham, N.C.: Duke University Press, 1999), 35–36.

41. Rosenzweig, "Die Tendenz ist antimystisch, nicht antigeistig," from *Briefe*, no. 330, "An Hans Ehrenberg" (Kassel, l, late Dec. 1921): 413–414.

42. Willi Goetschel, "Philosophy from the Outside In: Rosenzweig's Critical Project," *Filozofija I Društvo* 23.2 (2012): 65–76.

43. In R. Hirsch's address on the Schiller Centenary in *Collected Writings of Rabbi Samson Raphael Hirsch, Volume 9* (Feldheim, 1995), 137–152; and Matthias Morgenstern, "Rabbi S. R. Hirsch and his Perception of Germany and German Jewry," in *The German-Jewish Experience Revisited*, ed. Steven E. Aschheim and Vivian Liska (Boston: Walter de Gruyter, 2015), 207–229.

44. See Rosenzweig, "The New Thinking," in *Philosophical and Theological Writings*, trans. Paul Franks and Michael Morgan (Indianapolis: Hackett Publishing Company, 2000), 109ff; and Gordon, "Rosenzweig Redux," 15ff.

45. Brenner, *Renassiance of Jewish Culture*, 74–77.

46. Glossing an 1809 speech by Hegel celebrating the reopening of a classical *Gymnasium*, Peggy Kamuf writes, "The dividing wall of *Bildung*, therefore, is itself divided between that which effectively separates or holds apart so as to prevent contamination, and that which poses itself as a separation only in order to be overcome," in *The Division of Literature: Or, the University in Deconstruction* (Chicago: University of Chicago Press, 1997), 80.

47. Glatzer begins his account of the Frankfurt Lehrhaus by declaring Rosenzweig's "radically humanist and universalist orientation in many ways reminiscent of the *Bildungsideal* of Wilhelm von Humboldt" (105).

48. Readings, *The University in Ruins*, 204 and 222, which discuss the Rectoral Address of 1933; and Heidegger's *What Is Called Thinking?*, trans. J. G. Gray (New York: Harper and Row, 1968).

49. Peter E. Gordon, *Rosenzweig and Heidegger: Between Judaism and German Philosophy* (Berkeley: University of California Press, 2003), xxvii. Gordon begins with the famous Davos disputation in 1929 between Heidegger and Hermann Cohen, on which Rosenzweig reflected posthumously in "Vertauschte Fronten" [Exchanged Fronts], reproduced with commentary in Rosenzweig, *Philosophical and Theological Writings*, 140–152.

50. Martin Heidegger, "Plato's Doctrine of Truth," trans. Thomas Sheehan, in *Pathmarks*, ed. William McNeill (Cambridge: Cambridge University Press, 1998) 166–167.

51. Heidegger, *What Is Called Thinking?*, 15. Both essays by Heidegger are discussed in Iain Thomson, *Heidegger on Ontotheology: Technology and the Politics of Education* (Cambridge University Press, 2005).

52. For example, Schelling's 1802–1803 lectures *On University Studies*. See also Nietzsche's "On the Future of Our Educational Institutions," trans. J. M. Kennedy, in *The Complete Works*, vol. 6 (T. N. Foulis, 1909), 3–143, suppressed in his lifetime but avidly consumed by Heidegger when it finally saw light in 1935, not least for sentences like these: "*Bildung* begins with obedience, subordination, discipline, and subjection. Just as great leaders need followers, so those who are led need the leader [*der Führer*]" (140).

53. "Toward a Philosophical Orientation for Academics," trans. John Protevi, *Graduate Faculty Philosophy Journal* 14–5 (1991): 497–500; and Thomson, *Heidegger on Ontotheology*, 90ff. See also Gordon, *Rosenzweig and Heidegger*, 85ff.

54. Martin Heidegger, "The Self-Assertion of the German University and the Rectorate 1933/34: Facts and Thoughts," trans. Karsten Harries, *Review of Metaphysics* 38:3 (March 1985): 467–502.

55. See Michael Wimmer, "The Gift of *Bildung*: Reflections on the Relationship between Singularity and Justice in the Concept of *Bildung*," in *Derrida and Education*, ed. Gert J. J. Biesta and Denise Egéa-Kuehne (New York: Routledge, 2001), 150–175.

56. Theodor Adorno, *Theorie der Halbbildung* (Theory of Half-Education) (Adorno, Theodor: Suhrkamp, 2006).

57. From a root meaning "comingled substances with no change in character." The *Bavli* (b. *Shevuot* 39a) explains the formula, *Kol yisrael 'arevim zeh bazeh* (all Jews are guarantors for one another), as having both positive and negative implications.

58. Brenner, *Renaissance of Jewish Culture*, 89; and Weltsch Robert, "Introduction," *Yearbook of the Leo Baeck Institute* 2.1 (1957); 26 quote Glatzer (120) to that effect.

59. Compare the catalog of lectures given at the shadow-world counterpart to Lehrhaus, held in the Terezin *Konzentrationslager* from 1942 through 1944, the focus of the Makarova-, Makarov-, and Kuperman-edited *University Over the Abyss*.

60. Jacques Lezra, "Helen's List," *PMLA* 130.1 (2015): 163–166.

61. Gershom Scholem, *From Berlin to Jerusalem: Memories of My Youth*, trans. Harry Zohn (Philadelphia: Paul Dry Books, 2012), 154.

62. *Journal of Textual Reasoning* 1 (2002), jtr.shanti.virginia.edu/volume-1-number-1/cohen-why-textual-reasoning/.

63. See Peter Ochs on "*TR* sensibilities" in his introduction to "Jewish Sensibilities," issue 4.3 (May 2006), jtr.shanti.virginia.edu/volume-4-number-3/jewish-sensibilities/.

64. Norbert M. Samuelson, *A User's Guide to Franz Rosenzweig's Star of Redemption* (New York: Routledge, 1999), 102.

65. From a letter written shortly before his death, quoted in the introduction to Rosenberg, Faith Shattered and Restored, xiii.

66. Levinas, *Otherwise Than Being; Or, Beyond Essence*, trans. Alphonso Lingis (Pittsburgh, Pa.: Duquesne University Press, 1981), 24. "How is it that the 'what' . . . becomes a demand and a prayer, a special language inserted into the 'communication' of the given as an appeal for help, for aid addressed to another?"

INTERCHAPTER V: *BILDUNG* AND BUILT-INS

1. The term also makes a conspicuous appearance in the final sentence of "How Is Judaism Possible?" (1959) from the same volume: "Credit it! The signature is not false!" (254). I read "Signature" in greater detail in Adam Zachary Newton, *To Make the Hand Impure: Art, Ethical Adventure, the Difficult and the Holy* (New York: Fordham University Press, 2015), 144–148.

2. See Judith Baskin's "Jewish Studies in North American Colleges and Universities: Yesterday, Today, and Tomorrow," *Shofar* 32.4 (2014): 9–26; and Samuel G. Freedman, "Classes in Judaic Studies Drawing a Non-Jewish Class," *New York Times*, November 3, 2004.

3. From an advertised position for the program, www.h-net.org/jobs/job_display.php?id=49944.

4. From Marin Kavka's "What Does It Mean to Receive Tradition?" Kavka (author of *Jewish Messianism and the History of Philosophy* with a pertinent chapter on Rosenzweig), connects it to both a scene of reading and the "drama of becoming a self": "The person who walks into the Lehrhaus can do nothing but desire; the person who reads a text and tries on various conceptual personae develops options for action—and a Jewish identity—through the act of becoming another character" (193).

5. VENTILATING THE TRADITION: RASHBAM AND THE COEN BROTHERS

1. "Symposium: *A Serious Man*," *AJS Review* Vol. 35.02 (November 2011): 347–348.

2. Schreier, *Impossible Jew*, 169.

3. Shimon Gershon Rosenberg (Rav Shagar), *Faith Shattered and Restored Judaism in the Postmodern Age*, trans. Elie Leshem (Jerusalem: Maggid Books, 2017), 128.

4. On this meta-linguistic concept and its midrashic, intertextual implications, see Chana Kronfeld and Robert Adler Peckerar, "Tongue-Twisted: Itzik Manger between *mame-loshn* and *loshn-koydesh*," *In geveb*, August 13, 2015, https://ingeveb.org/articles/tongue-twisted-itzik-manger-between-mame-loshn-and-loshn-koydesh.

5. Ethan and Joel Coen, *A Serious Man* (London: Faber and Faber, 2009), 18.

6. A Coen brothers specialty, this theme is subject to aggressive and brilliant makeover in *Fargo*, the television extension of the CB film by the same name by Noah Hawley, which makes abundant use of isolated Jewish detail in much the same way as *ASM*.

7. The distinction and its several permutations are summarized in the entry on "Narrative Constitution" by Michael Scheffel on the online *Living Handbook of Narratology* at www.lhn.uni-hamburg.de/article/narrative-constitution.

8. In "Genre, Repetition, Temporal Order: Some Aspects of Biblical Narratology," in *A Companion to Narrative Theory*, ed. J. Phelan and P. Rabinowitz (Malden: Blackwell, 2005), 285–298, David Richter proposes a distinction between "Biblical narrative" and "Bible stories" (adapted pericopes that elide the inconsistencies of narrative structure as a whole).

9. The terms come from the title of Meir Sternberg, *The Poetics of Biblical Narrative: Ideological Literature and the Drama of Reading* (Bloomington: Indiana University Press, 1987).

10. Jane Kanarek, *Biblical Narration and the Formation of Rabbinic Law* (Cambridge: Cambridge University Press, 2014), 87.

11. See Robert Cover's landmark article, "Nomos and Narrative," *Harvard Law Review* 97:4 (1983): 4–68.

12. As the "twice told," it is discussed by José Ángel García Landa in his essay "Narrating Narrating: Twisting the Twice-Told Tale," in *Theorizing Narrativity*, ed. John Pier and José Ángel García Landa (Boston: Walter de Gruyter, 2008), 419–451.

13. On the expository role of the rabbinic text in relation to the perceived omnisignificance of the biblical text, see James Kugel, *Traditions of the Bible: A Guide to the Bible as It Was at the Start of the Common Era* (Cambridge, Mass.: Harvard University Press, 1999), 17ff.

14. Elaine Scarry, *The Body in Pain: The Making and Unmaking of the World* (New York: Oxford University Press, 1987), 188. On the *toldot* formula generally, see Matthew A. Thomas, *These are the Generations: Identity, Covenant, and the 'toledot' Formula* (New York: T & T Clark, 2011).

15. George M. Savran, *Telling and Retelling: Quotation in Biblical Narrative* (Bloomington: Indiana University Press, 1988), 46.

16. See Michael L. Satlow, *Jewish Marriage in Antiquity* (Princeton, N.J.: Princeton University Press, 2001); Lieve M. Teugels, *Bible and Midrash: The Story of the "Wooing of Rebekah" (Gen 24)* (Leuven: Peeters, 2005); and Gail S. Labovitz, *Marriage and Metaphor: Constructions of Gender in Rabbinic Literature* (Lanham, Md.: Lexington Books, 2009).

17. Sternberg, *Poetics of Biblical Narrative*, 92 and 182.

18. On this important question with its sizable secondary literature, see, for instance, the title essay from Bernard M. Levinson's *The Right Chorale: From the Poetics to the Hermeneutics of the Hebrew Bible* (Tübingen: Mohr Siebeck, 2008).

19. I build on the excellent study of the Rashbam by Hanna Liss, *Creating Fictional Worlds: Peshat Exegesis and Narrativity in Rashbam's Commentary on the Torah* (Leiden: Brill, 2011), which in turn owes a debt to the pathbreaking work of Eleazar Touitou's *Ha-peshatot ha-mithadeshim be-khol yom: 'Iyyunim beperusho shel Rashbam la-Torah* (Ramat Gan: Bar-Ilan University Press, 2003). The preferred edition of the Rashbam's commentary is *Der Pentateuch Commentar des R. Samuel Ben Meir*, trans. David Rosin (Breslau, 1881).

20. Ramban on Genesis 12:6; online commentary in Hebrew at www.sefaria.org/ Ramban_on_Genesis.

21. On the Ramban's synthetic approach to structures of repetition, see Michelle Levine, *Nahmanides on Genesis: The Art of Biblical Portraiture* Brown Judaic Series no. 350 (Providence: Brown University Press, 2010).

22. Robert Alter, *The Art of Biblical Narrative: Specimens of Stylistic and Structural Analysis* (New York: Basic Books, 1981), 53. See, as well, J. P. Fokkelman, *Narrative Art in Genesis: Specimens of Stylistic and Structural Analysis* (Eugene: Wipf and Stock, 2004).

23. *Midrash Rabbah*—Genesis 60:8. Online Hebrew version at www.daat.ac.il/ daat/ tanach/raba/shaar-2.htm.

24. *Midrash Rabbeinu Bachya* vol. 1, trans. Eliyahu Munk (New York-Jerusalem: Lambda, 2003), 366.

25. See *Midrash of Rabbi Moshe Alshich*, trans. Eliyahu Munk (New York-Jerusalem: Lamda, 2000), 152.

26. See James Price, *The Syntax of Masoretic Accents in the Hebrew Bible* (E. Mellen Press, 1990); and Aaron Dotan, ed., *Sefer diqduqe ha-te'amim le-rabbi Aharon Ben-Moshe Ben-Asher* (Jerusalem: Hebrew University, 1979 [1963]).

27. Nelly Altenberger, "Chayei Sarah: Shalshelet and Its Meanings," *Sefaria.org* https://www.sefaria.org/sheets/86693.?lang=bi.

28. The same combination occurs in Gen 39:8, on the word *vay'maen* ("and he adamantly refused"), as Joseph resists the advances of Potiphar's wife. The other two instances are Gen 19:16 on the word *vayitmah'mah* ("and he lingered"), as Lot wavers before leaving S'dom, and on *vayishhat* ("And he [Moses] slaughtered") in Lev 8:23, interpreted as expressing Moses's ambivalence in being excluded from anointment to the Priesthood.

29. See the general introduction by Robert A. Harris, "Medieval Jewish Biblical Exegesis," in *A History of Biblical Interpretation Vol 2: The Medieval through the Reformation Periods*, ed. Alan J. Hauser and Duane F. Watson (Grand Rapids: Eerdmanns, 2009), 141–183; also, Eran Viezel, "'The Anxiety of Influence': Rashbam's Approach to Rashi's Commentary on the Torah," *AJS Review* 40.2 (November 2016): 279–303.

30. *Torat Ḥayim* (Mosad ha-Rav Kook, 1988). *Mikrot Gedolot* in Hebrew, online at he.wikisource.org/wiki/מקראות_גדולות.

31. Bernard M. Levinson, "Literary Exegesis of Biblical Narrative: Between Poetics and Hermeneutics," in *Not in Heaven: Coherence and Complexity in Biblical Narrative* (Bloomington: Indiana University Press, 1991), 120–128.

32. Sternberg exhaustively tracks this scene in "Double Cave, Double Talk: The Indirections of Biblical Dialogue" in *Not in Heaven*, 128–157.

33. On *peshat* as "contextual" and possible Quranic influence, see Edward L. Greenstein, "Medieval Bible Commentaries," in *Back to the Sources*, ed. Barry Holtz (New York: Simon and Schuster, Inc., 1984), 213–259.

34. On this device, see Harris, *Discerning Parallelism: A Study in Northern French Medieval Jewish Biblical Exegesis* (Providence: Brown Judaic Studies, 2004).

35. Liss, *Creating Fictional Worlds*, 81ff. See also Mordechai Z. Cohen, "Rashbam Scholarship in Perpetual Motion," *Jewish Quarterly Review* 98.3 (Summer 2008): 389–408.

36. See, for instance, J. P. Fokkelman, *Reading Biblical Narrative: An Introductory Guide* (Louisville: Westminster John Knox Press, 2000), 112–122; Alter, *Art of Biblical Narrative*, 88–113; and Savran, *Telling and Retelling*.

37. *Sofer* ("scribal narrator-editor") is Rashbam's term of choice for Moses himself.

38. Georges Poulet, "The Phenomenology of Reading," *New Literary History* 1.1 (October, 1969): 53–68.

39. The Hebrew is *tamim t'heyeh im hashem elokecha*, "Be simple with the Lord, your God," on which Rashi comments, "Conduct yourself with Him with simplicity and depend on Him, and do not inquire of the future; rather, *accept whatever happens to you with [unadulterated] simplicity* and then, you will be with Him and to His portion."

40. Convergence-wise, it doesn't hurt that of the many commentaries attributed to Rashbam besides his commentary on the Pentateuch, two of the three that survive treat the Books of Job and Ecclesiastes, which feature men of semi-constant sorrow. On the third, see Hannah Liss, "The Commentary on the Song of Songs Attributed to R. Samuel ben Meïr (Rashbam)," http://www.medieval-jewish-studies.com/Journal/Vol1/article01.html.

41. Brian Richardson, *Unnatural Voices: Extreme Narration in Modern and Contemporary Fiction* (Columbus: Ohio State University Press, 2004). The term that it means to echo is "the disnarrated," developed by Gerald Prince in "The Disnarrated," *Style* 22.1 (Spring 1988): 1–8.

42. A general introduction to the concept and bibliography can be found at www.lhn.uni-hamburg.de/article/unnatural-narrative, on the online *Living Handbook of Narratology*. It features prominently in the fiction of Douglas Coupland.

43. The film features several misdirections: incongruities like the repeated use of "Hashem" by conservative Jews in 1960s Minnesota, solecisms (e.g., a *mezuzah* fastened to the wrong side of the doorway or a desk-size image of the Ten Commandments with its two columns reversed), and ritual errors as in the Bar Mitzvah scene.

44. Levinson, *Right Chorale*, 11.

45. Hegemony of narrative sequence does not exemplify the Coen Brothers' cinematic universe, anyway—from the labyrinth of connecting details in *Blood Simple* to the major plot elision in *No Country for Old Men*, from the cyclicality and stylizations of *Miller's Crossing* to the endless loop of *Inside Llewyn Davis*.

46. The fictional device has generated real-world scholarship: "The Mentaculus Vision" by Barry Loewer, in *Time's Arrows and the World's Probability Structure*, ed. Barry Loewer, Brad Weslake, and Eric Winsberg (Harvard University Press, forthcoming.)

47. The Hebrew root "Sh.B.Sh" happens to mean "error," as in textual corruption: *meshubash* is a corrupted or inaccurate text.

48. Dana Steven, "A Serious Man: A Seriously Good Coen Brothers Movie," *Slate*, October 1, 2009, www.slate.com/articles/arts/movies/2009/10/a_serious_man.html.

49. Jon S. Baird, "A Collaborative Narrative," *Diegetic Digest*, August 29, 2012, diegeticdigest.blogspot.com/2012/08/a-serious-man-collaborative-narrative.html.

50. David Denby, "Gods and Victims," *New Yorker*, October 5, 2009, 88.

51. Peter Rainer, "Movie Review: 'A Serious Man'," *Christian Science Monitor*, October 2, 2009, www.csmonitor.com/The-Culture/Movies/2009/1002/p17s02-almo.html.

52. See *Living Handbook of Narratology*, http://www.lhn.uni-hamburg.de/article/metalepsis-revised-version-uploaded-13-july-2016.

53. Adele Berlin, *Poetics and Interpretation of Biblical Narrative* (Sheffield: Almond Press, 1983), 62–63, 91, 92; and Simcha Kogut, "On the Meaning and Syntactical Status of הנה in Biblical Hebrew," in *Studies in Scripta Hierosolymitana*, vol. 31, ed. Sara Japhet (Jerusalem: Magnes Press, 1986), 133–154.

54. Rashbam, *Commentary on Genesis: An Annotated Translation*, trans. Martin I. Lockshin (E. Mellen Press, 1989).

55. Liss, *Creating Fictional Worlds*, 141.

56. As Jeffrey Adams expresses the same idea in *The Cinema of the Coen Brothers: Hard-Boiled Entertainments* (New York: Columbia University Press, 2015), "We are answerable to their texts. Our response is our responsibility" (200).

57. Benjamin, "Theses on the Philosophy of History," 253–264. See also Derrida's explanation of the concept as "heterogeneous and disjointed time" in *Specters of Marx: The State of the Debt, the Work of Mourning and the New International*, trans. Peggy Kamuf (New York: Routledge, 2006), 181.

58. On these and other linguistic misunderstandings, see Jonathan Boyarin's essay from the symposium "An Ugly Story?" *AJS Review* 35.2 (November 2011): 377–382.

59. Walter Benjamin, *The Correspondence of Walter Benjamin and Gershom Scholem, 1932–1940*, trans. Gary Smith, Andre LeFevere, and Anson Rabinbach (Cambridge, Mass.: Harvard University Press, 1992), 142.

60. Agamben might as well be describing Larry's empty conversations with assorted rabbis and lawyers, when he identifies "a legitimation crisis in which law is in force as the pure 'Nothing of Revelation'" (Agamben, *Homo Sacer*, 51; also quoted in Santner, *Psychotheology of Everyday Life*, 41).

61. Slavoj Žižek, "God without the Sacred: The Book of Job, the First Critique of Ideology," November 9, 2010, New York Public Library, nypl.org

/sites/default/files/ av/ transcripts/LIVE ZizekGod_11.9TranscriptQUERIES.pdf.

62. I draw here from André Aciman's concept of "mnemonic arbitrage" in his essay "Arbitrage," in *False Papers* (New York: Farrar, Straus and Giroux, 2011), 148–164.

63. Derrida, "Abraham, the Other," in *Judeities: Questions for Jacques Derrida*, ed. Bergo, Bettina, Joseph Cohen, Raphael Zagury-Orly, trans. Bettina Bergo and Michael B. Smith (New York: Fordham University Press, 2007), 34.

64. Franz Kafka, *Parables and Paradoxes*, ed. by Nahum N. Glatzer (New York: Schocken Books, 1995), 45.

65. (*PI*§107). In a diary entry reproduced in *Ludwig Wittgenstein: Private and Public Occasions*, ed. James C. Klagg and Alfred Nordmann (Lanham, Md.: Rowman and Littlefield, 2003), the philosopher writes, "I must be a very modern person since the cinema has such an extraordinarily beneficial effect on me. I cannot imagine any rest for the mind more adequate to me than an American movie," 29.

66. Bruns, *Hermeneutics Ancient and Modern* (New Haven, Conn.: Yale University Press, 1995), 207.

EPILOGUE: KNOTTED THREAD, MIDDLE GAME: AN *ENVOI*

1. See Trevor, H. Levere, *Affinity and Matter—Elements of Chemical Philosophy 1800–1865* (Philadelphia: Gordon and Breach Science Publishers, 1971). In Abraham Rees's *The Cyclopaedia; Or, Universal Dictionary of Arts, Sciences and Literature* Vol. 1 (London: Longman, 1819), a lengthy entry for "affinity" connects it with "gravitation," cohesion," and "adhesion" as various species of attraction.

2. David Shumway, "Disciplinary Identities," in *Affiliations: Identity in Academic Culture*, ed. Jeffrey R. Di Leo (Lincoln: University of Nebraska Press, 2003), 92.

3. Stephen Watt, "It Seems (Af)Filiation Is to Blame," in *Affiliations: Identity in Academic Culture*, ed. Jeffrey R. Di Leo (Lincoln: University of Nebraska Press, 2003), 125.

4. Maria Damon, "Memoirs of a Mutable Thoughter," in *Affiliations: Identity in Academic Culture*, ed. Jeffrey R. Di Leo (Lincoln: University of Nebraska Press, 2003), 238.

5. The metaphor appears in Levinas, *Otherwise Than Being*, 5–8; and greatly elaborated by Derrida in the essay, "At This Very Moment in This Work Here I Am," trans. Ruben Berezdivin, in *Rereading Levinas*, ed. Robert Bernasconi and Simon Critchley, (London: Athlone, 1991), 11–49.

6. Schreier, *Impossible Jew*, 12.

7. Saul Bellow, *Herzog* (New York: Penguin Books, 2003), 225.

8. It is safe to say that Robbins's documentaries, "Some of My Best Friends are Zionists" (2012) and "How Shlomo Sand Stopped Being a Jew" (2017) on the one hand, and Bellow's university fictions like *Mister Sammler's Planet* or *Ravelstein* on the other, inhabit rather different ideological worlds.

9. Bruce Robbins, *Secular Vocations: Intellectuals, Professionalism, Culture* (London: Verso, 1993), 30.

10. Neusner, *How to Grade Your Professors*, 38.

11. Likewise, see two important works by Paul Bové, *Mastering Discourse: The Politics of Intellectual Culture* (Durham, N.C.: Duke University Press, 1992), and *Intellectuals in Power: A Genealogy of Critical Humanism* (New York: Columbia University Press, 1986).

12. For example, *The Undercommons: Fugitive Planning* by Fred Moten and Stefano Harney, a platform for a reenergized Black Studies; see, in particular, chapter 2, "The University and the Undercommons: Seven Theses," published separately in *Social Text* 79 22. 2 (Summer 2004): 101–115.

13. For example, Sidonie Smith's *Manifesto for Humanities: Transforming Doctoral Education in Good Enough Times* (Ann Arbor: University of Michigan Press, 2015), or Mikhail Epstein's *Transformative Humanities: A Manifesto* (London: Bloomsbury, 2012).

14. Ferguson, Roderick A. *The Reorder of Things: The University and Its Pedagogies of Minority Difference* (Minneapolis: University of Minnesota Press, 2012), 232.

15. Ralph Waldo Emerson, *Essays and Lectures*, ed. Joel Porte (New York: Library of America, 1983), 53–54.

16. The Emersonian term reappears throughout Bercovitch's "Games of Chess: A Model of Literary and Cultural Studies," in *Centuries' Ends, Narrative Means*, ed. Robert Newman (Stanford: Stanford University Press, 1996), 15–57.

17. Stanley Cavell, *This New Yet Unapproachable America: Lectures After Emerson After Wittgenstein* (Albuquerque: Living Batch Press, 1989), 8.

18. Readings, *University in Ruins*, 223n12, and 227n10.

19. Cavell, *Unapproachable America*. Cavell explains that America is presently "unapproachable" for Emerson "both because there is nowhere else to go to find it, we have to turn toward it, reverse ourselves; and because we do not know if our presence to it is peopling it" (92–93).

20. A formative intellectual influence on all my work, Stanley Cavell passed away as this book was in production. Of many appreciations composed before and after, a passage from Mark Greif's "Cavell as Educator," *n+1* Issue 12: Conversion Experience, July 5, 2011, https://nplusonemag.com/issue-12/essays/cavell-as-educator, speaks to my purposes as a postscript:

"His career started with asking what is on this side of the chasm, where we all live, most of the time—what we are doing here. And what, in what we do here, will lead us to any other side. What acts, or speech, will erect a bridge from here to there, or lay a plank, or throw the philosopher's 'rope over an abyss'? Or what will move us, shuffling our feet, until perspective reveals the distance to the other side to be only a step, if life were differently viewed?"

WORKS CITED

Aciman, André. *Papers*. New York: Farrar, Straus and Giroux, 2000.
Adams, Jeffrey. *The Cinema of the Coen Brothers: Hard-Boiled Entertainments*. New York: Columbia University Press, 2015.
Adler, Eliyana R., and Sheila E. Jelen, eds. *Jewish Literature and History: An Interdisciplinary Conversation*. Bethesda: University Press of Maryland, 2008.
Adorno, Theodor. *Minima Moralia: Reflections from Damaged Life*. Trans E. F. N. Jephcott. London: Verso, 2006.
———. *Theorie der Halbbildung* [Theory of Half-Education]. Frankfurt am Main: Suhrkamp, 2006.
Agamben, Giorgio. *The Coming Community*. Trans Michael Hardt. Minneapolis: University of Minnesota Press, 1991.
———. *Homo Sacer: Sovereign Power and Bare Life*. Trans. Daniel Heller-Roazen. Stanford: Stanford University Press, 1998.
———. *The Man without Content*. Trans. Georgia Albert. Stanford: Stanford University Press, 1999.
———. *Potentialities: Collected Essays in Philosophy*. Trans. Daniel Heller-Roazen. Stanford: Stanford University Press, 1999.
———. "What Is a Paradigm?," http://www.maxvanmanen.com/files/2014/03/Agamben-What-Is-a-paradigm1.pdf.
Agnon, Yosef Shmu'el. *Only Yesterday*. Trans. Barbara Harshav. Princeton, N.J.: Princeton University Press, 2004.
Ahrens, Erich. "Reminiscences of the Men of the Frankfurt Lehrhaus." *Yearbook Leo Baeck Institute* 19.1 (1974): 245–253.
Alexander, Phillip S. "Jewish Studies in Comparative Contexts; Great Britain." In *Teaching Jewish Civilization: A Global Approach to Higher Education*. Ed. Moshe Davis. New York: New York University Press, 1995.
Alexander, Zaia. "Primo Levi and Translation." In *The Cambridge Companion to Primo Levi*. Ed. Robert S. C. Gordon. Cambridge: Cambridge University Press, 2007, 155–169.
Alshich, R. Moshe. *Midrash of Rabbi Moshe Alshich*. Trans. Eliyahu Munk. New York-Jerusalem: Lambda, 2000.

Alter, Robert. *The Art of Biblical Narrative*. New York: Basic Books, 1981.
———. *Canon and Creativity: Modern Writing and the Authority of Scripture*. New Haven, Conn.: Yale University Press, 2013.
———. "What Jewish Studies Can Do." *Commentary* (October 1974): 71–76.
Altmann, Alexander. *Jewish Studies: Their Scope and Meaning Today*. Hillel Foundation, 1958.
Amir, Yehudah. "The Distinctively Jewish Perspective in the Thought of Franz Rosenzweig". *Daat*. 6 (1961): 89–102 (Hebrew).
Arama, R. Isaac. *Akeydat Yitzchak*. Trans. Eliyahu Munk. New York-Jerusalem: Lambda, 2001.
Aravamudan, Srinivas. "The Character of the University." *Boundary 2* 37:1 (2010): 23–55.
Asad, Talal. *Formations of the Secular: Christianity, Islam, Modernity*. Stanford: Stanford University Press, 2003.
Aschheim. Steven E. *Culture and Catastrophe: German and Jewish Confrontations with National Socialism and Other Crises*. New York: New York University Press, 1996.
Attias, Jean-Christophe. *The Jews and the Bible*. Trans. Patrick Camiller. Stanford: Stanford University Press, 2015.
Attridge, Derek. "The Humanities without Condition: Derrida and the Singular Oeuvre." *Arts and Humanities in Higher Education* 13.1–2 (2014): 54–61.
Avery-Peck, Alan J., Bruce Chilton, William Scott Green, and Gary G. Porton, eds. *A Legacy of Learning: Essays in Honor of Jacob Neusner*. Leiden: Brill, 2014.
Augustine. *Confessions*, Book X. Ed. J. J. O'Donnell. New York: Oxford University Press, 2013. http://www.stoa.org/hippo/frame_entry.html.
Bahti, Timothy. "The Injured University." In *Logomachia: The Conflict of the Faculties*. Ed. Richard A. Rand. Lincoln: University of Nebraska Press, 1992.
Baḥya, R. ben Yosef Ibn Paḳuda. *Midrash Rabbeinu Bachya*. Trans. Eliyahu Munk. New York-Jerusalem: Lambda, 2003.
Baird, Jon S. "A Serious Man—A Collaborative Narrative." *Diegetic Digest*, August 29, 2012, http://diegeticdigest.blogspot.com/2012/08/a-serious-man-collaborative-narrative.html.
Baird, Robert. "Boys of the Wissenschaft." In *Judaism Since Gender*. Ed. Miriam Peskowitz and Laura Levitt. New York: Routledge, 1997.
Baker, Cynthia. *Jew*. New Brunswick, N.J.: Rutgers University Press, 2017.
Bakhos, Carol. "Method(ological) Matters in the Study of Midrash." In *Current Trends in the Study of Midrash*. Ed. Carol Bakhos. Leiden: Brill, 2006, 161–188.

Bakhtin, M. M. *Art and Answerability: Early Philosophical Essays.* Trans Vadim Liapunov and Kenneth Brostrom. Austin: University of Texas Press, 1981.
———. *The Dialogic Imagination: Four Essays.* Trans. Caryl Emerson and Michael Holquist. Austin: University of Texas Press, 1981.
———. *Speech Genres and Other Late Essays.* Trans. Vern W. McGee. Austin: University of Texas Press, 1986.
Band, Arnold J. "Jewish Studies in American Liberal-Arts Colleges and Universities." *American Jewish Year Book* 67 (1967): 3–30.
———. *Studies in Modern Jewish Literature.* Philadelphia: Jewish Publication Society, 2003.
Barnett, Ronald. *Being a University.* New York: Routledge, 2011.
Barthes, Roland. *Leçon.* Paris: Editions du Seuil, 1978.
Baskin, Judith R. "Jewish Studies in North American Colleges and Universities: Yesterday, Today, and Tomorrow." *Shofar* 32.4 (2014): 9–26.
Batnitzky, Leora. "Dialogue as Judgment, Not Mutual Affirmation: A New Look at Franz Rosenzweig's Dialogical Philosophy." *The Journal of Religion* 79.4 (October, 1999): 523–544.
———. *Idolatry and Representation: The Philosophy of Franz Rosenzweig Reconsidered.* Princeton, N.J.: Princeton University Press, 2000.
Baumgarten, Albert I. "Review of Aaron Hughes, *Jacob Neusner: An American Jewish Iconoclast.*" *Enoch Seminar*, March 4, 2017, http://enochseminar.org/review/12805.
Becher, Tony, and Paul Trowler. *Academic Tribes and Territories: Intellectual Enquiry and the Cultures of Disciplines.* Philadelphia: Open University Press, 2001.
Bell, Dean Phillip, ed. *The Bloomsbury Companion to Jewish Studies.* London: Bloomsbury, 2013.
Bell, Roger V. *Sounding the Abyss: Readings between Cavell and Derrida.* Lanham, Md.: Lexington Books, 1992.
Bellamy, Elizabeth. *Affective Genealogies: Psychoanalysis, Postmodernism, and the "Jewish Question."* Lincoln: University of Nebraska Press, 1997.
Bellow, Saul. *Herzog.* New York: Penguin Books, 2003.
———."Op-Ed- Papuans and Zulus." *New York Times Book Review*, March 10, 1994.
Benjamin, Andrew. *Of Jews and Animals.* Edinburgh: Edinburgh University Press, 2011.
Benjamin, Walter. *The Correspondence of Walter Benjamin and Gershom Scholem, 1932–1940.* Trans. Gary Smith, Andre LeFevere, and Anson Rabinbach. Cambridge, Mass.: Harvard University Press, 1992.
———. *Illuminations: Essays and Reflections.* Ed. Hannah Arendt. Trans. Harry Zohn. New York: Schocken Books, 1968.

———. "On Language as Such and on the Language of Man." Trans. Edmund Jephcott. In *Selected Writings Volume 1 1913–1926*. Ed. Marcus Bullock and Michael W. Jennings. Cambridge, Mass.: Belknap Press of Harvard University Press, 1996, 62–74.

———. *One-Way Street, and Other Writings*. Trans. Edmund Jephcott and Kingsley Shorter. London: Verso, 1978.

———. *Walter Benjamin, Early Writings (1910–1917)*. Trans. Howard Eiland et al. Cambridge, Mass.: Harvard University Press, 2011.

Bercovitch, Sacvan. "Games of Chess: A Model of Literary and Cultural Studies." In *Centuries' Ends, Narrative Means*. Ed. Robert Newman. Stanford: Stanford University Press, 1996, 15–57.

———. "The Philosophical Background to the Fable of Emerson's 'American Scholar.'" *Journal of the History of Ideas* 28.1 (January–March, 1967): 123–128.

———. *The Rites of Assent: Transformations in the Symbolic Constructions of America*. New York: Routledge, 1993.

Bergo, Bettina, Joseph Cohen, Raphael Zagury-Orly, eds. *Judeities: Questions for Jacques Derrida*. Trans. Bettina Bergo and Michael B. Smith. New York: Fordham University Press, 2007.

Berkovitz, Jay R. *Protocols of Justice: The Pinkas of the Metz Rabbinic Court 1771–1789*. Leiden: Brill, 2016.

Berlin, Adele. *Poetics and Interpretation of Biblical Narrative*. Sheffield: Almond Press, 1983.

Berman, Lila Corwin. "Jewish History Beyond the Jewish People." *AJS Review* 42.2 (November 2018), 269–292.

Bernard-Donals, Michael, ed. *Jewish Rhetorics: History, Theory, Practice*. Waltham: Brandeis University Press, 2014.

Bernasconi, Robert. "On Deconstructing Nostalgia for Community Within the West: The Debate Between Nancy and Blanchot." *Research in Phenomenology* 23.1 (1993): 3–21.

Bernstein, Jeffrey. "The Paradoxical Transmission of Tradition and Agamben's Potential Reading of the Rishonim." *Comparative and Continental Philosophy* 3.2 (2011): 225–242.

Berry, Rohan. "The Coen Brothers: Serious Men?" *Apercu*. August 26, 2011.

Best, Stephen, and Sharon Marcus. "Surface Reading: An Introduction." *Representations* 108.1 "The Way We Read Now" (Fall 2009): 1–21.

Biale, David. *Gershom Scholem: Kabbalah and Counter-History*. Cambridge, Mass.: Harvard University Press, 1979.

Biale, David, ed. *Cultures of the Jews: A New History*. New York: Schocken Books, 2002.

Biale, David, Michael Galchinsky, and Susannah Heschel, eds. *Insider/Outsider: American Jews and Multiculturalism*. Berkeley: University of California Press, 1998.

Bielik-Robson, Agata. *Jewish Cryptotheologies of Late Modernity: Philosophical Marranos*. New York: Routledge, 2014.

Black, Antony. *Guilds and Civil Society*. Ithaca: Cornell University Press, 1984.

Blum, Mark E. *Kafka's Social Discourse: An Aesthetic Search for Community*. Bethlehem, Pa.: Lehigh University Press, 2011.

Blumberg, Ilana M. *Houses of Study: A Jewish Woman Among Books*. Bison, 2009.

Blumenthal, David. "Jewish Studies and Religious Studies." Religious Education 81.1 (Winter 1986): 29–36.

———. "Where Does 'Jewish Studies' Belong?" *Journal of the American Academy of Religion* 44.3 (1976): 535–546.

Boelhower, William. *Through a Glass Darkly: Ethnic Semiosis in American Literature*. New York: Oxford University Press, 1987.

Boitani, Pietro. *The Bible and Its Rewritings*. Trans. Anita Weston. New York: Oxford University Press, 1999.

Bono, James J., Tim Dean, and Ewa Plonowska Ziarek, eds. *A Time for the Humanities: Futurity and the Limits of Autonomy*. New York: Fordham University Press, 2008.

Bourdieu, Pierre. *Homo Academicus*. Trans. Peter Collier. Stanford: Stanford University Press, 1988.

Bousquet, Marc. *How the University Works: Higher Education and the Low-Wage Nation*. New York: New York University Press, 2008.

Boustan, Ra'anan S., Oren Kosansky, and Marina Rustow, eds. *Jewish Studies at the Crossroads of Anthropology and History: Authority, Diaspora, Tradition*. Philadelphia: University of Pennsylvania Press, 2011.

Bové, Paul. *Intellectuals in Power: A Genealogy of Critical Humanism*. New York: Columbia University Press, 1986.

———. *Mastering Discourse: The Politics of Intellectual Culture*. Durham, N.C.: Duke University Press, 1992.

Boyarin, Daniel. *Intertextuality and the Reading of Midrash*. Bloomington: Indiana University Press, 1994.

———. "Jewish Studies as Teratology: The Rabbis as Monsters." *Jewish Quarterly Review* 88.1/2 (July–October 1997): 57–66.

———. "On the Status of the Tannaitic Midrashim: A Critique of Jacob Neusner's Latest Contribution to Midrashic Studies." *Journal of the American Oriental Society* 112. 3 (July–September 1992): 455–465.

———. *Socrates and the Fat Rabbis*. Chicago: University of Chicago Press, 2009.

———. "The Talmud as a Fat Rabbi: A Novel Approach." *Text and Talk* 28.5 (2008): 603–619.

Boyarin, Jonathan. "Responsive Thinking: Cultural Studies and Jewish Historiography." In *Modern Judaism and Historical Consciousness: Identities, Encounters, Perspectives.* Ed. Andreas Gotzmann and Christian Wiese. Leiden: Brill, 2007, 477–478.

———. *Thinking in Jewish.* Chicago: University of Chicago Press, 1996.

———. 2017 foreword, https://ingeveb.org/articles/yiddish-science-and-the-postmodern.

———. "An Ugly Story?" *AJS Review* 35.2 (November, 2011): 377–382.

Boyarin, Jonathan, and Daniel Boyarin. *Jews and Other Differences: The New Jewish Cultural Studies.* Minneapolis: University of Minnesota Press, 2008.

Braidotti, Rosi, and Paul Gilroy, eds. *Conflicting Humanities.* London: Bloomsbury, 2016.

Braiterman, Zachary. "'Into Life'??!—Franz Rosenzweig and the Figure of Death." *AJS Review* 23.2 (1998): 203–222.

———. "The Patient Political Gesture: Law, Liberalism, and Talmud." In *Judaism, Liberalism, and Political Theology.* Ed. Randi Rashkover and Martin Kavka. Bloomington: Indiana University Press, 2014, 241–265.

———. "Response to Jacob Neusner." *Religious Education* 95.1 (Winter 2000): 105.

———. *The Shape of Revelation: Aesthetics and Modern Jewish Thought.* Stanford: Stanford University Press, 2007.

———. "Teaching Jewish Studies in a Radically Gentile Space: Some Personal Reflections." *Religious Education* 94.4 (Fall 1999): 396–409.

———. "Too Jewish Studies (Response to Aaron Hughes)." *Jewish Philosophy Place*, May 8, 2014, https://jewishphilosophyplace.com/2014/05/08/too-jewish-jewish-studies-response-to-aaron-hughes/.

Brenner, Michael. *The Renaissance of Jewish Culture in Weimar Germany.* New Haven, Conn.: Yale University Press, 1996.

Brinner, William. "Introduction." *Judaism* 45.2 (Spring 1996): 131–133.

Bruce, Iris. *Kafka and Cultural Zionism: Dates in Palestine.* Madison: University of Wisconsin Press, 2007.

Bruford, W. H. *The German Tradition of Self-Cultivation: "Bildung" from Humboldt to Thomas Mann.* Cambridge: Cambridge University Press, 2010.

Bruns, Gerald. *Hermeneutics Ancient and Modern.* New Haven, Conn.: Yale University Press, 1995.

Buber, Martin. "Die Lösung" [The Watchword.] Zur Programmatik der Zeitschrift. *Der Jude* 1 (1916): 1–2.

———."Jewish Scholarship: New Perspectives." In *The Jew in the Modern World: A Documentary History.* Ed. Paul Mendes-Flohr and Jehuda Reinharz. New York: Oxford University Press, 2010, 214–242.

———. *The Letters of Martin Buber: A Life of Dialogue*. Ed. Nahum N. Glatzer and Paul Mendes-Flohr. Syracuse: Syracuse University Press, 1991.

Buber, Martin, and Franz Rosenzweig. *Scripture and Translation*. Trans. Lawrence Rosenwald, with Everett Fox. Bloomington: Indiana University Press, 1994.

Budick, Emily Miller. "Performing Jewish Identity in Philip Roth's *Counterlife*." In *Key Texts in American Jewish Culture*. Ed. Jack Kugelmass. New Brunswick, N.J.: Rutgers University Press, 2003, 75–88.

Bush, Andrew. *Jewish Studies: A Theoretical Introduction*. New Brunswick, N.J.: Rutgers University Press, 2011.

Cadav, Eduardo, Peter Connor, and Jean-Luc Nancy, eds. *Who Comes After the Subject* New York: Routledge, 1991.

Calvino, Italo. *Invisible Cities*. Trans. William Weaver. New York: Harcourt Brace Jovanovich, 1978.

Caplan, Marc. *How Strange the Change: Language, Temporality, and Narrative Form in Peripheral Modernisms*. Stanford: Stanford University Press, 2011.

———. "Review of *from Continuity to Contiguity: Toward a New Jewish Literary Thinking* by Dan Miron. *Journal of Jewish Identities* 4.2 (July 2011): 95–97.

Caputi, Mary, and Vincent J. Del Casino Jr., eds. *Derrida and the Future of the Liberal Arts: Professions of Faith*. London: Bloomsbury, 2013.

Casey, Edward S. *The Fate of Place: A Philosophical History*. Berkeley: University of California Press, 1997.

Cavell, Stanley. *Philosophy the Day After Tomorrow*. Cambridge, Mass.: Harvard University Press, 2005.

———. *A Pitch of Philosophy*. Cambridge, Mass.: Harvard University Press, 1994.

———. *This New Yet Unapproachable America: Lectures After Emerson After Wittgenstein*. Albuquerque: Living Batch Press, 1989.

Cerbone, David R. "Dwelling on Rough Ground: Heidegger, Wittgenstein, Architecture." In *Wittgenstein and Heidegger*. Ed. David Egan, Stephen Reynolds, Aaron Wendland. New York: Routledge, 2013, 245–260.

Chion, Michel. *Jacques Tati*. Cahiers du Cinema/Paris: Seuil, 1987.

Cheyette, Bryan. "Against Supersessionist Thinking: Old and New, Jews and Postcolonialism, the Ghetto and Diaspora." *Cambridge Journal of Postcolonial Literary Inquiry* 4.3 (September 2017): 424–439.

———. *Diasporas of the Mind: Jewish and Postcolonial Writing and the Nightmare of History*. New Haven, Conn.: Yale University Press, 2014.

Cielemęcka, Olga, and Monika Rogowska-Stangret. "Stigmergy as a Collective Research Practice." In *Imagine There Were No Humanities . . .*

Transdisciplinary Perspectives. Ed. Ines K. Ackermann, Katarzyna Chruszczewska, Ewa Róża Janion, Ágnes Máté, Natalia Obukowicz. Warsaw: Wydawnictwo DiG, 2015, 51–59.

Ciocan, Cristian, and Georges Hansel. *Levinas Concordance.* Dordrecht: Springer, 2005.

Clark, Timothy, and Nicholas Royle. "The University in Ruins." *Oxford Literary Review* 17 (1995).

Coen, Ethan, and Joel. Interview with Andrew O'Heir. "Goys, God, Dentistry, and 'A Serious Man.'" *Salon,* Oct. 1, 2009, www.salon.com/2009/10/01/coens/.

———. *A Serious Man.* London: Faber and Faber, 2009.

Cohen, Aryeh. "Why Textual Reasoning?" *Journal of Textual Reasoning* 1.1 (2002). http://jtr.shanti.virginia.edu/volume-1-number-1/cohen-why-textual-reasoning/.

Cohen, Gerald A. "Complete Bullshit." In *Finding Oneself in the Other.* Ed. Michael Otsuka. Princeton, N.J.: Princeton University Press, 2012.

Cohen, Gerson. "An Embarrassment of Riches: Reflections on the Conditions of American Jewish Scholarship in 1969." In *The Teaching of Judaica in American Universities.* Ed. Leon A. Jick. New York: Ktav Publishing, 1970.

Cohen, Hermann. "Die Errichtung von Lehrstühlen für Ethik und Religionsphilosophie an den jüdisch-theologischen Lehranstalten." *Monatsschrift für Geschichte und Wissenschaft des Judentums* 48.1 (January 1904): 2–21.

Cohen, Mordechai Z. "Rashbam Scholarship in Perpetual Motion." *Jewish Quarterly Review* 98.3 (Summer 2008): 389–408.

Cohen, Shaye. "Jacob Neusner, Mishnah, and Counter-Rabbinics: A Review Essay." *Conservative Judaism* 37 (1983): 48–63

Cohen, Shaye, and Edward L. Greenstein. *The State of Jewish Studies.* Detroit, Mich.: Wayne State University Press, 1990.

Cohen, Tom, ed. *Jacques Derrida and the Humanities: A Critical Reader.* Cambridge: Cambridge University Press, 2009.

Collini, Stefan. *Speaking of Universities.* London: Verso, 2017.

Conard, Mark. *The Philosophy of the Coen Brothers.* Lexington: University of Kentucky Press, 2012.

Cover, Robert. "Nomos and Narrative." *Harvard Law Review* 97.4 (1983): 4–68.

Cristaudo, Wayne. *Religion, Redemption, and Revolution: The New Speech Thinking of Franz Rosenzweig and Eugen Rosenstock-Huessy.* Toronto: University of Toronto Press, 2012.

Critchley, Simon. "With Being-With? Notes on Jean-Luc Nancy's Rewriting of Being and Time." *Studies in Practical Philosophy* 1.1 (1999): 53–67.

Cutter, William. "Jewish Studies as Self-Definition: A Review Essay." *Jewish Social Studies* 3.1 (Autumn 1996): 158–176.

Cutler, Yosl. *Muntergang. 2ṭe oyfl.* Nyu York: Farlag Signal Proletaren, 1934.

Davis, Moshe, ed. *Teaching Jewish Civilization: A Global Approach to Higher Education.* New York: New York University Press, 1995.

Davis, Ruth F. *Musical Exodus: Al-Andalus and Its Jewish Diasporas.* Lanham, Md.: Rowman and Littlefield, 2015.

DeCaroli, Steven D. "Visibility and History: Giorgio Agamben and the Exemplary." *Philosophy Today* 45 (2001): 9–17.

Denby, David. "Gods and Victims." *New Yorker,* October 5, 2009, 88–89.

Derrida, Jacques. *Archive Fever: A Freudian Impression.* Trans. Eric Prenowitz. Chicago: University of Chicago Press, 1995.

———. "The Eyes of Language: The Abyss and the Volcano." In *Acts of Religion.* Trans. Gil Anijdar. New York: Routledge, 2002, 189–227.

———. *Eyes of the University: Right to Philosophy 2.* Trans. Jan Plug et al. Stanford: Stanford University Press, 2004.

———. *Given Time: I. Counterfeit Money.* Trans. Peggy Kamuf. Chicago: University of Chicago Press, 1992.

———. *Judeities: Questions for Jacques Derrida.* Trans. Bettina Bergo and Michael Smith. New York: Fordham University Press, 2007.

———. *Monolingualism of the Other; or, the Prosthetics of Origin.* Trans. Patrick Mensah. Stanford: Stanford University Press, 1998.

———. *Specters of Marx: The State of the Debt, the Work of Mourning and the New International.* Trans. Peggy Kamuf. New York: Routledge, 2006.

———. *The Truth in Painting.* Trans. Geoff Bennington and Ian McLeod. Chicago: University of Chicago Press, 1987.

———. "Violence and Metaphysics: An Essay on the Thought of Emmanuel Levinas." In *Writing and Difference.* Trans. Allan Bass. Chicago: University of Chicago Press, 1967, 79–173.

———. *Who's Afraid of Philosophy? Right to Philosophy 1.* Trans. Jan Plug Stanford: Stanford University Press, 2002.

———. *Without Alibi.* Trans. Peggy Kamuf. Stanford: Stanford University Press, 2002.

Devisch, Ignaas. *Jean-Luc Nancy and the Question of Community.* London: Bloomsbury, 2014.

Diamond, James A. *Maimonides and the Shaping of the Jewish Canon.* Cambridge: Cambridge University Press, 2014.

Di Leo, Jeffrey R. "On Being and Becoming Affiliated." In *Affiliations: Identity in Academic Culture.* Ed. Jeffrey R. Di Leo. Lincoln: University of Nebraska Press, 2003, 101–114.

———. "Review of Louis Menand's *Marketplace of Ideas: Reform and Resistance in the American University.*" *Comparatist* 35 (May 2011): 249–254.

Dolgopolski, Sergey. *The Open Past: Subjectivity and Remembering in the Talmud*. New York: Fordham University Press, 2013.

———. *Other Others: The Political After the Talmud*. New York: Fordham University Press, 2017.

———. *What Is Talmud?* New York: Fordham University Press, 2009.

Dotan, Aaron, ed. *Sefer diqduqe ha-te'amim le-rabbi Aharon Ben-Moshe Ben-Asher*. Jerusalem: Hebrew University, 1979 [1963].

Edwards, Laurence L. "Rabbi Akiba's Crowns: Postmodern Discourse and the Cost of Rabbinic Reading." *Judaism* 49.4 (Fall 2000): 417–435.

Ehrlich, Carl S., and Sara Horowitz, eds. *Handbook of Jewish Studies*. Boston: Walter de Gruyter, 2016.

Eiland, Howard, and Michael Jenkins. *Walter Benjamin: A Critical Life*. Cambridge, Mass.: Harvard University Press, 2014.

Elbogen, Ismar. "A Century of Wissenschaft des Judentums." In *Studies in Jewish Thought: An Anthology of German Jewish Scholarship*. Ed. Alfred Jospe. Detroit: Wayne State Press, 1981.

Elman, Yaakov. "Review of Daniel Boyarin, *A Traveling Homeland: The Babylonian Talmud as Diaspora*," *AJS Review* 40.1 (April 2016): 168–171.

Elmarsafy, Ziad. "Aping the Ape: Kafka's 'Report to an Academy.'" *Studies in Twentieth-Century Literature* (1995): 159–170.

Emerson, Ralph Waldo. *Essays and Lectures*. Ed. Joel Porte. New York: Library of America, 1983.

Epstein, Mikhail. *The Transformative Humanities: A Manifesto*. London: Bloomsbury, 2012.

Erlewine, Robert. *Judaism and the West: From Hermann Cohen to Joseph Soloveitchik*. Bloomington: Indiana University Press, 2016.

Eubanks, Philip, and John D. Schaeffer. "A Kind Word for Bullshit: The Problem of Academic Writing." *CCC* 59:3 (February 2008): 372–388.

Fackenheim, Emil L., and Raphael Jospe. *Jewish Philosophy and the Academy*. Cranbury: Associated University Presses, 1996.

Fagenblat, Michael, ed. *Negative Theology as Jewish Modernity*. Bloomington: Indiana University Press, 2017.

Fenves, Peter. *The Messianic Reduction: Walter Benjamin and the Shape of Time*. Stanford: Stanford University Press, 2010.

Ferguson, Roderick A. *The Reorder of Things: The University and Its Pedagogies of Minority Difference*. Minneapolis: University of Minnesota Press, 2012.

Finkin, Jordan D. *A Rhetorical Conversation: Jewish Discourse in Modern Yiddish Literature*. Pennsylvania: University of Pennsylvania Press, 2010.

Fischer, Elli. "A Prayer at the Grave of Franz Rosenzweig." *Lehrhaus.com*, October 6, 2016, http://www.thelehrhaus.com/commentary-short-articles/grave-franz-rosenzweig.
Fisher, Philip. "Democratic Social Space: Whitman, Melville, and the Promise of American Transparency." *Representations* 24 (Fall 1988): 60–101.
Fokkelman, J. P. *Narrative Art in Genesis: Specimens of Stylistic and Structural Analysis*. Eugene: Wipf and Stock, 2004.
Fonrobert, Charlotte. "The New Spatial Turn in Jewish Studies." *AJS Review* 33.1 (April 2009): 155–164.
Fonrobert, Charlotte, Ishay Rosen-Zvi, Aharon Shemesh, and Moulie Vidas, eds. *Talmudic Transgressions Engaging the Work of Daniel Boyarin*. Leiden: Brill, 2017
Foox, Michael. "Rosenzweig and Institutions." *Social Dimensions of E-Communication*. New York: iUniverse, Inc., 2005, 54–58.
Foucault, Michel. "Des Espace Autres" [Of Other Spaces: Utopias and Heterotopias]. *Architecture, Mouvement, Continuité*, no. 5 (October 1984): 46–49. Trans. Jay Miskowiec.
———. *Diacritics* 16, no. 1 (Spring 1986): 22–27.
———. *Discipline and Punish: The Birth of the Priso*. Trans. Alan Sheridan. New York: Vintage, 1995.
———. *Les Mots et les Choses: Une Archéologie des Sciences Humaines* [The Order of Things]. New York: Pantheon Books, 1970.
Fraade, Steven D. "Jacob Neusner as Reader of the Mishnah, Tosefta, and Halakhíc Midrash." *Henoch* XXXI (2005), 259–270.
Frankel, Yonah. *Darchei HaAggadah ViHaMidrash*. Jerusalem: Givatayim, 1991.
———. "Hermeneutic Problems in the Study of the Aggadic Narrative." *Tarbiz* 47 (1978): 139–172 (Hebrew).
Frankel, Zacharias. *"Einleitendes." Monatsschrift für Geschichte und Wissenschaft des Judentums* 1 (1852): 1–6.
Frankfurt, Harry G. *On Bullshit*. Princeton, N.J.: Princeton University Press.
Franklin, Cynthia. *Academic Lives: Memoir, Cultural Theory, and the University Today*. Athens: University of Georgia Press, 2009.
Franks, Paul. "Everyday Speech and Revelatory Speech in Rosenzweig and Wittgenstein." *Philosophy Today* (Spring 2006): 24–39.
Freedman, Jonathan. "Do American and Ethnic American Studies Have a Jewish Problem; or, When Is an Ethnic Not an Ethnic, and What Should We Do about It?" *MELUS* 37.2 (Summer 2012): 19–40.
Fricke, Martin. "Die Kraft der Lehre—Rosenzweigs Beitrag zu einer performativen Religionspädagogik." *Proceedings of the Internationale Rosenzweig Gesellschaft* 1 (2014): 46–58.
———. "On Jewish Literature: A Polemical Position Paper, *SAJL* 31.1 (2012): 19–23.

Fuller, Randall. *Emerson's Ghosts: Literature, Politics, and the Making of Americanists*. New York: Oxford University Press, 2007.
Gabirol, Shlomo Ibn. *Selected Poems of Solomon Ibn Gabirol*. Trans. Peter Cole. Princeton, N.J.: Princeton University Press, 2001.
Gaon, Stella. "'As If' There Were a 'Jew': The (non)Existence of Deconstructive Responsibility." *Derrida Today* 7.1 (2014): 44–58.
———. "Communities in Question: Sociality and Solidarity in Nancy and Blanchot." *Journal for Cultural Research* 9.4 (October 2005): 387–403.
Garber, Marjorie. *Academic Instincts*. Princeton, N.J.: Princeton University Press, 2009.
Garber, Zev, ed. *Academic Approaches to Teaching Jewish Studies*. Lanham, Md.: University Press of America, 2000.
García Landa, José Ángel. "Narrating Narrating: Twisting the Twice-Told Tale." In *Theorizing Narrativity*. Ed. John Pier, José Ángel García Landa. Boston: Walter de Gruyter, 2008, 419–451.
———. "Unpacking Benjamin: A Note on Walter Benjamin's 'Unpacking My Library: A Talk about Book Collecting,'" 1988, http://www.unizar.es/departamentos/filologia_inglesa/garciala/publicaciones/benjamin.html.
Gass, William. "Deciding to Do the Impossible." *New York Times Book Review*, January 4, 1987, 25.
Geberoff, Joel. "Talmudic Stories about Angry and Annoyed Rabbis." In *A Legacy of Learning: Essays in Honor of Jacob Neusner*. Leiden: Brill, 2014, 82–109.
Gelley, Alexander. *Benjamin's Passages: Dreaming, Awakening*. New York: Fordham University Press, 2015.
Gibbs, Robert. *Correlations in Rosenzweig and Levinas*. Princeton, N.J.: Princeton University Press, 1992.
Gierke, Otto. *Community in Historical Perspective*. Trans. Mary Fisher. Cambridge: Cambridge University Press, 1990.
Ginsberg, Benjamin. *Fall of the Faculty: The Rise of the All-Administrative University and Why It Matters*. New York: Oxford University Press, 2011.
Ginsburg, Shai. "The Physics of Being Jewish; Or, On Cats and Jews." *AJS Review* 35.2 (November, 2011): 357–364.
Glatzer, Nahum N. "The Beginnings of Modern Jewish Studies." In *Studies in Nineteenth-Century Jewish Intellectual History*. Ed. Alexander Altmann. Cambridge, Mass.: Harvard University Press, 1964, 27–45.
———. "The Frankfort Lehrhaus." *Year Book Leo Baeck Institute* 1.1 (1956): 105–122.
———. *Franz Rosenzweig: His Life and Thought*. Indianapolis: Hackett Publishing Co., 1998.

Glenn, Susan A., and Naomi B Sokoloff, eds. *Boundaries of Jewish Identity*. Seattle: University of Washington Press, 2010.
Goethe, Johann Wolfgang von. *Faust, Part One*. Trans. David Luke. New York: Oxford University Press, 2008.
Goetschel, Willi. "Dialogic: Difference and Alterity in Hermann Levin Goldschmidt's Thought," 2005, www.dialogik.org/wp/wp-content /uploads/2010/12/Goetschel-Dialogic.pdf.
———. *The Discipline of Philosophy and the Invention of Modern Jewish Thought*. New York: Fordham University Press, 2013.
———. "Hermann-Levin Goldschmidt: A German-Jewish Philosopher." In *German Literature, Jewish Critics: The Brandeis Symposium*. Ed. Stephen D. Dowden and Meike Werner. Rochester: Camden House, 2002.
———. "Philosophy from the Outside In: Rosenzweig's Critical Project." *Filozofija I Društvo* 23.2 (2012): 65–76.
Goh, Irving. *The Reject: Community, Politics, and Religion After the Subject*. New York: Fordham University Press, 2015.
Goldberg, David Theo, and Michael Krausz, eds. *Jewish Identity*. Philadelphia: Temple University Press, 1993.
Goldberg, Harvey E. "Coming of Age in Jewish Studies; Or, Anthropology Is Counted in the Minyan." *Jewish Social Studies* 4:3 (Spring-Summer, 1998): 29–64.
Goldman, Harvey. *Max Weber and Thomas Mann: Calling and the Shaping of the Self*. Berkeley: University of California Press, 1988.
Goldschmidt, Hermann Levin. *Die Botschaft des Judentums*. Ed. Willi Goetschel. Vienna: Passagen Verlag, 1994.
———. *The Legacy of German Jewry*. Trans. David Suchoff. NewYork: Fordham University Press, 2007.
Goodman, Martin. "The Problems of Jewish Studies." *Zutot: Perspectives on Jewish Culture* 2 (2003).
Goodman, Martin, Jeremy Cohen, and David Sorkin, eds. *The Oxford Handbook of Jewish Studies*. New York: Oxford University Press, 2002.
Gordon, Peter E. *Rosenzweig and Heidegger: Between Judaism and German Philosophy*. Berkeley: University of California Press, 2003.
———. "Rosenzweig Redux: The Reception of German-Jewish Thought." *Jewish Social Studies* 8.1 (Fall 2001): 1–57.
Goshen Gottstein, Alon. "Four Entered Paradise Revisited." *HTR* 88:1 (1995): 69–133.
———. *The Sinner and the Amnesiac the Rabbinic Invention of Elisha Ben Abuya and Eleazar ben Arach*. Stanford: Stanford University Press, 2005.
Gourgouris, Stathis. *Lessons in Secular Criticism*. New York: Fordham University Press, 2013.

Granel, Gérard. *De l'Université*. Mauvezin: Éditions TER, 1982.
Gray, Richard T., Ruth V. Gross, Rolf J. Goebel, and Clayton Koelb. *A Franz Kafka Encyclopedia*. Westport: Greenwood Press, 2005.
Greenspahn, Frederick E. "The Beginnings of Judaic Studies in American Universities." *Modern Judaism* 20 (2000): 209–225.
Greenstein, Edward L. "Medieval Bible Commentaries." In *Back to the Sources: Reading the Classic Jewish Texts*. Ed. Barry Holtz. New York: Simon and Schuster, Inc., 1984, 213–259.
Greif, Mark. "Cavell as Educator." *n+1* Issue 12: Conversion Experience. July 5, 2011, nplusonemag.com/issue-12/essays/cavell-as-educator.
Groiser, David. "'Repetition and Renewal: Kierkegaard, Rosenzweig, and the German-Jewish Renaissance." In *Die Gegenwärtigkeit des Deutsch-Jüdischen Denkens*, hrsg. von *Julia Matveev und Ashraf Noor*. Munich: Wilhelm Fink, 2011, 265–301.
Grossman, David. "Letter from Israel: Fifty Is a Dangerous Age." Trans. Chaim Watzman. *New Yorker*, April 20, 1998, 55–58.
Guijarro, Albert, and Miguel Yus. *The Origin of Chirality in the Molecules of Life: A Revision from Awareness to the Current Theories and Perspectives of this Unsolved Problem*. Cambridge: RSC Publishing, 2009.
Halbertal, Moshe. *People of the Book: Canon, Meaning, and Authority*. Cambridge, Mass.: Harvard University Press, 1997.
Hammerschlag, Sarah. *The Figural Jew: Politics and Identity in Postwar French Thought*. Chicago: University of Chicago Press, 2010.
Handelman, Matthew. "Digital Humanities as Translation: Visualizing Franz Rosenzweig's Archive." *Transit* 10.1 (2015), http://transit.berkeley.edu/2015/handelman/.
Harpham, Geoffrey Galt. *The Humanities and the Dream of America*. Chicago: University of Chicago Press, 2011.
———. *Shadows of Ethics: Criticism and the Just Society*. Durham, N.C.: Duke University Press, 1999.
Harris, Robert A. *Discerning Parallelism: A Study in Northern French Medieval Jewish Biblical Exegesis*, Brown Judaic Series no. 341. Providence: Brown Judaic Studies, 2004.
———. "Medieval Jewish Biblical Exegesis." In *A History of Biblical Interpretation Vol 2: The Medieval through the Reformation Periods*. Ed. Alan J. Hauser and Duane F. Watson. Grand Rapids: Eerdmanns, 2009, 141–183.
Harrison-Kahan, Lori, and Josh Lambert. "Finding Home: The Future of Jewish American Literary Studies." *MELUS* 37.2, "The Future of Jewish American Literary Studies" (Summer 2012): 5–18.
Harshav, Benjamin. *The Meaning of Yiddish*. Berkeley: University of California Press, 1990.

Hart, Henry. "What Is Heaney Seeing in Seeing Things?" *Colby Quarterly* 30.1 (March 1994): 33–42.
Hartman, Geoffrey. *Criticism in the Wilderness: The Study of Literature Today.* New Haven, Conn.: Yale University Press, 1980.
———. "The Culture of Criticism." *PMLA* 99.3 (May 1984): 371–397.
———. "Editorial Note." *Critical Inquiry* 16.1 (Autumn 1989): 199–204.
———. "History-Writing as Answerable Style." *New Literary History* 2.1 "A Symposium on Literary History" (Autumn 1970): 73–83.
———. *A Scholar's Tale: Intellectual Journey of a Displaced Child of Europe.* New York: Fordham University Press, 2007.
Hartman, Geoffrey, and Sanford Budick, eds. *Midrash and Literature.* New Haven, Conn.: Yale University Press, 1986.
Hayes, Peter, and John K. Roth. *The Oxford Handbook of Holocaust Studies.* New York: Oxford University Press, 2013.
Heaney, Seamus. *The Government of the Tongue: Selected Prose, 1978–1987.* New York: Farrar, Straus and Giroux, 1988.
———. "An Interview with James Randall." *Ploughshares* 18 (Spring 1979).
———. *Seeing Things.* London: Faber and Faber, 1991.
———. "A Soul on the Washing Line: Interview with Seamus Heaney." *The Economist*, June 1991.
Heidegger, Martin. "Letter on Humanism." Trans. Frank A. Capuzzi. In *Basic Writings*. Ed. David Farrell Krell. New York: Harper and Row, 1977, 190–242.
———. "Plato's Doctrine of Truth." Trans. Thomas Sheehan. In *Pathmarks*. Ed. William McNeill. Cambridge: Cambridge University Press, 1998, 155–182.
———. "The Self-Assertion of the German University and the Rectorate 1933/34: Facts and Thoughts." Trans. Karsten Harries. *Review of Metaphysics*, 38:3 (March 1985): 467–502.
———. "Toward a Philosophical Orientation for Academics." Trans. John Protevi. *Graduate Faculty Philosophy Journal* 14–5 (1991): 496–497.
———. *What Is Called Thinking?* Trans. J. G. Gray. New York: Harper and Row, 1968.
Heller, Scott. "The New Jewish Studies: Defying Tradition and Easy Categorization." *Chronicle of Higher Education*, January 1999, A21.
Herberg, Will. "Rosenzweig's 'Judaism of Personal Existence': A Third Way between Orthodoxy and Modernism." Commentary 10.6 (December 1950): 541–549.
Herzog, Anabel. "'Monolingualism' or the Language of God: Scholem and Derrida on Hebrew and Politics." *Modern Judaism* 29.2 (May 2009): 226–238.

Heschel, Abraham Joshua. *Heavenly Torah: As Refracted through the Generations.* Ed. and trans. Gordon Tucker. London: Bloomsbury, 2006.

Heschel, Susannah. "Jewish Studies as Counterhistory." *Insider/Outsider American Jews and Multiculturalism.* Ed. David Biale, Michael Galchinsky, Susannah Heschel. Berkeley: University of California Press, 1998, 101–115.

Heschel, Susannah, and Sarah Imhoff. "Where Are All the Women in Jewish Studies?" *The Forward*, July 3, 2018, forward.com/culture/404416/where-are-all-the-women-in-jewish-studies/.

Hidary, Richard. *Rabbis and Classical Rhetoric: Sophistic Education and Oratory in the Talmud and Midrash.* Cambridge: Cambridge University Press, 2017.

Ḥizkuni (Hezekiah ben Manoah). *Chizkuni Torah Commentary.* Trans. Eliyahu Munk. New York: Ktav Publishing, 2013.

Hoffman, Anne Golomb. "Topographies of Reading: Agnon through Benjamin." *Prooftexts* 21.1 (Winter 2001): 71–89.

Hofmann, Michael. "Dazzling Philosophy: *Seeing Things* by Seamus Heaney." *London Review of Books* 13.15 (August 15, 1991): 14–15.

Hollander, Dana. *Exemplarity and Chosenness: Rosenzweig and Derrida on the Nation of Philosophy.* Stanford: Stanford University Press, 2008.

Holtz, Barry W. "Across the Divide: What Might Jewish Educators Learn from Jewish Scholars?" *Journal of Jewish Education* 72 (2006): 5–28.

Horowitz, Sara R. "The Paradox of Jewish Studies in the New Academy." In *Insider/Outsider American Jews and Multiculturalism.* Ed. David Biale, Michael Galchinsky, Susannah Heschel. Berkeley: University of California Press, 1998, 116–129.

Horwitz, Rivka. "Franz Rosenzweig—On Jewish Education. *Journal of Jewish Thought and Philosophy* 2.2 (1993): 201–218.

Hughes, Aaron W. *Jacob Neusner: An American Jewish Iconoclast.* New York: New York University Press, 2016.

———. *Jacob Neusner on Religion: The Example of Judaism.* New York: Routledge, 2016.

———. "Jewish Studies Is Too Jewish." *The Chronicle Review of the Chronicle of Higher Education*, March 24, 2014.

———. *The Study of Judaism: Authenticity, Identity, Scholarship.* Albany: State University of New York Press, 2013.

Humboldt, Wilhelm von. "Theorie der Bildung des Menschen." In *Werke in fünf Bünden: Vol. I. Schriften zur Anthropologie und Geschichte.* Ed. Andreas Flitner and Klaus Giel. Darmstadt: Wissenschaftliche Buchgesellschaft, 234–240.

Hutchens, B. C. *Jean-Luc Nancy and the Future of Philosophy.* New York: Routledge, 2005.

Jaschik, Scott. "The Lost Tribe." *Inside Higher Ed*, December 28, 2009, www.insidehighered.com/news/2009/12/28/jews.

———. "The New Jewish Studies." *Inside Higher Ed*, December 21, 2005, www.insidehighered.com/news/2005/12/21/jewish.

Jay, Martin. "1920. The Free Jewish School Is Founded in Frankfurt am Main under the Leadership of Franz Rosenzweig." In *Yale Companion to Jewish Writing and Thought in Germany*. Ed. Sander Gilman and Jack Zipes. New Haven, Conn.: Yale University Press, 1997, 395–400.

———. "Response to George Mosse and David Myers." *Judaism* Issue 178, Vol. 45.2 (Spring 1996): 159–162.

Jepsen, Per. "Philosophy of Education as Reflection of Political Forms." In *Politics in Education*. Ed. Peter Kemp and Asger Sørensen. Berlin: Lit Verlag, 2012, 100–109.

Jospe, Alfred. "The Frankfurt Lehrhaus: A Model for American Jewish Education?" In *To Leave Your Mark: Selections from the Writings of Alfred Jospe*. Ed. Eva Jospe and Raphael Jospe. New York: Ktav Publishing, 2000, 80–83.

Jospe, Rafael. "Hillel's Rule." *The Jewish Quarterly Review* 81.1/2 (July–October 1990): 45–57.

Joy, Eileen A., and Christine M. Neufeld. "A Confession of Faith: Notes Toward a New Humanism." *Journal of Narrative Theory* 37. 2 "Premodern to Modern Humanisms: The BABEL Project" (Summer 2007): 161–190.

Kafka, Franz. *The Complete Stories*. Ed. Nahum N. Glatzer. New York: Schocken Books, 1995.

———. *Letters to Felice*. Trans. James Stern. New York: Schocken Books, 2016.

———. *Parables and Paradoxes/Parabeln und Paradoxe*. Ed. Nahum N. Glatzer. New York: Schocken Books, 1995.

Kalman, Jason. "A Serious Man." *AJS Perspectives* (Fall 2010): 53–54.

Kamuf, Peggy. *The Division of Literature: Or, the University in Deconstruction*. Chicago: University of Chicago Press, 1997.

Kanarek, Jane. *Biblical Narration and the Formation of Rabbinic Law*. Cambridge: Cambridge University Press, 2014.

Kandiyoti, Dalia. "What Is the 'Jewish' in 'Jewish American Literature'?" *Studies in American Jewish Literature* 31.1 (2012): 48–60.

Kant, Immanuel. *The Conflict of the Faculties*. Trans. Mary J. Gregor. Norwalk, Conn.: Abaris Books, 1979.

Kavka, Martin. *Jewish Messianism and the History of Philosophy*. New York: Cambridge University Press, 2004.

———. "Two Study-Houses: Authority in Goldschmidt and Jewish Tradition." Zurich: Stiftung Dialogik, 2013.

———. "What Does It Mean to Receive Tradition? Jewish Studies in Higher Education." *Crosscurrents* (Summer 2006): 180–197.
Katz, Claire Elise. *Levinas and the Crisis of Humanism*. Bloomington: Indiana University Press, 2013.
Kern-Ulmer, Brigette. "Franz Rosenzweig's Judische Lehrhaus in Frankfurt: A Model of Jewish Adult Education. *Judaism* 39 (Spring): 202–214.
Klagg, James C., and Alfred Nordmann, eds. *Ludwig Wittgenstein: Private and Public Occasions*. Lanham, Md.: Rowman and Littlefield, 2003).
Klein, Diane. "Should We Take 'A Serious Man' Seriously?" *Three Jews, Four Opinions*, January 6, 2010, www.threejews.net/2010/01/should-we-take-serious-man-seriously.html.
King, Lynnea Chapman. *The Coen Brothers Encyclopedia*. Lanham, Md.: Rowman and Littlefield, 2014.
Kiperwasser, Reuven. "Review of Daniel Boyarin's *Socrates and the Fat Rabbis*." *Jewish History* 25 (2011): 377–397.
Koch, Richard. "Das Freies Jüdisches Lehrhaus in Frankfurt am Main." *Der Jude* 7 (1923): 116–120.
Kogut, Simcha. "On the Meaning and Syntactical Status of הנה in Biblical Hebrew." In *Studies in Scripta Hierosolymitana*, vol. 31. Ed. Sara Japhet. Jerusalem: Magnes Press, 1986, 133–154.
Koltun-Fromm, Ken. *Material Culture and Jewish Thought in America*. Bloomington: Indiana University Press, 2008.
Kramer, Michael. "Race, Literary History, and the 'Jewish' Question." *Prooftexts* 21.3 (2001): 287–349.
Kreber, Carolin. *The University and Its Disciplines: Teaching and Learning Within and Beyond Disciplinary Boundaries*. New York: Routledge, 2009.
Kronfeld, Chana, and Robert Adler Peckerar. "Tongue-Twisted: Itzik Manger between *mame-loshn* and *loshn-koydesh*." *In geveb*, August 13, 2015, https://ingeveb.org/articles/tongue-twisted-itzik-manger-between-mame-loshn-and-loshn-koydesh.
Kugel, James. *Traditions of the Bible: A Guide to the Bible as It Was at the Start of the Common Era*. Cambridge, Mass.: Harvard University Press, 1999.
Kun, Joshua. *Audiotopia: Music, Race, and America*. Berkeley: University of California Press, 2005.
Labovitz, Gail S. *Marriage and Metaphor: Constructions of Gender in Rabbinic Literature*. Lanham, Md.: Lexington Books, 2009.
LaCapra, Dominick. "The University in Ruins?" *Critical Inquiry* 25:1 (Autumn 1998): 32–55.
Lear, Jonathan. *Happiness, Death, and the Remainder of Life*. Cambridge, Mass.: Harvard University Press, 2000.

Lentricchia, Frank. *Ariel and the Police: Michel Foucault, William James, Wallace Stevens* Madison: University of Wisconsin Press, 1988.

Levenson, Alan. "The Conversionary Impulse in Fin de Siècle Germany." *Leo Baeck Institute Yearbook* 40 (1995): 107–122.

Levenson, Alan, and Jeffrey Schein. "Will the Real Franz Rosenzweig Please Stand Up? Two Reflections on Two Educational Essays." *Journal of Jewish Education* 76.2 (2010): 151–163.

Levere, Trevor, H. *Affinity and Matter—Elements of Chemical Philosophy 1800–1865.* Philadelphia: Gordon and Breach Science Publishers.

Levi, Primo. *The Periodic Table.* Trans. Raymond Rosenthal. New York: Schocken Books, 1984.

———. "Postfazione." 1. Franz Kafka, *Der Proze?* Trans. Primo Levi as *Il processo.* Einaudi, 1983.

Levinas, Emmanuel. *Beyond the Verse: Talmudic Readings and Lectures.* Trans. Gary D. Mole London: Athlone Press, 1994.

———. *Difficult Freedom: Essays on Judaism.* Trans. Seán Hand. Baltimore: Johns Hopkins University Press, 1990.

———. *Humanism of the Other.* Trans. Nidra Poller. Champaign: University of Illinois Press, 2003.

———. *Nine Talmudic Readings.* Trans. Annette Aronowicz. Bloomington: Indiana University Press, 1990.

———. *Otherwise Than Being: Or, Beyond Essence.* Trans. Alphonso Lingis. Pittsburgh, Pa.: Duquesne University Press, 1981.

———. "Signature." Ed. Adriaan Peperzak. *Research in Phenomenology* 8.1 (1978): 175–189.

———. *Unforeseen History.* Trans Nidra Poller. Champaign: University of Illinois Press, 2004.

Levine, Michelle. *Nahmanides on Genesis: The Art of Biblical Portraiture* Brown Judaic Series no. 350. Providence: Brown University Press, 2010.

Levine, Nachman. "Reading Crowned Letters and Semiotic Silences in Menahot 29b." *Journal of Jewish Studies* 53.1 (2002): 35–48

Levinson, Bernard M. "Literary Exegesis of Biblical Narrative: Between Poetics and Hermeneutics." In *Not in Heaven: Coherence and Complexity in Biblical Narrative.* Bloomington: Indiana University Press, 1991, 120–128.

———. *The Right Chorale: From the Poetics to the Hermeneutics of the Hebrew Bible.* Tübingen: Mohr-Siebeck, 2008.

Levinson, Julian. "Is There a Jewish Text in This Class? Jewish Modernism in the Multicultural Academy." *Michigan Quarterly Review* 42.1 Jewish in America, Part Two. (Winter 2003), hdl.handle.net/2027/spo.act2080.0042.122.

Levinson, Yehoshua. *The Twice Told Tale: A Poetics of the Exegetical Narrative in Rabbinic Midrash.* Jerusalem: Magnes Press, 2005.

Levitt, Laura S. "The Awkward Silence in The Wake of Jacob Neusner's Passing." *Religion Dispatches,* December 7, 2016, religiondispatches.org/the-awkward-silence-in-the-wake-of-jacob-neusners-passing/.

Levy, Gabriel. "Hermeneutics in A Serious Man." *Coen: Framing Religion in Amoral Order.* Ed. Elijah Siegler. Waco: Baylor University Press, 2016, 222–232.

———. *Judaic Technologies of the Word: A Cognitive Analysis of Jewish Cultural Production.* New York: Routledge, 2012.

Lewandowski, Joseph D. "Unpacking: Walter Benjamin and His Library." *Libraries & Culture* 34.2 (Spring 1999): 151–57.

Lezra, Jacques. "Helen's List." *PMLA* 130.1 (2015), 163–166.

Lieberman, Saul. "A Tragedy or a Comedy? *The Talmud of the Land of Israel: A Preliminary Translation and Explanation* by Jacob Neusner." *Journal of the American Oriental Society* 104.2 (April/June 1984): 315–319.

Lim, Timothy H. *The Formation of the Jewish Canon.* New Haven, Conn.: Yale University Press, 2013.

Linnitt, Carol. "Film Review: A Serious Man," *Journal of Religion and Film* 13.2 (2009), digitalcommons.unomaha.edu/cgi/viewcontent.cgi?article=1499&context=jrf.

Liska, Adam. "The Myth and the Meaning of Science as a Vocation." *Ultimate Reality and Meaning* 28:2 (2005), 149–164.

Liska, Vivian. *German-Jewish Thought and Its Afterlife: A Tenuous Legacy.* Bloomington: Indiana University Press, 2017.

———. *When Kafka Says We: Uncommon Communities in German-Jewish Literature.* Bloomington: Indiana University Press, 2009.

Liss, Hannah. "The Commentary on the Song of Songs Attributed to R. Samuel ben Meïr (Rashbam)," www.medieval-jewish-studies.com/Journal/Vol1/article01.html.

———. *Creating Fictional Worlds: Peshat Exegesis and Narrativity in Rashbam's Commentary on the Torah.* Leiden/Boston: Brill, 2011.

Loveland, Kirsten. "The Association for Jewish Studies: A Brief History." AJS Annual Conference, December 21, 2008. www.ajsnet.org/ajs.pdf.

Lovlie, Lars, Klaus Peter Mortensen, and Sven Erik Nordenbo, eds. *Educating Humanity: Bildung in Postmodernity.* London: Wiley-Blackwell, 2003.

Lynch, Deirdre Shauna. *Loving Literature: A Cultural History.* Chicago: University of Chicago Press, 2015.

Mack, Michael. *German Idealism and the Jew: The Inner Anti-Semitism of Philosophy and German Jewish Responses.* Chicago: University of Chicago Press, 2003.

Maechler, Stefan. *The Wilkomirski Affair: A Study in Biographical Truth*. New York: Schocken Books, 2001.
Magid, Shaul. *American Post-Judaism*. Bloomington: Indiana University Press, 2013.
———. "The Intolerance of Tolerance: *Makhloket* and Redemption in Early Hasidism." *Jewish Studies Quarterly* 8 (2001): 326–368.
Makarova, Elena, Sergei Makarov, and Victor Kuperman. *University Over the Abyss: The Story Behind 520 Lecturers and 2,430 Lectures in KZ Theresienstadt 1942–1944*. Jerusalem: Verba Publishers Ltd, 2004.
Martinon, Jean-Paul. *On Futurity: Malabou, Nancy and Derrida*. Basingstoke: Palgrave Macmillan, 2007.
Marty, Éric. *Radical French Thought and the Return of the "Jewish Question."* Trans. Alan Astro. Bloomington: Indiana University Press, 2015.
McCance, Dawne. *Medusa's Ear: University Foundings from Kant to Chora L*. Albany: State University of New York Press, 2004.
Meir, Ephraim. *Dialogical Thought and Identity: Trans-Different Religiosity in Present Day Societies*. Berlin and Boston: Walter de Gruyter and Magnes, 2013.
———. *Differenz und Dialog*. Berlin: Waxmann, 2011.
———. *The Rosenzweig Lehrhaus: Proposal for a Jewish House of Study in Kassel Inspired by Franz Rosenzweig's Frankfurt Lehrhaus*. Ramat Gan, 2005.
Menand, Louis. *The Marketplace of Ideas: Reform and Resistance in the American University*. New York: W. W. Norton & Company, 2010.
Mendes-Flohr, Paul. "The Freies Jüdisches Lehrhaus." *Jüdische Kultur in Frankfurt am Main von den Anfängen bis zur Gegenwart*. Ed. Karl Erich Grözinger. Vienna: Harrassowitz Verlag, 1997, 217–230.
———. *From Mysticism to Dialogue: Martin Buber's Transformation of German Social Thought*. Detroit: Wayne State University Press, 1989.
———. *German Jews: A Dual Identity*. New Haven, Conn.: Yale University Press, 1999.
———. "The Jew as Cosmopolitan." In *Divided Passions: Jewish Intellectuals and the Experience of Modernity*. Detroit: Wayne State University Press, 1991, 313–423.
Mendes-Flohr, Paul, and Jehuda Reinhartz. *The Jew in the Modern World: A Documentary History*. New York: Oxford University Press, 2011.
Meskin, Jacob, and Harvey Shapiro. "'To Give an Example Is a Complex Act': Agamben's Pedagogy of the Paradigm." *Educational Philosophy and Theory* 46.4 (2014): 421–440.
Mevorach, Yishai. *Te'ologyah shel ḥoser: 'al emunah shele-aḥar ha-tohu* [Theology of Absence: On Faith After Chaos]. Tel Aviv: Resling Publishing, 2016.

Meyer, Michael. "Two Persistent Tensions Within Wissenschaft Des Judentums." *Modern Judaism* 24.2 (May 2004): 105–119.
Meyerowitz, Rael. *Transferring to America: Jewish Interpretations of American Dreams.* Albany: State University of New York Press, 1995.
Mikraot gedolot ha-Keter. Ed. Menaḥem Cohen. Tel Aviv: Bar-Ilan University, 1992.
Milder, Robert. "'The American Scholar' as Cultural Event." *Prospects* 16 (1991): 119–147.
Miller, Joshua L., and Anita Norich. *Languages of Modern Jewish Culture: Comparative Perspectives.* Ann Arbor: University of Michigan Press, 2016.
Miron, Dan. *From Continuity to Contiguity: Toward a New Jewish Literary Thinking.* Stanford: Stanford University Press, 2010.
Miyoshi, Masao, and Harry Harootunian, eds. *Learning Places: The Afterlives of Area Studies.* Durham, N.C.: Duke University Press, 2012.
Monroe, Jonathan. "Philosophy, Poetry, Parataxis." *The European Legacy: Toward New Paradigms* 14.5 (2009): 599–611.
Morin, Marie-Ève. *Jean-Luc Nancy.* Cambridge: Polity Press, 2012.
Morris, Leslie. "Placing and Displacing Jewish Studies: Notes on the Future of a Field." *PMLA* 125. 3 (May 2010): 764–773.
Mosès, Stéphane, and Sigrid Weigel, eds. *Gershom Scholem: Literatur und Rhetorik.* Koln: Bohlau Verlag, 2000.
Mosse, George L. "Central European Intellectuals in Palestine." *Judaism* Issue 178, Vol. 45.2 (Spring 1996): 134–141.
———. *German Jews Beyond Judaism.* Cincinnati: Hebrew Union College Press, 1985.
Moten, Fred and Stefano Harney. "The University and the Undercommons: Seven Theses." *Social Text* 79 22. 2 (Summer 2004): 101–115.
Mouffe, Chantal. "Democratic Politics and the Question of Identity." In *The Identity in Question.* Ed. John Rajchman. New York: Routledge, 1995, 33–46.
Muecke, Mikesch. "The Dialectics of the Collector: On Museums, Images, and Practical Recollections." In *Essays on Architecture and Other Topics.* Ames, Ia.: Culicidae Architectural Press, 2006, 45–70.
Musil, Robert. *The Enthusiasts.* Trans. Andre Stone. New York: Performing Arts Journal Publications, 1983.
———. *The Man without Qualities.* Trans. Sophie Wilkins. New York: Alfred A. Knopf, 1995.
Myers, David M. "The Fall and Rise of Jewish Historicism: The Evolution of the Akademie für die Wissenschaft des Judentums (1919-1934)." *Hebrew Union College Annual* 63 (1992): 107–144.

———. "The Ideology of Wissenschaft des Judentums." In *History of Jewish Philosophy*. Ed. Daniel Frank and Oliver Leaman. New York: Routledge, 1997, 706–721.

———. "A New Scholarly Colony in Jerusalem." *Judaism* 178, Vol. 45.2 (Spring 1996): 142–158.

———. *Resisting History: Historicism and its Discontents in German-Jewish Thought*. Princeton, N.J.: Princeton University Press, 2003.

———. "Rethinking the Jewish Nation: An Exercise in Applied Jewish Studies." *Havruta Journal* (Winter 2011): 26–33.

———. "The Scholem-Kurzweil Debate and Modern Jewish Historiography." *Modern Judaism* 6.3 (October 1986), 261–286.

Nabokov, Vladimir. *Bend Sinister*. New York: Vintage, 1990.

Naeh, Shlomo. "The Script of the Torah in Rabbinic Thought (B): Transcription and Thorns." *Leshonenu* 71 (2010): 89–123 (Hebrew).

Nancy, Jean-Luc. *Being Singular Plural*. Trans. Robert Richardson and Anne O'Byrne. Stanford: Stanford University Press, 2000.

———. "*La Comparution* /The Compearance: From the Existence of 'Communism' to the Community of 'Existence.'" Trans. Tracy B. Strong. *Political Theory* 20.3 (August 1992): 371–398.

———. *The Disavowed Community*. Trans. Philip Armstrong. New York: Fordham University Press, 2016.

———. *The Inoperative Community*. Trans. Peter Conner. Minneapolis: University of Minnesota Press, 1986.

———. "Of Being-in-Common." *Community at Loose Ends*. Ed. The Miami Theory Collective. Minneapolis: University of Minnesota Press, 1991.

———."Philosophie und *Bildung*." In *Wer hat Angst vor der Philosophie?: Eine Einführung in Philosophie*. Ed. Norbert Bolz. München: Wilhelm Fink, 2012, 177–194.

———. "Sharing Voices." *Transforming the Hermeneutic Context*. Ed. Gayle Ormiston and Alan Schrift. Albany: State University of New York Press, 1990.

Neeman, Ehud. *Omer va-esh : she'arim le-haguto ule-hayav shel Franz Rosenzweig* [*Utterance and Fire: Pathways to the Thought and Life of Franz Rosenzweig*]. Alon Shevut: Mechon Herzog, 2016.

Neuman, Abraham A. "The Dropsie College for Hebrew and Cognate Learning Basic Principles and Objectives." *The Jewish Quarterly Review* 57 (1967): 18–46.

Neusner, Jacob. "Anti-Semitism: No Ifs or Buts." *Jewish Advocate*, March 31, 1988, 2.2

———."'Being Jewish' and Studying about Judaism." Atlanta: Emory University, 1977.

———. *Canon and Connection: Intertextuality in Judaism*. Lanham, Md.: University Press of America, 1987.

———. "The Case of James Kugel's Joking Rabbis and Other Serious Issues." In *Wrong Ways and Right Ways in the Study of Formative Judaism*. Atlanta: Atlanta Scholars Press, 1988, 59–73.

———. *Death and Birth of Judaism: The Impact of Christianity, Secularism, and the Holocaust on Jewish Faith*. New York: Basic Books, 1987.

———. *From Description to Conviction: Essays on the History and Theology of Judaism*. Atlanta: Scholars Press, 1987.

———. "Foreword" to Theodore Pappas. *The Martin Luther King, Jr. Plagiarism Story*. Rockford, Ill.: Rockford Institute, 1994.

———. *How to Grade Your Professors: And Other Unexpected Advice*. Boston: Beacon Press, 1984.

———. *The Idea of Purity in Ancient Judaism*. Leiden: E.J. Brill, 1973.

———. "Intertextuality and the Literature of Judaism." *American Journal of Semiotics* 7.1/2 (2008): 153–182.

———. "Jewish Studies and Academic Anti-Semitism." *Indianapolis Jewish Post* (December 2, 1987): 10–11.

———. "Jewish Studies Rises, but we Pay the Price." *The Forward*, September 7, 2010.

———. *Judaism, the Evidence of the Mishnah*. Chicago: University of Chicago Press, 1981.

———. *Lectures on Judaism in the Academy and in the Humanities*. Atlanta: Scholars Press, 1990.

———. *New Humanities and Academic Disciplines: The Case of Jewish Studies*. Eugene: Wipf and Stock, 2004.

———. *Rabbinic Judaism: The Documentary History of the Formative Age, 70–600 CE*. Bethesda, Md.: CDL Press, 1994.

———. "Review of Daniel Boyarin's *Intertextuality and the Reading of Midrash*," *Journal for the Study of Judaism* 21 (1990): 254–258.

———. "Teaching Jewish studies 'under gentile auspices' versus the academic study of religion, including Judaism: Response to Zachary Braiterman." *Religious Education* 95.1 (Winter 2000): 95–96.

———. "What's Jewish about Jewish American Poetry?," *Judaism* 47:4 (1998): 487–489.

Neusner, Jacob, and Noam Neusner. *Reaffirming Higher Education*. New York: Transaction, 2000.

Newton, Adam Zachary. "A Tale of Two Jewish Studies: From Ron Meshbesher to the Rashbam." *Studies in American Jewish Literature* 36.2 (2017): 117–157.

———. *To Make the Hand Impure: Art, Ethical Adventure, the Difficult, and the Holy.* New York: Fordham University Press, 2015.
Nietzsche, Friedrich. "On the Future of Our Educational Institutions." Trans. J. M. Kennedy. In *The Complete Works*, vol. 6. T. N. Foulis, 1909, 3–143.
———. "We Philologists." In *Complete Works*, vol. 8. Trans. J. M. Kennedy. HardPress Publishing, 2013.
Novick, Peter. *That Noble Dream: The "Objectivity Question" and the American Historical Profession.* Cambridge: Cambridge University Press, 1988.
Oakley, Francis. *Community of Learning: The American College and the Liberal Arts Tradition.* New York: Oxford University Press, 1992.
Ofrat, Gideon. *The Jewish Derrida.* Syracuse: Syracuse University Press, 2001.
O'Leary, Timothy. "Governing the Tongue: Heaney Among the Philosophers." *Textual Practice* 22.4 (2008): 657–677.
Ouaknin, Marc-Alain. *The Burnt Book: Reading the Talmud.* Trans. Llewellyn Brown. Princeton, N.J.: Princeton University Press, 1995.
Pagis, Dan. *Hebrew Poetry of the Middle Ages and the Renaissance.* Berkeley: University of California Press, 1991.
Peck, Abraham J., ed. *The German-Jewish Legacy in America, 1938–1988: From Bildung to the Bill of Rights.* Detroit: Wayne State University Press, 1989.
Peeters, Benoit. *Derrida: A Biography.* Trans. Andrew Brown. Cambridge: Polity Press, 2013.
Pelikan, Jaroslav. *The Idea of the University: A Reexamination.* New Haven, Conn.: Yale University Press, 1992.
Pollack, Benjamin. *Franz Rosenzweig's Conversions: World Denial and World Redemption.* Bloomington: Indiana University Press, 2014.
Pollin-Galay, Hannah. *Ecologies of Witnessing: Language, Place, and Holocaust Testimony.* New Haven, Conn.: Yale University Press, 2018.
Pomson, Alex. "Franz Rosenzweig and the Elementary School Teacher: A Midrashic Re-viewing of an Experiment in Adult education. *Journal of Jewish Education* 71 (2005): 261–277.
Portnoy, Edward A. "Modicut Puppet Theatre: Modernism, Satire, and Yiddish Culture." *TDR: The Drama Review* 43.3 (T 163) (Fall 1999): 115–134.
Poulet, Georges. "The Phenomenology of Reading." *New Literary History* Vol. 1, No. 1, "New and Old History" (October, 1969): 53–68.
Prell, Riv-Ellen. "Ethnographers and History: A Conversation Located in Jewish Studies." *American Jewish History* 98.1 (January, 2014): ix–xvi.

———. *A Serious Man* in Situ: 'Fear and Loathing in St Louis Park." *AJS Review* 35.2 (November, 2011): 365–376.
Price, James. *The Syntax of Masoretic Accents in the Hebrew Bible*. E. Mellen Press, 1990.
Prince, Gerald. "The Disnarrated," *Style* 22.1 (Spring 1988): 1–8.
Putnam, Hilary. *Jewish Philosophy as a Guide to Life: Rosenzweig, Buber, Levinas, Wittgenstein*. Bloomington: University of Indiana Press, 2008.
———."Reading Rosenzweig's Little Book." *Argumenta* 1.2 (2016): 161–168.
Rainer, Peter. "Movie Review: 'A Serious Man'," *Christian Science Monitor*, October 2, 2009, www.csmonitor.com/The-Culture/Movies/2009/1002/p17s02-almo.html.
Rand, Richard A., ed. *Logomachia: The Conflict of the Faculties*. Lincoln: University of Nebraska Press, 1992.
Rashbam (R. Samuel ben Meir). *Commentary on Genesis: An Annotated Translation*. Trans. Martin I. Lockshin. E. Mellen Press, 1989.
———. *Der Pentateuch Commentar des R. Samuel Ben Meir*. Herausgegeben von Dr. David Rosin. Breslau, 1881.
———. *Hachut Hameshulash* vol. 2. Trans. Eliyahu Munk. New York-Jerusalem, 2003.
Readings, Bill. *The University in Ruins* (Cambridge, Mass.: Harvard University Press, 1996).
Redmon, Allen. *Constructing the Coens: From Blood Simple to Inside Llewyn Davis*. Lanham, Md.: Rowman and Littlefield, 2015.
Rees, Abraham. *The Cyclopaedia; Or, Universal Dictionary of Arts, Sciences and Literature* London: Longmans, 1819.
Reinhard, Kenneth and Julia Reinhard Lupton. "Jewish Studies and the Secular University: Religion Between Culture and Philosophy," 1999, www.jcrt.org/archives/01.1/reinhard_lupton.html.
Reiss, Tom. *The Orientalist: Solving the Mystery of a Strange and Dangerous Life*. New York: Random House, 2005.
Richards, Robert J. *The Tragic Sense of Life: Ernst Haeckel and the Struggle over Evolutionary Thought*. Chicago: University of Chicago Press, 2008.
Richardson, Brian. *Unnatural Voices: Extreme Narration in Modern and Contemporary Fiction*. Columbus: Ohio State University Press, 2004.
Richter, David. "Genre, Repetition, Temporal Order: Some Aspects of Biblical Narratology." In *A Companion to Narrative Theory*. Ed. J. Phelan and P. Rabinowitz. Malden: Blackwell, 2005, 285–298.
Ritterband, Paul, and Harold Wechsler. *Jewish Learning in American Universities: The First Century*. Bloomington: Indiana University Press, 1994.
Robbins, Bruce. *Secular Vocations: Intellectuals, Professionalism, Culture*. London: Verso, 1993.

Robertson, Lisa Ann. "'Universal Thump': The Redemptive Epistemology of Touch in *Moby-Dick*." *Leviathan* 12.2 (June 2010): 5–20.

Robinson, Ira. *Translating a Tradition: Studies in American Jewish History.* Boston: Academic Studies Press, 2008.

Rosenbaum, Fred. "Lehrhaus Then and Now." W. Schmied Kowarzik, ed. *Der Philosoph Franz Rosenzweig (1886–1929) Internationaler Kongress- Kassel 1986. Bd. I: Die Herausforderung jüdischen Lernens.* Freiburg-München, 1988, 353–360.

Rosenberg, Shimon Gershon (Rav Shagar). *Faith Shattered and Restored Judaism in the Postmodern Age.* Trans. Elie Leshem. Jerusalem: Maggid Books, 2017.

Rosenstock-Huessy, Eugen. *Speech and Reality.* Ed. Clinton C. Gardner. Eugene: Wipf and Stock, 2013.

Rosenzweig, Franz. *Briefe und Tagebücher (Franz Rosenzweig Gesammelte Schriften).* The Hague: Martinus Nijhoff, 1979

———. *Der Mensch und sein Werk. Gesammelte Schriften, III: Zweistromland. Kleinere Schriften zu Glauben und Denken.* Ed. Annemarie Mayer, Reinhold Mayer. Dordrecht: Martinus Nijhoff, 1984.

———. *Franz Rosenzwei's "The New Thinking."* Trans. Alan Udoff and Barbara Galli. Syracuse: Syracuse University Press, 1999.

———. *God, Man, and the World: Lectures and Essays.* Trans. Barbara Galli. Syracuse: Syracuse University Press, 1998.

———. "The Impossibility and Necessity of Translation." In *Translating Literature: The German Tradition from Luther to Rosenzweig.* Ed. André Lefevere. Assen: Van Gorcum, 1979, 110–112.

———. "Of *Bildung* There Is no End." Trans. Michael Zank. In *Textual Reasonings: Jewish Philosophy and Text Study at the End of the Twentieth Century.* Ed. Peter Ochs and Nancy Levene. London: SCM Press, 2002, 229–250.

———. *On Jewish Learning.* Ed. N. N. Glatzer. New York: Schocken Books, 1955.

———. *Philosophical and Theological Writings.* Trans. Paul Franks and Michael Morgan. Indianapolis: Hackett Publishing Company, 2000.

———. *Understanding the Sick and the Healthy. A View of World, Man, and God.* Trans. N. N. Glatzer. Cambridge, Mass.: Harvard University Press, 1999.

———. *Zweistromland: Kleinere Schriften zu Glauben und Denken.* Ed. Reinhold and Annemarie Mayer. Dordrecht: Martinus Nijhoff, 1984.

Roth, Laurence. "Unpacking My Father's Bookstore." In *Modern Jewish Literatures: Intersections and Boundaries.* Ed. Sheila Jelen, Michael Kramer, and L. Scott Lerner. Philadelphia: University of Pennsylvania Press, 2011, 280–302.

Roth, Philip. *The Counterlife*. New York: Farrar, Straus and Giroux, 1986.
Rousso, Henry. *The Latest Catastrophe: History, the Present, the Contemporary*. Trans. Jane Marie Todd. Chicago: University of Chicago Press, 2014.
Royle, Nicholas. "Yes, Yes, the University in Ruins," *Critical Inquiry* 26.1 (Autumn 1999): 147–153.
Rubenstein, Jeffrey. "Elisha ben Abuya: Torah and the Sinful Sage (*Ḥagigah* 15a–b)." *Talmudic Stories: Narrative Art, Composition, and Culture*. Baltimore: Johns Hopkins University Press, 1999, 66–104.
———. "Theodicy and Torah." In *Stories of the Babylonian Talmud*. Baltimore: Johns Hopkins University Press, 2010, 182–201.
Rubenstein, Jeffrey L., and Shaye J. D. Cohen, eds. *Rabbinic Stories*. Mahwah, N.J.: Paulist Press, 2002.
Rubinstein, Ernest. *An Episode of Jewish Romanticism: Franz Rosenzweig's "Star of Redemption."* Albany: State University of New York Press, 1999.
Sagi, Avi. *The Open Canon: On the Meaning of Halakhic Discourse*. Trans. Batya Stein. New York: Continuum, 2007.
Said, Edward. *Humanism and Democratic Criticism*. New York: Columbia University Press, 2004.
———."Secular Criticism." In *The World, the Text, and the Critic*. Cambridge, Mass.: Harvard University Press, 1983, 1–30.
Saiman, Chaim N. *Halakhah: The Rabbinic Idea of Law*. Princeton, N.J.: Princeton University Press, 2018.
Salusinszky, Imre, ed. *Criticism in Society*. New York: Methuen, 1987.
Samuelson, Norbert M. *A User's Guide to Franz Rosenzweig's Star of Redemption*. New York: Routledge, 1999.
Santner, Eric. *On the Psychotheology of Everyday Life: Reflections on Freud and Rosenzweig*. Chicago: University of Chicago Press, 2001.
Satlow, Michael L. *Jewish Marriage in Antiquity*. Princeton, N.J.: Princeton University Press, 2001.
———. "Jewish Studies: Not so Good: Review of Aaron Hughes's *The Study of Judaism*." H-Judaic (May 2014).
Savran, George M. *Telling and Retelling: Quotation in Biblical Narrative*. Bloomington: Indiana University Press, 1988.
Scannell, Paddy. "The Life of the University." In *Making the University Matter*. Ed. Barbie Zelizer. New York: Routledge: 2011, 17–22.
Scarry, Elaine. *The Body in Pain: The Making and Unmaking of the World*. New York: Oxford University Press, 1987.
Scheindlin, Raymond P. *Wine, Women, and Death: Medieval Hebrew Poems on the Good Life*. New York: Oxford University Press, 1986.
Scholem, Gershom. "Bekenntnis über unsere Sprache." In *Juden in der Weimarer Republik*. Ed. Walter Grab and Julius H. Schoeps. Berlin: Burg, 1986.

———. "Bertrachtungen eines Kabbala-Forschers," *Du* (April 1955), 64–65.

———. *From Berlin to Jerusalem: Memories of My Youth*. Trans. Harry Zohn. Philadelphia: Paul Dry Books, 2012.

———. *The Fullness of Time: Poems*. Trans. Richard Sieburth. Jerusalem: Ibis Editions, 2003.

———. *The Messianic Idea in Judaism and Other Essays on Jewish Spirituality*. New York: Schocken Books, 1971.

———. *On the Possibility of Jewish Mysticism in Our Time and Other Essays*. Ed. Avraham Shapira. Trans. Jonathan Chipman. Philadelphia: Jewish Publication Society, 1997.

Schorsch, Ismar. *From Text to Context: The Turn to History in Modern Judaism*. Lebanon: University Press of New England, 2003.

Schreier, Benjamin. *The Impossible Jew: Identity and the Reconstruction of Jewish American Literary History*. New York: New York University Press, 2015.

———. "Review of *From Continuity to Contiguity: Toward a New Jewish Literary Thinking* by Dan Miron." *Comparative Literature Studies* 50.4 (2013): 695–698.

Schulz-Grave, Isabell. *Lernen im Freien Jüdischen Lehrhaus*. Oldenburg, 1998.

Schwartz, Seth. "Historiography on the Jews in the 'Talmudic Period' (70–640 ce)." In *The Oxford Handbook of Jewish Studies*. Ed. Martin Goodman. New York: Oxford University Press, 2004, 79–114.

Schwartz, Shuly Rubin. *The Emergence of Jewish Scholarship in America: The Publication of the Jewish Encyclopedia*. Cincinnati: Hebrew Union Press, 1991.

Schwehn, Mark R. *Exiles from Eden: Religion and the Academic Vocation in America*. New York: Oxford University Press, 1993.

Schweid, Eliezer. "Rosenzweig's Contribution to the Curriculum of Jewish Thought." In *Paradigms in Jewish Philosophy*. Ed. Raphael Jospe. Cranbury: Associated University Presses, 166–181.

Scott, A. O. "Calls to God: Always a Busy Signal," *New York Times*, October 2, 2009.

Seery, John E. *America Goes to College: Political Theory for the Liberal Arts* (Albany: State University of New York Press, 1997.

Sefaria: a Living Library of Jewish Texts Online. www.sefaria.org/.

Seidman, Naomi. *A Marriage Made in Heaven. The Sexual Politics of Hebrew and Yiddish*. Berkeley: University of California Press, 1984.

———. "On Translating and not Being Jonathan Boyarin." *In Geveb*, ingeveb.org/blog/on-translating-and-not-being-jonathan-boyarin.

Sestershenn, Raimund, ed. *Das Freie Jüdische Lehrhaus—Eine Andere Frankfurter Schule*. Munich and Zurich, 1987.

Shandler, Jeffrey. "Serious Talk," *AJS Review* 35.2 (November, 2011): 349–355.
Shapiro, Harvey. *Educational Theory and Jewish Studies in Conversation: From Volozhin to Buczacz*. Lanham, Md.: Lexington Books, 2013.
Shattuck, Roger. *Forbidden Knowledge: From Prometheus to Pornography*. New York: Harcourt Brace Jovanovich, 1996.
Shelleg, Assaf. *Jewish Contiguities and the Soundtrack of Israeli History*. New York: Oxford, 2014.
Sherratt, Yvonne. *Hitler's Philosophers*. New Haven, Conn.: Yale University Press, 2014.
Shostak, Debra B. *Philip Roth: Countertexts, Counterlives*. Columbia: University of South Carolina Press, 2004.
Shumway, David. "Disciplinary Identities." In *Affiliations: Identity in Academic Culture*. Ed. Jeffrey R. Di Leo. Lincoln: University of Nebraska Press, 2003, 89–100.
——. And Ellen Messer-Davidow. "Disciplinarity: An Introduction." *Poetics Today* 12 (Summer 1991): 201–225.
Silberstein, Laurence J. "Jewish Studies, Textualism, and the Crisis of the Humanities." *Shofar* 4.3 (Spring 1986): 8–16.
Simmel, Georg. *The View of Life: Four Metaphysical Essays with Journal Aphorisms*. Trans. John A. Y. Andrews and Donald N. Levine. Chicago: University of Chicago Press, 2015.
Simon, Ernst. "Franz Rosenzweig and Jewish Education." *Conservative Judaism* 18.2 (Winter 1964): 10–24.
Simon, Josiah B. *Introducing Hegel and the State: The Early Rosenzweig, Biography, and History*. Albuquerque: University of New Mexico Press, 2006.
Skocpol, Theda. *Diminished Democracy: From Membership to Management in American Civic Life*. Norman: University of Oklahoma Press, 2003.
Smith, Sidonie. *Manifesto for the Humanities: Transforming Doctoral Education in Good Enough Times*. Ann Arbor: University of Michigan Press, 2015.
Sperling, Baruch, A. Levine, and B. Levy. *Students of the Covenant: A History of Jewish Biblical Scholarship in North America*. Atlanta: Scholars Press 1992.
Stangl, Chris. *The Exploding Kinetoscope*: "Secret Test!: *A Serious Man*, Oct 29, 2009, explodingkinetoscope.blogspot.com/2009/10/secret-test-serious-man-2009.html.
Stanley, Timothy. "A Serious Man," *Bible and Critical Theory*, vol. 9, num1&2 (2013): 1–34.
Staten, Henry. *Wittgenstein and Derrida*. Lincoln: University of Nebraska Press, 1984.

Stein, Dina. *Textual Mirrors: Reflexivity, Midrash, and the Rabbinic Self.* Philadelphia: University of Pennsylvania Press, 2012.
Steiner, George. "The Mandarin of the Hour—Michel Foucault." *New York Times Book Review*, February 28, 1971.
Stern, David. "Introduction." *Poetics Today* 19.1, "Hellenism and Hebraism Reconsidered: The Poetics of Cultural Influence and Exchange I" (Spring 1998): 1–17.
Sternberg, Meir. "Double Cave, Double Talk: The Indirections of Biblical Dialogue." In *Not in Heaven: Coherence and Complexity in Biblical Narrative.* Bloomington: Indiana University Press, 1991, 128–157.
———. *The Poetics of Biblical Narrative: Ideological Literature and the Drama of Reading.* Bloomington: Indiana University Press, 1987.
Stevens, Dana. "A Serious Man: A Seriously Good Coen Brothers Movie." *Slate*, October 1, 2009, www.slate.com/articles/arts/movies/2009/10/a_serious_man.html.
Stevenson, Frank W. "Horizontality and Impossibility in Kafka's Parabolic Quests." *CLCWeb: Comparative Literature and Culture* 14.5 (2012), doi.org/10.7771/1481-4374.2147.
Strauss, Herbert A. "A Program for Jewish Studies." In *Conference on Intellectual Policies in American Jewry.* Ed. Herbert Strauss. New York: American Federation of Jews from Central Europe, Inc., 1972, 20–38.
Suchoff, David. "Family Resemblances: Ludwig Wittgenstein as a Jewish Philosopher." *Bamidbar* 2.1 (2012): 75–92.
———. *Kafka's Jewish Languages: The Hidden Openness of Tradition.* Philadelphia: University of Pennsylvania Press, 2012.
Svensson, Patrik, and David Theo Goldberg, eds. *Between Humanities and the Digital.* Cambridge, Mass.: MIT Press, 2015.
Taylor, Mark C. *Crisis on Campus: A Bold Plan for Reforming Our Colleges and Universities.* New York: Alfred A. Knopf, 2010.
———. "End the University as We Know It." *New York Times*, April 26, 2009, sec. A23, www.nytimes.com/2009/04/27/opinion/27taylor.html.
Teugels, Lieve M. *Bible and Midrash: The Story of the "Wooing of Rebekah" (Gen 24).* Leuven: Peeters, 2005.
Thomas, Matthew A. *These are the Generations: Identity, Covenant, and the 'toledot' Formula.* New York: T & T Clark, 2011.
Thomas, Michael. *The Reception of Derrida: Translation and Transformation.* Basingstoke: Palgrave Macmillan, 2006.
Thomson, Iain. *Heidegger on Ontotheology: Technology and the Politics of Education.* Cambridge: Cambridge University Press, 2005.
Tirosh-Samuelson, Hava, ed. *Women and Gender in Jewish Philosophy.* Bloomington: Indiana University Press, 2004.

Tollerton, David. "Job of Suburbia? A Serious Man and Viewer Perceptions of the Biblical." *Journal of Religion and Film* 5.2 (October 2011), digitalcommons.unomaha.edu/jrf/vol15/iss2/7.
Torat Ḥayim. Yerushalayim: Mosad ha-Rav Kook, 1988.
Touitou, Eleazar. *Ha-peshaṭot ha-mitḥadeshim be-khol yom:ʿIyyunim beperusho shel Rashbam la-Torah*. Ramat Gan: Bar-Ilan University Press, 2003.
Trowler, Paul, Murray Saunders, and Veronica Bamber, eds. *Tribes and Territories in the Twenty-First Century: Rethinking the Significance of Disciplines in Higher Education*. New York: Routledge, 2012.
Udel, Miriam. *Never Better! The Modern Jewish Picaresque*. Ann Arbor: University of Michigan Press, 2016.
Valley, Eli. "Metamorphosis." *The Forward* (November 25, 2009).
Vendler, Helen. *Seamus Heaney*. Cambridge, Mass.: Harvard University Press, 1998.
Vidas, Moulie. *Tradition and the Formation of the Talmud*. Princeton, N.J.: Princeton University Press, 2014.
Viezel, Eran. "'The Anxiety of Influence': Rashbam's Approach to Rashi's Commentary on the Torah." *AJS Review* 40.2 (November 2016): 279–303.
Vološinov, V. N. *Marxism and the Philosophy of Language*. Trans. Ladislav Matejka and I. R. Titunik. Cambridge, Mass.: Harvard University Press, 1986.
Wacquant, Loïc J. D. "For a Socio-Analysis of Intellectuals: On *Homo Academicus*." *Berkeley Journal of Sociology* 34 (1989): 1–29.
Walcott, Derek. *The Prodigal*. New York: Farrar, Straus and Giroux, 2004.
Ware, Owen. "Dialectic of the Past/Disjunction of the Future: Derrida and Benjamin on the Concept of Messianism." *Journal for Cultural and Religious Theory* 5.2 (April 2004): 99–114.
Wasserman, Mira Beth. *Jews, Gentiles, and Other Animals: The Talmud After the Humanities*. Philadelphia: University of Pennsylania Press, 2017.
Weber, Max. "Science as a Vocation." In *Max Weber, Essays in Sociology*. Trans. and ed. H. H. Gerth and C. Wright Mills. New York: Oxford University Press, 1946, 129–156.
———. "Wissenschaft als Beruf." *Gesammlte Aufsaetze zur Wissenschaftslehre*. Tübingen: Mohr-Siebeck, 1922, 524–555.
Weber, Samuel. "The Future of the Humanities: Experimenting." *Culture Machine* 2 (2000).
———. "The Future of the University: The Cutting Edge." In *Ideas of the University*. Ed. Terry Smith. Sydney: Sydney University Press, 1996, 43–75.
———. *Institution and Interpretation*. Stanford: Stanford University Press, 2002.

Weiss, Meir. *The Bible from Within: The Method of Total Interpretation*. Jerusalem: Magnes Press, 1984.
Weller, Barry. "Pleasure and Self-Loss in Reading." *ADE Bulletin* 99 (Fall 1991): 8–12.
Weltsch, Robert. "Introduction." *Yearbook of the Leo Baeck Institute* 2.1 (1957): 9–27.
Wiener-Dow, Leon. *The Going: A Meditation on Jewish Law*. New York: Palgrave MacMillan, 2017.
———. *U'vlekhtekha Va'derekh* (Hebrew). Tel Aviv: Bar-Ilan University Press, 2017.
Williams, Jeffrey J. "History as a Challenge to the Idea of the University." *JAC* 25.1 (2005): 55–74.
Wimmer, Michael. "The Gift of *Bildung*: Reflections on the Relationship between Singularity and Justice in the Concept of *Bildung*." In *Derrida & Education*. Ed. Gert J. J. Biesta and Denise Egéa-Kuehne. New York: Routledge, 2001, 150–175.
Wimpfheimer, Barry Scott. "The Dialogical Talmud: Daniel Boyarin and Rabbinics." *Jewish Quarterly Review* 101.2 (Spring 2011): 245–254.
Wirth-Nesher, Hana, and Michael P. Kramer, eds. *The Cambridge Companion to Jewish American Literature*. Cambridge: Cambridge University Press, 2003.
Wittgenstein, Ludwig. *Culture and Value*. Trans. Peter Winch. Oxford: Basil Blackwell, 1980.
———. *Philosophical Investigations*. Trans. G. E. M. Anscombe: Blackwell, 1948.
Wolosky, Shira. "A Jewish-American Poetics." In *Cambridge Companion to Jewish-American Literature*. Ed. Michael Kramer and Hana Wirth-Nesher. Cambridge: Cambridge University Press, 2003, 250–268.
Wood, Abigail. "The Cantor and The Muezzin's Duet: Contested Soundscapes at Jerusalem's Western Wall." *Contemporary Jewry* 35.1 (April 2015): 55–72.
Wortham, Simon. *Rethinking the University: Leverage and Deconstruction*. Manchester: Manchester University Press, 1999.
Wortham, Simon, and Christopher Fynsk. *Counterinstitutions: Jacques Derrida and the Question of the University*. New York: Fordham University Press, 2006.
Wortham, Simon, and Gary Hall. *Experimenting: Essays with Samuel Weber*. New York: Fordham University Press, 2007.
Yadin-Israel, Azzan. *Scripture and Tradition: Rabbi Akiva and the Triumph of Midrash*. Philadelphia: University of Pennsylvania Press, 2015.
Yerushalmi, Yosef Hayim. *Zakhor: Jewish History and Jewish Memory*. Seattle: University of Washington Press, 1982.

Zank, Michael. "Franz Rosenzweig, the 1920s, and the <<e-mail>> moment of textual reasoning." In *Textual Reasonings: Jewish Philosophy and Text Study at the End of the Twentieth Century*. Ed. Peter Ochs, Nancy Levene. London: SCM Press, 2002, 229–250.

———. "The Rosenzweig-Rosenstock Triangle." *Modern Judaism* 23 (2003): 74–98.

Zipperstein, Steven J. "Home Again?" *Judaism: A Quarterly Journal of Jewish Life and Thought* 44.4 (Fall 1995): 10–12.

Žižek, Slavoj. *The Abyss of Freedom/Ages of the World*. Ann Arbor: University of Michigan Press, 1997.

———."God without the Sacred: The Book of Job, the First Critique of Ideology." New York Public Library, November 9, 2010.

Zunz, Leopold. "On Rabbinical Literature." In *The Jew in the Modern World: A Documentary History*. New York: Oxford University Press, 2011, 221–223.

INDEX

"Abraham, the Other" (Derrida), 188
Aciman, André, 235n62
Aḥer (R. Elisha ben Abuya), 74; 215n34
Academic Instincts (Garber), 12–13
adhan/azzan, 62, 72
adhesion, xi, 20–21, 191–192
Adler, Mortimer, 44
Adorno, Theodor, 14, 150, 165, 166
affiliation, 191, 192, 194
Agamben, Giorgio, 17, 67, 71–75, 79, 81, 112, 118, 195, 216, 234n60
Agnon, Yosef Shmu'el, 81, 138, 151, 212n1
Association for Jewish Studies, 30, 37, 38, 163, 165–167, 209n15
Akademie für die Wissenschaft des Judentums, 135, 139, 225n20
Akiva, R., 53–54
Alexander, Philip, 25
allegory, 8, 11, 27, 33, 96, 106, 118, 147, 194
Alshich, R. Moshe, 232n25
Alter, Robert, 54, 173
Altmann, Alexander, 208n10
"American Scholar, The" (Emerson), 197–198
Appelfeld, Aharon, 31
Arama, R. Isaac, 173
'arevut, 151
Arnold, Matthew, 44
Asad, Talal, 20, 168
Ashkenaz, 20, 129
aspect/content (Scholem), 42
Attridge, Derek, 210n26
Auden, W. H., 69
Audiotopia (Kun), 3–4
Auerbach, Eric, 62
Azariah, R. El'azar ben, xii

Ba'al Makhshoves, 42
Babel, Isaac, 58
Bahti, Timothy, 51, 94–97, 155–156

Baḥya, R. ben Yosef Ibn Paḳuda, 174
Baker, Cynthia, 205n40, 215n32
Bakhtin, Mikhail, 24, 44–48, 83, 94, 102, 115, 210n32
Baldwin, James, 120
Band, Arnold J., 39, 41–42, 207n3
Barnett, Ronald, 213n13
Baron, Salo, 38, 41, 93, 133
Barthes, Roland, 193
Baskin, Judith, 208n7
Batnitzky, Leora, 134
Bauhaus, 137
"Bauleute, Die" (Rosenzweig), 138, 142
Becher, Tony, 218n12
Being and Time, 148
"'Being Jewish' and Studying About Judaism" (Neusner), 111ff., 219n21
beit midrash, 62, 88, 113, 127, 132, 136, 150, 226n26
Bekhor Shor, Yosef ben Yitzḥak, 69
belonging, 21, 24, 37, 72, 74–75, 77, 109, 208n13
Bellow, Saul, 107, 198
Bend Sinister (Nabokov), 87
Benjamin, Walter, 14, 23, 31, 42, 44, 55–57, 60, 73, 185–186, 188, 191, 215n33
Bercovitch, Sacvan, 1–8, 11, 22, 24, 25, 27, 28, 43, 47, 61, 64, 75, 99, 166, 199–200, 236n16
Bericht, 6, 8, 10–11
Berkowitz, Jay, 201n4
Berlin, Adele, 174
Berliner Kindheit um Neunzehnhundert (Benjamin), 42
Bernasconi, Robert, 76
Biale, David, 40, 63
Bielik-Robson, Agata, 13, 14
Bildung, xii, 6, 25, 39, 48, 67, 73, 134, 140, 141, 143–150, 152, 156, 158, 164, 199, 227n46, 228nn52,55

273

Bildungsfrage (Heidegger), 148–149
Bildungsproblem (Rosenzweig), 144ff.
"Bildung und Kein Ende" (Rosenzweig), 127, 140, 141, 152, 156, 158
Blanchot, Maurice, 216n44
Bloom, Allan, 44, 95
Body in Pain, The (Scarry), 171
Borge, Jorge Luis, 58
Borge, Viktor, 55
Bourdieu, Pierre, 92, 95, 207n3
Bousquet, Marc, 203n23
Boustan, Ra'anan S., 19, 208n8
Boyarin, Daniel, 16–17, 95, 98, 115–116, 219n19
Boyarin, Jonathan, 21, 46, 204n35, 205n35
Boym, Svetlana, 44
Braiterman, Zachary, 18, 98, 120–121, 136–137, 205n38
Brenner, Michael, 134, 144, 224n4, 227n39
Brod, Max, 1, 31
Brodsky, Joseph, 69
Bruns, Gerald, 27, 33
"Brücke, Die" (Kafka), 126
Buber, Martin, 33, 189
Budick, Emily, 203n13
Bush, Andrew, 19–20, 22, 163

Cahan, Abraham, 120
Calvino, Italo, 52–53, 58
Canetti, Elias, 31
canon, 25, 29, 98, 101, 102, 103, 127
Caplan, Marc, 18
Cavell, Stanley, 26, 161, 199, 200, 222n50, 236nn19,20
Charney (Niger), Shmuel, 42
Cheyette, Bryan, 208n13
chirality, 28
"Chors des Fragenden" (Rosenzweig), 128, 149, 200
Coen, Ethan and Joel, 26, 165, 167, 169, 177ff., 230n6, 233n45
Coetzee, J. M., 202n7
Cohen, Aryeh, 157
Cohen, Hermann, 132
Cohen, Shaye, 218n14
community, 2, 18, 21, 31–33, 37, 45, 53, 60, 67, 71–80, 85, 118, 147, 160, 162, 195–196, 199, 200
"community of *dissensus*" (Readings), 67

"community of the question" (Derrida), 71, 200
Conrad, Joseph, 212n3
Coming Community, The (Agamben), 73, 74, 112
Confessions (Augustine), 11
Conflict of the Faculties, The (Kant), 48
Copeland, Aaron, 58
Costello, Elizabeth, 202n7
counterlife, 1, 7–8, 9, 11, 22, 61, 128, 166, 192, 198, 200
Counterlife, The (Roth), 7
Cover, Robert, 230n11
Criticism in the Wilderness (Hartman), 104
Culture and Imperialism (Said), 102
Cutler, Yosl, 29, 167

dalet amot, 95, 157
Dangor, Achmat, 58
Debord, Guy, 215n35
De Man, Paul, 220n33
denarration, 166, 168, 177, 180–182, 185, 187
Denby, David, 179
Der Jude, 32
Derrida, Jacques, 15, 25, 29, 31, 41–45, 48, 49–54, 63–64, 66–67, 71, 77, 94–96, 99–101, 103, 116, 125, 131, 137, 149, 155, 185–186, 188, 196, 197, 200, 211n42, 212n9, 234n57
"Des Espace Autres: Hétérotopies" (Foucault), 132–133, 135–137
Dickens, Charles, 123, 161
differend, 110–111
Di Lampedusa, Giuseppe Tomasi, 57, 212n5
Discipline of Philosophy, The (Goetschel), 13–15, 143, 210n29
Dolgopolski, Sergei, 79, 216n48
Dubnow, Simon, 41

Edwards, Laurence L., 115
Elbogen, Ismar, 208n10
Ellison, Ralph, 58–59
Elman, Yaakov, 16–18
Emerson, Ralph Waldo, 2, 24, 26, 197–200
"End of the Tether, The" (Conrad), 212n3
Erlich, Shoshke, 42
"Exchanged Fronts" (Rosenzweig), 228n49
experimentum linguae (Agamben), 74

Fagenblat, Michael, 223n56
Faust, Part 1 (Goethe), 140–141
Ferguson, Ronald, 106, 107, 195
Fichte, Johann Gottlieb, 145
fill renoué (Levinas), 26, 193
Finkel, Fyvush, 178
Fish, Stanley, 146
Fisher, Philip, 224n4
Flusser, Vilém, 211n39
Fokkelman, J. P., 231n22, 232n36
Foucault, Michel, 25, 132, 135, 137, 151, 152, 225n13
Fraade, Steven D., 219n17
Frankel, Yonah, 222n51
Frankel, Zacharias, 41, 48, 52, 210n35
Frankfurt Freies Lehrhaus Judaica, 25, 46, 127, 131, 133, 138, 153, 226n27
Frederick the Great, 49
Freedman, Jonathan, 202n5
Freud, Sigmund, 58
Frost, Robert, 52, 69
"Future of the Profession, The" (Derrida), 49

"Games of Chess" (Bercovitch), 198, 236n16
Garber, Marjorie, 12–15, 92, 141, 198
García Landa, José Ángel, 211n3, 230n12
Gass, William, 7
Gates, Henry Louis, Jr., 120
"Gemeinschaft" (Kafka), 31–33, 88, 91, 105
Gierke, Otto von, 76
Ginsburg, Benjamin, 216n46
Glatshteyn, Yankev, 58
Glatzer, Nahum M., 128, 129, 130, 133–134, 138, 142, 143, 153–154
Goethe, Johann Wolfgang von, 140–141, 145, 158, 191
Goetschel, Willi, 13–15, 143, 210n29, 225n22, 226n19, 227n47
Goldberg, Leah, 42
Goldschmidt, Hermann Levin, 128, 142, 210n28
Gordon, Peter E., 129–130, 147, 224n8, 228n49
Goshen Gottstein, Alon, 215n34
Gourgouris, Stathis, 21, 51–52, 213n12
"Government of the Tongue, The" (Heaney) 91
"Goy's Teeth, The," 179–180, 182, 184
Graetz, Heinrich, 41

Graff, Gerald, 97, 146
Granel, Gérard, 149
granello di sale e di senape, il, 28
Greif, Mark, 236n20
Gropius, Walter, 136
Groiser, David, 158–159

Ha'am, Ahad, 42
Habermas, Jürgen, 146
Haeckel, Ernst, 2, 202n2
Haggadah, 23, 26, 111
Halivni, David Weiss, 161
Halkin, Shimon, 42
Hallo, Rudolf, 138
Harpham, Geoffrey Galt, 61–62, 72, 97, 119–120, 142–143
Hartman, Geoffrey, 88–89, 103–104, 108, 109, 111, 121, 220n33
Hasidism, 84
ḥavruta, 89
Hawthorne, Nathaniel, 47
Ḥayei Sarah, 170
ḥazanut, 62
Heaney, Seamus, ix, 68–71, 72, 80, 81, 83, 85, 91, 93, 121, 197, 213
Heidegger, Martin, 25, 49, 131, 136, 147–151, 228
Heine, Heinrich, 14, 42
Herberg, Will, 130
Herzl, Theodor, 1
Heschel, Abraham Joshua, 93, 120
Heschel, Susannah, 43, 63, 84
heterotopia, 25, 132–133, 135–137, 146, 151, 160, 193
Hillel, 63–66, 69, 212n7
Hirsch, Samson Raphael R., 143, 145
Ḥizkuni (Hezekiah ben Manoah), 173
Horowitz, Sara R., 204n30
Hughes, Aaron, 19, 218n7
humanities, x, 14–16, 20, 24–25, 35, 37, 43–45, 47, 51, 54, 58, 61, 63, 67, 76, 87ff., 124–125, 196
Humanities and the Dream of America, The (Harpham), 61–62
Humboldt, Wilhelm von, 44, 48, 145, 146, 227n47
Hutchins, Robert Maynard, 44
hypomochlion, 51–52, 187

Ibn Ezra, R. Abraham, 174
Ibn Gabirol, Shlomo, 70, 71, 80, 81, 121

"Ich könnte mir einen anderen Abraham" (Kafka), 187–188
Idea of Purity in Ancient Judaism, The (Neusner), 90
Idel, Moshe, 58
Imhoff, Sarah, 84
Impossible Jew, The (Schreier), 19–22, 23
"Injured University, The" (Bahti), 51, 96–98
Inoperative Community, The (Nancy), 75, 76, 78, 215n38
interdisciplines (Ferguson), 106–107
"Investigations of a Dog" (Kafka), 2–4, 8, 11, 27, 32, 80
Invisible Cities (Calvino), 52–53

Jay, Martin, 136, 208n12, 226n25
Jewish Quarterly Review, The, 165
"Jewish Studies and the Secular University" (Reinhard/Lupton), 63–67
Jewish Studies at the Crossroads (Boustan, et al.), 19, 168
Johnston, Daniel, 118, 217
Jospe, Alfred, 138
Jospe, Rafael, 64

Kafka, Franz, 1, 2–11, 15–17, 28, 31–33, 42, 80, 88, 91, 93, 96, 105, 126, 134, 135, 137, 139, 156, 162, 186–188, 202n7
Kampfplatz, 45, 54, 65, 73, 78, 91
Kamuf, Peggy, 227n46
Kandinsky, Wassily, 120
Kant, Immanuel, 14, 25, 44, 45, 48–51, 61, 63, 75, 93, 96, 145, 155, 197, 211n42
Kaplan, Mordechai, 64
Katchor, Ben, 31, 58
Kavanaugh, Patrick, 69
Kavka, Martin, 142, 208n7, 226n26, 229n30
Keats, John, 69
Keller, Helen, 123
Kierkegaard, Søren, 206n57
Kimḥi, R. David (Radak), 174
Klausner, Yosef, 42
Kleist, Heinrich von, 104
kohen gadol, 65
Kramer, Michael, 205n39
"Kreisel, Der" (Kafka), 134–135
Kronfeld, Chana, 230n4
Kun, Joshua, 3–6, 7, 8, 25, 27, 47, 62, 64, 139, 200

Kundera, Milan, 221n38
Kurzweil, Baruch, 42, 120, 209n17, 218n9

LaCapra, Dominick, 23, 192, 193, 206n53, 222n48
Lear, Jonathan, 202n8, 210n38
leaven, 28
Lefebvre, Henri, 225n13
Lehrhaus, 25, 46, 127–133, 134, 136–143, 145–147, 149–158, 224, 226n26, 229n59
"Lehrhaus Address, The," 140–141
Leibowitz, Yeshayahu, 30
Lessing, Gotthold Ephraim, 14
Lessons in Secular Criticism (Gourgouris), 213n12
lever/leverage, xi, 25, 35ff., 71, 78, 83–86, 94, 96–97, 126, 133, 143, 147, 150, 154–156, 157, 192, 196, 200
Levi, Primo, 28, 192
Levinas, Emmanuel, xii, 21–22, 26, 30, 53, 57–58, 64, 66–68, 70–71, 74, 76, 95, 106, 117, 118, 123–124, 160, 162, 172, 191–192, 193, 200, 205n36, 229n66, 229n1
Levinson, Bernard M., 231n18
Lezra, Jacques, 153
Lichtenstein, Rav Aharon, 130
Lieberman, Saul, 41, 93, 98, 218n14
"Life as Transcendence" (Simmel), 35, 48
Liska, Vivian, 207n2, 214n26
Liss, Hannah, 175, 183
list, 153
literatoyre, 167
Lupton, Julia, 63–67
Luzzatto, Shmuel David, 225n11
Lynch, Deidre, 97
Lyotard, Jean-François, 67, 110, 111

Maharal (Yehuda Loew ben Bezalel), 166
Maharil (R. Yaakov ben Moshe Levi Moelin)129–130
makhlokes/ maḥloḳet, 93–95, 111, 115, 120, 121, 219n16
Mandel'shtam, Osip and Nadezhda, 68
Manger, Itzik, 167, 230n4
Marketplace of Ideas, The (Menand), x, 13, 61, 98, 153, 195, 201n6
Marvell, Andrew, 109

Matalon, Ronit, 58
"Means of Identification" (Levinas), 20–21, 66, 70, 118, 191–192
Meir, Ephraim, 128, 225n11
Melville, Herman, 32, 47, 208n6
Menand, Louis, x, 13, 61, 98, 153, 195, 201n6
Mencken, H. L., 217n3
Mendele Moykher Sforim, 124
Mendelssohn, Moses, 14, 42
Mendes-Flohr, Paul, 212n6, 226n30
Menippean satire, 115–116
mentaculus, 177, 233n46
Merleau-Ponty, Maurice, 123
Meskin, Jacob, 215n33
messianische Kraft (Benjamin), 23, 185
Meyer, Michael A., 210n35
Meyerowitz, Rael, 203n9
Mezzrow, Mezz, 58
midrash, 19, 54, 65, 82, 104, 115–116, 127, 171, 173, 221n34, 224n2
Midrash Rabbah, 231n33
Mikraot gedolot, 232n30
Milosz, Czeslaw, 69
Mill, J. S., 100, 101
Minima Moralia (Adorno), 165, 166
Miron, Dan, 11, 193
Mishnah, 25, 64, 95, 116, 219n16; Tractate *Kelim* 5:10, 92
mochlos, 87, 93, 94, 115, 121, 128, 143, 195
"*Mochlos*, or the Conflict of the Faculties" (Derrida), 25, 48–52, 54, 63, 149, 155
Molodowsky, Kadya, 31
Mon Oncle (Tati), xii
Morris, Leslie, 52–54
Mosley, Walter, 58
Mosse, George L., 208n12
Moten, Fred, 236n12
Mouffe, Chantal, 214n26
"Music of America, The" (Bercovitch), 2–4, 11, 22, 43
Musil, Robert, ix, 139
Muskeljudentum (Max Nordau), 50
Myers, David M., 52, 54, 135

Nabokov, Vladimir, 87
Naḥmanides, 172, 174
Nancy, Jean-Luc, ix, 36, 67, 71, 72, 74–76, 77, 78–79, 80, 123
"Neues Denken, Das" (Rosenzweig), 143, 159
"Neues Lernen" (Rosenzweig), 136, 138, 139
Neusner, Jacob, 19, 20, 25, 26, 37, 41, 87–122, 133, 132, 139, 152, 156, 158, 163, 165, 193, 194, 195, 209n15, 218nn11,14, 220nn27,35, 221nn29–30, 222nn45–46
New Humanities and Academic Disciplines (Neusner) 105
Newman, John Henry, 44
New Yet Unapproachable America, This (Cavell) 222n50, 236n19
Nietzsche, Friedrich, 1, 49, 129, 228n52
Nobel, Rabbi Nehemia Anton, 138
Novick, Peter, 97
Nussimbaum, Lev/Kurban Said, 22

Oakley, Francis, 100, 214n24
Once Upon a Time in China (Hark), xii
One-Way Street (Benjamin), 60
On Jewish Learning (Rosenzweig), 127
"On Language as Such and on the Language of Man" (Benjamin), 185–186
"On Leaving Saragossa" (Ibn Gabirol), 70–71
Only Yesterday (Agnon), 217n50
"On Rabbinical Literature" (Zunz), 42, 48
"On the Future of Our Educational Institutions" (Nietzsche), 228n52
Other Others (Dolgopolski), 79–80
Ouaknin, Marc-Alain, 93, 121
Ozick, Cynthia, 31

Pagis, Dan, 31
Pappenheim, Bertha, 138
paraergon (Derrida), 212n9
"Pardes" (Agamben), 74–75, 112, 215n36
partes extra partes (Nancy), 35, 36, 178
Periodic Table, The (Levi), 28
Philosophical Investigations (Wittgenstein), 112, 189, 235n65
Philosophy of Right (Hegel), 49
Pinsky, Robert, 68
pitchfork, 24, 60ff.
"Pitchfork, The" (Heaney), 68
"Placing and Displacing Jewish Studies" (Morris), 52–54
Plato, 118
"Plato's Doctrine of Truth" (Heidegger), 147

Plaskow, Judith, 120
Poller, Nidra, 211n42
Pollin-Galay, Hannah, 201n4
potenza, la (Agamben), 27, 74, 75
Poulet, Georges, 176
Prell, Riv-Ellen, 181
prenant appel sur un pied (Derrida), 60, 63, 200
Prince, Gerald, 233n41
Professionals, The (Brooks), 194

Radak (R. David Kimḥi), 174, 182
Ramban, 231n21
Rawidowicz, Simon, 58
Rashbam (R. Samuel ben Meir), ix, 26, 31, 175, 183, 231n19, 233n40
Rashi (R. Shlomo Yitzchaki), 173, 175, 176, 177, 178, 233n39
"reading for the list," 153
Readings, Bill, ix, xi, 14, 23, 43–45, 53, 66–67, 71, 74–74, 76, 78–79, 84, 95, 102, 103, 104, 109–111, 142, 145–147, 149, 152, 192, 196, 199, 200
Reaffirming Higher Education (Neusner), 96
Redmon, Allen, 184–185
Rees, Abraham, 235n1
"Reflections on Modern Jewish Studies" (Scholem), 38–42
Reinhard, Kenneth, 63–67
Renan, Ernest, 10
renarration, 166–169, 170ff.
Reorder of the Things, The (Ferguson), 106, 107, 195
"Report to an Academy, A" (Kafka), 4–6, 10–11, 15, 32, 80
Richardson, Brian, 177
Ringelblum, Emmanuel, 31
Rites of Assent (Bercovitch), 62
Ritterband, Paul, 72
Robbins, Bruce, 26, 119–120, 194–195
Rosenstock-Huessy, Eugen, 120
Rosenzweig, Franz, xii, 14, 18, 25, 26, 46, 58, 87, 90, 109, 112, 120, 122, 127–160, 164, 166, 193, 195, 200, 210n32, 224n7, 225nn15,18, 227nn39,47, 228n49
Roskies, David, 54
Roth, Henry, 30
Roth, Philip, 7, 8, 10, 22, 27, 58, 93, 125, 193, 195, 198
Rothberg, Michael, 208n13

Rubenstein, Jeffrey, 212n8, 215n34
Ruin the Scared Truths (Bloom), 109
ruins, 35, 43, 44, 199

Sadan, Dov, 42
Sagi, Avi, 219n16
Said, Edward, 21, 102, 192, 195
Saiman, Chaim N., 201n5
salt/mustard, 28
Santner, Eric, 58
satire, 27–28, 29, 33, 106, 189, 206n60
Savran, George M., 172, 232n36
Scannell, Paddy, 206n54
Scarry, Elaine, 171–172, 176
Schelling, Friedrich Wilhelm Joseph von, 145
Schiller, Friedrich, 145
Schleiermacher, Friedrich, 145
Scholem, Gershom, ix, x, 9, 27, 35, 38–42, 46, 59, 62, 63, 71, 85, 98, 120, 135, 151, 153, 186, 187, 188, 199, 209n17, 218n9
Scholes, Robert, 97
Schopenhauer, Friedrich, 152
Schorsch, Ismar, 208n12
Schreier, Benjamin, 19, 22–23
Schulz, Bruno, 31
Schwartz, Seth, 218n9
Sciar, Moacyr, 58
Sebald, W. G., 123
"Secular Criticism" (Said), 21, 192, 205n47
Secular Vocations (Robbins), 26, 119, 194
Sefaria.org, 130
Serious Man, A (Coen Brothers), 167–170, 177–187
se'or sheba'isa, 28
Sepharad, 20, 58
Shagar (Rav Shimon Gershon Rosenberg), 130, 159, 166
shalshelet, 173, 176, 178, 179, 232n37
Shammai, 63–67, 69, 212nn7,8
Shandler, Jeffrey, 180, 182
Shape of Revelation, The (Braiterman), 18, 137
Shapiro, Harvey, 19
"Shekinah" (Agamben), 74, 112
Shelleg, Assaf, 222n42
Shiloah, Amnon, 222n42
Sholem Aleichem, 47, 124
Shostak, Debra, 203n12

Shumway, David, 192
Sidney, Sir Philip, 12
"Signature" (Levinas), 162, 229n1
Simmel, Georg, 35, 47, 58
Skocpol, Theda, 216n46
Smith, Morton, 93
Socrates and the Fat Rabbis (Boyarin), 115–116
Soloveitchik, Rav Joseph B., 30
Spinoza, Baruch, 14
Spitzer, Leo, 62
Star of Redemption, The (Rosenzweig), 48, 154
Steiner, George, 133
Steinschneider, Moritz, 40, 210n35
Sternberg, Meir, 174, 232n32
Strauss, Herbert, 138
Strauss, Leo, 138, 151
Suchoff, David, 207n2, 226n28
swerve, xi, 195

Talmud Bavli, xii–xiii, 63, 74, 117, 228n57; Tractate b. *Bava Batra* 7b, 157; Tractate b. *Bava Metsi'a* 59b, 92, 218n13; Tractate b. *Berakhot* 17a, 28; Tractate b. *Ḥagigah* 3b, xii, 94; Tractate b. *Ḥagigah* 14b, 74, 118; Tractate b. *Menaḥot* 29b, 112, 116, 117; Tractate b. *Shabbat* 31a, 63; Tractate b. *Shevuot* 39a, 228n57; Tractate b. *Yevamot* 64a, 81; Tractate b. *Yoma* 69b, 28
tanur shel Akhnai, 91, 218n13
tarbut ha–maḥloket, 95
Taylor, Mark C., 203n23
Textual Reasoning, Journal of, 156ff.
Thelehrhaus.com, 129–130, 131, 156, 218n13, 224n7
Thinking in Jewish (Boyarin), 21, 54, 204n35
Tirosh-Samuelson, Hava, 204n25
toldot, 171, 231n14
Tolstoy, Lev, 107, 118
Tönnies, Ernst, 76
travailler le cadre, 24, 64
Treasure of the Sierra Madre, The (Huston), xii
Touitou, Eleazar, 231n19
Trowler, Paul, 218n12
Tusculanes (Cicero), 101

University in Ruins, The (Readings), 43–44, 66–67, 73, 76, 145
"Unpacking my Library" (Benjamin), 55–57
Urzelle (Rosenzweig), 154

Vaihinger, Hans, 45
Valley, Eli, 202n1
Vidas, Moulie, 75, 215n37
Viner, Meir, 42

Walcott, Derek, 58, 68, 71
Was Heisst Denken (Heidegger), 148
Wasserman, Mira Beth, 216n48
Weber, Max, 55, 118–119, 120, 148, 191, 223n58
Weber, Samuel, 206n57
Wechsler, Harold, 72
Weller, Barry, 107–108
Weltsch, Felix, 1
"What Is a Paradigm" (Agamben), 73
"Why Textual Reasoning?" (Cohen), 157
Wilkomirski, Benjamin/Bruno Doessekker, 22
Winckelmann, Christian Herman, 152
"Wir Philologen" (Nietzsche), 1
"Wissenschaft als Beruf" (Weber), 55, 118–119
Wissenschaft des Judentums, 11, 17, 20, 39, 44, 46, 61, 71, 98, 106, 128, 131–135, 136, 139, 144, 150, 187, 199, 204n35, 210n35
Wittgenstein, Ludwig, 79, 89, 112, 136, 189
Wolfson, Harry, 93
Wood, Grant, 217n1
"Wünsche sind die Boten des Vertrauens" (Rosenzweig) 141, 150, 164, 229n4
Wyneken, Gustave, 215n33

Yeats, William Butler, 104
Yerushalmi, Yosef Haim, 58

Zank, Michael, 139, 144, 151, 154, 156, 227n39
"Zeit ist's" (Rosenzweig), 134, 141, 152
Žižek, Slavoj, 166, 186, 187
Zunz, Leopold, ix, 42, 46, 48, 52, 65, 120, 133, 149, 210n35
Zweistromland (Rosenzweig), 159

Adam Zachary Newton is University Professor Emeritus at Yeshiva University. Among his books are *Narrative Ethics*, *The Elsewhere*, and *To Make the Hands Impure* (Fordham).

www.ingramcontent.com/pod-product-compliance
Lightning Source LLC
Chambersburg PA
CBHW030435300426
44112CB00009B/1020